Everything You Should Know About

CHELATION THERAPY

D0564909

Everything You Should Know About

CHELATION THERAPY

by MORTON WALKER, D.P.M.
and HITENDRA H. SHAH, M.D.

KEATS PUBLISHING   NEW CANAAN, CONNECTICUT

DISCLAIMER

This book about chelation therapy has been written and published strictly for informational purposes. In no way should it be used as a substitute for your own physician's or other health professional's advice.

While Morton Walker, D.P.M., and Hitendra H. Shah, M.D., are collaborating here as coauthors, Dr. Walker is the professional medical journalist reporting on such health care information and Dr. Shah is the physician expert who uses chelation therapy as one of his medical practice modalities.

You should not consider educational material in this book to be the practice of medicine, although almost all the facts have come from the files, publications, and personal interviews of informed physicians who diagnose and treat cardiovascular and peripheral vascular diseases and their patients who have suffered from such conditions.

If you, as a potential user of knowledge received from these pages, require opinions, diagnoses, treatments, therapeutic advice, correction of your lifestyle, or any other aid relating to your health or to chelation therapy, it is recommended that you consult either Dr. Shah, the other physicians contributing material for this book or a chelating physician trained by the American Board of Chelation Therapy and who follows the *Protocol of the American College for Advancement in Medicine for the Safe and Effective Administration of EDTA Chelation Therapy,* as revised in February 1989.

These statements are to be considered disclaimers of responsibility for anything published here. The coauthors and publisher provide the information in this book with the understanding that you may act on it at your own risk and also with full knowledge that health professionals should first be consulted and that their specific advice for you should be considered before anything that is being presented here.

EVERYTHING YOU SHOULD KNOW ABOUT CHELATION THERAPY

Previously published as *Chelation Therapy: How to Prevent or Reverse Hardening of the Arteries.*

Copyright © 1997 by Morton Walker, D.P.M. and Hitendra H. Shah, M.D.

All Rights Reserved

No part of this book may be reproduced in any form without the written consent of the publisher.

Library of Congress Cataloging'in'Publication Data
Walker, Morton.
    Everything you should know about chelation therapy / by Morton Walker and Hitendra H. Shah.
        p.   cm.
    Revised ed. of: Chelation therapy. New York : M. Evans, 1980.
    Includes bibliographical references and index.
    ISBN: 0-87983-730-6
    1. Arteriosclerosis—Treatment. 2. Ethylenediaminetetraacetic acid—Therapeutic use. 3. Chelation therapy. I. Walker, Morton. Chelation therapy. II. Shah, Hitendra M. III. Title.
RC692.W263 1997
616.1'36061—dc21   97-7973
                                                               CIP

Printed in the United States of America

Published by Keats Publishing, Inc.
27 Pine Street (Box 876)
New Canaan, Connecticut 06840-0876

Dedication to
Wallis W. "Chip" Wood

Who, in 1980, held abiding faith in the value of this senior author's message. After thirty-two publishers had rejected the finished manuscript, Chip Wood, through his '76 Press, issued the first hardcover book to educate medical consumers about EDTA chelation therapy for preventing or reversing hardening of the arteries. Subsequently, 318,000 copies were distributed to readers around the world with many lives and limbs being saved.

CONTENTS

FOREWORD

I am former chairman of the Board of Trustees and former president of the American College for Advancement in Medicine (ACAM), a group of traditionally trained physicians who have broken from precedent and offer the controversial, but highly beneficial, chelation therapy. Dr. Morton Walker has described the intravenous technique of chelation with the disodium salt of ethylene diamine tetraacetic acid (EDTA) in this carefully researched, well-documented, and entirely correct book. He has taken an exceedingly technical medical subject and provided us with an entertaining, clear, and easy-reading explanation of what chelation therapy is, how it works in the body, the method of administration, how much it costs, the time it takes to administer, what happens from its administration, why people need it and want it, who are the beneficiaries, when it is given, and a thousand other answers to questions potential patients may have.

Dr. Walker has also documented the opposition to chelation therapy and presented its history—the whole story. There are many ramifications to this opposition, something the author dug into so that he provides us more than just the medical marvels of a treatment. He has, in fact, shown some failures in our modern system of health care delivery.

Today's overutilized, overpublicized heart surgery is a good example of our failure to deal effectively with causes of hardening of the arteries. Instead, we spend billions of dollars treating the results of occlusive arterial disease. Excellent medical studies have shown that most bypass heart patients do no better (and many do *worse*) than those who receive much safer drug therapy at a mere fraction of the cost. Yet even drug therapy does not address itself to the basic causes of heart disease. In spite of well-controlled studies demonstrating the shortcomings of experimental bypass surgery for coronary heart disease, the use of this surgical procedure by American hospitals and physicians is increasing so rapidly that it has become the largest single item in our entire federal medical budget.

Change is obviously needed and long overdue. Rather than concentrating on some new methods of funding this failing health care system, we must first redirect our thoughts and efforts to develop and practice true preventive medicine concepts as an integral part of a new health delivery system. Indeed, this must be a national priority item.

We all seem to need more motivation to follow a healthier lifestyle long before our health has deteriorated to the point that it becomes obvious to us or to our physician. Fortuitously, technological developments at this time have resulted in the growth of highly sophisticated, yet entirely painless, methods of "noninvasive" testing of our circulatory status. These techniques allow your physician to determine accurately how much circulatory impairment you have before recognizable symptoms, such as leg cramps, appear. Such testing provides us with an important form of feedback information that can help motivate us to incorporate important changes in how we live into our daily routine. Such actions performed not for a day, not for a month, but for a lifetime will demonstrably improve our health and slow down or even prevent (reverse?) our hardening of the arteries.

Too bad that almost all major medical progress initially encounter broad skepticism and even open hostility from the leaders of the orthodox medical community. After all, their basic beliefs are usually challenged by any significant breakthrough in medical knowledge. This negative response is largely due to the well-documented thirty- to fifty-year time lag that occurs between the initial discovery of a major new concept and its later broad general acceptance by the medical world. The history of penicillin, vitamin C, iodine, niacin, and even the acceptance of modern surgical antisepsis are all classic examples that demonstrate this unfortunate fact.

Today this delay may be even further aggravated by government regulations and interference intended to control the *costs* of medical care and administered with typical bureaucratic inefficiency through gigantic, virtually uncontrollable government agencies, best exemplified by the Food and Drug Administration of the federal government. Their resistance to change is assisted by the usual skepticism of "orthodox" members of medical societies and even medical boards, which are usually under the direct control of organized medicine. These impediments to progress are further aided by the physicians' reluctance to be innovative, due to the constant threat of malpractice suits as well as by the pressure of peer-group opinion. In addition, the economic interests of health insurance companies cause them to place additional barriers in the path of medical progress. We now have government-sanctioned peer review committees and other quasi-governmental health planning agencies that, collectively, threaten to halt invaluable medical advances. Without innovation, there is no progress.

Of course, this is all done in the name of the "consumers," who are told they need this protection because they are not able to decide on health care matters for themselves. Why? The agencies warn that consumers might be subject to some form of quackery or even fraud.

Unfortunately, no one explains to consumers that in these efforts to "protect" them, there can be more real danger to their health than from all the health quacks in the world. They may finally be denied all innovative treatments until they become "approved" at some distant time—which may be years after they are dead. They might have spent the remaining funds in their estate trying to help themselves, even trying unproved therapies. So it doesn't appear that the bureaucrats are really operating in the consumer's best interest after all. Who will protect us from a government grown too big and too powerful?

It is my belief that the facts and information contained in *Everything You Should Know About Chelation Therapy* will motivate citizens of the industrialized West to maintain their own good health, along with maintaining their medical freedom of choice, before it becomes truly too late for either. This means that all of us must generally discuss significant medical concepts such as "informed consent" and "benefit-to-risk ratios." Americans and other Westerners should think for themselves so that we can once again return to that unique climate of medical freedom that allowed the United States to become one of the great world leaders in medical progress.

Dr. Morton Walker, aided by Hitendra Shah, M.D., has done all of us a service by investing his skill as a medical journalist in this subject of chelation therapy. Admittedly, it has been a controversial subject in medicine and because of that, the authors have had a difficult time in getting this book published.

Use of the information in *Everything You Should Know About Chelation Therapy* can save lives—yours, mine, and the lives of a million and a quarter other Americans who die each year from the effects of occlusive arterial disease. We have the potential to live the full span of human life—120 years—if we take care of our health. This book will help you approach that lifespan with a quality of living immeasurably improved over anything you have now. All that's needed is that you act upon the information written here.

Garry F. Gordon, M.D., former Chairman of the Board of Trustees and past president, the American College for Advancement in Medicine, Payson, Arizona 85541

PREFACE

In early spring 1976, when I was preparing the proposal for a book on techniques to reverse hardening of the arteries, one of the scientists I consulted, Elliot M. Goldwag, Ph.D., said to be sure and include chelation therapy. "What's that?" I asked.

Perhaps like you, I was newly exposed to the therapeutic wonders of EDTA chelation. My investigations have since convinced me that chelation therapy has the ability to save the lives of more than three million Americans annually.

The steady but ubiquitous hardening of our arteries drains vitality from the cells and tissues of the body. It disables and kills by blocking blood circulation to the heart, brain, internal organs, or limbs. It narrows arterial channels, reduces blood flow, cuts off oxygen, suffocates blood vessels themselves, and prevents nourishment from reaching the anatomical areas these starved arteries supply. Yet, treatment taken with an intravenous infusion of EDTA chelation reverses each of these pathological processes. My twenty-one years of research since I learned of the therapy, interviewing more than five hundred physicians who give the injections and several hundred patients who have taken them, has proved beyond question that medical science has a potent tool to stop the diseases derived from the degeneration of our arteries.

Every second person who dies in this country each year is killed, directly or indirectly, by degeneration of the arteries. But the absolute reversal of the clogging mechanism in arteries can be accomplished without surgery, without pain, and without radiation. The chemotherapy used is nontoxic, nutritional, medicinal, comfortable, and involves physician participation. It does ask you to change your lifestyle, as an essential part of altering the degeneration process within the arteries.

People in North America, Europe, Australia, New Zealand, Japan, China, and other parts of the industrialized world do not have to die prematurely from hardening of the arteries. This book tells you how to reverse the process.

This book can save your life. I hope you will use it!

Morton Walker, D.P.M.
Stamford, Connecticut
April 1, 1997

ACKNOWLEDGMENTS

This is the fourth revised, updated and completely rewritten version of a book first published in 1980. Most of the information is new and never before publicized.

Hundreds of contributors assisted us in bringing you the information: chelation therapy patients who told me their stories, the physicians who administered their treatments, the patients' loved ones who filled in objective details, their friends and neighbors who verified the facts I uncovered and medical librarians who dug into archives.

In gathering research material, we had a lot of other help, too. I want to acknowledge the diligent efforts of Garry F. Gordon, M.D., of Payson, Arizona, past chairman of the Board of Trustees and past president of the American College for Advancement in Medicine (ACAM), who supplied me with a great deal of clinical journal material and case histories. Dr. Gordon remained a continuous source of inspiration, even when the subject of chelation therapy kept getting rejected by publishers.

I thank my coauthor, Hitendra H. Shah, M.D., medical director of the Institute of Holistic Medicine, 22807 Barton Road, Grand Terrace, California 92313; telephone (909) 783-2773; teleFAX (909) 783-6625. Dr. Shah has provided me with vast amounts of new material—patient case histories, the chelating detoxification program, the chelation exercise, published clinical journal articles, documents from his cardiovascular practice, and more for this updated and revised book on chelation therapy.

Originally earning his medical degree in Bombay, India, and working as a hospital staff physician there, Dr. Shah immigrated to the United States. He took a five-year medical residency, first in general surgery at Brookdale Hospital and then in radiation therapy at Kings County Hospital, Downstate Medical Center of the State University of New York. Both institutions are located in Brooklyn, New York. Since he had focused on making a career in cancer radiotherapy, Dr. Shah took an extra year of fellowship training in radiation oncology at the University of California Medical Center at Irvine.

But then he realized that administering conventional, allopathic radiation treatment to dying cancer patients did nothing much to improve the quality of their lives. Consequently, Dr. Shah turned to holistic medicine—chelation therapy being among its foundations—not only to preserve human life but also to offer prolongevity to those patients who adopt concepts of whole person healing. He is a diplomate candidate of the American Board of Chelation Therapy and an active participant in programs of the American College for Advancement in Medicine.

I appreciate the input of the now-deceased Harold W. Harper, M.D., of Los Angeles, also a former president of the Academy, who set up appointments with colleagues and provided me with his own experiences. I thank Bruce W. Halstead, M.D., of Colton, California, past president of ACAM; Yiwen Y. Tang, M.D., of Reno, Nevada; and Charles H. Farr, M.D., Ph.D. of Oklahoma City, Oklahoma, all of whom furnished case histories and illustrative materials, and shared their own experiences with chelation techniques. Warren M. Levin, M.D., of New York City unselfishly granted me much of his time; and Norman E. Clarke, M.D., "the grandfather of EDTA chelation," provided a scientific treatise on atherosclerosis he had prepared for a medical meeting.

Of everyone, Joan Walker, my loving and patient spouse, deserves the most thanks because she suffered through the periodic publisher rejections with me. She had as much investment in time—having lost my attention during its writing—from my involvement with this book. Furthermore, she was my built-in editor who helped cull the vast amount of medical material into the more manageable manuscript that finally evolved.

The more I researched, the greater was my realization that this story was the most important piece of medical journalism I had ever undertaken. In uncovering facts for you, Joan and I have learned how to preserve our own lives and health, too.

Morton Walker, D.P.M.

INTRODUCTION

As you will learn in detail in the chapters to follow, chelation therapy is a form of artery cleansing. This therapy reduces calcium deposits which glue together plaque material that blocks blood flow through the vessels. The treatment involves intravenous injection of small amounts of an amino acid that has the unique and valuable property of powerfully attracting ionic calcium. When the amino acid comes in contact with this calcium, it becomes bound (chelated) to it. Then, the amino acid–calcium complex that's formed gets excreted through the kidneys into the urine or through the liver into the intestinal tract and finally passes out of the body as a waste product. This binding property of the amino acid provides the basis for chelation therapy to clean away arterial obstructions.

During the past forty years, the chelation process has been a primary source of saving the lives of more than ten million North Americans who had been close to death from myocardial infarction, atrial fibrillation, congestive heart failure, angina pectoris or other types of cardiovascular disease. The number of stories showing the benefits of chelation therapy are too many to retell or even to count. And except for some details that are idiosyncratic to the individual patient, most of the stories of near-death and recovery sound the same.

At first, the tales told are of conventional medical practices that were ruining a person's quality of life. There were procedures that brought no relief of symptoms or drugs that caused serious side effects. Some techniques were highly invasive and harmful. There were reports of allopathic physicians—even including cardiologists—who were careless or uncaring or unskilled or ignorant. The health situation for that particular victim of cardiovascular disease, given the case history, was exceedingly bleak. Death seemed near; perhaps the individual's suffering was so great that death was almost welcome.

And then something really uplifting happens: the patient or members of the patient's family or friends discover the existence of chelation therapy. Everything related to the sick person's health gets better. Improvement of body and brain is gladly accepted by the patient, family, and friends, but that doesn't stop them from asking why this beneficial method of therapy wasn't routinely recommended before the patient's life had been put in such jeopardy. You'll learn the answer to that question in the following chapters.

The Case History of Lindley M. Camp

Allow us to tell you the case history of one such victim who had numerous cardiac complications. Sixty-eight-year-old Lindley M. Camp of Cantonment, Florida, wants this story of cardiovascular rehabilitation told and offers both his home telephone number and E-mail address so that you may learn the truth of what he has written (telephone (904) 968-3780 and E-mail keylation@aol.com).

"While at home on January 13, 1995, I developed severe angina pains, and my wife took me to the emergency room of West Florida Regional Hospital," writes Mr. Camp. A retired employee of Merrill Lynch & Co., a stock brokerage firm, Mr. Camp presents us with a personal account of recovery from his very serious heart disorder and its associated complications. He wants fellow patients with cardiovascular disease to possess all possible information for helping themselves in the same safe way that he saved his own life. Until he proceeded with chelation therapy to solve his severe health problem, he had harrowing experiences with two cardiologists and their form of cardiac medicine as it is practiced in the United States.

"I laid in the CCU [coronary care unit] for two days while being monitored [by the hospital's personnel]. My wife, Sherry, stayed with me continuously. It seemed strange to us that we had not seen my regular physician, a cardiologist, from the time I was admitted to the CCU. We knew that he had been notified by the admitting office. Near the end of the second day, Sherry left for our home to bathe, change clothes, run some errands, and telephone my doctor," said Lindley Camp. "She did reach him and asked what he was going to give me as treatment, since I had been hospitalized and merely monitored for forty-eight hours. The doctor seemed unsure about my identity as his patient, and then he admitted that he didn't know what treatment would be administered.

"Puzzled about his uncertainty, Sherry requested the physician (whom we had known quite a considerable period and had visited three weeks earlier for my routine checkup) to return her call when he had decided on the treatment. At this point in their conversation (almost as a hint to get his mental processes going), she asked if he was 'considering angioplasty.' In answer, the cardiologist remarked that this was a possibility," Mr. Camp said. "Approximately twenty minutes later, he did call back to my wife and told her that, in fact, he was going to perform angioplasty, for it was a necessary procedure to save my life. When Sherry returned to the hospital that evening, however, she was told by the nurses that another cardiologist would be performing the angioplasty."

Angioplasty and Complicating Myocardial Infarction

Having a history of heart impairment for the prior ten years, Lindley M. Camp was now experiencing recurrent angina pectoris, a pain in the center of his chest, induced by exercise and relieved by rest. Angina pectoris occurs when the demand for blood by the heart exceeds the supply of the coronary arteries, usually resulting from coronary artery atheroma, an abnormal mass of fat deposit in the artery wall. Still, on that day in early January, this particular angina pain struck the patient so suddenly and severely, he agreed with his wife that the hospital was where he belonged.

In standard cardiovascular practice, angioplasty is considered a viable invasive surgery for severe angina pectoris. Angioplasty to correct angina pain involves the insertion of a balloon-tipped catheter into the artery at the site of its partially obstructive fatty plaque lesion (atherosclerosis). The inflation of the balloon can rupture the artery's innermost layer (the intima) along with its middle layer (the media) to dramatically dilate the obstruction. Still, angioplasty is not any sort of cure for atherosclerosis. About 25 percent of all atherosclerotic lesions reocclude inside an operated artery within a few days or weeks. Then the cardiac surgeon may try angioplasty again, for frequently the reoccluded artery can be redilated successfully. There's a proven risk of complication, however. Repeat X-ray examination (angiography) of the operated blood vessel one year later has revealed that the central opening of the artery through which blood flows (the lumen) becomes abnormal, with damage in 70 percent of the blood vessels undergoing the procedure.

Angioplasty is classified as an alternative to bypass surgery only in the patient with suitable anatomic lesions (pathology). The procedure's current risk is comparable to bypass surgery in the following ways: (1) death of the patient (mortality) takes place in an average of 2 percent of the operated cases; (2) heart attack appearing as death of a segment of heart muscle (myocardial infarction or MI) takes place as a complication in 4 percent of the operated patients; (3) emergency bypass surgery, sometimes required during the angioplasty itself, must be undertaken to accomplish resection (repair) of the damaged intima, with recurrent obstruction in 5 percent of angioplasties. In a highly experienced cardiologist's hands, the rate of initial angioplasty success is perhaps 85 percent. Performed by less experienced operators, the failure rate for angioplasty is recorded at three out of every ten heart patients who undergo the procedure.[1]

"While the doctor was inserting the angioplasty balloon into my coronary artery, I underwent a documented mycardial infarction," Lindley Camp wrote in his February 1, 1996 letter to Ms. Kate Mann, an executive with Empire Blue Cross/Blue Shield of Middletown, New York. (He provided this letter for reproduction here, so that you would have the details of his case history.)

Later, in a telephone interview with me, Mrs. Sherry Camp stated that the cardiac surgeon actually created this MI, because "Lindley, who was awake during the procedure, shouted for him to take out the balloon. But the surgeon ignored his pleas."

"I was put into the hospital's coronary care unit," continued Mr. Camp's letter. "The evening after this operative procedure and heart attack took place (on January 15), my wife and daughter came up to see me in the CCU after attending Sunday evening church services. According to them, I looked chipper, responsive, and ate my dinner. And the 3:00 P.M. to 11:00 P.M. shift nurse reported that my condition was stable and I was resting comfortably. My family left the hospital believing that their prayers had been answered and that I was recovering.

The Patient Reacts Adversely to Ativan® Injection

"Then, later in this same shift, the male nurse on duty injected my IV with a drug called Ativan® to help me sleep. From his observations, no side effects were noted on my chart. When the nursing shift changed for the hours of 11:00 P.M. to 7:00 A.M., the next male nurse also injected Ativan® into my IV and noted on the chart that my air passages were swelling and that I was having trouble breathing. He recorded further that Ativan® administration should be discontinued. Yet, at some point between 6:00 A.M. and 7:00 A.M., during the next shift change, another nurse came into my room and injected my intravenous feeding again with Ativan®," stated Mr. Camp.

"Slightly after 8:00 A.M., my wife arrived at the hospital, pressed a buzzer outside the CCU doors, and when my 7:00 A.M. to 3:00 P.M. duty nurse came out, asked that she be paged in the waiting room when my regular cardiologist walked into my room to check on my progress. You see, the usual hours for visitors began at 9:00 A.M., and Sherry wouldn't venture inside the cardiac care unit before the appropriate time," said Mr. Camp. "The nurse didn't tell my wife about what had taken place earlier with the drug injections.

"So she sat in the family reception area until 9:00 A.M. and then entered my hospital room. Upon seeing me, Sherry was shocked by my poor condition. She saw that I was deteriorated from the robust way I had appeared the previous evening. She asked the nurse what happened to me," Mr. Camp explained. "The nurse admitted, 'Well, somebody gave Mr. Camp a *third* dose of Ativan® during the hectic shift change early this morning, and they kinda didn't know what the right hand was doing from the left.' She then laid out for Sherry how I had gone into congestive heart failure. Now I was having my breathing supported by a respirator and other machines that hadn't been hooked up to me the previous evening."

According to the *Physician's Desk Reference®*, the drug Ativan® (injectable lorazepam) is produced by Wyeth-Ayerst Laboratories, a Division of American Home Products Corporation of Philadelphia, Pennsylvania. It has antianxiety and sedative effects and is administered for purposes of producing sleepiness or drowsiness, relief of preoperative anxiety and lack of recall of events related to the day of surgery. Adverse effects include partial airway obstruction for the patient or the creation of excessive sedation when other drugs are being used. Patients over the age of fifty receiving Ativan® seemingly have more profound and prolonged sedation which may require the use of equipment to maintain an open airway.[2]

"When the doctor finally arrived, of course, my wife had words with him about what had occurred. While standing outside my room (with her arms crossed over her chest), she confronted him. He reached over and pulled her arms down to her sides and said this situation with the drug wasn't his problem; she must speak to the head nurse and put in a complaint, which she did," wrote Mr. Camp. "The head nurse acted as if no serious harm had come from the incident, despite Sherry telling her that there had to be some accountability by somebody for what happened to me. After that, the nursing personnel and doctors said nothing further about mishandling of the drug. Remaining in the CCU, two days later I was taken off the respirator and other extra equipment.

"Meantime, because of this fiasco, I changed cardiologists from my first long-time doctor to the second one who had performed the angioplasty, even though I suspected that this second doctor actually was the cause of my experiencing an MI," affirmed Mr. Camp. "As it happens, these two experienced heart doctors are partners in the same group practice. But the first cardiologist didn't seem to care about me, so I felt I had to change. In another few days the second cardiologist had me discharged from the hospital, and I went home to recuperate.

"On February 16, 1995, I visited the hospital as an outpatient to undergo an echocardiogram in order to determine the extent of heart damage from the infarction," Mr. Camp continued. "We didn't learn the answer to that question. Sherry and I returned for a consultation with my former cardiologist in his office on February 21. He discussed what medications should be added or changed—nothing more. He didn't tell us how much heart damage I had experienced."

Steady Deterioration of His Health

"From February to November, my general health went downhill steadily to the point that I could barely shuffle to the mailbox at the end of my driveway and back. It was necessary for me to discontinue my water aerobics class which I enjoyed attending three times a week. I was too weak. Most of each day I slept or remained groggy from swallowing thirteen prescription medicines daily," he said. "Even though my medications were changed during these months, I continued to decline.

"Because I felt close to death, at the start of the 1995 Thanksgiving holiday week, Sherry again drove me to the West Florida Hospital emergency room, and this time I was admitted with a diagnosis of congestive heart failure. Confining me for several days, the medical staff injected me with an intravenous form of Lasix™ [the trademark for a water pill or diuretic]. I was allowed to go home Thanksgiving Day. But on December 4, I was forced to return to the emergency room once more with congestive heart failure, plus I received the additional diagnosis of atrial fibrillation with a possible blood clot," asserted the patient.

Atrial fibrillation is a heart condition marked by rapid, unsystematic contractions of the upper heart chambers, the atria. This causes the lower chambers (the ventricles) to beat irregularly at the rate of 130 to 150 a minute. The atria may discharge a dangerously high number of more than 350 electric impulses per minute. The lower chambers cannot contract in response to all these impulses, and the heart's contractions become disordered. Atrial fibrillation occurs most often in heart diseases such as those reported by Lindley Camp, as mitral stenosis and atrial infarction. The rapid pulsations result in a decreased amount of blood pumped to the body. The disorganized contractions of the atria can cause blood clots to form in the atria.

"During this additional hospital admission, I told my second cardiologist that I thought he was the cause of my heart attack, which at first he denied, but then he agreed that this might have been possible. He also said that he needed to perform another echocardiogram and at the same time do a cardioversion (see below) to reset my heart," said Mr. Camp. "I agreed and signed the necessary legal forms."

Echocardiography (also called ultrasonic cardiography) is a noninvasive method of diagnosis that studies the structure and motion of the heart. Ultrasonic waves directed through the heart are reflected backward, or echoed, when they pass from one type of tissue to another, such as from heart muscle to blood. This test can find tumors in the upper heart chambers and fluid in the sac around the heart (pericardial effusion). It can measure the parts of the lower chambers and spot problems with the movement of the valve between the upper and lower chambers on the left side of the heart (the mitral valve).

Cardioversion involves restoring the heart's normal rhythm by giving an electric shock through two metal paddles placed on the patient's chest. Cardioversion is used to treat atrial fibrillation and for severe arrhythmias. The electric voltage is given by placing one of the metal paddles, covered with a thick layer of special paste, below the heart on the left side of the chest. The other paddle is placed over the upper right chest. The device is first set at a low level of voltage. If the normal rhythm of the heart does not resume, shocks of up to 400 watts per second can be given.

The patient must sign an informed consent before cardioversion can start. Diuretics and digitalis are withheld for twenty-four to seventy-two hours. Nothing is given by mouth for six to eight hours before the treatment. A sedative is taken an hour before cardioversion. Afterward, the patient must stay in bed. A constant graph of the heart's electric impulses is watched (called electrocardiographic monitoring). Oxygen is administered if needed. Cardioversion will usually work to restore the heart's normal rhythm as it did for Lindley Camp.

"My cardioversion was performed at approximately 1:30 P.M., and the doctor sent me home around 5:00 P.M. that same day (December 6). But I felt terribly weak and could barely make it into the house from the car," Mr. Camp explained. "Then on December 8, around 5:00 A.M., I awakened Sherry to take me back to the emergency room for the third time. I remember that it was a Friday. I could barely breathe and was wheezing all through the night. During this hospital stay, the cardiologist came into my room with Sherry sitting there and informed us that the heart attack I had sustained during the angioplasty in January had damaged 40 percent of my heart and the front muscle wasn't moving. He wanted to be sure that this large amount of heart muscle loss was a fact, so he told me I needed to take a treadmill stress test. I replied, 'No, I'm too weak!' He then said that he wanted to perform another heart catherization [an angiogram] and follow up this diagnostic test with a coronary artery bypass operation. What he offered was hardly good news!"

The Camps Consult with Julian Whitaker, M.D.

"As it happens, Sherry and I spent a week during September 1995 at the Whitaker Wellness Institute in Newport Beach, California, under the treatment supervision of Julian Whitaker, M.D. Therefore, learning that I needed open heart surgery, I asked my Florida cardiologist to contact Dr. Whitaker for input on my condition," reported Mr. Camp.

"Well, he became visibly agitated and said outright, 'I don't agree with Dr. Whitaker's medical practice!' Sherry asked him if he would at least talk to Dr. Whitaker if we could contact him over the telephone. The cardiologist consented and we called Dr. Whitaker to tell him what was happening to me. They spoke together, and my Florida cardiologist agreed to put magnesium into my IV [intravenous] feeding. The doctor came back into my room that Friday evening and stated that he would give us until Monday to decide what we wanted to do and that I could receive the magnesium drip until then."

Julian Whitaker, M.D., is a diplomate in chelation therapy, who has become renowned as an outspoken critic of organized medicine through the editing of his monthly newsletter, *Dr. Julian Whitaker's Health & Healing™: Tomorrow's Medicine Today,* published by Phillips Publishing, Inc. of Potomac, Maryland. Dr. Whitaker's newsletter has a verified circulation to more than 750,000 subscribers. Practicing medicine for over twenty-three years, Dr. Whitaker received degrees from Dartmouth College and Emory University. He has long been an advocate of a healthy, nontoxic approach to living an active life. He is the author of five books. Dr. Whitaker's Wellness Institute has helped thousands find a healing, safe approach to living, and to reverse the effects of heart disease, arthritis, diabetes, and many other diseases.

Dr. Julian Whitaker has taken a stand against angioplasty. But it is one of those procedures which are "allowed" to be covered by health insurance companies. Dr. Whitaker writes: "It may surprise you to realize that what is 'allowed' or 'not allowed' has *nothing to do with scientific documentation of benefit.* In fact, many of the 'unallowed' therapies have far more scientific evidence of benefit than some of the 'allowed' therapies that are used in their place. Most of the time it boils down to money: *The [medical] profession will invariably 'allow' the therapy that is the most lucrative, even if a safer and less expensive therapy is available.* You might think that the insurance companies would object to this, but they actually have no say on what is or is not allowed.

"For instance," continues Dr. Whitaker, "percutaneous transluminal angioplasty. This is the procedure where a balloon is inserted into the small arteries to the heart, then inflated to open up blocked arteries. This is not only an unproven therapy, it's not even a good idea. As early as 1983, it was clearly shown that the ideal angioplasty candidates—men with mild symptoms and one or two clearly defined blockages—had a death rate with conservative therapy of less than 1 percent. Therefore, to stick a balloon inside one of these arteries only makes the problem worse. The procedure itself carries a death rate of 2 percent (one out of fifty), and in those that are 'successful,' the artery will snap shut—sometimes more severely—in 30 percent in less than a year.

"In spite of this, angioplasty is an 'approved' therapy, and in fact, the cardiologist who is doing angioplasty is paid by the number of arteries he balloons. If he knows that the [health] insurance company will pay an additional $500 to 1,500 for ballooning a second artery, he might be encouraged to 'help the patient' and do just that. As an allowed therapy, medical insurance companies are currently dishing out about $2.25 billion a year, or roughly $6 million per day, for this unproven therapy," Dr. Whitaker reports.[3]

"As an aside, I might add that we have been shocked at the cardiologist's bad news about the extent of my heart damage," observed Mr. Camp. "This amount of damage was never revealed to us during my February consultation after undergoing the echocardiogram. I can't be sure if the information of 40 percent heart muscle death is completely true, for I sense that the information was used on us as a fear tactic to get me to give the doctor permission to perform the more dangerous and costly procedures. These, I fear, would have killed me."

Dr. William Watson Administers Chelation Therapy

"During that weekend, we contacted Dr. William Watson of Milton, Florida, and related all of the above to him. He agreed with Dr. Whitaker that I must not have any further invasive procedures," wrote Mr. Camp. "Both Dr. Whitaker and Dr. Watson spoke on the phone about my condition and were of like opinion. My wife and I completely agreed with them, and I asked Dr. Watson if I could come to his clinic for an evaluation as soon as I was strong enough. (You should know that after being discharged on Tuesday morning, December 12, 1995, I was in Dr. Watson's office at 4 o'clock that same afternoon.)"

William N. Watson, M.D., is in general practice in Milton, Florida with specialties in surgery, bariatrics and chelation therapy. By his study and experience, Dr. Watson has moved up to an examination level that recognizes his having attained the status of diplomate/candidate with the American Board of Chelation Therapy. He participates as an active physician/member of the American College for Advancement in Medicine, the specialty organization that investigates and advocates chelation therapy.

"On Monday morning, December 11, my cardiologist came into the hospital room, listened to my chest, and asked if I was ready to sign the papers giving him permission to do another angioplasty or a coronary artery bypass operation. I told him that I didn't want any further invasive procedures and that I wouldn't sign the papers. He allowed me to stay in the hospital until the following morning (Tuesday), and I was discharged," Mr. Camp said.

"As of July 16, 1996, I have received eighty-two chelation treatments including intravenous infusions of hydrogen peroxide (H_2O_2), dimethyl sulfoxide (DMSO), vitamin C, and vitamin B_6 at a cost of $8,200 to me. I have been able to drop two arthritic medications (Flexiril® and propoxyphene), and I have also been able to eliminate all but four of the thirteen heart prescriptions," asserted Mr. Camp. "My blood pressure now runs around 124/63; I can look down without getting dizzy and lightheaded; my weight is decreasing; my libido has improved; I'm taking some short walks through our neighborhood; my hearing has improved; my color has improved; aging spots are diminishing; and I have an overall sense of well-being—all of these positive results [occurred from receiving chelation therapy] without having to resort to expensive and life-threatening heart surgery."

Remember, you are reading a letter written by Lindley Camp to the Empire Blue Cross/Blue Shield Health Insurance Company which is mainly interested in how much money it can get away with not paying for its clients' medical care. That's why the patient is putting emphasis on cost saving. His goal is to receive reimbursement for money he had expended for chelation therapy.

"I was an employee of Merrill Lynch & Co. from 1952 until my disability retirement in 1986. I don't wish to waste my former employer's money by having very expensive heart surgery and endless invasive procedures which only contribute to my deterioration. Before receiving chelation therapy, my ability to function as a husband, father, and man were greatly diminished. I am so encouraged since I have been receiving these treatments; however, I need financial help in order to continue or I might need to resort to open heart surgery. Chelation treatments could run possibly to $10,000 over a period of one and a half years, at $100 per treatment," Mr. Camp continued. "I am currently taking three per week. Economically and healthwise, this makes more sense than Empire BC/BS paying up to and maybe more than $100,000 for open heart surgery, heart catherization, angioplasty, treadmill tests, etc.

"Ms Mann, I appreciate your interest in my case, and I am enclosing a book for your information, *The Chelation Way,* authored by Dr. Morton Walker. If you require any further information, please telephone me at (904) 968-3780. I look forward to hearing from you," concluded Lindley M. Camp.

On May 30, 1996, Mr. Camp provided us with records of his health history, the letter you've just read to Empire Blue Cross/Blue Shield, and an additional written explanation of what had transpired relating to his health and finances during the prior four months. The following is what he states:

"I'm enclosing information regarding my health history which we have discussed several times over the phone. You may use any of this information in any of your books," Mr. Camp writes. "Since my letter dated February 1, 1996 to Kate Mann (Empire BC/BS), my health has greatly improved. I previously was on thirteen heart medicines [each day] and a cholesterol reducer. I am now on four: Lanoxin®, Lasix®, Betapace®, and Coumadin®. I'm slowly weaning myself away from the 0.25 mg of Lanoxin® by taking four capsules (50 mg each) of the herbal remedy, hawthorne extract (including 300 mg of hawthorne berries). Dr. Watson believes that I may have to stay on Coumadin® throughout my lifetime.

Illness Symptoms Improve for Lindley Camp

"I want you to know, Drs. Walker and Shah, that as I got into chelation therapy, H_2O_2 therapy, DMSO therapy, as well as vitamins and herbs, I began to slowly wean myself down to the four prescriptions that I now take. My newest Florida cardiologist [the third], who respects Dr. Watson's practice and is a personal friend of his, knows that I have done this. He is also aware of all my treatments under Dr. Watson and my affiliation with Dr. Julian Whitaker," Mr. Camp says.

"My blood pressure is now normal and is checked weekly when I have my chelation treatments. As of this date, I have had sixty-eight combined treatments of chelation, hydrogen peroxide and DMSO. I was going [for treatment] three times weekly and have now cut back to twice weekly. My [blood] cholesterol level was 257 and is now 123," reports Mr. Camp, "triglycerides were 194 and are now 80. Most important, my ejection fraction has increased from 40 to 53."

The improved ejection fraction number is highly significant for indicating the patient's better heart health. Ejection fraction (EF) is the proportion of blood that is released during each contraction of the ventricle (the lower heart chamber) compared with the total volume of blood released by both, the upper and the lower ventricles. The greater an injection fraction reading, the stronger a heart muscle is pumping.

"My skin color is much better," continued Mr. Camp. "I no longer experience dizziness when I bend over, am clear-headed, and my overall feeling of wellness has improved remarkably. However, if I eat salt, don't drink my half-gallon of water daily, or expose myself to prolonged heat, I experience swelling, weight gain, congestion, and thus find it difficult to sleep. Sherry and I recently decided to throw all refined sugars and sugar products out of the kitchen. This, along with drinking a lot of water, has resulted in substantial weight loss for me. I now weigh 196.5 pounds versus 212 while I was in the hospital in December 1995. I expect to continue to lose some additional weight. My maintenance goal is 185 pounds.

Empire Blue Cross/Blue Shield Pays for Chelation Therapy

"I want to tell you about how I received reimbursement [for chelation therapy] from Empire BC/BS. As you saw from my letter to Kate Mann, I detailed my problems and asked for help with the chelation therapy payments. She has been with Blue Cross/Blue Shield for years, and she told me, 'This is the first request for chelation reimbursement from anyone.' And, she stated that I should get the word out to chelation therapy users regarding reimbursement by their insurance companies. (I am writing to Dr. Whitaker about this in case he wants to mention it in his newsletter.) I never submitted a claim to Medicare because they stated they will only pay for chelation therapy if you have hypercalcemia, digitalis intoxication, or lead poisoning," Mr. Camp said. "I have received total payments of $6,064 [up to May 30, 1996]. I also informed Ms. Mann that I would appeal any denial to higher officers of Merrill

Lynch (my former employer of thirty-six years who pays for my health care insurance with Empire BC/BS). In phone conversations with Ms. Mann, I stressed the total bill for chelation therapy of $10,000 vs possibly $100,000 for open heart surgery. In addition to my letter, I sent her a copy of your book, *The Chelation Way,* which she said was most enlightening and very helpful to the insurance company personnel when making their decision. (She stated, 'We have never before heard of chelation therapy.')"

Mr. Camp received a letter from Empire Blue Cross/Blue Shield extending his reimbursement for chelation therapy to July 27, 1996. The previous cutoff date for payment had been May 17, 1996. This reimbursement extension will now cover a total of $7,562 worth of chelation therapy costs.

"My former cardiologist [the second one who performed the angioplasty] was very closed-minded and negative about any alternative therapies," wrote Mr. Camp. "The cardiologist noted in my hospital file record, which I was able to obtain a copy of [and mail to Dr. Morton Walker], that after a six-month probation period under Dr. Whitaker, 'he (referring to me) must sell his soul to me.' Well, I have to reply sharply: 'No, doctor, I didn't go out the back door of West Florida Regional Hospital in a hearse as you had planned!'

"So, Dr. Walker, please let me know if you want further information. I really appreciate being able to stay in touch with you, and am looking forward to reading the rewritten edition of your upcoming book," Mr. Camp concluded.

Chapter One

YOU CAN REVERSE

HARDENING OF THE

ARTERIES

From the womb of darkness and the cocoon of indifference is emerging a form of treatment that will eventually be added to the armamentarium of the alert and concerned physician.

—RICHARD E. WELCH, M.D.
Let's Live, April 1976

New Life for Old Arteries

While golfing under the Southern California sun George W. Frankel, M.D., of Long Beach, California, chief of otolaryngology at two hospitals and staff ear, nose and throat specialist at three others, was seized by severe chest pains. His golfing partners returned him to the club house, and after resting Dr. Frankel visited his cardiologist.

Following electrocardiograms and treadmill tests, a coronary angiogram was performed at the hospital. Dr. Frankel was told by the cardiologist and a chest surgeon that his angiogram revealed obstructing plaques in the left main coronary artery. They recommended a triple coronary artery bypass. This operation must be done as soon as possible, the specialists said, in order to avoid coronary occlusion and, possibly, sudden death.

Coronary artery bypass surgery involves the removal of one of the major veins from the patient's thigh and its use to bypass the arteries feeding the heart that are being occluded. Such a surgery entails several serious hazards. There is a 10 to 15 percent possibility of a heart attack while on the operating table; there can be later aggravated deterioration of the arteries bypassed; there is a 20 to 30 percent possibility of occlusion of the new graft within two years; and there is the possibility of the reappearance, after a few years, of similar chest pains, with little or no chance of relief by additional surgery. Although the mortality of this operation at this writing is approximately 5 to 12 percent, the morbidity, better known as the *complications,* still exist in another 10 to 15 percent of the cases done. That is, one patient in fifteen will die *during the operation;* one in seven will suffer complications *after* the surgery.

Physicians experience fear of life-threatening procedures as does anyone else, and this ear, nose and throat specialist was no exception. Dr. Frankel was not anxious to face major surgery on his heart, but there seemed to be no alternative. Consequently, he did agree, and the surgery was scheduled to be performed in a few days. Then fate changed his course. Seven units of blood were needed for standby during the operation, but the Red Cross could not obtain this blood until after the Christmas and New Year holidays. His heart surgery was therefore rescheduled for two weeks later.

During his wait, Dr. Frankel discussed his condition with many of his colleagues and friends. One friend, whom Dr. Frankel described to us as "a very dear colleague who went to medical school with me, interned with me, and later became a prominent internist in New York," told of another individual with a similar condition. That person went through a treatment called *chelation,* a medical therapy that apparently reduced the amount of calcium in the obstructing plaques of the coronary arteries and reduced the amount of calcium in other areas of the vascular system.

Dr. Frankel, eager to try any logical, safe and painless avenue that might avoid the very real potential of death offered by heart surgery, began to search for clinical literature on the subject at the Los Angeles County Medical Association Library. He was amazed to find numerous medical journal articles on chelation therapy, a treatment he had never heard of before. After careful study of these many references, the patient ventured on what he hoped to be a journey to save his life. He entered an Alabama hospital which was run by H. Ray Evers, M.D.

"I saw people come in with diabetic ulcerative lesions and gangrenous lesions that cleared up in a matter of ten or twelve days, and I could not believe my eyes," said Dr. Frankel. "I saw one patient who was admitted after being told elsewhere that his leg would have to be amputated because of gangrene, and, daily, after chelation therapy, I watched with my mouth agape, as the leg came back to normal. I acted as a sort of assistant to Dr. Evers by making rounds with him every day. He was a very determined man who worked twenty of every twenty-four hours."

There was something else that Dr. Frankel could hardly believe. Prior to treatment, anginal pains had seared his chest when he walked only ten or twelve steps. After he received only ten chelations, the pain disappeared entirely. He went on to take twenty chelation treatments in Alabama and felt 75 percent better than before. He decided to put off having the heart surgery indefinitely. In the event he needed surgery later, the patient knew that his chance of survival was considerably enhanced by the remarkable improvement he experienced from his chelation treatments.

The physician–patient gave himself another eighty-eight chelations at home—with the help of a nurse-anesthetist for the intravenous injections—a total of 108 treatments in all. "And I want to tell you that I have not had an angina since," says Dr. Frankel. "I carry a full work load. I do approximately ten to fifteen surgeries every week, and these are microsurgeries of the ear. I carry a full practice. I play golf. I swim twenty laps in my pool every day, and I cannot speak with any but the greatest praise for the men who are attempting to make chelation an accepted form of therapy."

* * * * *

After enjoying an outing in very hot weather Roland C. Hohnbaum, D.C., then fifty-four years old, a chiropractor in Richmond, California, noticed that an ulcer had developed on his left foot. Such an ulcer was highly dangerous for Dr. Hohnbaum, since he is a long-term diabetic. Even with knowledge of the ramifications of diabetic ulcers, the chiropractor told himself "this can't happen to me. I'm different!" But he was not different, and the gangrenous course of arteriosclerosis complicated by diabetes began its insidious creep from his toes upward.

"It grew worse and worse, and finally I was forced down and was flat on my back for about two months," said Dr. Hohnbaum. "I had an internist at the Alta Bates Hospital in Berkeley, California, in whom I had a lot of confidence. He took care of my case in the beginning but then he became frightened, too, saying that I'd have to go to the hospital because I was going to lose my toes."

Also quite frightened himself, Dr. Hohnbaum knew it was time to make some major decisions. He rejected the amputation because of gangrene, since he knew that a decision to operate just *started* at the toes. Gangrene is known to spread, slowly and steadily, and eventually may require amputation below the knee, above the knee, or even at mid-thigh. Besides, the combination of hardening of the arteries and diabetes was by now showing effects in his other foot, too. It possibly meant having both feet cut off.

Because he refused hospitalization and surgery, Dr. Hohnbaum was denied further treatment by both his internist and the consulting vascular surgeon. Afflicted as he was, the patient had to engage in his own self-help program at home by bringing in dietary factors and anything else he could use to improve his health. He prayed that his condition might begin to show some improvement.

"I finally found out about Dr. Tang with the chelation therapy," the chiropractor said, while tears formed in his eyes, "and this was a life-saver for me. I don't think I can say any more than that I—I have feet under me now."

When Dr. Hohnbaum visited Yiwen Y. Tang, M.D., F.A.B.F.P. of Reno, Nevada, he arrived on crutches and in pain. "The patient was in immediate need of amputation of his two legs below the knee," Dr. Tang told me. "His life was in imminent danger. He could bear nothing on his feet—not hosiery—certainly not shoes." Dr. Tang supplied me with photographs which depict the condition of Dr. Hohnbaum's feet. After careful diagnostic studies, Dr. Tang began Dr. Hohnbaum on chelation treatments.

"The pre-chelation tests also indicated clogging of my carotid artery, making me a prime target for stroke," said Roland Hohnbaum.

Within a week of having the first treatment the patient could put on socks. Two months after the last of fifteen chelations, he wore shoes and returned to work full time. The chiropractor completely healed with no evidence of anything having happened to his feet.

"Post-chelation tests show my carotid artery now clear of occlusion," Dr. Hohnbaum told me. "There is no doubt that the atherosclerosis which accompanied my diabetes has been abated."

Dr. Hohnbaum's case and thousands of others like his have changed medical thinking in this country about diabetic gangrene. The condition had previously been diagnosed as irreversible, but diabetic ulcers and gangrene now can be cured by chelation therapy (see photographs 1-1, 1-2, 1-3, 1-4).

Photograph 1-1

Photograph 1-2

Photograph 1-4

Photograph 1-3

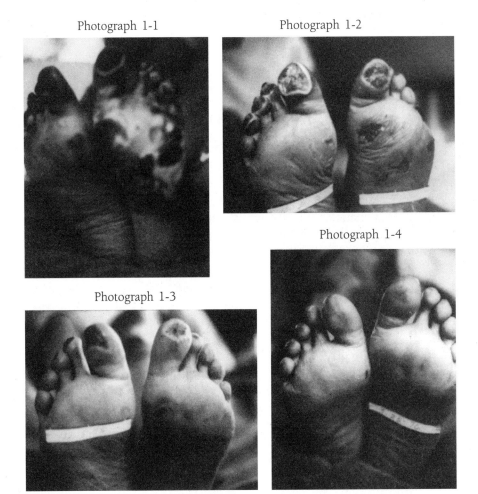

Photograph 1-1 shows the feet of Roland C. Hohnbaum, D.C., two days before his scheduled operation for amputation because of diabetic gangrene and ulcerations. He could bear nothing on his feet, not even hosiery, because of the pain. Following standard medical procedure, both legs would have been cut off below the knees. After just one week of chelation therapy, however (*Photograph 1-2*), the gangrene has been reversed and the ulcerated areas are beginning to heal. Two months after the last of fifteen chelation treatments (*Photograph 1-3*), the diabetic gangrene was eliminated and Dr. Hohnbaum wore shoes and returned to work full time. Two months later (*Photograph 1-4*), all ulcerations have disappeared and Dr. Hohnbaum's feet are completely normal. Gangrene has been reversed.

Dr. Hohnbaum added a postscript to his story. He said, "I am still haunted by the flat statement made to me by a vascular surgeon whom I had met after my feet were all healed. Upon seeing the photographs of my gangrenous feet, the surgeon said, 'If you had been my patient and your feet looked like these pictures, there is no question—I would have amputated!'"

* * * * *

During the Thanksgiving holidays, Lester I. Tavel, D.O., of Houston, Texas made a visit to his friend, Harold W. Harper, M.D., of Los Angeles, California. Dr. Tavel complained of no particular health problem, but as doctors will do for each other, Dr. Harper performed a physical examination on his colleague. At the examination's conclusion, Dr. Harper advised his friend to take chelation treatment as a precautionary measure against occlusial artery disease. Then Dr. Harper gave Dr. Tavel chelation materials to use for self-treatment at home.

"But being an osteopathic physician, I made my own diagnosis and came to the decision that there was nothing wrong with me," confessed Dr. Tavel during our interview. "I did not give myself chelation therapy."

Five months later, Dr. Tavel suffered a heart attack, a paroxysmal atrial tachycardia with a pulse rate running at 200 beats per minute. It took three electric shocks of 25, 50, and 100 volts each to cardiovert the victim back to a near-normal rate. An X-ray examination of his chest showed the patient's heart enlarged, filling practically the whole chest cavity. He remained in the intensive care unit of St. Luke's Hospital, Houston. Knowing of the risks that went with open-heart surgery, however, such an operation was not even considered by the osteopathic physician, his attending physicians, or his family.

As soon as Dr. Tavel could be moved, his wife flew with him to Dr. Harper's office in Los Angeles. Since her husband was unable to take more than three or four steps without experiencing tremendous shortness of breath, Mrs. Tavel pushed him in a wheel chair. The patient's ankles were swollen to the size of footballs.

Dr. Harper set up intravenous chelation in an apartment-hotel suite he had made ready for his friend. At the end of three weeks, in which he received fifteen treatments, the patient's heart began to return to its usual size. In another week, upon X-ray examination, it again appeared completely normal.

"You know, Los Angeles has a lot of streets with 45-degree inclines,"

Dr. Tavel later told us. "Well, by the time I had received thirty chelations in about six weeks, I was walking up the hill in front of my hotel. I walked up steps, too. My resting pulse rate was 84 beats per minute and by the time I reached the top of the hill, it increased to 110. Then it dropped back to 84 upon my resting within a minute afterwards."

"What Lester didn't know at the time," said Dr. Harper, "is that his electrocardiogram (EKG) and enzyme studies indicated he had acute myocardial infarction (a local area of death) in the heart muscle. I began to administer therapy as soon as my emergency medical workup for him was over. After about the first five treatment days, his shortness of breath began to go away. The edema (swelling) was down. He was able to eat again. His color changed from pasty white to something near his natural ruddiness.

"In the first week Lester was able to walk without being totally tired, as he had been when he arrived. His glucose tolerance test level had dropped to 15 milligrams percent (normal blood sugar is near 90) so I instituted a nutritional program during his treatment days," Dr. Harper revealed.

"I took a second X-ray series after about ten chelations. His heart size showed close to normal, but not quite. Lester's enzyme studies and blood sugar had returned to normal, though, and his EKG returned to normal within a two-week period." In fact, the EKG didn't even point to ischemia (inadequate circulation of blood).

"Follow-through at the end of thirty treatment days showed my patient's heart size comparable to the way it had been when I saw him the previous November. Comparison X-ray films attested to the heart sizes as being exactly the same. There were no fluid levels in his lungs— no congestion—no edema. Lester was able to go home at the end of six weeks," concluded Dr. Harper.

"I checked myself quite cautiously," Dr. Tavel added. "I ran a heck of a lot of BUNS (blood-urea-nitrogen tests for toxicity) and creatinines (urine tests) after I got home, and I didn't have any problems with those or any other toxic symptoms.

"I did notice many things about myself improve—my prior dyspnea (frequent rapid breathing) was relieved; my fatigue was relieved; my limbs were warmer," Dr. Tavel said. "I had a regrowth of hair on my legs, and I had an increased libido (sex drive) that my wife enjoyed. I gave myself ten more chelation treatments at home, and I've been taking six treatments a year since.

"About thirty days ago I had another chest X-ray that showed my heart size remaining normal. An independent group of cardiologists then evaluated my EKGs and rechecked about thirty-five of my laboratory tests, including all the heart enzyme tests and liver enzyme tests. All the diagnostic findings were back to normal as if I never had experienced a heart attack," Dr. Tavel assured us.

* * * * *

A triple coronary artery bypass was avoided; a gangrenous foot was not amputated, and the foot was restored to normal; a heart attack victim rejects open-heart surgery, instead has a fluid enter his veins, and now says he is completely recovered. Can these stories possibly be true?

Every case history you will read about in this book is authentic. Every one you will read, we have double-checked for truth and accuracy. Dr. Tavel's story struck us as most dramatic. His heart problem had him closer to death than anyone ought to be, and still recover. We therefore took the opportunity to triple-check his story and sought out and interviewed a person who worked for Dr. Tavel at the time of his attack. We spoke with Deborah Triche, a registered nurse employed by Dr. Tavel and his former associate, Dr. John Mohney.

Nurse Triche retold the story of Dr. Tavel's heart attack that we have described. She said, "I was the technician who recorded Dr. Tavel's EKGs and submitted them to our cardiological EKG service. The heart doctors on the service read the recordings and computerize their reports. Each time a patient has an EKG taken, it is compared to the one taken of him previously.

"Well, after Dr. Tavel's chelation therapy was completed, I asked one of the cardiologists about the comparisons between his pretherapy and posttherapy EKGs. The cardiologist said, 'You know, Dr. Tavel's heart was severely damaged before the treatment, but now following chelation it shows no after-effects on the EKG at all.' I was amazed," said the nurse.

The History of Chelation Therapy

Chelation therapy is a well-recognized treatment for lead poisoning. It has been used to remove this poison metal from the bodies of children and other patients for almost fifty years. The treatment has also been applied for reversal of hardening of the arteries with great success. Although not well recognized for anti-atherosclerotic purposes, chelation therapy is extensively documented in the medical literature, with at least 2,150 clinical and laboratory journal articles published in the English language. We have included a reference list of some of these articles in the footnotes and appendix. The articles provide additional supportive scientific evidence of the treatment's safety and efficacy.

Chelation therapy is not a new procedure. It was introduced into the United States in 1948, but it had been employed as a chemical medical treatment in Europe long before that. Presently, about two thousand physicians in this country offer the intravenous treatment. Approximately twenty-five million injections have been administered by them to around one million North American patients and many thousands of Europeans, Australians, etc.

The goal of the physician who gives chelation therapy is to restore adequate blood flow through his patient's occluded arteries and to relieve symptoms of arterial insufficiency anywhere in the body. This mode of therapy relieves the symptoms caused by atherosclerotic plaque that hardens and obstructs blood vessel walls. How it does this is the subject of some controversy and debate at this time. In this book, we shall present all of the known or currently held medical theory, established physiological or pathological facts, and the practical application of chelation therapy for atherosclerosis. Our investigative medical reporting comes from clinical and laboratory journal articles, interviews with patients who experienced the treatment and physicians who give the injections, and our own investigations.

Chelation therapy administered to a patient is known to bind, or "chelate," divalent and trivalent metals in the human body. These metals have two or three combining bonds or valences. In the *concept of valence* in chemistry, the elements which do *not* combine with hydrogen—such as the metals—are said to have positive valence. Some of the metals, such as calcium, iron, zinc, lead, and mercury have two or three valences; they are *divalent* or *trivalent.*

The substance used to bring about chelation therapy is able to remove ionic calcium (a divalent metal) from the bloodstream and probably from the walls of the blood vessels, either directly or indirectly. This chemical substance is employed in the chelation intravenous injection. It carries dissolved liquid calcium from the bloodstream to the patient's kidneys and out of the body in the urine. The removed blood calcium is then replaced from the abnormal or unhealthy metastic calcium deposits. These deposits act as a loose glue binding together the components of atherosclerotic plaque, so that the metastatic calcium leaves the plaque and ionizes in the blood. What happens to the plaque when it loses its glue? It breaks up and leaves the body.

Alterations in calcium and other divalent metals in the blood produce beneficial improvements in arterial enzyme function. They stabilize cellular membranes and enhance cellular function.

The ultimate effect of these physiological changes is an increased blood flow and an improvement in elasticity of hardened arteries. In addition, there is a much-improved tissue perfusion through the capillaries, by decreasing the wall rigidity of red blood cells. Also, red blood cell aggregations are reversed. This decreases platelet "stickiness" by improving platelet membrane function. These net results appear to give "new life to old arteries."

The Medical Alternative to Surgical Treatment for Hardening of the Arteries

The basic chemical agent employed in chelation therapy, which we shall describe in the next chapter, has been shown by more than two hundred studies to be safe and effective against lead poisoning and other heavy metal contaminations. It is approved for this use by the Food and Drug Administration (FDA). The same mechanism that makes the drug a beneficial antidote against poisoning from lead makes it equally useful against excess serum calcium. Even so, chelation treatment to reverse hardening of the arteries is vigorously opposed by much of the American medical establishment.

Our contention is that American medical consumers have the right to know about all their medical alternatives. Individual physicians have a legal and moral responsibility to inform patients of the various treatment choices available. This responsibility should be fulfilled regardless of whether the physician agrees or disagrees with the therapy.

As it stands now, a person who is suffering from hardening of the arteries generally received incomplete information for this condition. The arteriosclerotic patient is not told of chelation therapy by his vascular surgeon—perhaps because most physicians don't know anything about the treatment themselves. In other instances physicians who think they know all about chelation may base their knowledge on hearsay and totally misleading information and not on any scientific study. They may, as a result, choose not to inform a patient who is contemplating bypass surgery or limb amputation about chelation therapy. Their reasons may be honorable. It might be that these physicians do not believe the treatment could really be effective. Legally, however, under prior court decisions, doctors must inform patients of *every* alternative—even if they personally reject one or more of the choices.

Chelation therapy is an alternative to painful, high-risk treatments, such as cardiovascular surgery with its high mortality rate, or to vasodilator drugs with their many side effects. Cardiovascular operations are prohibitively expensive and limited in their use, but these operations are terribly popular today. Surgery is restricted by the size of the blood vessels that can be operated upon. Tiny blood vessels cannot undergo surgical procedures, while in contrast chelation therapy can be used throughout the entire circulatory system.

In contemporary chelation treatment there have been *no known fatalities* as a result of its use. Conversely, death during or soon after bypass surgery is reported to range from 5 to 12 percent, depending on the experience of the heart surgeon and his staff. In surgical bypass the severity of the disease in the patient also plays a part. In fact, a study done by the National Institute of Health, which was reported to the medical community in March 1977, states that no one should have a bypass operation except for the relief of intractable angina. Yet, nine out of ten of these same kinds of severe cardiac cases are reported entirely relieved of symptoms with chelation therapy. Obviously, the risk factor is almost eliminated.

That NIH report went on to say that general medical treatment rather than surgery was demonstrated to be safer and more effective for coronary arteriosclerosis cases.

The Status of Chelation Therapy in the United States

Legal problems connected with the main chelating agent that is used in this country are tied exclusively to economics. For instance, where the chelation agent once was accepted and recommended for the treatment of "occlusive vascular diseases" such as angina and was even paid for by health insurance companies, it appears now to have lost this official status as a result of a change in federal regulations. There are exceptions, of course, as in the situation of Lindley M. Camp, reported to you in the Introduction. The patents on the chelation drug expired in 1968. Because of this expiration, compliance to prove effectiveness under the new guidelines of federal regulations would cost drug manufacturers millions of dollars. Drug companies cannot recover their money when the drug is no longer patentable. They therefore have no further interest in developing and marketing the product.

To attempt the licensing of a new drug, from scratch, in accordance with the safety and efficacy guidelines of the Food, Drug and Cosmetic Act as amended in 1962, and as currently enforced, involves up to ten years of trials and at least $200 million to $300 million in expenses. Such a great investment in time and money is required simply to get Food and Drug Administration approval. Then millions of dollars for advertising campaigns to physicians are necessary. Although not new, an unknown treatment like chelation therapy would need to be explained very carefully to practicing physicians in the United States.

It comes down to a matter of too many dollars and too much time required to bring chelation therapy to the American people. The plain and undeniable truth is that people are dying from atherosclerosis in part because of a lack of chelation therapy acceptance. The nonacceptance is caused by an absence of significant pharmaceutical industry investment potential.

Falling within the jurisdiction of the FDA are all those substances used in medical treatment which are construed to be either unlicensed new drugs or unsafe food additives. This includes safe and well-known substances such as aspirin, vitamin C and nasal sprays, when used for a "new" purpose. The substance employed for chelation therapy is a safe food additive used in salad dressings (such as Hellmann's *Real* Mayonnaise®) and many other foods. It is listed on the GRAS list (generally recognized as safe by the FDA). Indeed, it is a licensed drug that is *not new* at all.

It is not banned if it is to be used for treatment of metallic poisoning. The agent is also used, and with U.S. government sanction, for treatment of radioactive contamination. A story in the "Medicine" section in the March 21, 1977 issue of *Newsweek* magazine told of Harold McCluskey, a 64-year-old chemical operator, who had inhaled the largest recorded human dose of the isotope americium-241. His life was saved, sight restored and radiation sickness prevented by the calcium salt of that same chelating agent which is banned from use against hardening of the arteries.[1]

The FDA ban is enforced even though the medication is the "drug of choice" for dealing with hardening of the arteries in other countries. For example, when atherosclerosis affects the legs of citizens of the former Czechoslovakia, this intravenous chelation injection treatment is given. The Czechs give full credit to American physicians for the discovery, but it remains bureaucratically suppressed in the United States.

The American Medical Association's department of medicine does not approve of chelation therapy for arteriosclerosis either. Its status and worth for reversing hardening of the arteries "must be regarded with skepticism," says the AMA. And other doctors have referred in stronger terms to the various stories told by chelated patients. "Anecdoted medicine is bulls**t," says Alfred Soffer, M.D., of Chicago, a prominent internist, who was executive director of the American College of Chest Physicians. Dr. Soffer is a leading critic of chelation therapy.[2]

Most insurance companies today will not compensate holders of their health insurance policies for chelation treatment for arteriosclerosis. The patients are denied any reimbursement. The insurance industry has labeled the therapy "not usual, reasonable or customary" and generally refuses payment on those grounds, even if, because of chelation, the patient avoids hundred of thousands of dollars in bills for bypass surgery (which the insurance companies *do* pay).

Chelation Certainly Is "Reasonable" to Reynolds Hall

Although chelation is controversial, it certainly is "reasonable" to Reynolds Hall, age fifty-five, of Melbourne, Florida. It should be "usual and customary" also, he says, because the treatment for him generated a miracle.

Reynolds Hall is blind in his left eye as a result of a childhood accident. While shaving in the morning, he suddenly went blind in his right eye as well. "When my right eye went out, I couldn't see the mirror in front of me," Hall recalled to *Today* staff writer Howard Wolinsky.[3] (*Today* is a Gannett newspaper published in Brevard County, Florida.)

Hall said the vision in his right eye improved somewhat on its own during the time he was visiting physicians who specialize in eye and brain surgery. He was still considered legally blind when he was admitted to Brevard Hospital in Melbourne.

"After the testing was done, the docs said there was nothing they could do for me," Hall said.

Robert Rogers, M.D., of Melbourne, Hall's general practitioner, suggested chelation therapy since Hall suffers from arteriosclerosis. His hardening of the arteries had been so severe that the circulation of blood to his left leg had clogged completely and the leg had been amputated.

Dr. Rogers suggested that the arteriosclerosis apparently was blocking arteries deep in Hall's head, causing the blindness to his remaining eye. The physician gave the patient intravenous chelation therapy while he was in the hospital in hopes of removing any blockage.

"After I took seven treatments, the miracle took place. I could see," said Hall. "I was looking across the room and about fifteen feet away I could read some tiny writing on the TV. It said 'Hospital Communications Systems.' I got real excited and called Dr. Rogers. When the doctor got to the hospital *he* couldn't even read the words. [The print was so small.]"

When an ophthalmologist checked his vision, it was found that Hall was 20/15 in his right eye—better than normal 20/20. In a letter that he wrote, another physician, Robert Sarnowski, M.D., a neurosurgeon in the Melbourne area, attested to the "dramatic" improvement in Hall's vision.

Our Personal Note to the Reader

At this point in our writing we must interject a personal note about what you have read so far and what is to come. Usually, the conclusion that an objective observer draws, especially someone trained in science and medicine, like us, is that Dr. Soffer's remark is correct. More often than not, anecdotal medicine is nothing more than "buffalo dew." In the past we have believed that to be true. But what must an investigative medical journalist and a practicing physician do when they are exposed to story after story and to one case history after another that reports potentially imminent death, blindness, amputation, paralysis and other problems among people, and upon visiting those people to check their stories, they see them presently free of all signs of their former health problems. This has happened to us! About 500 individuals who were victims of hardening of the arteries are much changed. We have talked with them. They have become *former* victims. Now they are vibrant, productive, youthful looking, vigorous, full of zest for life, and they enthusiastically endorse chelation therapy as the cause of their prolonged good health.

We have checked most of what they said and turned up not a single untruth. Whether or not the scientific method accepts anecdotal evidence, information about the effects of chelation therapy on hardening of the arteries deserves to be revealed. All persons whom we interviewed or corresponded with delivered their messages of recovery with ardor. They wish to share their sense of renewed health and well-being with others who are suffering or will suffer. Consequently, we decided to bring a number of their messages to you in this book. You may want the same thing that these people have found—freedom from hardening of the arteries.

Chapter Two

WHAT THE CHELATION PROCESS IS

There are no such things as incurables; there are only things for which man has not found a cure.

—BERNARD BARUCH, Address to the President's Committee on Employment of the Handicapped, May 1, 1954

"Physician, Heal Thyself"

His grandfather died at age fifty of a heart attack.

His father, also at age fifty, became blind from a degenerative disease of the retina. Later, his father suffered multiple strokes and died from hardening of the arteries at fifty-five years of age.

His maternal grandmother was also afflicted by strokes and died at age sixty.

Many uncles and aunts added to his well-established family history of death by arterial occlusive disease.

Harold W. Harper, M.D., was quite aware that his background had him in perpetual danger—to be struck down anytime with acute symptoms of arteriosclerosis and to die in an instant. Dr. Harper did die from hardening of the arteries, but his colleagues estimate that chelation therapy allowed him eight more years of living than he ordinarily would have had.

When Dr. Harper was thirty-two years old and out of medical school just two years, his blood pressure stood at 220/150, and he weighed 358 pounds. Colleagues advised the new physician to leave the profession because the stress of medical practice was adding unduly to all his other atherosclerotic risk factors. Cardiologists offered him only two more years of survival.

By performing personal research on obesity and hypertension, Harold Harper developed a method that helped him lose 155 pounds. This massive weight loss somewhat decreased his high blood pressure and thus reduced the danger from those two particular cardiac killers.

Being apprehensive about his irrevocable family history of arteriosclerosis, however, Dr. Harper took the precaution of carrying nitroglycerin tablets in his shaving kit wherever he traveled. He knew it was only a matter of time before he would be hit with a heart attack. His logic was that nitroglycerin might provide an immediate blood flow through the coronary arteries, until he could arrive at some emergency medical facility.

It came six years later, while he relaxed with friends aboard a sixty-five foot houseboat on Lake Powell, located between Arizona and Utah. They had been fishing and playing penny-ante poker.

Dr. Harper's first sensation of something gone wrong began with a headache "like little men inside my head with sledge hammers who were trying to get out," he later recalled. Another pain began just below his left breast at the rib margin. The pain rose slowly upward to his left shoulder, neck, jaw, and down the left arm. "This is it!" he told himself. "My time has come!"

In those first few seconds Dr. Harper felt as if a truck tire was weighing down upon his chest, with the truck still attached. It was a repressive feeling—a restrictive thing—which made him sweat profusely. Large beads of perspiration popped out on his forehead and ran like rivulets down his face. He rose to get the nitroglycerin from his shaving kit, but, upon taking the first step, he fell flat on his face and broke his nose. There the man lay, face down, semiconscious and unable to move or talk. His companions stared in shock at his still form. Although he attempted to manipulate an index finger to let his stunned friends know he was still alive, even that the physician could not do.

The man who had been seated at Dr. Harper's left stood to help him, and he too fell like a sack of potatoes across the victim's body. The poker player on the right attempted to get up, but he collapsed across the table as well. The card player who sat opposite just slumped over.

The reason for these reactions was a not uncommon occurrence in boating. Their boat had been traveling at five knots in the face of a wind blowing exactly five knots. Gases coming from the motor had been held in place, stagnant. Internal combustion engines create carbon monoxide, which, when inhaled, combines with hemoglobin, the oxygen-carrying component of the blood. This limits the oxygen-supplying capability of the body and can be very dangerous. Among the first symptoms and signs are headache and unconsciousness. The four card players were poisoned by carbon monoxide engine exhaust, and carbon monoxide poisoning provoked Dr. Harper into a heart attack.

When he figured out the cause of the four companions' unconsciousness, the charter houseboat captain turned the boat into the wind, set the automatic pilot and dragged the men onto the deck. Three of them finally were able to stand. The heart patient was awake but had no ability to move except to wiggle a few fingers. Dr. Harper was paralyzed. His friends let him lie on the deck breathing fresh air until their party arrived at a landing. By fast powerboat they took him to a small airport and flew him for hospitalization near his home.

By the time the fishermen reached Los Angeles, paralysis had left the patient, and, at Dr. Harper's request, his friends took him to his office instead of to a hospital. There, using his own equipment, his medical staff gave the doctor an electrocardiogram, heart enzyme tests and a full examination. The tests indicated that he was over the acute stage of the heart attack. He had undergone a limitation of circulatory exchange across the coronary vessels, the main point of his arterial weakness. Dr. Harper and the staff members decided that any hospitalization would be ineffective. He rested at home. The patient thereafter took time off from work for three days and then returned to medical practice on a modified work schedule which lasted only three weeks. Then he worked full tilt as before.

Periodically, the physician experienced anginal pain with pressure in the chest. His episodes of pain occurred when he worked very hard or walked up several flights of stairs without stopping to rest. He took no additional medical treatment, however, and kept at his regular routine that included twelve-hour work days.

"I continued with occasional chest pain for two years. I had been exploring for some way to get over the cardiac problem—do something for myself—but until then I knew that there was nothing to be done," Dr. Harper said during the course of a few interviews. He knew that the usual medical treatments with vasodilators and low cholesterol or low-fat diets were almost worthless. When doctors see the ineffectiveness of such a routine, they naturally become skeptics. Since it is a leading cause of death, many physicians have come to regard arteriosclerotic heart disease as the normal attrition of old age. But that could not be the case for him. Dr. Harper was not quite ready to accept that old age philosophy for himself, since at that time he was just forty years old.

The Physician Learns of Chelation Therapy

"In February, 1972, I attended the annual meeting of the National Academy of Metabology in New York City. One of the lectures I tape recorded was delivered by H. Ray Evers, M.D. He spoke on the use of chelation therapy for heart disease. This doctor from a little town in Alabama had a dramatic story to tell about the treatment. Frankly, I didn't pay much attention. It just sounded too miraculous. I am, after all, a scientifically trained person unable to believe the type of miracle clinical response that Dr. Evers was describing," Dr. Harper admitted.

"Yet I couldn't push Evers' words out of my mind. That night in my hotel room I listened over again to the tape I had recorded. It made biochemical sense. I mulled it over for days. Back in Los Angeles I set a researcher to gathering all the literature about chelation that could be found. The medical librarians pulled out everything in their stacks and photocopied hundreds of pages of information.

"During his lecture, Dr. Evers had invited any physician who wanted to learn more about chelation to visit with him at the Columbia General Hospital in Andalusia, Alabama, where he then practiced. After delaying two weeks, my curiosity got the better of me. I had my secretary telephone to tell the man I was flying in to find out more—examine patient history charts—observe the people under care—and make a decision about his results."

"I reviewed 150 history charts and made hospital rounds with Dr. Evers beginning at 5:30 A.M., the next morning. He worked long hours. I noted patient response," said Dr. Harper. "People came from all over the U.S.—Florida, Alaska, Oregon, Wyoming, Connecticut, Maryland, Montana and from foreign countries also. Patients had to be met at the plane because Andalusia is a tiny town 85 miles from the Montgomery (Alabama) Airport.

"People heard of the treatment through relatives. Word can get around fast when some unusually effective response is taking place," Dr. Harper continued. "I saw patients who had come with Raynaud's disease, others with purple extremities, gangrenous lesions on the legs

and feet, and the whole range of arteriosclerotic conditions. And I saw
these conditions heal. They healed well! I was shocked! I decided to
go home and perform the technique on myself. Dr. Evers explained to
me how I could acquire the chelating solution and make the mixture.
I became my own first patient for chelation therapy.

"I took serial EKGs on myself during the treatment. After just three
treatments my electrocardiograms returned to normal for the first time
since I had entered medical school almost twelve years before. My EKGs
have remained normal since. My blood pressure became normal. My
anginal pain went away and has not returned. That has been for eight
years now," Dr. Harper said.

Chelation Therapy Helps to Widen Narrowed Arteries

The most promising treatment for premature aging of arteries, the most
common form of which is atherosclerosis, is intravenous chelation therapy. This injection treatment apparently widens arteries that are narrowing and closing off blood flow. It reverses pathology of some of the
most serious life-threatening problems that affect human beings, including coronary heart disease, stroke, peripheral vascular disease, gangrene
of the extremities, high blood pressure, diabetes; kidney disorders of
many types, including kidney stones; senility, reduced vision, thyroid
and adrenal disturbances, psoriasis, scleroderma, emphysema, Parkinson's disease, multiple sclerosis, hypercalcinosis, heavy metal poisoning,
rheumatoid arthritis and some other forms of arthritis, and a variety of
malfunctions and disabilities *where the basic issue is an interference with
the flow of blood to a cell, tissue, organ or body part.*

Chelation therapy helps to deliver adequate nutrients and oxygen and
removes toxic waste. The treatment acts through the mechanism of
"chemical endarterectomy." At one time it was described as a sort of
chemical "rotary-powered snake" that cleans out clogged blood vessels
the way a septic engineer unclogs your home sewage pipes. Its action
was said to take place at the microscopic or cellular level and there was
no risk of something breaking off and causing damage elsewhere. Now
chelating physicians know that the treatment is not any kind of chemical
rotorooter. It cleans arteries of atherosclerotic plaque in another way.

The chelation technique makes use of a liquid "engineer," the chelation solution, which is a remarkable man-made amino acid called *ethylene diamine tetraacetic acid,* abbreviated EDTA. The EDTA solution has the unique property of binding with divalent or trivalent metals, including toxic heavy metals. It also combines with other minerals that when present in excess may bind with cellular constituents and apparently diminish the cellular enzyme function required to maintain cellular viability within the arteries. Thus the solution flushes the cells.

EDTA picks up ionic trace minerals complexed with various cell wall constituents and travels with them to the kidneys. There they are eliminated through the genitourinary tract. To a lesser extent, the solution and combined constituents go through the liver and thence are sent out through the gastrointestinal tract. Testing reveals that a measurable and definite amount of ionized blood calcium is eliminated from the body this way. Almost none of this is the calcium that has been bound into bones and teeth, but rather it is metastatic or pathologic calcium lightly bound to components within the arterial wall and even to the walls of the platelets and blood cells. Thermograms taken before and after the chelation treatment reveal that areas of impaired circulation are frequently restored to normal by this fascinating and efficient liquid engineer called EDTA.

We have said that chelation heals a variety of malfunctions and disabilities where the basic issue is an interference in the blood supply. In fact, any system of treatment which brings fresh blood and oxygen to the tissues can be expected to aid in the healing process. Cleansing the blood by chelation does just that. When used properly, it is extremely scientific and highly effective.

When chelation is taken along with regular exercise, proper nutrition, and a balanced nutritional supplement program, the full-treatment regimen offers us the greatest promise for life extension and optimization of health. Early researchers have found chelation therapeutic benefits were "not lasting." The reason for that is clear now! No effort was made at that earlier time to improve the patients' lifestyles. No one enforced the full-treatment regimen then as knowledgeable chelation physicians require today. Unless a complete change in lifestyle is practiced, no medical therapy can succeed.

Chemical chelation cleans the blood of metastatic or pathological calcifications which are laid down on the intima, or from broken-off plaque which is floating free in the blood vessel lumen. *Metastatic calcium* is the stuff that combines with the proteins or the lipids in blood to help form atheromatous sclerosing plaques. *Metastatic calcium* impairs cellular function required to constantly repair damaged arteries. *Metastatic calcium* forms the hardening elements inside and around the walls of aging arteries. *Metastatic calcium* decreases circulation and interferes with life. Reverse the pathological calcification or prevent metastasis of calcium from happening in the first place, and we have markedly increased our chance to live our full lifespan.

The Natural Process of Chelation

The process of chelation is going on constantly in nature. It takes place in the bodies of living organisms, both plant and animal, as a natural function. Chelation is the means by which plants and animals are able to utilize inorganic minerals. For example, chlorophyll, the green matter of plants, is a chelate of magnesium. Hemoglobin, the oxygen-carrying pigment of human red blood cells, is a chelate of iron. The formation and function of enzymes, the protein substances which control most of our functions in the body, are all products of chelation. Aspirin, citric acid and cortisone are known to function at least partially as chelating agents.

The chelation process, in fact, may be responsible for the effectiveness of almost all the drugs used in medicine to overcome disease. Without it they could not act and react with the body's physiology. Some of the most basic and yet complex chemical reactions found in nature and in man are encompassed by the chelation process.

As a process in plant and animal biology, this reaction has been recognized for over thirty years. It is a biochemical process which is fundamental in:

- Food digestion and assimilation.
- The formation of numerous enzymes.
- The functions of enzyme systems.
- The synthesis of many hormones.
- The detoxifying of certain (toxic) chemicals.
- The detoxifying of certain metals, such as lead, arsenic and mercury.
- The movement of vitamins, minerals, hormones and other nutrients across membranes of body tissues as part of transport systems.

The chelation mechanism controls many of our bodily functions. These same principles are applied in chelation therapy to treat hardening of the arteries and the diseases that result from this hardening effect.

The Definition of Chelation

The word *chelation* (pronounced *key-lay-shon*) is derived from the Greek word *chele* meaning *claw*, such as the claw of a lobster or crab. In effect, the chelate substance offers a firm, pincerlike binding of certain chemicals to a bivalent metal or other mineral. Chelation incorporates the metal or mineral ion into a heterocyclic ring structure. Certain chemicals are used to close this ring and grasp calcium or other metals with this claw-like action so that they are encircled or sequestered by the complex ring structure, thereby losing their toxic properties.

Writing in the September 1962 *Illinois Medical Journal,* John H. Olwin, M.D., and J. L. Koppel, Ph.D., both from the Coagulation Research Laboratory, Department of Surgery, Presbyterian-St. Luke's Hospital, Chicago, said:

> Chelation is the process by which certain chemical agents bind metals to form ring complexes. When such a chelate is formed, the action becomes an integral part of a stable ring structure and ceases to act as a free ion. The stabilities of the resulting chelates depend upon the cation involved, one which is more weakly bound being displayed by another which is more strongly bound. It is upon this property that the clinical usefulness of chelation therapy depends.

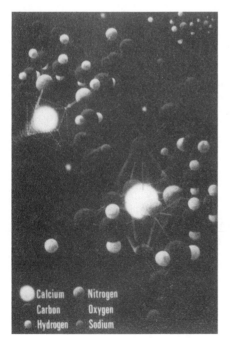

Calcium Nitrogen
Carbon Oxygen
Hydrogen Sodium

This illustration depicts how the molecule of ethylene diamine tetraacetic acid, or EDTA, works in the chelating process. The EDTA molecule, disodium salt, is shown in the upper right of the drawing, before chelation has begun. Then, in the upper left, the disodium EDTA attracts a divalent metal, calcium, the chief culprit for atherosclerotic plaque. The ionic calcium is drawn into the very center of the EDTA molecule. Finally, a chelate is created in the form of an octahedron (double pyramid), as the calcium ions are locked into an EDTA disodium salt ring. *(Drawing by Robert H. Knabenbauer, supplied courtesy of World Life Research Institute.)*

The disodium salt of ethylene diamine tetraacetate, or EDTA, is the weakly bound cation replaced by other cation minerals higher up in the electromotive scale. A *cation* is an ion carrying a charge of positive electricity. Thus, disodium EDTA forms stronger soluble complexes with cations such as barium, beryllium, cadmium, calcium, chromium, cobalt, copper, lead, iron, magnesium, manganese, mercury, nickel, strontium and zinc. That's why, as Drs. Olwin and Koppel suggest:

> The use of chelating agents in the treatment of certain clinical conditions is not new. It is perhaps best known for its benefits in heavy metal, particularly lead, poisoning. Its use in other conditions, such as scleroderma, porphyria, cardiac arrhythmias, and atherosclerosis in some of its clinical manifestations, is less well known.

EDTA grasps metals, including calcium, with this claw-like action and encircles or sequesters them within a complex ring. They lose their physiologic and toxic properties this way. Therefore, when chelation takes place, the calcium or heavy metal comes in contact with EDTA, or some other chelating agent, and becomes imprisoned by the ring. The sodium is never dropped, and so the sodium is apparently not toxic. It is simply excreted by the body intact with the EDTA. Excess lead or other toxic metals are excreted from the system along with the EDTA. The "toxic" element is trapped by the chelator, like the claw of a crab holding something in its pincers.

The ability of EDTA amino acid to grasp or bind with the ionic calcium found in metastatic or pathological calcium deposits is phenomenal. It seems to be catalytic in its power to excrete or mobilize calcium far beyond the dose of the medicine itself. Some of this reaction takes place because of the parathormone (the hormone of the parathyroid gland) response to the induced hypocalcemia during the infusion of the drug. We will describe in depth the mechanism of action of EDTA in Chapters Four and Five.

As potential users of this life-extending treatment, we should be aware that chelation is as old as life on this planet. All biological processes are involved in the phenomenon. It is only in recent years, however, that chelation has emerged as a very valuable therapeutic technique for purposes of predictable health improvement.

The History of EDTA Chelation

In interviews with Bruce W. Halstead, M.D., who is a biotoxicologist and director of the World Life Research Institute in Colton, California, we learned that EDTA was first synthesized by Mr. F. Munz, a German chemist. Then it was developed by the I. G. Farben Industries as a result of the geopolitical problems created by Adolf Hitler. Germany required the product in its fabrics and textiles industries. In due course, EDTA was patented in 1930, as reported in the *American Journal of Laboratory and Clinical Medicine* ("Regarding EDTA," 1930). Working with some older components, I. G. Farben finally brought out the agent in 1931 as a substitute for citric acid as a coating or preservative of fibers.

Chelation therapy was first employed in medicine in 1941 with the use of sodium citrate in lead poisoning. This usage was reported in an article, "Treatment of lead poisoning with sodium citrate" by S. S. Kety and T. V. Letonoff (*Proc. Soc. Exp. Biol. MED. 46* [1941], 476–477).

EDTA was patented in the United States in 1949 by Frederick Bersworth, a biochemist at Georgetown University, for the Martin-Dennis Company. Several papers on EDTA were published in the early 1950s.

Dr. Halstead said, "EDTA is known to all analytical chemists. There are entire books devoted to it. The number of articles in the field of analytical chemistry dealing with EDTA number into the thousands. One of the values of this agent is its precise nature. At least in an *in vitro* situation (in the test tube) you can literally mathematically predict how EDTA is going to act and approximately to what extent it is going to chelate."

In a March 1976 appearance before the Advisory Panel on Internal Medicine of the Scientific Board of the California Medical Association (CMA), Norman E. Clarke, Sr., M.D., a cardiologist of Birmingham, Michigan, told the Scientific Board of his pioneering activities with chelation therapy.

"I learned about EDTA in 1953 from Dr. Albert J. Boyle, Professor of Chemistry at Wayne State University, Detroit, and from Dr. Gordon B. Myers, who then was Professor of Medicine at the same university and a well-known cardiologist. Drs. Boyle and Myers had preliminary experience in treating two patients at University Hospital, Detroit, who had calcified mitral (heart) valves. The patients were almost completely incapacitated," Dr. Clarke told the CMA. "The doctors were pleased with the results (of chelation treatment) because they obtained very satisfactory return of cardiac function. But they [Drs. Boyle and Myers] did not have the opportunity or the time to go on with it (their research). Dr. Boyle asked if I would—because then I was chairman of the research department of Providence Hospital, Detroit—undertake a study of EDTA in cardiovascular diseases, which I did.

"I knew, having been in cardiology quite a number of years [since 1921], that arteriosclerotic cardiovascular disease was a helpless, hopeless situation for the cardiologist. I had to start by trying to find out whether it was safe [EDTA]; what was the best dosage; were there any side effects; and how would we standardize its use as a treatment?

"Well, of course," Dr. Clarke continued, "the first couple of years we treated only hospital patients where we had them under excellent control. We started with a rather large dosage [10 gm] and had some side reactions consisting primarily of signs of a B-6 [Vitamin B-6—pyridoxine] deficiency. Some males' scrotum lost a complete cast of skin, but it was absolutely painless and with no sensation of discomfort. After finding the proper dosage, of course, all those things have never happened again. And even with those large doses we had no unusual or serious side effects. Ultimately, we determined, and for a long time gave, 5 grams, and later determined that 3 grams was the proper dose.

"In the last twenty-three years of my experience with EDTA chelation I would say conservatively, because after all those years you don't keep accurate records with all you do, but conservatively I have given at least 100,000 to 120,000 infusions of EDTA and seen nobody harmed," the chelation specialist said. "I've never seen any serious toxicity whatsoever. I've seen only benefits."

The veteran cardiologist went on to describe more success with diabetes and other cases of chest pain. Then Dr. Clarke said, "Another field in which I have found [EDTA] most effective is cerebrovascular senility. I am extremely impressed with that, not only by the improvement in the patients but from the economic factor today. All you have to do is go into one of those old folks' homes and see the senile people sitting around and you'll recognize immediately not only the economic problems but the physical and mental problems that they and their families go through."

Dr. Clarke, who was eighty-eight years old himself at the time, concluded his remarks to the California Medical Association's advisory panel assembled to hear about chelation therapy. He said, "After all these years and with all that experience, I am just as certain as can be that EDTA chelation therapy is the best treatment that has ever been brought out for occlusive vascular disease."

With Dr. Clarke's longtime successful experience with EDTA, it is almost appalling that the medical profession in the United States has continued to reject it.

Dr. Marvin Penwell Does Not Reject Chelation Therapy

During his osteopathic medical practice in Linden, Michigan, Marvin D. Penwell, D.O., a diplomate in chelation therapy, readily accepted the intravenous infusion of EDTA as the means to restore cardiovascular and peripheral vascular health for his numerous patients. As recently as May 1996, while attending the semiannual scientific sessions of the American College for Advancement in Medicine held in Orlando, Florida, Dr. Penwell furnished us with seven significant case reports of patients who so benefited. Here are a few of those cases.

Fifty-nine-year-old Stewart Franklin of Flint, Michigan, an assembly-line foreman at the Ford Motor Company, had an advanced gangrenous condition of his left great toe. But this turned out to be only one of his health problems. Laboratory tests taken by Dr. Penwell revealed that Mr. Franklin was a poorly controlled diabetic with severe peripheral vascular disease in both legs.

The diabetes was brought into focus and treated clinically by Dr. Penwell, but this did not clear up the gangrene. It looked like his big toe would require amputation. And if the peripheral vascular surgeon being consulted so judged, the man might lose his left leg as well.

Before referring the patient for surgery, Dr. Penwell decided first to try administering twenty intravenous infusions of EDTA chelation therapy. Exactly as shown for Dr. Roland Hohnbaum's situation with diabetic gangrene that is illustrated in Chapter One, the chelation treatments saved Stewart Franklin's left limb. There was no reason to amputate at the conclusion of twenty chelations.

In another patient's case, Paul Micholis of Detroit, Michigan, age forty-eight, a supervisor at the truck and bus assembly plant in Flint, was sent to Dr. Penwell by a local radiologist who knew of benefits afforded by chelation therapy. Mr. Micholis was a chain smoker who repeatedly developed extreme fatigue and was found to be hypertensive. What actually brought him in for chelation treatment, however, was leg pain from intermittent claudication (calf muscle spasm from lack of blood) and frequent episodes of chest pain from mild angina pectoris.

Despite his refusal to give up cigarette smoking, Paul Micholis's response to chelation therapy was exceedingly dramatic. At the end of twenty treatments with IV EDTA, his energy had returned to a high level. The leg pain he had been experiencing disappeared altogether so that this plant supervisor could walk anywhere he wanted through the huge truck assembly building without any difficulty. Also, his chest pain no longer bothered him, and the high blood pressure was reduced after only four treatments. Repeated blood pressure examinations indicated that the patient remained normotensive rather than hypertensive.

Mr. Micholis was uncooperative and didn't discontinue his unhealthy lifestyle as Dr. Penwell recommended. A healthful diet, the taking of nutritional supplements, discontinuance of smoking and other improvements in the way the patient lived were all ignored. Instead, the assembly-line supervisor told Dr. Penwell that he would return for more chelation injections when he needed them.

Dr. Penwell remained uncertain as to his own desire to once again try to counteract this person's self-destructive manner of living. Before the patient found it necessary to return for another life-saving program of chelation therapy, Dr. Penwell had relocated his practice to Florida.

Chapter Three

THE THERAPEUTIC EFFECTS OF EDTA CHELATION

EDTA chelation therapy makes good sense to me as a chemist and medical researcher. It has a rational scientific basis, and the evidence for clinical benefit seems to be quite strong. Metallic ions play an important role in the formation of atherosclerotic plaque. EDTA removes those ions with relative safety and without surgery. Published research and extensive clinical experience show that EDTA helps to reduce and prevent atherosclerotic plaques, thus improving blood flow to the heart and other organs. The scientific evidence indicates that a course of EDTA chelation therapy might eliminate the need for bypass surgery. Chelation has an equally valid rationale for use as a preventive treatment.

—LINUS PAULING, Ph.D.
From the Foreword to *A Textbook on EDTA Chelation Therapy*, 1989

Chelation Therapy Alters the Course of Parkinson's Disease

In a hotel room in Kansas City, Missouri, during a semiannual meeting of the American College for Advancement in Medicine (ACAM), nine physicians discussed their experiences with administering chelation therapy. One of them was Sibyl W. Anderson, D.O., who had practiced osteopathic medicine with her husband, Leon Anderson, D.O., in Jenks, Oklahoma. This is what Sibyl Anderson said:

My husband, Dr. Leon Anderson, was the first patient we ever treated with chelation. He had a tremor in his right hand and experienced difficulty performing routine functions such as tying his shoelaces. He went for an examination to our favorite neurologist in Tulsa, Oklahoma. The doctor was unable to give a definite diagnosis of Parkinson's disease, *paralysis agitans,* because it was in such an early stage, but he couldn't say he didn't have Parkinsonism. He did not offer any treatment or advice except that Dr. Leon should come back if it got worse.

Parkinson's disease, also known as *shaking palsy,* is a neurological syndrome usually resulting from arteriosclerotic changes in the basal ganglia. It is characterized by rhythmical muscular tremors, rigidity of movement, a peculiar rapid or hastening acceleration of gait, droopy posture, and masklike countenance of the patient.

"Whether the problem was in the hand or the brain, we felt the best thing we could do was to get good nutrition into the tissues so the body could do its own healing," Dr. Sibyl said. "We worked on my husband's dietary and vitamin and mineral supplement program, but the fundamental key to curative treatment that we used was EDTA chelation.

"After only five EDTA treatments Dr. Leon really began to see a difference in his tremor. He could use his hands for all the little things we have to do for ourselves that you don't actually think about until you can't do them. He took thirty chelation treatments altogether and eliminated any problem with Parkinson-like symptoms. Dr. Leon has taken a short series of intravenous EDTA yearly,." Dr. Sibyl Anderson said. "His problem had begun in 1970, but he keeps it controlled with Chelation Therapy so that medical practice has continued for him without interruption."

EDTA Chelation Reverses Blindness

She described another person, a prominent, fifty-eight-year-old attorney from Tulsa, Oklahoma, who visited Drs. Sibyl and Leon Anderson. The man asked if they could help him get better nutrition to his retina. He had been blind in one eye for seven years. One month prior to his visit to the two osteopathic physicians he had lost the central vision of his other eye.

The patient already had made the rounds of the best eye specialists in Tulsa, Oklahoma City and San Francisco. After going through thorough evaluations and laser beam treatments, he had been sent home with no hope of ever being able to see to read, except with aid from an inverted television camera. The attorney was told by the ophthalmologists that he could never again drive a car or perform many of the essential activities necessary for a busy law practice. The patient's diagnosis of *macular degeneration* was made by each of his three ophthalmologists.

The *macula retinae* is a small, orange-yellow oval area, 3 by 5 millimeters, on the inner surface of the retina slightly below the optic disk near the rear pole of the eyeball, and therefore is the visual axis. At its center is the *fovea centralis,* which provides the best visual acuity under photopic conditions. If it degenerates, as in macular degeneration, blindness results. This is what happened to the Tulsa attorney.

The attorney's wife had read Adelle Davis's book, *Let's Get Well.* Adelle Davis had mentioned that the use of vitamin A injections and other nutrients was helpful with treatment of *retinitis pigmentosa,* another retina problem. The couple wondered if injections of vitamin A might be useful as an aid for the near-blind patient in his particular problem as well. They thought it might be worth a try.

"Dr. Leon and I discussed nutrition in general with the couple, gave specific diet instructions and prescribed an oral vitamin program. Also we injected both vitamin A and vitamin E," Dr. Sibyl Anderson said. "Even with this approach we needed to get the nutrients to the retina directly, so our first thought was chelation treatments which we felt would open up the retinal blood supply.

"Since we had not treated a patient with macular degeneration before, we called Dr. H. Rudolph Alsleben in Anaheim, California, whom we had heard was treating a number of patients daily with intravenous chelation," said Dr. Sibyl. "Dr. Alsleben encouraged us to start treatments immediately. He said that he had some very good response with retinal problems.

"Our own patient's vision at this time was 20/400 (legally blind) in the right eye, and he had no corrective lens on the left eye, having lost the central vision in that eye seven years previously," the osteopathic physician said.

"The attorney's wife was very conscientious in following the nutritional program and giving her husband his supplements. Her cooperation was essential in his treatment. They were both very disciplined and delightful to work with," she said. "We proceeded to administer chelation therapy." Dr. Anderson told about her patient's progress as a result of the treatment.

She said, "At the end of two and one-half months he was able to read the newspaper with a special corrective lens, and at three and one-half months he could resume driving and read normally with the new corrective lens. Also at this time, the left eye had improved sufficiently for a corrective lens. It is interesting to note that the medical literature states that a patient with macular degeneration can expect continual loss of vision and should change his occupation and mode of living to adjust to his problem."

Dr. Anderson concluded, "Over a year's time this attorney took 105 treatments. During this period several doctors contributed their expertise, including Dr. H. Ray Evers and Dr. Morgan Raiford. My patient's visual acuity at the end of one year was 20/35. He continues to take the intravenous EDTA treatments periodically."

The attorney took 134 chelations. "His general health also has *much* improved," Dr. Sibyl Anderson said.

Intravenous Chelation Aids Multiple Sclerosis

We learned of a man who had taken intravenous chelation to aid multiple sclerosis. He had walked with the assistance of two canes when he arrived at the chelation clinic. After receiving just one week of chelation treatment, he gave up the use of one cane and walked with better balance and more strength. Prior to that, he had been under ordinary medical care for multiple sclerosis and his condition had not shown any improvement. This man had not been made aware that he was an MS patient until May 1973, although his family knew possibly a year before that.

Alvin Kavaler, fifty years old, of West Hartford, Connecticut, is a former insurance salesman who is confined to his home presently because of his MS condition. He confirmed some of the things we had heard about his improvement following chelation therapy, but not all of them.

Mr. Kavaler said, "I would be reluctant to say that chelation therapy is any kind of cure for multiple sclerosis. It's not! Although I experienced improvement after taking the treatment, I think probably it came from a change in some other physical problems I had that I didn't know about. In any case, I have encouraged many MS-affected people to go for chelation since the treatment is an aid to relieving symptoms of poor circulation. I am convinced that most of our discomforts as MS patients come from circulatory difficulties. Unfortunately, the usual

M.D. seems to think that anything bothering an MS victim is due to MS. Not so! For instance, my feet had always felt ice cold. This condition had been bothersome for as long as I can remember. A few weeks after I took my first eighteen bottles of chelation solution I realized that my feet—and the rest of me, too—were warm, and they have remained warm. This comfort has been an exciting new experience for me—to have a warm-feeling body, hands and feet all of the time. I know that many multiple sclerosis patients are troubled by feelings of coldness all over."

Multiple sclerosis is a chronic, slowly progressive disease of the central nervous system characterized clinically by a lot of symptoms and signs which come and go intermittently. There are visual disturbances, transient weakness, stiffness or fatigability of a limb, interference with walking, bladder control difficulties, occasional dizziness, and other troubles that slowly get worse.

Obviously, chelation is no cure-all, but the attitude of American medicine is too often to do nothing except for what is accepted by the medical mainstream.

A Chelation Pioneer Tells of Giving 16,000 Infusions

John H. Olwin, M.D., Clinical Professor of Surgery at Rush Medical College in Chicago, a seventy-year-old vascular surgeon whose coauthored paper is quoted in Chapter Two, described his experiences with giving chelation therapy. Dr. Olwin made an appearance before the ad hoc committee of the Advisory Panel on Internal Medicine of the Scientific Board of the California Medical Association. His appearance occurred immediately before Dr. Clarke made his presentation, which is described in the last chapter. From the notarized transcript of that hearing, we offer Dr. Olwin's testimony about the therapeutic effects that EDTA chelation achieves.

First, Dr. Olwin recounted how he became acquainted with EDTA chelation. "Some sixteen years ago," he said, "a biochemist in the department of surgery of one of our medical schools asked me if I were using chelation therapy on my patients with obliterative atherosclerosis. I asked him what chelation therapy was, and he explained. I subsequently talked with Dr. Clarke, Dr. Al Boyle, and Drs. Lawrence E. Meltzer and

J. Roderick Kitchell, who are coauthors of papers on chelation, and who practice in Philadelphia.

"I then went to the Veteran's Hospital in Hines, Illinois, where I was the attending [physician] on the vascular service," Dr. Olwin said. "There I began using this treatment according to the schedule of Drs. Kitchell and Meltzer on our patients on whom we had written off the legs because of obliterative atherosclerosis. We were awaiting these patients' consent for amputation. We began using this material [EDTA] and saved a number of limbs. The necrotic dead areas of skin or flesh were limited; they dropped off; the limbs warmed; the nails and hair began to grow [following administration of chelation therapy], and after several of these experiences I began to use EDTA chelation in my private practice.

"Over the past fifteen years," Dr. Olwin told the CMA review committee members, "I have used it for between 335 and 350 patients, representing something over 16,000 infusions of about three grams each, in most instances. Seventy-five of these patients have been on chelation therapy for more than five years, and twenty-five of those seventy-five for more than ten years."

Dr. Olwin asked and answered a compelling question: "What are the effects that we observe? Well first there is relief of claudication. Patients can walk farther. Some of them say they can walk as far as they could normally.

"There is relief of the ischemic pain.

"There is a warming of limbs, both subjective and objective.

"There is an arrest of gangrene.

"There is a regrowth of hair and nails.

"There is a relief of angina.

"There is healing of the ischemic ulcers . . .

"Some patients with thrombophlebitis migrans, even those on controlled anticoagulant therapy, will have recurring episodes of thromboembolism, but we are able to reduce this materially—in some instances eliminate the recurrence of thrombophlebitis—by adding to the anticoagulant routine intermittent doses of EDTA," the vascular surgeon said. (*Thrombophlebitis migrans* is a creeping or slowly advancing inflammation of a vein with secondary thrombus formation. It appears in first one vein and then another.)

"Another observed effect is the increase in capillary blood flow. You can observe the flow in the conjunctival [eye membrane] vessels. There is extreme sludging of blood in most patients with atherosclerosis. Without exception, over a period of time, the flow in capillaries as seen in the eye is improved after treatment of several months with EDTA.

"We have seen improvement in mental processes," Dr. Olwin assured his reviewing peers. "In the early stages we noted that these people with gangrenous limbs and gangrenous toes were not as mentally sharp as they had once been. One young executive who had lost his job because of mental disturbances returned to work after he had been treated with EDTA.

"Some of our neurologists became interested in this and with their cooperation, we treated thirteen patients with chronic brain syndrome. Four of these [patients] showed clinical improvement. Three of them showed reversal of [abnormal] EEGs [electroencephalograms] and one of them had a return to a normal EEG, a man in his late seventies. He went on to die at the age of eighty-three of a perforated duodenal ulcer.

"We see an improvement in ECGs [another way to abbreviate EKG electrocardiograms]. This is not my field, but some of my colleagues have observed and some of my patients have experienced an improvement in this [heart] condition."

Psychological and Internal Medical Benefits As Well

Dr. Olwin, a peripheral vascular specialist, ordinarily works fifteen hours a day operating on blood vessels and amputating limbs. Yet here is a vascular surgeon who dramatically saves arms and legs by the intravenous infusion of a chemical. Where possible, he substitutes medicine for surgery.

He said, "I've been taking this chelation for myself for ten years, almost every third week for maybe five years, and now about every two weeks. As far as I know, my chemistry's normal. All my functions are normal. And I expect to continue to work for an indefinite period."

There were a number of psychological and internal medical benefits that Dr. Olwin observed in addition to his work with peripheral vascular disease. For instance, some of his patients reported that they enjoyed an increase in libidinous drive and sexual potency. He told the California Medical Association reviewers the following anecdote:

"An eighty-year-old brilliant lawyer in Chicago had had a chronic brain syndrome for many years. His neurologist asked about this chelation treatment; I explained the experience that we'd had, and the family wished to have the elderly man treated. The patient was treated in collaboration with the neurologist, and after about a year there was no improvement in his [the patient's] chronic brain syndrome.

"However, the eighty-year-old man's wife called me one day and asked, Is this supposed to increase sexual desire?' I said, 'We've had that recorded.' And she replied, 'Well, James has not been interested in sex for fifteen years and last night he tried to make love to me!'

"Perhaps this effect was an indication that the man's sexual problem was not a functional affair but an organic change. It seems reasonable that if blood supply is being improved, all organs of the body may benefit from this improvement," Dr. Olwin conjectured.

In other instances the specialists cited the reduction of insulin requirement for diabetics. He said, "One of our patients, a juvenile diabetic, who was almost blind and taking seventy-five units of insulin, had after a series of treatments, a reduction of thirty-five units of insulin."

The vascular surgeon showed color slides during his CMA presentation. The slides included indisputable tables of results and "before and after" photographs of patients with a variety of problems. His tables and charts indicated blood fat metabolism alterations.

Dr. Olwin said, "We observed a reduction in lipid levels in all patients in which we have done any studies in lipid levels. This [chelation effect] must be an enzymatic action. The mechanism is still unclear. The lipid reduction returns to the pretherapy levels after four to six weeks on termination of the therapy. And [lipid levels] can again be reduced after the therapy is restarted. In three instances we have had recanalization of main arterial channels."

(To explain: Dr. Olwin said that he saw a *recanalization,* a new opening, in major blood vessels after there had previously been complete blockage in these vessels by thrombotic occlusion. The new arterial opening forms by organization of the thrombus with creation by the body of new capillaries that let blood flow through, where before, blockage prevented it. That is *collateral circulation* or recanalization. The body part that is about to die of blood starvation now will receive blood nutrition and live.)

Dr. Olwin added, "I had one patient, a man who had claudication for six months; after about twenty-two months [of chelation], his pulses recurred in his feet and arteriography clearly indicated that there had been a recanalization of an obstruction at the level of the abductor tendon [in the lower thighs]." (The patient Dr. Olwin was telling about, a war veteran, had actually been rolled on a stretcher bed into the operating room to have his leg amputated. But Dr. Olwin put in an arterial graft as a bypass instead and immediately started him on chelation therapy.) "The graft closed several weeks later, but there had apparently been enough of the effect of EDTA that his gangrene sloughed. And this is the foot at some weeks later." The slide that Dr. Olwin flashed on the screen showed the man's foot was healed—his leg saved.

He described another patient: "A woman of forty-five had had endarterectomy [surgical removal of an artery's lining along with its occluding atheromatous deposits] of both common iliac arteries [major blood vessels in the abdominal area that supply the entire lower portion of the body]. About three months later, despite anticoagulant therapy, these arteries closed," Dr. Olwin said. "Chelation was started; anticoagulants were continued; around eighteen months later she reopened both iliac arteries. These arteries have remained open under continuous anticoagulants and intermittent chelation therapy," Dr. Olwin told the CMA investigating panel.

Chelation Therapy Improves Memory

During our many interviews, Warren M. Levin, M.D., F.A.A.F.P. of New York City, described his personal experience with giving himself chelation therapy. He said, "I went through a full preventive medical checkup including cardiac stress testing and was pronounced 'fit as a fiddle.' However, my father had died at the age of fifty-six with a coronary. Also, I'm short, relatively stocky, and have been eating what I now consider unhealthy food for the first forty years of my life—until I learned better. I know that I have been undergoing the same sort of degenerative changes of hardening of the arteries like everyone else. I think that in the past few years, by altering my lifestyle with regular daily exercise and better eating habits, I have slowed down the pathology. Nevertheless, I wanted to do more than just slow it down. I wanted to eliminate atherosclerosis from my body altogether, if I could. So despite my feeling in really fine health. I took a series of twenty chelation treatments.

"About eight weeks after I finished self-administered chelation, I suddenly realized that a very important memory change had taken place in me. My memory was much improved," said Dr. Levin. "I have always been blessed with a pretty good brain—high I.Q. and all that—and now I am able to remember long unused addresses and telephone numbers. I had no problem with that kind of remembering. My annoyances would occur in the middle of a workday in this unbelievably hectic office—allergy tests being taken—chelations being given to patients—physical examinations going on—and other activities.

"I might be examining one person and have another waiting in my consultation room," Dr. Levin continued. "The telephones would be ringing. My nurse might ask me about service charges or appointments for patients—sixteen different inputs coming at me at once. Then I may walk into my consultation room from the examining room and have to stop to ask myself, 'What did I come in here for?' Often I'd have to turn around and go back to the examining room to see my patient or look at the chart, and then it would come to me. I'd realize, 'Oh yes, I was supposed to get that order blank' or fill out the form on my desk."

Dr. Levin assured us, "That sort of memory lapse doesn't happen to me anymore. The whole pattern has modified dramatically. There is absolutely no question in my mind that my improved memory is a direct result of chelation therapy. I will be taking chelation at fairly regular intervals indefinitely. It's the best *preventive medicine* that we have to offer in this country to eliminate hardening of the arteries for somebody in my state of health and at my age of sixty-one years."

Other Benefits of EDTA Chelation

What? A treatment to improve the memory, stop parkinsonism, aid multiple sclerosis, reverse blindness, recanalize blocked arterial channels, lower insulin requirements for diabetics, restore libido and sexual potency, dissolve thromboses, reverse gangrene, relieve claudication pain—EDTA chelation does all that? Yes, and there is more.

In their book, *How to Survive the New Health Catastrophes,* H. Rudolph Alsleben, M.D., and Wilfrid E. Shute, M.D., explain some additional chelation therapeutic effects that occur with intravenous administration of the synthesized amino acid, disodium ethylene diamine tetraacetic acid (EDTA). This substance provides the following beneficial effects.[1]

- prevents the deposit of cholesterol in the liver.
- reduces blood cholesterol levels.
- causes high blood pressure to drop in 60 percent of the cases.

- reverses the toxic effects of digitalis excess.
- converts to normal 50 percent of cardiac arrhythmias.
- reduces or relaxes excessive heart contractions.
- increases intracellular potassium.
- reduces heart irritability.
- increases the removal of lead.
- removes calcium from atherosclerotic plaques.
- dissolves kidney stones.
- reduces serum iron and protects against iron poisoning and iron storage disease.
- reduces heart valve calcification and improves heart function.
- detoxifies several poisonous venoms.
- reduces the dark pigmentation of varicose veins.
- heals calcified necrotic ulcers.
- reduces the disabling effects of intermittent claudication.
- improves vision in diabetic retinopathy.
- decreases macular degeneration.
- dissolves small cataracts.

In a small, self-published book prepared for his patients, osteopathic physician and surgeon Martin Dayton, D.O., M.D., of Sunny Isles (North Miami Beach), Florida, provides a partial list of pathological signs, symptoms, conditions and illnesses which are reported to improve following the use of intravenous chelation therapy. Dr. Dayton, who has been designated a diplomate by the American Board of Chelation Therapy, has offered this treatment to his patients for over seventeen years. In alphabetical order, here is the listing of human and animal body and brain conditions which improve from receiving chelation therapy:

age spots
angina pectoris
arteriosclerosis (cerebral, coronary, and peripheral)
Buerger's disease
bursitis
cardiac rhythm irregularities
chronic obstructive lung disease
cirrhosis of the liver
congestive heart failure
coronary heart disease
dementia of the Alzheimer's type
diabetes mellitus
diabetic retinopathy
digitalis intoxication
elevated blood cholesterol
elevated blood fats
enlarged heart
erectile failure
fatigue

free radical pathology
gangrene
gas poisoning
generalized impairment of the
  blood circulation
hair loss
headaches
heavy metal poisoning
hypercalcemia
hyperlipidemia
hypertension
hypoglycemia
immune system dysfunction
impotence
insomnia
intermittent claudication
iron toxicity
kidney disease
lead toxicity
lessened blood flow in legs
lupus erythematosus
macular degeneration
malaise
male sexual dysfunction
memory loss
mental malfunction
mercury toxicity
mood instability
multiple sclerosis
neuralgia
neuropathy
nuclear radiation poisoning
osteoarthritis
osteoporosis
Parkinson's disease
Peyronie's disease
post-stroke syndrome
psoriasis
Raynaud's disease
renal insufficiency
rheumatoid arthritis
schizophrenia
scleroderma
senile dementia
skin ulcers
skin wrinkles
strokes
tachycardia
thrombophlebitis
toxic metal syndrome
transient ischemic attack
vasculitis
vertigo
vision impairment (cataracts,
  glaucoma)
vitality diminished

Review of the medical literature on this subject indicates that the value of EDTA chelation therapy has been well tested and carefully reported. Some major institutions have underwritten studies of the intravenous therapy. Grants-in-aid research on EDTA chelation therapy have been given by

1. The National Institutes of Health
2. The U.S. Public Health Service
3. The National Institute of Arthritis and Metabolic Diseases
4. The University of California, Los Alamos Scientific Laboratory
5. The American Cancer Society

6. The Charles S. Hayden Foundation
7. The Else U. Pardee Foundation
8. The Oscar Meyer Foundation
9. The U.S. Atomic Energy Commission
10. The John A. Hartford Foundation
11. The Providence Hospital Research Department, Detroit, Michigan
12. The Equitable Life Assurance Society, Bureau of Medical Research
13. The U.S. Public Health Department, Division of General Medical Sciences
14. The Mayo Clinic and Mayo Foundation

The scientific literature indicates that there has been a high degree of success in achievement of therapeutic benefits through the use of chelation therapy.

Just what does EDTA chelation therapy do inside the body? What is the substance's mechanism of action? How is it able to unharden arteries, widen arterial tunnels and make so many people feel a variety of benefits? The next chapter will answer these questions.

Chapter Four

The Internal Mechanism of EDTA Chelation

Preventive medicine has moved into the space age, where the latest technology is employed to detect the earliest deterioration, so that maximum extension of useful life span may be attained. . . . Since chelation therapy appears to offer a nontoxic life extension in research animals and beneficial effects in man, it is clearly desirable to increase its efficacy. To do this most efficiently, all possible mechanisms of action should be identified.

—Garry F. Gordon, M.D.
and Robert B. Vance, D.O.,
Osteopathic Annals, February, 1976

Nick Jurich Won the War Waging in His Arteries

Our arteries are ongoing battle scenes. They fight skirmishes with the pernicious forces in our unhealthy environment. All of us undergo the same sort of internal strife, and most of us succumb eventually to effects of this pathogenic stress. Our arteries develop atheromatous plaques that choke off our blood supply to the limbs, the heart or the brain.

Crippling deformity and finally death almost came to Nicholas Jurich, a real estate broker in Pittsburgh, Pennsylvania. In 1971 Mr. Jurich had a serious brush with the pathogenic stress common in our industrialized environment. It took the form of a rear-end automobile collision. The resulting whiplash injury he suffered set off a chain reaction of severe physical complications.

During the two years that followed his accident, Nick Jurich's metabolism went awry. He was afflicted with a near-fatal trace mineral deficiency, malfunctioning of his glandular organs, aggravation of a dormant arthritic condition and intense chest pains. Most alarming were the spells of unconsciousness that struck him without warning from an unknown cause. Repeated bouts of sudden blackouts landed the man in the hospital.

The Pittsburgh physicians put the patient through numerous laboratory tests that turned up no specific diagnosis. The doctors confessed they were puzzled and called in consultants. In futility, the several specialists finally prescribed Dilantin that Jurich was to take for at least one year and possibly for the rest of his life. The use of such a medication was an outright experiment, since only symptoms were being treated. They failed to find the source of the patient's problem and prescribed empirically. But harsh toxic effects from Dilantin, such as slurred speech, constant drowsiness, blurred vision and continuous tiredness could have ensued if Nick Jurich had followed the physicians' orders. He did not!

An enthusiastic referral by a visiting friend, who owned a health food store, motivated Nick Jurich to telephone from his Pittsburgh hospital room for an appointment with Dr. Ray Evers. The patient left his bed and flew south for diagnosis and eventual treatment.

Jurich received a total of 117 blood vessel-flushing chelations, administered intermittently from June 16, 1973 to November 30, 1975.

"My various symptoms cleared up," Jurich said. The blackouts disappeared. They had come from a severe deficiency of body minerals and inadequate oxygen supplied to the brain by his inadequate arterial circulation. The chelation treatments restored the circulation by opening formerly blocked blood vessels.

"Where I walked with great difficulty before from a prior acute onset of rheumatoid arthritis, now I could walk longer distances, although a little awkwardly. My joint swelling went down and most of the pain went away. My metabolism stabilized; glandular functioning seemed to improve considerably; my energy and mental alertness returned. Dr. Evers not only used chelation therapy, but he also built me up with an optimum diet, vitamins and chelated minerals. Now I'm able to hike far and wide without feeling any claudication pain in my legs," the man said.

Jurich spoke with enthusiasm to friends about his treatment results, so that others with symptoms of hardening of the arteries also made the trip to Dr. Evers' clinic. "In our community we've seen case after case of wonderful recovery from a variety of circulatory conditions," he said. "Carmen Carulli, a Braddock, Pennsylvania policeman is one of them. Carmen read an article about my friends who had chelation in the *Pittsburgh Press*. During that week he was waiting for Texas heart surgeon Dr. Denton Cooley to accept him for an examination appointment.

"Carmen traveled south for chelation care instead of going through open heart surgery. He took almost seven weeks of chelation treatment. Believe it or not, Carmen Carulli went back to work without the need of any heart operation," Jurich said.

The Story Police Officer Carmen Carulli Told

We searched for Officer Carulli to check out his story. This is what he told us:

"In September, 1969 I had a severe heart attack and was put in intensive care for three weeks. I was out of work for three months and then returned to the force.

"Three years later I again began to get this awful angina pain and finally needed hospitalization. This time I returned to work within a few weeks.

"About a year and a half later, one night while on duty at two o'clock in the morning, I picked up a man off the street and was socked for a third time by terrible chest pains—the same angina as before. The doctors quickly put me in the hospital. I was hospitalized that time for four weeks, and a heart specialist from Pittsburgh performed an angiogram on me. That angiogram caused me awful angina pain while I laid there on the table. When the catheter went in and hit an artery I felt terrible, and the doctors quickly pulled it out. The angiogram showed that I had three coronary artery blockages, 85 percent clogging of one, 80 percent in another, and 75 percent in the third.

"My cardiologist said that I was beyond surgery—that I was a goner! Well, I couldn't accept such a depressing outlook, so after some time I called down to Houston, Texas, to make an appointment for an evaluation by Dr. Denton Cooley. His secretary scheduled me for an examination in a week. But six days later, as I was getting ready to catch a plane for Houston, the same secretary phoned to say that Dr. Cooley couldn't see me because he was attending a convention, or something. It looked to me like I might die and nobody would care. That's when I found out about Dr. Evers and chelation therapy," Carmen Carulli told me.

"I telephone Dr. Evers and made an appointment to see him. Even though I was confined to a wheelchair—I was that weak—had angina at any exertion—my friends made sure that I managed the trip. One or the other of them pushed my wheelchair on and off the plane. I brought along my bag full of medicines. There were all kinds of heart pills that I thought I could not live without.

"After he examined me, Dr. Evers had me throw all the darn pills in the garbage, and he started the chelation injections. When I took three bottles of that EDTA stuff I started walking around the hospital. The fourth day I walked three city blocks and each day I added on distance.

"Remember what I'm telling you! When I went down there I was in a wheelchair—couldn't walk at all because of the angina pain," emphasized the policeman. "At the sixth day about fifteen of us, all were Dr. Evers' patients, went to New Orleans to see the city. It was a windy, blustery day. I walked fifteen blocks in that gusty wind without any recurrence of my chest pain. And I haven't had any angina since. I stayed in Dr. Evers' hospital for six-and-a-half weeks and returned to get ready for work one week after I came home. Then I went back to work.

"The Braddock Police Department wouldn't let me come back on duty unless I did my job. I put in a full eight hours daily walking the beat, and police work is pretty rough nowadays. I get into some scraps—bodily pick up 200-pound drunks off the street—walk up apartment house steps maybe three, four, five flights at a time. I'm obligated to do whatever I'm assigned, and I do it. I wouldn't be around here if it wasn't for the grace of God, Dr. Evers and chelation therapy," said police officer Carmen Carulli.

Officer Carulli is robust, wide-shouldered, vigorous, built like a bull and as tough a cop as you would see on any inner city street corner in New York, Chicago or Detroit. He spoke emphatically and demanded prepublication approval of what we would write about him. Carulli did not change anything when we sent him copy for correcting, except that he gave *God* part of the credit for his recovery.

By now, you may be wondering about the mechanism by which this widening of narrowed arteries takes place. We will present a full disclosure of the internal decalcification process using EDTA chelation therapy in the balance of this chapter and in the next.

Information Sources Advising Us on the Chelation Mechanism

Recognizing that until now therapies available for patients suffering with arteriosclerosis have truly been inadequate, the physician who is conscientious and who reads the information to follow will not disdain its value. Chelation therapy deserves study. The material is frankly awesome when one considers that its use can save a million or more lives each year, lives ordinarily lost to hardening of the arteries.

The well-informed physician, before administering this treatment, will want to review the entire literature on cardiovascular chemotherapy that employs synthetic chelating agents. The chief agent among them is *disodium edetate*, known generically as *disodium ethylene diamine tetraacetic acid (EDTA)*.

It is possible that this book may be the first place a physician comes across a full description of the chelation therapeutic technique. The victim of hardening of the arteries or a victim's family member may bring this book to the physician to ask if EDTA chelation is the way to hold onto a patient's limb or to snatch the patient from impending death. A physician may use this book's references to help him make that decision. That is why so much scientific and medical material is included in these next few chapters.

Furthermore, the physician who has his or her curiosity aroused might also interview some patients who have taken chelation treatments. We have discovered these people to be quite open and cooperative. They want to share their experience and good fortune with others who may benefit.

In the United States and many other Western countries, arteriosclerosis is the most frequently encountered chronic disease.[1,2,3,4] It is implicated in the death of at least every second decedent of our population. And the ratio of deaths caused by hardening of the arteries is increasing annually. The early onset of this disease in over 60 percent of twenty-one-year-old men was documented by autopsy findings in Korea and Vietnam casualties.[5,6] Nobody is immune to the arterial onslaught.

EDTA chelation therapy can reverse those staggering statistics. A most comprehensive summary of the derivation and development of EDTA chelation is presented in an article, "EDTA Chelation Therapy for Arteriosclerosis: History and Mechanism of Action," authored by Garry F. Gordon, M.D., and Robert B. Vance, D.O. The article is published in *Osteopathic Annals,* February 1976, Volume 4, Number 2, copyright by Insight Publishing Co., Inc., Alfred J. Arsenault, Publisher, 150 East 58th Street, New York, New York, 10022.

Reasons Why Chelation Treatment Is Not Widespread

In their article and in our interviews the coauthors informed us that the administration of chelation therapy is gradually becoming more common for treatment of arteriosclerosis. A number of published medical papers already attest to that.[7-23]

Along with the considerable interest among physicians who have informed themselves about the therapy, however, controversy also surrounds the use of EDTA in several chronic degenerative disease processes.[24-26] That is unfortunate for many patients. Controversy causes doctors to shrink back from using a remedy. They are fearful of being criticized by their physician peers. Although they don't want to be the last to use some treatment, most doctors do not want to be the first, either.

All possible mechanisms of action of chelation therapy for producing the observed beneficial effects are still incompletely documented. And this incomplete understanding of why and how it works becomes a useful argument employed by medical opponents of the method. Except for those listed in Chapter Three, insufficient medical interests has been shown in EDTA chelation by large clinical research institutions. There has, in fact, been no full-scale study of the technique. Such a study is needed and has become one of our goals for writing this book.

When delineations become firmly established, improved chelating agents will undoubtedly be developed. They are likely to decrease the inconvenience, time involved and cost of repeated intravenous infusions. This inconvenient administration technique and the general lack of familiarity with chelating agents[27] are two additional reasons for the serious delay in the widespread utilization of chelation therapy in medical practice. In the meantime, masses of people will continue to die from hardening of the arteries because the average conventionally trained American physician has not been educated to the therapy's mechanisms of effective action.

EDTA Mechanisms of Actions Science Understands

Bruce W. Halstead, M.D., former president of the American College for Advancement in Medicine, has written an extensive work on *The Scientific Basis of EDTA Chelation Therapy,* published by Golden Quill Publishers, Inc., P.O. Box 1278, Colton, California 92324. He told us, "I have reviewed most of the world scientific literature on EDTA, and I am totally convinced that chelation therapy is on solid scientific ground from the molecular to the clinical level."

Dr. Halstead directed our attention to the fundamental action that takes place when EDTA enters an individual's blood vessels. He said, "We find in the course of about the fourth or fifth decade of an adult living in the United States and in most of the developed countries of the world, where atherosclerosis is running rampant, that there is a steady increase in the calcium component in his blood. Along with this extra calcium there is a decline—a depression—in forty-six of the ninety-eight enzyme systems in his body that are active in one facet or another of arterial metabolism. This extra calcium inevitably must cause hardening of the arteries. However, the EDTA chelate directs its activities to the diffuse ionic calcium, which is the particular component that affects those enzyme systems. As a result of the law of mass action, calcium being a very dominant factor, it comes out in excessive quantities during the process of chelation, in an *in vivo* situation. [*In vivo* means that chemical reactions occur in living organisms.]

"EDTA is able to step in there, run through the arterial lumen, and play two roles. It is an intracellular membrane stabilizing agent. It removes metallic ions that serve as catalysts in terms of lipid peroxidation and membrane destruction. This first role is possibly the most significant one that EDTA plays, but we are just beginning to understand it," Dr. Halstead said.

"The second significant role of EDTA chelation we *do* understand quite well. Chelation begins to destroy some of the calcium complexes that are inhibiting the enzyme systems. It corrects the shifted enzyme balance that is producing insoluble calcium substance which piles up during the formation of atherosclerotic plaque in the intima wall. EDTA does this by chelating out the insoluble calcium."

Dr. Halstead offered us a summary of the primary actions of EDTA. They are as follows:

1. EDTA reduces the excess ionic calcium which causes inhibition of the enzyme systems of the arterial wall.
2. EDTA tends to stabilize the intracellular membranes of the cells of the arteries, and thus protects the biochemical integrity of the cells.
3. EDTA assists in maintaining the electrical charge of the platelets in the bloodstream and thereby reduces clumping and blood clots.

"The end result of ionic calcium buildup," said Dr. Halstead, "is the production of an oxygen deficiency state [hypoxia] which triggers off a vicious biochemical cycle of events leading to cellular dysfunction, molecular alterations, a gradual buildup of atherosclerotic plaques, and finally death.

"This biochemical cycle is a series of interacting events involving a complex of nutritional deficiencies, an excessive buildup of metal ion complexes, an accumulation of polluting toxic agents, physical inactivity, and finally an oxygen deficiency state, which is the end result of atherosclerosis," Dr. Halstead explained. "If you examine the overall picture critically, it readily becomes apparent on a rational biochemical basis as to how EDTA functions in reversing hardening of the arteries. EDTA has only one unique ability and that is to be able to form metal ion complexes—to remove these metals from the body."

How EDTA Actually Works in the Blood

What are the chelating agent's actual clinical mechanics? How does it work to take calcium out of atheroscolerotic plaque? How may the artery's narrow lumen be widened? These are but a few of the hundreds of questions we endeavored to answer by checking references and asking authorities.

EDTA first binds with the circulating unbound serum calcium to

form a calcium–EDTA complex. Much of this complex is excreted in
the kidney and bypasses the normal renal conservation of calcium. Drs.
Gordon and Vance confirmed its kidney action in their article. They
wrote:

> Approximately 80 percent is cleared through the kidney in the first six
> hours, and 95 percent in the first 24 hours. Some of the EDTA-calcium
> complex may dissociate, and calcium is dropped when a metal such as
> lead or chromium, for which EDTA has a higher affinity, becomes
> available.

Vance and Gordon went on to explain that the loss of calcium
through the kidney produces a transient lowering of serum calcium
with a concomitant decrease in serum phosphorus, as well as an increase
in serum magnesium. All of these chemical alterations with serum heavy
metals are beneficial to the heart muscle's contraction by means of an
action potential across the membranes.[28] Also, there is a possible holding
in balance of electrons.[29] Altogether a person experiences a number of
improvements in myocardial contraction and generalized advantageous
heart function and heart rate from the EDTA chelation mechanism.[11,30,31]

The body's homeostatic mechanisms are trying to return the serum
calcium to normal levels. It makes this attempt partly through increasing
parathormone levels. The initial calcium loss is replaced from the relatively easily changed calcium states of the body.[32-34] Some of the replacement is provided by metastic (pathologic) calcium that is deposited in
scattered remote tissues including the blood vessel walls. Some of it
also leaches from the available surface calcium of the skeletal system.

The human body is capable of replacing calcium into the blood at
the rate of 50 mg per minute. Based on this physiological fact, up to
seven times the accepted dose of EDTA could be given in as little as
one-tenth the normal administration time—in fifteen minutes instead of
in three hours or more as it is administered now—without serious ill
effect. EDTA is obviously quite a safe therapeutic aid. We shall discuss
safety of use or any possible toxicity of EDTA further in Chapter Seven.

There is no usual complication with the agent's employment, but if
a patient develops *hypocalcemia tetany* with the normal dose, his taking
magnesium as a nutritional supplement will correct this.[35] *Hypocalcemia*
is an abnormally low level of calcium in the circulating blood and
commonly denotes subnormal concentrations of calcium ions. *Tetany* is
a disorder marked by intermittent tonic muscular contractions, accom-

panied by fibrillary tremors, paresthesias and muscular pains; the hands are usually affected when tetany is present.

The increase in parathormone levels, if frequently repeated, leads to activation of osteoblastic bone activity. *Osteoblasts* are the bone-forming cells that build the osseous matrix. Thus new bone can form during or following the chelation process. Instead, EDTA chelation stimulates new bone formation.

Bone formation from EDTA use takes place in the following manner: The continued osteoblastic activity, when maintained for a sufficient time, continues to remove calcium from the blood serum so that soft-tissue pathologic calcium in plaques continues to diminish in order to meet this need caused by the increased bone uptake of calcium. A therapeutic cycle continues: EDTA takes up serum calcium and disposes of it as waste—parathormone activates bone-forming cells—bones grow stronger and require more calcium for their buildup—more atherosclerotic plaques give off loosely bound pathologic calcium to satisfy the bone cells' demand—the arteries soften and widen steadily in the process. The beneficial effects of chelation therapy are observed to go on for many months following treatment, since bone formation continues at an increased rate and keeps causing dissolution of metastatic calcium.

The late Carlos P. Lamar, M.D., F.I.C.A., one of the original pioneers of calcium chelation in atherosclerosis, had described the reduction in visible aortic calcification with simultaneous apparent decalcification of previously osteoporotic vertebral bones. *Osteoporosis* is a porous condition characterized by scanty, thin and reduced skeletal tissue.[15,18,19] He mentioned seeing improved joint function as arthritic joint calcium deposits are decreased. For that reason, symptoms of arthritis are dissipated. The deformity in a joint may remain, as with Nick Jurich, but mobility returns and pain goes away.

Another advantageous side effect of the chelation mechanism, the strengthening of bones and teeth, can be explained in this way: As reversal of hardening of the arteries takes place, bones and teeth get stronger, because ionic and metastatic calcium that may have avoided being grasped by the chelation claw go into reinforcing existing bone. Thus, hardened arteries get softer and softened bones and teeth get harder from EDTA chelation therapy.

Chapter Five

ADDITIONAL INTERNAL ACTIONS of EDTA CHELATION

The medical importance of chelating agents hinges on the fact that metals play many critical roles in the life of living organisms. In the human body metabolism depends not only on sodium, potassium, magnesium and calcium, but also to a considerable degree on trace amounts of iron, cobalt, copper, zinc, manganese and molybdenum. On the other hand, certain other metals, even in minuscule amounts are highly toxic to the body. It is apparent, therefore, that chelate drugs with appropriate properties could play several different therapeutic roles. Various chelating agents might be designed (1) to seek out toxic metals and bind them in compounds that will be excreted, (2) to deliver essential trace metals to tissues or substances that require them and (3) to inactivate bacteria and viruses by depriving them of metals they need for their metabolism or by delivering metals to them that are harmful. All three of these hopes have been realized.

—JACK SCHUBERT,
Scientific American, 1966

Chelation Therapy Smooths Skin Wrinkles

Charles H. Farr, M.D., Ph.D., medical director of the Genesis Medical Center of Oklahoma City, Oklahoma, noticed that after treating several hundred patients with chelation therapy, these people appeared to grow younger. Dr. Farr surmised that the mechanisms through which chelation helps the arterial system are essentially the same for the rest of the body. Skin changes that give a younger appearance certainly could occur. Internal actions of EDTA chelation have a relationship to the elastic tissue and collagen tissue in skin.

Elastic tissue, or *elastin,* is the major connective tissue protein of elastic structures such as in large blood vessels and the skin. It affords these structures the ability to stretch, yield to change and then resume shape or size.

Collagen is the major protein of the white fibers of connective tissue, cartilage and bone. It has a tendency to overcome the effects of elastin.

One of the factors of aging is that there is a gradual loss of elastic tissue with a buildup of collagen tissue. Thus there is a hardening effect not only of the blood vessels but of the skin and other organs as well.

Patients who have been chelated do remark about changes that they notice in their skin. It becomes smoother—appears much younger than before—wrinkles disappear to a degree.

In order to document these skin changes, Dr. Farr has taken thousands of photographs of patients before and after chelation therapy. Also, he has made microphotographs (pictures of skin sections visualized under the microscope). As an example, Photograph 5-1 shows a patient with crows feet at the corner of the eye. The crows feet furrows were wrinkled deeply at the time of photographing, which was August 12, 1994. In photograph 5-2, the same eye area, photographed October 8, 1995, shows the skin remarkably improved in appearance after chelation therapy. It looks younger, smoother, much healthier and with a loss of wrinkles. This finding, which occurs in some people very rapidly and in others a little slower, is quite consistent.

Skin Biopsies Depict Calcium Deposits

"I was not sure what was accounting for these skin changes," Dr. Farr said, "and this led me to begin doing skin biopsies in order to correlate them with changes in the cellular components themselves. I found two very significant changes that I could document."

Dr. Farr looked at the skin biopsies that were stained specifically to depict calcium deposits in the skin before and after chelation therapy. He found that metastatic calcium (the calcium in excess of what the

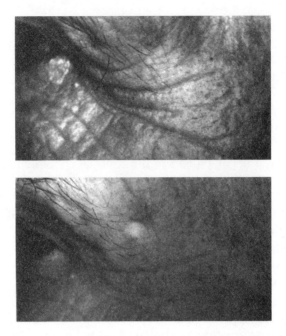

Chelation therapy can smooth skin wrinkles, as these before and after photographs reveal. Photograph 5-1 shows a patient with crow's feet, but after chelation (Photograph 5-2), these furrows are remarkably improved.

body requires) was much less after chelation. This indicates that chelation therapy removed the excessive calcium from the skin.

Dr. Farr said, "I also found that along the basement layer of skin there is some type of fatty tissue or fatty deposit unidentified as yet. These fatty deposits that were white and milky had something to do with the age and texture of the skin.

When a biopsy slice was made through the skin itself, chelation therapy was shown to have greatly reduced the white fatty material.

"From these studies of literally thousands of biopsies and microphotographic views of skin folds, we can deduce that reduction of metastatic calcium deposits have increased the health status of the skin," Dr. Farr said. "The same improved health status should be reflected throughout the entire body because the internal actions of EDTA chelation affect every cell in the body and not just the skin."

Additional Internal Actions of EDTA Chelation

In their *Osteopathic Annals* article[1] Dr. Gordon and Dr. Vance told of additional internal results from EDTA chelation. Some of the effects do occur quickly following intravenous infusion. They are likely to be the cause of exceedingly dramatic changes in severely involved people. Although not limited to the mechanical actions which we will describe now, the following benefits also occur.

Calcium is reduced in extracellular fluid, and this is among the most important benefits of the EDTA internal action. The reduction produces a decrease in intracellular free calcium ions that lessens smooth vascular muscle tone or contraction. The result will be the arrest or relief of spasms as in multiple sclerosis or in convulsions as in epilepsy.[2]

EDTA Infusion Has a Mild Pain-Killing Effect

EDTA may work in a way similar to papaverine. *Papaverine* is a nonnarcotic drug with a mild analgesic action. EDTA causes analgesia through an inhibition of phosphodiesterase enzyme.[3]

Phosphodiesterase enzyme produces an increase in the concentration of cyclic adenosine monophosphate (AMP), an enzyme, resulting in increased breakdown of glycogen to glucose for easier and more effective sugar utilization by the body.[4]

EDTA Infusion Enhances the Effects of Medication

EDTA medication is directly administered into the vascular compartment by intravenous injection. This infusion produces effective tissue drug levels far above those obtained with oral medication. There is consequent potential for medication effects far superior to those obtained with known oral vasodilators.

EDTA Protects Cell Membranes

The protective mechanism of EDTA is initiated when a cell membrane is invaded by a toxic mineral such as cadmium, lead, tin, mercury, calcium, or iron. When EDTA gets near such a damaged membrane, it binds with the toxic mineral. The chelating agent grasps the destructive particle and pulls it out of the membrane; ultimately, both the EDTA and the toxic mineral are excreted by the kidneys. Meanwhile, the damaged cellular membrane is coated by enzyme systems and interspersed with beneficial coenzymes such as vitamin E and selenium. Thanks to EDTA chelation, a sick cell has become a healthy one.

EDTA Cleans Lysosomes, the "Toilets" of the Body

Lysosomes are small structures inside cells that help to flush a cell of its waste products, similar to the action of a toilet in the home. When toxic trace metals such as lead, mercury, cadmium[5,6] or excess levels of calcium or zinc[7] block the lysosomal membrane, the function of the lysosome will be blocked, too. Intracellular lysosome function may have been impaired by the accumulation of intracellular heavy or toxic metals over the years at the lysosomal membrane. Chelation therapy cleans from the lysosome an accumulation of unwanted waste which may be impairing lysosomal function. Blockage contributes to the development of many chronic degenerative diseases such as arthritis, multiple sclerosis, lateral sclerosis, parkinsonism and more.[8] Removal of these heavy metals will allow the lysosome (the cell septic system) to detoxify more efficiently—even to improve myocarditis due to lead poisoning.[9]

In Chapter Two, we described EDTA as a "chemical rotary snake" that pushes out arterial blockage, or in effect clears the human "pipes." The lysosome is where the metaphor almost proves itself. Any toilet that becomes stopped-up begins to back up. Like a septic system, lysosomal membranes that are blocked cannot get rid of toxic materials. Because EDTA is an amino acid, it does not just float in the bloodstream, but it also profuses through the tissues, the capillary bed and in the tissue fluids, pulling out toxic metals from the trillions of cells of the body. When EDTA gets near a cellular membrane, it binds with any toxic divalent mineral, which is a heavy metal such as lead, tin, mercury, and others that are impairing membrane function and contributing to free-radical damage and lipid peroxidation of these important cellular membranes. The chelating agent pulls out that toxic mineral. Toxins are then floated from the cell by osmosis because there is a greater concentration inside the cell than outside, and that toxin eventually will be excreted from the kidneys. EDTA, therefore, is a membrane stabilizer which works differently than vitamin E and is potentially more powerful.

Why Calcium Is Affected More Than Other Serum Minerals

EDTA is a very effective chelating agent for calcium because of the wonderful way that nature organized things. The pH of the bloodstream is 7.2 to 7.4. The disassociation curve of minerals with EDTA shows that the mineral most commonly available in the pH range of 7.2 to 7.4 is calcium. Calcium is present in greater amounts than anything else. EDTA takes out lead, mercury, cadmium, zinc, magnesium, manganese, iron, and many other divalent minerals, but calcium seems to form the major metallic complex with EDTA at the normal pH of the bloodstream.

Harold W. Harper, M.D., explained that EDTA chelation is virtually an exchange process. "Calcium not only comes off the atherosclerotic plaque. It also affects the calcium pool in the body," Dr. Harper said. "If the physician injects into his patient *dicalcium* EDTA, he will primarily cause an exchange ion or removal of the next heaviest element, which is *lead*. If he injects disodium EDTA, it will exchange with the next higher element at that pH level, which is *calcium*. That is why we inject *disodium* EDTA rather than dicalcium EDTA. The sodium will apparently remain intact in the EDTA molecule and leave the body without increasing the salt load. One of the first and certainly the most prevalent divalent elements EDTA comes in contact with will be calcium. It will bind with that mineral at the bloodstream's 7.2 to 7.4 pH and move toward the kidneys for excretion as calcium EDTA," Dr. Harper explained.

In addition, we learned from conversations with Garry F. Gordon, M.D., that if the calcium EDTA is allowed by the body to recirculate, it will combine with the next higher mineral in the electromotive series (the periodic table of elements) with highly predictable stability constants. These minerals, which are toxic, include cadmium, mercury and particularly lead. EDTA in the recirculated calcium form removes the toxic minerals from the body as waste.

Special urine tests such as the twenty-four-hour urine analysis for calcium, the Cockcroft-Gault Equation, and the Sulkowich test are used to confirm how much calcium is coming out of an individual's body. The degree of unhardening of his or her patient's arteries is to an extent measurable by the physician in this way.

Thus the primary effects of the EDTA treatment occur within six hours; however, as we explained in Chapter Four, the chelation mechanism continues long afterward. For instance, the bones and teeth get stronger because metastatic calcium is absorbed into them over time. Once the process is initiated, therefore, additional excessive metastatic calcium, and other heavy toxic elements, continue to be removed from the lysomal and other cellular membranes.

EDTA Infusion Helps Adjust the Zinc–Copper Ratio

One of the most important ratios in avoiding coronary heart disease is the zinc–copper ratio, which EDTA specifically helps adjust. It improves lipid metabolism, too.[7]

In addition, many enzyme systems become reactivated. Some of these reactivated enzyme systems themselves then work more efficiently to repair damage in the body. Metabolism within the cells functions more normally with this increased cellular efficiency. EDTA acts in this way as a catalytic agent within the body to help make it more able to bring itself into its own desirable balance—known as *homeostasis.* That is why the initial improvement often seen clinically at the time of chelation is not the only effect. The benefits from EDTA infusion continue for sixty to ninety days afterward, and occasionally the maximum improvement is seen even beyond ninety days. This is what Dr. Halstead explained in Chapter Four as the first and most significant role played by EDTA. It is this function as an *intracellular membrane stabilizing agent* that provides the optimum beneficial effects. Dr. Halstead called EDTA "an amazing substance for human betterment."

EDTA Chelation Has an Anti-Aging Effect

The incidence of aging is slowed down by EDTA infusion. One reason why this occurs is that EDTA alters tryptophan metabolism.[10] *Tryptophan* is an amino acid component of proteins, which when lowered in bodily content, extends the lifespan of an individual. This is an anti-aging effect of EDTA chelation which should be investigated by gerontologists.

Plaque Particles Dissolve at Their Tops

If microscopic particles of calcium are uniformly dispersed in atherosclerotic plaque, the EDTA grasps them rapidly.

Dr. Harper told us, "Plaque particles come off not at the base of the plaque but at the top where the bloodstream's eddying currents come in contact with it. Plaque does not project into the lumen like a mountain top but rather like a molehill. Since EDTA attacks plaque where the eddying currents touch, dissolution takes place at the plaque's 'molehill' top where it projects into the lumen to narrow the tunnel that allows blood flow through that artery."

On the other hand, our investigations revealed that if the particles are macroscopic and irregularly dispersed, the calcium will be removed slowly, owing to the particle's small surface-to-volume ratio.[11-15] This probably is one of the reasons why some patients are helped more quickly than others. Their problems are caused by small-size calcium particles, while other patients are more resistant to help and a few may eventually require some direct intervention in the form of surgery for localized blockages that respond too slowly to the infusions of EDTA. Incidentally, the same patient may show both types of calcium deposits, microscopic and macroscopic, even in the same blood vessel, so that many areas in the body having both types of calcium deposits are helped.

Two instruments that measure blood circulation or volume—the *thermogram,* a regional temperature map of the body obtained without direct contact by infrared sensing devices, and the *plethysmogram,* a recording of the volume of blood flow in a body part or organ—show that capillary bed perfusion is markedly improved by EDTA chelation. Probably this happens at least partially as a result of lowered blood viscosity as well as lowered serum lipids.[13]

Lowering the lipids contributes to decreasing rouleaux formation by the red blood cells. *Rouleaux* is the stacking or clumping together of these red blood cells just like coins rolled into a wrapper. EDTA has been shown to decrease this type of red cell aggregation. This reduced aggregation speeds blood circulation. Also, decreasing aggregation may be a source of direct benefit to the red blood cells by decreasing the rigidity of their cell membranes. The improved capillary bed perfusion as well as improved peripheral blood flow could also come from the decreased resistance in the blood vessels[16] and other vascular structures induced by the decalcification of elastic tissues with associated decrease in cross-linkages in these tissues.[17-19] Improved capillary bed perfusion could also occur from what Gus Schreiber, M.D., of Dallas, Texas, described in an unpublished paper[20]—the decrease in basement membrane thickening, particularly in diabetics. Dr. Schreiber performed electron microscope studies of thigh muscle biopsies before and after these biopsied patients underwent chelation therapy.

Rheumatoid Arthritis Symptoms Reduce or Disappear

In the last chapter we described the elimination of Nicholas Jurich's rheumatoid arthritic symptoms. This may be from collagen tissues having their synthesis augmented by the high parathormone levels. Higher parathormone levels, you may recall, are produced in response to the abnormally low levels of calcium in the circulating blood due to the binding of serum calcium by EDTA and its subsequent elimination through the kidneys. Rheumatoid arthritis and other collagen diseases are involved with degradation of mucopolysaccharide and protein connective tissues. Parathormone alters the turnover of these tissues and thus affects rheumatoid arthritis pathology.[21]

Chelation Can Prevent Arthritis

Parathyroid stimulation by EDTA chelation alters the turnover rate of mucopolysaccharides and protein connective tissue components, as we described above.[22] This is important because mucopolysaccharide is a complex of protein and sugar, which when disordered in metabolism causes diseases that include various defects of bone, cartilage and connective tissue. Arthritis of various types will be the result.

By altering membrane calcium components, EDTA chelation increases red blood cell membrane flexibility.[20,23] Greater flexibility allows the red blood cells to fold more easily to conform to the tiniest of capillaries, which may be even smaller than the cells themselves. As a result, *sickle cell anemia* has been reported in the journal of *Hospital Practice* to improve from EDTA injection because of the reduced cell wall rigidity.[24] Less rigidity also permits potassium to enter into the cells more readily.[25,26]

High Blood Pressure Is Lowered

For a variety of reasons, administration of EDTA chelation lowers the patient's blood pressure levels. This may come from increased excretion of cadmium from kidney tissue cells,[27] the decreased peripheral resistance[16] through increased resiliency of blood vessels after removal of calcium[17-19] and decreased vascular spasm. Moreover, reduced hypertension takes place from increased serum magnesium that we previously mentioned.[28]

EDTA Protects the Liver

EDTA infusions protect against cirrhosis or impairment of liver function in high-fat diets.[23] We already said that it improves lipid metabolism,[29,30] but it also enhances glucose metabolism in diabetic patients.[31,32]

EDTA Chelation Alters Elastin Cross-Linking

EDTA chelation alters cross-linking of elastin, the major connective tissue protein of elastic structures.[17,18] In large blood vessels and elsewhere elastin is a yellow, elastic fibrous mucoprotein. This elastic alteration happening in the aorta has profound consequences, since this cross-linking of macromolecules by free radicals and calcium is now thought to be a basic aging mechanism.[33,34]

Chelation Assures the Presence of Adequate Zinc

By means of its binding with zinc, EDTA chelation assures more adequate levels of crucial unstable zinc.[35] Three components—the lactate dehydrogenase enzyme (LDH) of skeletal muscle and nicotinamide adenine dinucleotide enzyme (NAD) involved in degrading lactate and priming the change of glycogen into glucose, and any damaged cardiac muscle—are improved in their "demand-adaptation" by this change in zinc status.[36]

Chelation Offers Psychological Relief

After having no viable approach for relief of significant illnesses, the medical profession now has available EDTA chelation. It is a therapy highly acceptable by patients. Not only does it bring physiological benefit but psychological comfort as well. This psychological relief is destined to be the cause of removing people's anxiety about dying or losing a limb or an organ. Lowering anxiety levels is proven already,[37,38,39] with resulting vasodilation similar to that taught in "hand-warming" in biofeedback training.

Chelation Therapy Reduces Insulin Requirements for Diabetics

The war inside our arteries against atherosclerotic pathology continues without surcease. Every time another infusion with EDTA is given, more beneficial actions occur—more battles against arterial hardening are being won. To illustrate, requirements are reduced temporarily, and good control may be obtained in some diabetics simply by extending this action through repeated infusions at appropriate monthly or bi-monthly intervals.[31,35]

Diabetes mellitus has a well-known relationship to atherosclerosis that is of great importance in chelation therapy. In a study of a large group of patients with atherosclerosis who were without clinical features of diabetes, 56 percent were found to have latent disturbances of carbohydrate metabolism. The insulin disturbances were highest among those with advanced coronary artery heart disease.

In Dr. Norman E. Clarke's series of many thousands of patients with advanced forms of occlusive vascular disease, those with diabetes mellitus responded best to chelation therapy. Dr. Clarke told us that there has been a great reduction in insulin requirements among his patients. He checks their insulin needs frequently and lowers them gradually to avoid a severe insulin crisis. Other chelating physicians have repeated this same observation.

A reduced insulin requirement among diabetics taking chelation therapy has a speculative cause. The role of the pancreas in occlusive vascular disease with its insulin production may also include its islet cells as the source of elastase as its influence in medial elastin metabolism.

EDTA Manages Hyperlipidemia

Plasma lipid levels decrease by an average of 33 percent[7,36,37] so that long-term hyperlipidemias are more easily managed.

Arterial Walls Become More Flexible

Elasticity is restored to rigid, nonstretchy arterial walls. Dr. Clarke explained that the cholesterol in the atheromatous plaque is the product of prior degenerative reactions within the arterial wall. There is thickened fibrocollagenous tissue producing localized intimal enlargement at points of excess hemodynamic stress. Dr. Farr pointed this out earlier in this chapter when he illustrated the formation of skin wrinkles. The collagen deposition antedates the increase in local lipids within the arterial wall. The local intimal enlargements arise from what has been thought were stimulated fibroblasts. More recently, however, it has been demonstrated to be mutant daughter cells from the medial smooth muscle cell proliferating expressly—described as the "monoclonal hypothesis."

Restoration of Medial Elastic Tissue

Medical investigation of human aortas has demonstrated alteration in the medial elastic tissue, with calcium content increased prior to the appearance of any atherosclerotic plaque. An abundance of mucopolysaccharides in the arterial ground substance serves as fibrillar cement, and enzyme inhibitors of proteolyses that are present in young arteries and permit restoration of arterial wall injury. In older arteries this restoration process is much reduced, but EDTA chelation seems to allow for its return and rejuvenation, through restoration of enzyme function.

There are largely nonsulfated mucopolysaccharides in the arterial wall that decrease with age while the sulphated mucopolysaccharides increase. We learned from Dr. Clarke that sulphated mucopolysaccharides consist chiefly of chondroitin sulphate that has a high affinity for calcium. In the biologically aging artery, a change occurs in certain colloids with splitting and fragmentation of elastic fibers.

A group of arteriosclerotic people were found to have a mean yield of nine elastase units, while another group of young people (who died through violence) had an average of 208 elastase units. Elastase, like insulin, is formed in the pancreas.

More Lives Saved in Intensive Care and Emergencies

EDTA chelation is projected by Drs. Gordon and Vance to have lifesaving advantages for patients in intensive-care facilities. More people will leave those facilities alive through the use of this intravenous agent while they are present in the hospital.

EDTA chelation offers protection against the precipitation of lipoproteins that are produced by heparin. *Heparin* is the complex anticoagulant principle which prevents platelet agglutination and thrombus formation. Precipitation happens in the presence of divalent metals such as calcium.[40,41] Heparin is commonly used during acute heart attacks as crisis care, sometimes without the emergency physician recognizing the danger of increasing ischemia. *Ischemia* is the local lack of oxygenated blood, which is an anemia, due to mechanical obstruction to the blood supply of the heart. *Ischemia* also is defined as a necrosis (death) of a section of the heart through precipitation of prebeta lipoproteins in the presence of stress hormones.[42] By binding calcium and other divalent cations, EDTA chelation can prevent this heparin lipid-precipitation and improve cardiac arrhythmias (irregularities of the heart beat) as well.[25,26]

EDTA Infusion Dissolves Small Thrombi

Another important benefit of the internal EDTA chelation mechanism is the dissolving of small thrombi while the chelating agent is being injected. Dr. Olwin suggested in his presentation in Chapter Three that this benefit does take place. The lowered serum calcium produced by the infusion provides less likelihood of abnormal clotting. To prolong these benefits, the infusions could be given more slowly, such as over a twelve-hour period rather than the two and a half to six hours that they are given now (see Chapters Seven and Eight for the method of administration).

Other Diseases Become Treatable

Chelation therapy holds out the promise of success for treatment of various other diseases, as well. These include arthritis,[21,22] porphyria,[40] renolithiasis (kidney stones),[41] scleroderma,[42] lead poisoning,[43] calcium and certain other metal poisonings.[44] We have already emphasized that hypertension is helped.[16,27] There is improvement or restoration of vision in macular degeneration of the retina, as in the case history that Drs. Sibyl and Leon Anderson revealed in Chapter Three.

Physicians who employ chelation therapy for vascular occlusive disease, some of whom have joined together in the American College for Advancement in Medicine (ACAM), find that their patients experience a remarkable return of function, in addition to relief of symptoms. The statistical overall probability of significant improvement of patient functions has been calculated at better than 80 percent.[45] This ACAM combine of enlightened doctors is overcoming the widespread resistance of such therapy.

Chelation Maintenance Is Important

Often the patients voluntarily return after one or two years for a short series of chelation infusions to prevent any loss of benefits they enjoy. They understand that the arteriosclerotic process is an ongoing degeneration of arterial walls. Our bodies constantly skirmish with this deteriorating disease. Knowing this, some people feel so gratified with their health improvement, having previously suffered severely from ill-health, that they continue to add to their total number of chelation treatments over the years.

There does not appear to be any limit to how many repeat infusions can be taken.[14,29,45] Individuals have received over 500 infusions in a ten-year period; and where the medical history had shown several strokes or myocardial infarctions before chelation with EDTA, they frequently have had no further events during this extended treatment time.

Some, who have full knowledge of chelation advantages, employ the EDTA therapy for other things: a program of illness prevention in advance of any health problem developing, as had Dr. Warren E. Levin (described in Chapter Three); or a preparedness procedure for improved postoperative healing when major surgery is scheduled for the near future, as had Dr. Oswald B. Deiter, whom we shall describe in the next chapter.

Thus, sclerosis of the heart and blood vessels now no longer has to be the end product of the human body's war against our deteriorated environment. Dr. Harper said that the theoretical and practical mechanism for reversal of hardening of the arteries is what we have needed. That mechanism is now available—EDTA chelation therapy. Potential victims of hardening of the arteries should consider putting it to use immediately. Physicians can acquire the necessary materials and may use the method to offer their patients a virtually nontoxic therapy with potential life-extension benefits. To do this, the technique for administration of EDTA must be understood by both the beneficiary and the benefactor—the patient and the doctor. We shall provide the details of this technique's total method of administration in Chapters Seven and Eight. However, first you need to know in advance about the makeup of the ingredients that you might have infused into your blood vessels. We will therefore furnish information about the EDTA solution components next. Let us look at the materials included in the infusion bottle.

The Uses and Occurrences of EDTA Chelation

Although it is difficult to estimate the extent to which chelating agents are used in treatment of heavy metal poisonings, use of these agents have become the therapy of choice in a number of them. . . . So well established has this form of therapy become that, by and large, uncomplicated cases involving the use of these agents for more commonly seen metal poisonings, i.e., lead, are no longer reported in the literature.

—Harry Foreman, Ph.D.
Federation Proceedings on the
Biological Aspects of Metal
Binding, 1961

EDTA Chelation as a Preoperative Preparation

Oswald B. Deiter, D.O., of Ridgewood, New Jersey described himself as a practicing "ten-fingered osteopath." It was two months prior to an operation Dr. Deiter was planning to undergo on his left knee and about one month after he had completed three weeks of daily chelation therapy administered to him by H. Ray Evers. M.D. The patient had made EDTA chelation a part of his preparation for the operation. It was a precaution he had evaluated carefully and elected to adopt.

Dr. Deiter's knee was shot through with osteoarthritis from recurrent injuries. Football once was his forte in college, but knee trauma which he had sustained then caused the osteopathic physician to suffer now. In addition, Dr. Deiter had horses fall on him on three separate occasions over the years when he rode to the hounds. His knee condition was much aggravated. To overcome the pain, the physician was scheduled to have a plastic and metal prosthesis inserted into the left knee joint.

Where once this man had been very active in sports, now in his late sixties he sometimes required a wheelchair to get around. An ardent fisherman with a twinkle in his eye, a dry wit, a good sense of humor and an upbeat outlook, Dr. Deiter longed to become vigorous and sprightly once again. Having the knee surgery might accomplish that, he believed.

The knee operation was carried out at the Harkness Pavilion, Columbia Presbyterian Hospital, New York City. To insure quick healing through improved circulation, Dr. Deiter had taken precautionary preoperative therapy with chelation. Whether chelation treatment really did stimulate faster postoperative repair, the patient has no way of knowing for certain. He said, "I can tell you that surgery got rid of my degenerative arthritis problem, and I'm completely free of arthritic pain now. I can't prove that chelation helped me to heal more effectively—there's no way to measure—but I suspect it did. The treatment didn't do anything to actually repair my left knee, but now I don't need a wheelchair to get around anymore."

The osteopath also had prepared himself with other preoperatives. Well in advance of surgery, for instance, he built up his body with heavy doses (megadoses) of vitamins and chelated minerals, especially chelated zinc. *Zinc* is prescribed as a nutrient for patients by alert physicians and surgeons before and after optional surgery because it is known to speed healing.

"My general body condition improved very much," he said. "I took chelation to clean out as much atheromatous plaque as possible from my arteries, and I've observed changes in myself which proved that this happened. My blood pressure reduced from 160/110 to 130/70, and it has remained at that level. I showed rather pronounced varicosities in both legs before chelation treatment, but now I've lost the varicose veins in my left leg and about 60 percent of them in the right leg.

"I had trouble previously with moving my right hand due to arthritic problems and old injuries," said the osteopathic physician, "but now I have complete movement of my right hand—no limitation from traumatic arthritis anymore. On this right hand, also, I have what has been labeled a skin cancer. Two years ago the dermatologist wanted to cut it out. I didn't proceed with the skin surgery—just kept the area covered with a vitamin E ointment. Since I've had intravenous chelation, that skin cancer has almost disappeared from my right hand. It is gradually clearing up."

Chelation Results the "Ten-Fingered Osteopath" Observed in Others

Dr. Deiter described a woman he observed at Dr. Evers' clinic. She had been confined at separate times in two nationally known hospitals. Hardening of the arteries of the brain and body had affected her ability to speak and to walk. "She could do neither," he said. His description implied that the woman looked like a Dachau concentration camp prisoner. She weighed less than 89 pounds.

"After having one week of intravenous chelation," said Dr. Deiter, "I heard the woman begin to utter noises. At the end of two weeks she carried on a haltingly soft conversation. In three weeks she was marching around the clinic lobby talking with anyone who would listen. She gained weight and filled out. Her two sons, who alternated weeks staying with her, took her for long walks and other forms of exercise. I watched these really astounding changes take place in that patient and in others from chelation therapy."

The "ten-fingered osteopath" concluded with the description of a second dramatic case. A forty-six-year-old woman from Texas had been brought to the Evers clinic by her husband. "She had been quite active in her church and community," Dr. Deiter explained. "She had been a loving wife and mother and an excellent homemaker, her husband told me, but now she was absolutely demented. She failed to recognize her husband or her grown children or her friends. Suddenly she had gone out of her mind from something affecting her cranial arteries—some dementia. Then Dr. Evers found out the cause. A hair analysis performed on her by the medical staff at the clinic found the woman to be supersaturated with mercury—heavy metal toxicity.

"After being given just a week of daily chelation," Dr. Deiter continued, "the patient went through a marked personality change for the better. She regained her senses! Twenty-four-hour urine specimens taken every third day showed that mercury toxin was just pouring out of her in the hundreds of milligrams because of her receiving the EDTA infusions. While she remained to take more treatment, her husband went home to enlist the help of his city's board of health and all of the various shopkeepers and trade persons they dealt with to uncover the source of massive mercury doses that had been poisoning his wife," Dr. Deiter explained.

Original Use of EDTA for Heavy Metal Toxicity

The original use of disodium ethylene diamine tetraacetic acid (EDTA) in the United States, in fact, was for the treatment of heavy metal toxicity. In this country, the agent was first applied against lead poisoning in workers employed by a battery factory. Lead, a toxic heavy metal, was removed from the bloodstream and other body storage areas of workers by means of intravenous infusion.

EDTA chelation was also of interest to the U.S. Navy to remove lead from the arteries of sailors who absorbed it while they painted the Navy's ships and dock facilities. The therapy is still used for that purpose.

The medical potential of the chelating agent was demonstrated dramatically in 1951 when EDTA saved the life of a child suffering from lead poisoning (see "Chelation," by Harold F. Walton, *Scientific American,* June 1953).

Physicians observed that patients who had both lead poisoning and arteriosclerosis began to improve exceedingly well following chelation treatments with EDTA. Seeing their vascular conditions change for the better, the doctors started to treat others with vascular conditions who did not have lead poisoning. It was no surprise that patients with just occlusive vascular disease improved, too. In fact, the investigation of the medical uses of chelating agents has produced a voluminous literature, and chelate drugs have been developed for the treatment of a wide range of diseases from metal poisoning to cancer. The latest is for treatment in radioisotope saturation.

Besides citric acid and aspirin, other common chelating agents are cortisone, terramycin, and adrenalin. There are a host of additional chelating compounds, natural and synthetic, probably numbering in the tens of thousands.

Full Food and Drug Administration (FDA) approval has never been given for EDTA use against occlusive vascular disease, however. Intravenous infusion is the only route used because the chelating substance is poorly absorbed and not readily tolerated when taken by mouth. It does not cross the intestinal membrane well, with only 5 percent absorbed on the average. The stomach gets upset when EDTA is swallowed in its therapeutic form, although it is a common additive to many foods.

Chelation with EDTA remains an approved method for lead detoxification from the human body. It is excellent for that purpose, and this was confirmed as far back as 1961 during the *Federation Proceedings on the Biological Aspects of Metal Binding* from which we took the quotation at the beginning of this chapter. The State University of New York, Downstate Medical Center College of Medicine in Brooklyn, used calcium EDTA to treat hyperactivity of children, with excellent results. The medical authorities there believe that these children may have benefited because their hyperactivity may have represented an increased susceptibility to lead toxicity. They did not have true "lead poisoning" by accepted definition.

Heavy-metal toxicity is much more prevalent throughout the world and even more serious than is commonly recognized.[1] It is apparently more effectively diagnosed with hair analysis[2] than with conventional blood and urine tests.[3] Previously accepted "safe levels" of heavy-metal exposure have been found to cause or aggravate many chronic diseases.[4] Hyperactivity in children,[5,6] myocarditis[7] and neuropathy due to lead[4] and hypertension due to cadmium are among those heavy-metal toxicity diseases now recognized. After chelation, repeated hair analysis confirms the decrease in heavy metals as well as the improved trace minerals levels after adequate nutritional supplements are taken. Failure to show these changes may suggest the need for further reevaluation by the chelating physician. The physician will probably look for continued unrecognized heavy-metal exposure, as well as potential absorption or excretion defects in trace mineral metabolism.

Vitamin and Mineral Therapy Is Needed

Zinc and chromium deficiencies are readily diagnosed with hair testing in order to eliminate all potential causes of arteriosclerosis,[1,8,9] as well as to help maintain chelation benefits, and to achieve even greater improvement with the maximum elimination of symptoms. Hair analysis also contributes to greater chelation safety by avoiding potential aggravation of mineral deficiencies (such as zinc and chromium) through early recognition of these increased needs of some patients. Today's chelating physicians minimize the potential for EDTA toxicity by providing appropriate mineral and vitamin therapy along with the intravenous injections.[10,11,12]

Chelation therapy is known to bind and thus remove certain of the B-complex vitamins[11] particularly pyridoxine, as well as many essential trace metals,[12,13,14] notably zinc and chromium. It is therefore logical that clinicians using chelation therapy had to become keenly aware of the recent developments regarding the benefits of these vitamins and minerals in arteriosclerosis.[15,16] Mineral therapy and vitamin therapy are integral additions to the chelation therapy program. Hair analysis for evaluation of the patient's trace mineral status is performed routinely.[17-20] The program of treatment against hardening of the arteries, obviously, then, is not confined to EDTA chelation therapy alone. The anti-atherosclerotic program includes suggestions for dietary supplementation, vitamins, chelated minerals, special foods and other items.

Soviet physicians employed a chelator called *Unithiol* with a multivitamin administration in coronary arteriosclerosis. The Russians encourage the use of vitamin and mineral supplements for their people. They cited several sources in their 1973 and 1974 articles regarding the use of vitamins and Unithiol in arteriosclerosis.[21,22] The Soviet medical scientists concluded that such early treatment with dietary supplements and chelation is the most successful anticoronary approach. They recommend this combination treatment for the prevention of arteriosclerosis in the aging as well. This comprehensive approach of chelation, mineral and vitamin therapies may explain the great success some of today's clinicians are seeing in treating vascular disease. It is truly a "holistic" approach. Other informed and forward-looking doctors are beginning to use these holistic concepts as a more total treatment program for their patient's health problems. It includes nutritional therapy and chelation therapy, among other things.

Varieties of the Chelation Agents

Chelation agents are somewhat like aspirin in that all of the mechanisms by which they exert their beneficial effects are presently still not known.

We outlined a number of recognizable benefits provided by EDTA chelation in Chapters Four and Five, but there are probably more as yet unacclaimed.

The Russian chelating agent that we mentioned, Unithiol, employs a sulfhydryl group as the chelator.[22,23] When combined with orthomolecular nutrition (the use of megadose nutritional supplements) and regular exercise, this approach is so successful that some knowledgeable Russian physicians use it for an anti-aging procedure. It turns back the clock on the wearing out of tissues and reduces the incidence of hardening of the arteries for many older people.[23] As the foundation principle for reversal of hardening of the arteries, Russian physicians are providing their patients with an excellent program. A similar program is used in the former Czechoslovakia.

In 1972, the Czechoslovakian article "Chelates in the Treatment of Occlusive Atherosclerosis"[23] concluded that EDTA was the treatment of choice for vascular disease producing intermittent claudication of the legs.

It should thus be clear that all of us in the Western world have at least four choices by which to govern how and when we might live and die. Until now, only two of these choices have been offered. The choices are: (1) the extreme of simply watching and waiting for the expectant death caused by hardening of the arteries; (2) the other extreme of traditional medicine's totally inadequate "medical" *palliation* for the relief of arteriosclerotic symptoms in whatever organ the disease happens to strike;[24] (3) the intermediate between these of vascular surgery as a life-preserving technique, which consists of rather radical surgical procedures; or (4), what this book shows you as a fourth choice, the preventive and reversal treatment with EDTA chelation and nutritional therapies. Which choice would you select?

Commercial and Medical Chelation Substances

The chemical principle of chelation has been in use for at least a century in many industrial processes. For example, the softening of water is a process of chelation. Certain ion exchange materials, such as zeolite (used to soften water), are chelates. Zeolite is a complex sodium compound. When it comes in contact with hard water, it exchanges sodium for calcium and magnesium, which are the two minerals that make water hard. No lather forms when soap is added to hard water; a scummy precipitate drops out instead. Zeolite chemically forms sodium carbonates and sulfates to provide softened water. That is exactly how EDTA and other chelating agents work.

Chelation also forms the basis for the action of some of the other more commonly used detergents. Just as the chelating physician does for patients, the modern homemaker employs the principle of chelation when she uses detergents to wash clothes and dishes. Detergents form soluble chelates with calcium and magnesium that are readily washed out by water rinsing. That way no scum builds up as a ring around the dishwashing machine, bathtub, or wash basin.

The chelation process is used extensively in modern medicine. In addition to those already mentioned, such pharmaceuticals include penicillin, penicillamine, tetracycline, strepromycin, bacitracin, oxytetracycline, polymyxin, ammonia, cyanide ion, glycine, oxine, dipyridyl, tetraethyllithuram, vitamin B-12, isoniazid, aminosalicyclic acid and many others. Each chelating agent has a varying affinity for a variety of cations, depending on the various spatial arrangement of the ligand molecule and many additional chemical and physical factors.

For the educational benefit of physicians and physical chemists who are among our readers, we will list a few of the chelating agents used in medicine to directly achieve a desired chelation effect. These chelating agents are:

- Diethylenetriaminepentaacetate (DTPA)
- Cyclohexane trans 1, 2-diaminetetraacetate (CDTA)
- Ethylenediaminetetraacetate (EDTA)
- Isipropyllenediaminetetraacetate (IPDTA)
- Bis (-aminoethyl) ether tetraacetate (BAETA)
- (2-hydroxyethyl) ethylenediaminetetraacetate (HEEDTA-N)
- (2-hydroxycyclohexyl) ethylediaminetetraacetate (HCDTA-N)
- Nitrilotriacetate (NTA)
- Ethylenediamine di (0-hydroxyphenylacetate) (EDDHA)
- (2-hydroxyethyl) iminodiacetate (HEIDA-N)
- Di (hydroxyethyl) glycine (DHEG-N, N)
- 2,2-dimethylthiazoladine-4carboxylic acid (DTAC)
- 2,3 dimercaptoproponol (BAL)

The earliest medical therapeutic use for which the chelation principle was applied was with dimercaprol or *British antilewisite (BAL)*, discovered during World War II by Professor R. A. Peters and co-workers in Oxford, England. BAL is an antidote against the vesicant poison gas lewisite. By chelating the three arsenic atoms in the lewisite molecule, it renders the gas harmless and easily removable from the skin by water or from the body tissues in the urine. BAL became the first chelating agent used in the routine treatment of arsenic and other metal poisons during the 1940s. Unfortunately, BAL's own irritating effects on living tissues severely limited its widespread employment. Subsequently, other chelating agents were sought that could be used internally with fewer undesirable side effects. That is why EDTA came into common use for therapeutic purposes.

For suppliers of EDTA, see Appendix C.

The Chemical Formula of EDTA

EDTA has been designated by a variety of names by scientists in the papers they have published. Various names given to EDTA have included disodium ethylene-diamine tetraacetate; disodium ethylenediamine tetraacetic acid; edathamil; endrate; edathamil calcium disodium; disodium endrate; Sequestrene; disodium Versenate; triolone-B; disodium EDTA; and perhaps others. Its chemical formula is:

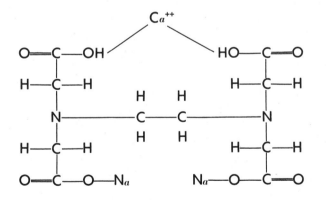

In the presence of a bivalent metallic cation such as calcium, (Ca++), each of the two-OH radicals releases their hydrogen atom, replacing it with each of the two calcium cation metallic valences, thus firmly sequestering the cation within a chelate ring (also see Figure 2-1). Then the formula of disodium EDTA changes to:

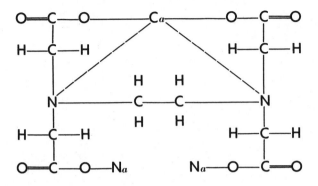

The first report of experimental control of serum calcium levels *in vivo* was made by Popovici and co-workers in 1950.[25] In 1951 Rostenberg and Perkins[26] used EDTA topically in the treatment of dermatitis appearing in nickel and cobalt miners. That same year Proescher[27] discovered that EDTA had some anticoagulant properties, leading to the finding of its strong calciotropism. *Calciotropism* is the attraction or grasping quality for calcium cations floating in the blood. More published clinical papers kept coming after that, and any search of the medical literature will turn up several hundred clinical papers published during the 1950s.

Research reports came from scientists in Switzerland, Germany, France, England, the United States, Japan and Australia. The Australian National University, in fact, listed 175 references in 1960. Probably the most attention-demanding papers for our purposes were Dr. Clarke's two reports, published in 1955 and 1956. They gave dramatic descriptions of the successful treatment of vascular disease with the removal of calcium from arteries by intravenous EDTA. Dr. Clarke's papers also told of the correction of an apparently terminal case of uremia which we discuss in detail in the next chapter. It was in a patient who had progressive nephrocalcinosis (calcification of the kidney), studied by X-ray during its evolution for several years.[28,29]

Chapter Seven

THE PROTOCOL FOR ADMINISTERING EDTA CHELATION THERAPY— PART ONE

In view of the repeatedly confirmed safety of this therapy and of its possible great benefits in the preservation of usable and enjoyable life and health for the many millions of people affected by calcific atherosclerosis and other calcium metastatic lesions, a concerted study of large numbers of institutional volunteer subjects (in homes for the elderly, in long-term care facilities, and in prisons) should be carried out, with matched controls receiving intravenous placebo solutions. All subjects should be thoroughly studied before and during therapy and for prolonged follow-up periods, by all available means including perhaps vascular biopsy studies. Only a mass investigation of this type can clarify the role of chemical endarterectomy in the prevention, early correction and late palliation of the metabolic disturbances which result from reduced blood supply through arteries with lumens narrowed by atherosclerotic plaques.

—CARLOS P. LAMAR, M.D.
Journal of the American Geriatrics Society, March, 1966

How to Increase American Life Expectancy

Chelation therapy allows a person with occlusive vascular disease to optimize his response to all the various forms of therapy he takes. As a single-modality approach, EDTA chelation is unsurpassed. It must be combined, however, with a comprehensive, multitherapeutic approach that includes reestablishment of optimum metabolic equilibrium through diet, exercise, reduced stress and nutritional supplementation. Then there is an unexcelled effect. This is the orthomolecular-holistic approach in which occlusive vascular disease processes will be generally controlled and possibly reversed.

All known risk factors for hardening of the arteries must be identified, treated and eliminated, if possible. For example, defective lipid metabolism must be improved with diet, nutritional supplements and hormones, instead of the current inadequate practice of surgical expediency or the other extreme of watching and waiting. Look at the prevalent practice of American medicine today—we wait for a crisis after watching a disease pattern take hold. Then we attack the problem—not infrequently using expensive and dangerous surgical procedures. Fortunately, a few enlightened physicians have had the honesty to look at what they are doing and make changes.

Current forms of orthodox American crisis-oriented medicine for hardening of the arteries invariably arrive but too little, too late. And chelation or supplemental nutrition is not even included as one of these orthodox therapies. We believe arteriosclerosis and other forms of chronic, degenerative disease that confront Americans can be reduced and even eliminated through application of these orthomolecular-holistic medical concepts, which is the practice of preventive medicine in its most ideal form.

Holistic medicine holds great validity, for through its practice the number of illnesses that affect all people can be much more effectively controlled—and at far lower costs in lives, dollars and time.

The intravenous approach for the administration of EDTA has been made part of the holistic approach. However, this technique to increase every American's life expectancy no doubt can be improved upon. Someday, perhaps, one infusion might do the work of several. This improvement would lower the cost associated with current administration techniques and thus increase acceptance of the concept, not only for the restoration of blood flow through diseased vessels, but also for the amelioration and prevention of several other disease processes. Until that general acceptance by the people and their physicians occurs, the components, administration technique and costs of intravenous chelation are not likely to change much. Our fear is that acceptance may come too late to have this important therapy included in any forthcoming national health program. If that be the case, its availability to the American people could be seriously threatened by the ever-present red tape of bureaucratic regulations usually associated with government-controlled medicine.[1-7]

The FDA-Approved Placebo-Controlled, Double-Blind Study of Chelation Therapy

In 1987, the American College for Advancement in Medicine (ACAM) received $300,000 in research grants from two private foundations to fund two randomized, placebo-controlled, doubled-blind studies of EDTA chelation therapy for atherosclerosis. The research protocol was designed by ACAM members in consultation with the United States Food and Drug Administration (FDA). Subsequently, after prolonged study, the FDA approved this Investigational New Drug (IND) study's design along with its protocol. Additional funding and donated services came thereafter from physicians, patients and the two research institutions where the studies were launched, Walter Reed Army Hospital in Washington, D.C., and Lederman Army Hospital in San Francisco, California.

It was anticipated that the IND research being conducted by the U.S. Army's clinical investigators who were completely unbiased, with no previous connection to EDTA chelation therapy, would be completed during the 1990–1991 period. Because of the Persian Gulf War, however, this did not happen. Nearly all of the clinical investigators were removed from the study to pursue matters associated with that war's mobilization. Peripheral vascular improvements for participating patients were quite apparent even with the double-blind study code never having been broken, but the clinical results remain in limbo. The study has yet to be completed.

Still, some good has come out of the disappointment befalling patients who want to receive chelation treatment and physicians who routinely administer it. Now vast numbers of cardiovascular- and peripheral vascular-impaired people have available an FDA-approved protocol for the safe and effective administration of EDTA chelation therapy. What follows is an explanation of that lengthy and medically technical protocol, which is suitable for use by a doctor of medicine (M.D.), a doctor of osteopathy (D.O.), or a doctor of naturopathy (N.D.), who is licensed to administer intravenous (IV) infusions. Twice each year, usually at its semiannual meeting, ACAM conducts courses to train physicians in the clinical use of EDTA chelation therapy. It's not recommended that any health professional administer EDTA chelation therapy for atherosclerosis until such training is received.

The full protocol for administering IV ethylene diamine tetraacetic acid may be acquired by contacting the American College for Advancement in Medicine, 23121 Verdugo Drive, Suite 204, Laguna Hills, California 92653; telephone (714) 583-7666 or (800) 532-3688; teleFAX (714) 455-9679. Please note that the ACAM protocol for EDTA administration and the ACAM physician membership roster are each so long that they will not be teleFAXed by ACAM.

Safe and Effective EDTA Chelation Therapy

When the FDA finally approved the design and protocol for chelation therapy's Investigative New Drug (IND) application, this governmental agency had already made a search for reports of adverse or poor results, including serious side effects, stemming from the treatment's administration. No unfavorable evidence of that type was found. Indeed, the FDA went so far as to officially request from all state and regulatory agencies across the United States any information relating to deaths, deleterious effects, poor results, no results, patient complaints, physician condemnations or any other expressions of opposition to intravenous infusion with EDTA to accomplish chelation therapy for athersclerosis. In response, no reports of that kind were received by the FDA.

The safety of IV EDTA, properly administered, was not an issue with FDA officials during planning sessions with clinical researchers when the IND research protocol was designed. For rats, for instance, IV EDTA is equivalent in toxicity to the amount of nicotine in tobacco inhaled from their "smoking" three cigarettes.[8] A large body of published research was presented to the FDA showing that EDTA is safer than most other approved therapies.[9]

Relative Safety and LD-50 of EDTA

Bruce W. Halstead, M.D., discussed the possible toxicity of EDTA with the California Medical Association's review committee on chelation therapy when he appeared at its March 1976 hearing. Dr. Halstead said, "A great many statements have been made by a number of different organizations regarding the great hazard in the toxicity, the so-called nephrotoxicity of EDTA. In the field of toxicity we usually evaluate the toxicity of a substance based on its *LD-50*. We talk about a measure where the toxic ingredient produced death in about 50 percent of the organisms."

In explanation of Dr. Halstead's statement, we'll inform you about toxicity and LD-50. You must have two particular values to discuss the toxicity of any drug intelligently. One value is the optimum effective dose, and the other is the toxic dose of LD-50. *This LD-50 is the dose which, given over a specified period of time, will kill half the subjects the drug is being administered to.* The toxic dose divided by the therapeutic dose is the *therapuetic index.* This therapeutic index tells researchers and physicians how dangerous a drug or other substance is to living organisms, especially people.

If the therapeutic index is small, the compound or drug is toxic; if it is large, it is nontoxic. For example, if 1.0 gram per day is the optimum dose of a drug and 2.0 grams per day is the LD-50, the therapeutic index is two. Obviously, this would be a very dangerous drug because the therapeutic index is small. Insulin may fall into this dangerous class. It has a low therapeutic index, and users know that insulin has to be administered with great caution. EDTA has an exceedingly high therapeutic index and is safer even than aspirin.

Dr. Halstead explained, "The LD-50 of EDTA is approximately 2,000 milligrams per kilogram of body weight, based on oral repetitive studies. And these studies have now been exhaustive and enormous. We find that the toxicity of EDTA can be compared to something we already are familiar with. That is the toxicity of aspirin. Aspirin's toxicity is 558 milligrams per kilogram of a person's body weight. So essentially, EDTA is about three and a half times *less* toxic than aspirin."

You can understand, therefore, that by Dr. Halstead's definition of EDTA toxicity this synthetic amino acid is less than one-third as toxic as aspirin. Aspirin is legally used as the treatment of headache, but EDTA has a much more important use. It improves blood flow to the heart, the head and the limbs.

Dr. Halstead's statement on the safety of nontoxicity of EDTA chelation therapy was confirmed in previous published reports.[10,11] EDTA has a wide safety spread of ten to 120 times between the therapeutic recommended dose and the LD-50. Recognition of the depletion of trace minerals such as magnesium, zinc, chromium, manganese, and iron[11,12,13] and vitamin B depletion with appropriate replacement has markedly improved its safety toward the high end of the scale. Even *teratogenesis,* the disturbed growth processes involved in the production of a malformed fetus, once reported in animals, was completely prevented with the administration of zinc.[15] Thus with an understanding of the mechanism of its action, the safety of EDTA, when given in recommended doses, is firmly established.[10,16]

Most criticisms of chelation therapy originate from individuals with vested interests in competing therapies such as representatives of the pharmaceutical industry, physicians supported in some way by pharmaceutical companies, coronary artery bypass surgeons, cardiologists, chest surgeons, peripheral vascular specialists who perform amputations, spokespersons parroting the National Council Against Health Fraud and others.

Even with the multimillion infusions given to hundreds of thousands of Americans, plus many thousands more patients in Europe, South America, Australia, New Zealand and Asia, reports of death from chelation therapy have been nonexistent since 1954. Dr. Norman E. Clarke, Sr., M.D., a cardiologist who was chairman of the department of research at Providence Hospital in Detroit, admits to having used inordinately large doses of EDTA at a time when the treatment had been almost untried previously. Of course, as with any type of medication, idiosyncratic allergic reactions may occur with the intravenous infusion of EDTA.

Nephrotoxicity of Chelation Therapy

The initial use of EDTA in 1954, as mentioned previously, was associated with two deaths[17,18] for which serious overdosages of up to 10.0 gm per infusion are blamed. Later, the recommended dose was lowered to 5.0 gm and then to 3.0 gm;[19] but it was only after the development and use of the electron microscope and other careful studies that this question of potential toxicity was fully clarified.[20-22] The conclusion of these studies was that the term "nephrotoxic," which Dr. Levin had referred to as "transient kidney malfunction," is *not* justified with EDTA. The change seen in the kidney is a normal physiologic mechanism for removal of toxic products through the kidney. There is *no* long-term damage or development of later kidney complications associated with EDTA when the intravenous technique is properly employed. After all, even water and air can be toxic when applied improperly.

Dr. Clarke wrote a report on the death of one of these EDTA-associated patients. It was in his early investigation of EDTA that one of Dr. Clarke's chelation cases, a sixty-eight-year-old mechanic identified as W. McL., who had his first attack of angina in 1947, might possibly have had his death hastened from a high-dose-related EDTA infusion. That was more than forty-three years ago. Dr. Clarke stated, "The patient's activities had been unlimited until early 1953. Then he had a diseased gall bladder removed in November 1953, after which he improved until January 1954, when angina pectoris increased rapidly."

In February 1954, Dr. Clarke gave the patient fifteen intravenous injections of 5.0 grams each within less than three weeks (a total of 75 grams). This amount was about three times what is now considered to be the usual and customarily acceptable dosage. A few days later the man had a convulsion, lost consciousness and died within a few hours. His autopsy disclosed that he also had previously unrecognized kidney disease, which further points out the necessity of first determining kidney function in all patients before they receive chelation.

Dr. Clarke continued with his report: "At necropsy [autopsy] they demonstrated extensive atherosclerosis. In some zones the atheromatous material containing lipid was diminished, and in other zones there was necrosis and degeneration of supporting stroma and slight polymorphonuclear infiltration. The coronary arteries section showed intense medical sclerosis with calcification and general narrowing of the lumen, but no atheroma. The kidneys had tubular nephritis and glomerulitis that was considered to be terminal. There was no vacuolization of the kidney cells. The coronary pathology was medical sclerosis with no occlusion or atheroma."

As an interpretation of this medical autopsy report offered by Dr. Clarke, the innocent lay reader should be told that the patient was probably doomed to die momentarily no matter what treatment he received. The disease in the man's kidneys alone could be the cause of his death. Or the mechanic could have died from coronary artery blockage.

As an explanation of that long ago case, Dr. Clarke has said, "That was during the early period when we were giving up to 10 grams of EDTA. We didn't know what to give, it being the first use of the compound on atherosclerosis of humans. We soon found that it was too high a dosage. We reduced it to 5 grams and later decided the correct dose was established at 3 grams."

There has not been a reported death from intravenous infusion of EDTA for forty-three years. The EDTA maximum dose given today is 3 grams (20 cc) for a usual number of one, two or maybe three treatments per week.

In support of Dr. Clarke, Dr. Halstead pointed out the significance of glomerulitis and nephritis mentioned in this 1954 case. This sort of support is needed currently, even though you may find this talk about toxicity highly technical—even monotonous. Why is it needed? Because if you ask your traditional physician about whether or not you should take chelation therapy, he is going to quote you rumors he may have heard about this same 1954 case.

Dr. Halstead said, "It so happens that because of the work of Dow Chemical Company and others in producing versenate EDTA, which is used extensively for various food products, blood constituents and other things, there have been very extensive studies in rats to determine whether or not there is any degree of renal [kidney] damage. In none of these reports have they ever reported glomerular nephritis. And if Dr. Clarke's case involves glomerular nephritis, we're talking about a patient complication—not EDTA toxicity: The fact that a person is being treated with EDTA and has atherosclerosis is no guarantee that he does not have pre-existing glomerular nephritis from other sources. He may have a host of other complications. Many of us don't just have arteriosclerosis. There are many other unknown entities.

"The dosage level is a very important point, too," said Dr. Halstead. "If the person was given 5 to 10 grams of EDTA per day, he was far beyond the dosage range that is considered normal and accepted therapeutic dosage today."

Commenting on those first two deaths with EDTA therapy which were reported in the medical literature in 1955 and 1956, Garry F. Gordon, M.D. of Payson, Arizona suggested a comparison. Dr. Gordon said, "The doses of EDTA used in those cases were 5 or 10 grams. You can compare this to an intake of water. Make the comparison! If you drank a year's supply of water in one week, you'd die, too. Nonetheless, opponents of this therapy will continue to dwell on those singular cases, and any other negative stories they can twist to make it appear chelation is unsafe. They ignore the hundreds of thousands of people who are treated successfully each year with no complications of any kind."

Findings on EDTA Safety by the Chelation Pioneer

Dr. Clarke, the chelation therapy pioneer, referring to EDTA safety, advised, "Among the extensive publications verifying the therapeutic safety of EDTA is a work by Oser, Oser and Spencer, published in 1963,[23] that 'found EDTA generally considered to be quite innocuous.' In another study of theirs EDTA was fed in two times accepted strength for twelve weeks to weaning rats, 'it caused no signs of body injury,' they wrote."

Dr. Clarke also said, "Doolan and Schwartz of the United States Naval Medical Research Institute in 1967[20-22] studied the effect of EDTA on the kidneys and reported 'the label of nephrotoxicity (for EDTA) is unjustified.'

"Meltzer and Kitchell of the Hahnemann Medical School," Dr. Clarke continued, "published a report based on 2000 consecutive infusions of 3.0 gm of EDTA and 'found *no* serious side effects or *toxicity* from EDTA when administered in 3.0 gm doses—can be used over prolonged periods without evidence of toxicity.'[10]

"An unusual study on rotifers by Sincock was published in 1975 in the *Journal of Gerontology*. Sincock found 'significant increase in [rotifer] body calcium content with aging' and 'regular brief immersion periods [of rotifers] in a solution of EDTA with withdrawal of body calcium by chelation produced extension of lifespan and reproduction period'." *Rotifers* are a form of many-celled aquatic microorganisms that have rows of cilia at one end, which in motion resemble revolving wheels. The rotifers were treated every other day of their lives with EDTA and lived 50 percent longer than controls.[24]

Dr. Clarke concluded, "From these and similar reports of which there are many, and from my own years spent in observing the therapeutic results and possible toxic effects of EDTA therapy and extensive clinical studies undertaken and published in 1955 and 1956, I conclude that EDTA deserves a place in the armament of the medical profession, even if it could help no more people than does our lauded present cancer therapy."

Kidney failure has sometimes occurred in patients with preexisting renal insufficiency who were given repeated infusions of EDTA without being properly monitored in accordance with this protocol. The chelating substance is potentially toxic to kidneys. An excessive dose, or a therapeutic dose given too rapidly, may cause renal damage. Precautions are taken by trained chelating physicians who follow this protocol. They closely monitor their patient's kidney function, especially if there is a preexisting renal insufficiency; otherwise, further impairment can occur.[25,26,27]

The kidney's glomerular filtration rate (GFR) must be measured as endogenous twenty-four-hour urinary creatinine clearance, for it diminishes in direct linear relationship with kidney impairment. (The kidney glomeruli are tufts or clusterlike structures composed of many tiny blood vessels which filter the blood as it passes through the kidneys.) The most reliable early finding of adverse kidney effects from IV EDTA is a progressively rising serum creatinine measured or computed during a twenty-four-hour urine collection. (Many chelating physicians use a computer program in their offices to calculate creatinine clearance and the optimal dose of EDTA for each patient.)

Even when they are anxious to conform to their physicians' requests, it's not unusual for people in unsupervised home environments or some other type of outpatient setting to fail to collect timed, complete and accurate specimens for the doctor's determination of GFR creatinine clearance during a full period of twenty-four hours. Therefore, the chelating doctor's use of the Cockcroft–Gault equation is more accurate for such calculation than asking a patient to perform the necessary steps: collecting urine, storing it under refrigeration and carrying it to the clinic for measurement.[28]

The highly accurate, modified creatinine clearance equation originally described in 1976 by Drs. D. W. Cockcroft and M. H. Gault is presented in Table 7-1.[29]

TABLE 7-1
COCKCROFT–GAULT EQUATION FOR CREATININE CLEARANCE

Creatinine Clearance (ml/min) = $\dfrac{(140 - \text{age in years}) \times (\text{wt in kg})}{72 \times \text{serum creatinine in mg/dL}}$

For women, multiply the above result by 0.85.
If creatinine is measured nonfasting, multiply the above result by 1.15.

EDTA DOSE to be administered in each infusion is computed as:
50 mg/kg of lean body weight × (creatinine clearance divided by 100)
Correct for creatinine clearance only if greater than 100.

LEAN BODY WEIGHT ALWAYS USED IN ABOVE COMPUTATIONS

Lean body weight for males is computed at 50 kg plus 2.3 kg for each inch of height over 5 feet.

Lean body weight for females is computed at 45.5 kg plus 2.3 kg for every inch of height over 5 feet.

Actual weight is used for thin patients, whenever actual weight is less than computed lean body weight.

The Cockcroft–Gault equation for measuring creatinine clearance, which is a significant test in determining continued kidney viability, takes into account the patient's age, sex, lean body weight and fasting or nonfasting state. It accurately computes the patient's creatinine clearance. It has become a well-accepted physiological mathematical formula for figuring out creatinine clearance without making the patient gather his or her urine in a gallon jug during the course of a full day and night.[30,31]

IV EDTA for Patients with Impaired Kidneys

It's been erroneously rumored that the intravenous infusion of EDTA harms kidney function. That is incorrect! IV EDTA does not do damage to normally functioning kidneys (the renals). In fact, chelation therapy actually enhances the kidneys' performance. At least three studies reported in the medical literature testify to improved kidney function following EDTA chelation and multivitamin-trace mineral therapy.[32,33,34]

Supposed pathology created by IV EDTA in humans with normal kidneys is not pathology at all. Observed temporary glomerular alteration consists of vacuolization of the renal tubules, which resembles that of sucrose nephrosis but is not. Tubular secretion makes no accompanying contribution because the chelate is presented to the luminal side of the tubular cells. The vacuolization is unaccompanied by any significant evaluation of serum creatinine or urea nitrogen. Rather, the vacuolization is due to the process of pinocytosis, independent of any metal binding process.[35,36,37] If the ACAM protocol is ignored, however, and an overdose of EDTA or excessive chelation therapy is administered the result can be nephrotic lesions with kidney impairment. This is especially true when toxic metal chelates are formed. (See Figure 7-1)

Pinocytosis is the process by which fluid is taken into a cell. The cell membrane develops a pouchlike space, fills with fluid from outside the cell, and then closes around it, forming a tiny pond of fluid in the cell. It's a normal process which clears out of the glomeruli within twenty-four to forty-eight hours after the discontinuance of chelation therapy.

When a person's renals are impaired, their inability to work properly may be short term (acute) or long term (chronic). The condition of impairment is marked by the patient's producing low amounts of urine with a rapid buildup of nitrogen wastes in the blood. But the extent of

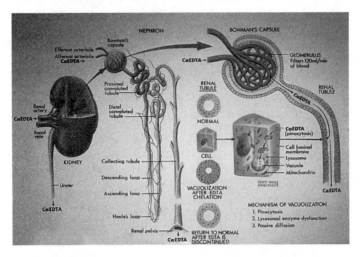

Figure 7-1. Depicted is the excretion of calcium ethylene diamine tetraacetic acid (CaEDTA) through the kidneys as it traverses anatomical components of the organ. When the patient is properly treated by following the accepted protocol, vacuolization usually disappears within twenty-four to forty-eight hours. (Courtesy of R.H. Knabenbauer (artist) and Bruce W. Halstead, M.D., Medical Director of the World Life Research Institute in Cotton, California.)

impairment is only a relative contraindication of the patient's receiving IV EDTA, and the *Protocol* approved by the FDA in 1987 allowed for such relativity. Strictly for purposes of the *Protocol,* the American College for Advancement in Medicine and the FDA divided an individual's kidney impairment into three degrees of insufficiency: (1) mild, (2) moderate and (3) severe.

Mild renal insufficiency is a loss of up to one-third of the patient's normal kidney function and requires monitoring before and during chelation therapy. The blood's creatinine content must be known. In addition, the patient's measured or computed endogenous twenty-four hour urinary creatinine clearance (CC) or the Cockcroft–Gault equation then come into play. The Cockcroft–Gault equation is accurate for detecting a decrease in kidney function, ranging from 50 to 80 ml per minute of CC. Normal CC is above 100 milliliters (ml) per minute (min).

In patients with normal kidney function, the recommended dose of intravenous EDTA for safety and optimum benefit is 50 mg per kg of lean body weight, up to a maximum of 5.0 g of EDTA. Given in a 500 cc bottle of the carrying vehicle (normal saline or something else as described in the next chapter), 30 mg of EDTA amounts to the inclusion of 20 cc into that vehicle. In contrast, when the urinary creatinine clearance is less than 100 ml/min, the EDTA dose is reduced proportionate to the amount by which creatinine clearance is less than 100 ml/min. For example, if CC is 70 ml/min, the dose of EDTA is 70 percent of the dose needed for 50 mg/kg lean body weight. If CC is 50 ml/min, the administered dose of EDTA is one-half of the dose calculated for 50 mg/kg of lean body weight.

Mild renal insufficiency, with at least two-thirds of normal GFR remaining, causes serum creatinine to range between 1.1 and 1.5 mg/deciliter (dL), which is still within the normal range. The CC (creatinine clearance) reading is a more accurate test than either the blood serum creatinine or the blood–urea–nitrogen (BUN) tests.

Moderate renal insufficiency is the loss of one-third to two-thirds of normal kidney function. Twenty-four-hour CC will be approximately 30 to 60 ml per minute, and serum creatinine ranges from approximately 1.6 to 2.7 mg/dL. After 50 percent of GFR is lost, serum creatinine increases rapidly. These impaired patients do show improvement in kidney function following a course of chelation therapy, but they must be monitored carefully with frequent renal function tests while receiving and directly following such treatment.

A moderately renal-impaired patient is not a candidate for IV EDTA if he or she experiences any rapid decrease in renal function following an infusion. But most of these kidney-damaged people do tolerate IV EDTA well when the dose, rate and frequency of treatments are adjusted to tolerance. Making judgments in accordance with readouts of kidney function tests is the way a trained chelating physician keeps his or her patient safe while using chelation therapy.

Severe renal insufficiency is the loss of two-thirds or more of normal GFR, shown by a twenty-four-hour creatinine clearance of 30 ml per minute or less, depending on body weight. The test for serum creatinine will read out at about 2.8 mg/dL or higher. This kidney-impaired patient should only receive IV EDTA under close supervision of a physician. IV EDTA may be used for an otherwise untreatable and life-threatening illness such as mercury poisoning for which EDTA is the only therapy.

Perhaps a patient with severe renal insufficiency will benefit from a reduced dose of EDTA administered over six or more hours at an interval of seven to fourteen days, or more, between infusions. For such a calculated risk of complete renal failure, it's vital to measure or compute the twenty-four-hour CC before each infusion. Informed consent in advance is mandatory for the patient.

Renal failure is the complete acute or chronic inability of the kidneys to work. Treatment requires that one restrict the amount of water and protein taken in and probably eliminate the use of diuretics. When medical measures no longer are effective, long-term kidney filtering (dialysis) is often begun, and a kidney transplant is considered.

It's the experience of most chelating physicians that kidney function improves over time from the patient's receiving IV EDTA chelation therapy, and patients can subsequently tolerate larger doses of EDTA.

Other Contraindications for IV EDTA

A pregnant woman should avoid taking chelation therapy, except if radiation toxicity or toxic metal syndrome from high dosages of metallic poisons such as lead, mercury, cadmium, copper, iron, aluminum, manganese or others is life-threatening.

Someone in congestive heart failure may undergo IV EDTA only if careful control of fluid and electrolyte balance, diuretic therapy, sodium restriction and the prevention of potassium and magnesium depletion are maintained.

The presence of significant liver disease is a relative contraindication of chelation therapy, but it may be given if no other treatment is available. IV EDTA does not worsen a moderate degree of liver impairment, but the liver complication requires resolution first.

While EDTA injections do not add to their medical risks, people taking long-term anticoagulation therapy such as with warfarin should have frequent monitoring of their prothrombin times. Certainly, heparin would be omitted from the infusion solution for such patients. (See Chapter Nine for a full listing of the ingredients in an IV chelation therapy solution.)

Theoretically, IV EDTA chelation therapy could reactivate arrested tuberculosis by dissolving calcified granuloma within the lungs which contains latent tubercle bacilli. This has never been reported, but it's possible. Yet, arrested tuberculosis or a positive tuberculin test is not a contraindication to chelation therapy.

At the same time that it removes heavy metals and other toxic minerals, intravenous EDTA depletes essential nutritional trace elements. Consequently, prior to and immediately following chelation therapy, the patient's trace element status should be determined by means of all or some of the following tests: urine measurement, hair mineral analysis and blood examination.

Urine creatinine measurement shows creatinine correction for dilutional variations caused by water intake and output as well as how much of the trace elements are coming out in the urine.

Hair analysis offers a comparison to other mineral contents shown currently in blood and urine tests, because the hair contains element material gathered over months of time.

Blood testing is less accurate for trace elements and certainly is more expensive, but it has a place in advising what minerals are being removed by chelation therapy.

Replacement of essential trace elements being lost by the chelation procedure is necessary. Patients should routinely take nutritional supplements that contain a balance of essential minerals and trace elements, especially those detected in urine and hair. Zinc is especially susceptible to depletion along with pyridoxine (vitamin B_6). Supplementing nutritionally with all the vitamins of the B complex, plus vitamins C, E, beta carotene, and selenium, is a good idea. If utilizing zinc as a supplement, it's mandatory to take selenium at the same time, or a selenium deficiency can be potentiated. Copper supplementation can cause a relative zinc deficiency, and high doses of zinc can bring on a copper deficiency. Supplementing with iron is not recommended. Since it's synergistic with chelation therapy, the use of magnesium supplementation is frequently advantageous.

Dr. Shah tells his chelating patients not to take vitamin and mineral supplements in the morning of the chelating treatment day. He also advises them to avoid milk products because they overload the body with too much calcium, and digitalis because it gets removed by the procedure.

Possible Side Effects of IV EDTA Chelation Therapy

Too rapid infusion of disodium EDTA for chelation therapy will cause a marked drop in the blood's content of calcium ions (hypocalcemia). Thus, *hypocalcemia* is a condition of insufficient calcium ions in the blood. While mild hypocalcemia has no symptoms, severe hypocalcemia produces irregular heart beat, muscle spasms and burning or prickling feelings of the hands, feet, lips and tongue which are not uncommon side effects. Correction is easily achieved by stopping the IV drip or decreasing the rate of infusion.

Possibly there will be the more serious situation of *hypocalcemic tetany,* a condition marked by cramps, convulsions, twitching of the muscles and sharp bending of the wrist and ankle joints. The treatment requires that calcium be given by mouth or through the veins in the form of calcium gluconate.

An excessive body burden of lead already present in the patient without having been detected prior to the start of chelation therapy could cause *lead nephrotoxicity.* Lead poisons those tiny filtering units of the kidney called *nephrons.* They resemble tiny funnels with long stems, each with two twisted tubes. A kidney contains approximately 1.25 million nephrons, and each is made up of a renal corpuscle containing a ball of blood vessels (a glomerulus) surrounded by its Bowman's capsule and several long tubes. Urine is formed in the renal corpuscles and in the tubes by the processes of filtration, reabsorption and release. The collecting tubes carry the urine to the kidney, the pelvic area and the ureters. By performing their job efficiently, the excess amounts of lead floating in the blood will be taken up by EDTA and cause a poisoning of the kidney (lead nephrotoxicity). Lead toxicity should have been spotted before the chelation treatment began or immediately after the first infusion by measuring lead relative to urine creatinine.

Occasional allergic reactions to chelation therapy may show as a result of ingredients other than EDTA which are added to the solution, or by a chemical preservative in one of those ingredients. The actual solution components most likely to be allergens would be lidocaine or procaine and chemical preservatives contained in water-soluble vitamins. It's best not to allow preservatives to be part of any ingredient in the EDTA injection formula. Injectible antihistamines are the corrective agents for allergies.

Superficial phlebitis in the form of local irritation at the infusion site may be a complication. This condition is minimized by the addition of 1,000 to 5,000 units of heparin to each infusion solution. Also, buffering the solution to physiologic pH with bicarbonate prevents phlebitis, which may be overcome quickly with the application of moist heat to the site of local irritation. It's best not to inject into leg veins for any of the EDTA infusions.

Dr. Warren Levin once said, "A doctor who puts needles into veins often enough is sure to inadvertently irritate a vein somewhere along the line. There is always the possibility of inducing an inflammation with clot formation, called *thrombophlebitis*. Generally this thrombophlebitis is not the kind of a clot in the vein that breaks off and travels through the circulatory system and produces problems. It is a local inflammatory response to irritation. The body takes care of the inflammation over time. The local thrombophlebitis can be annoying, but it's of no serious consequence to the patient and can occur during any infusion and not just from chelation."

Vitamin E is known to prevent this particular problem of local inflammation—or, in large doses, vitamin E seems to speed recovery from local thrombophlebitis.

"If someone is in heart failure or has severe high blood pressure," Dr. Levin continued, "giving extra sodium (which is a main component of the salt solution) intravenously is probably not a good idea. That individual would be one of the patients for whom I might use distilled water, 5% glucose or normal saline solution.

"Furthermore, allergy to one or all of the substances in any infusion is always a possibility. Allergic reactions can be serious enough to warrant temporarily discontinuing the therapy. It has been my good fortune not to have any serious allergic reactions to chelation therapy in this office," smiled the physician.

Dr. Levin added, "If the needle slips out of the vein and fluid seeps into the tissues, it can feel painful and irritating, but no significant or long-term harm ensues. The reaction is about like a bee sting.

Patients with a history of congestive heart failure need to be observed closely during chelation therapy. In such cases, sodium content of the IV solution must be reduced with the avoidance of saline, Ringer's lactate and other vehicles containing sodium. Also, the infusion drip should be slowed to go into the vein for from four to six hours, and the carrier solution should alternatively be reduced to 250 ml rather than 500 ml. Such a reduction may be required for the patient with markedly decreased cardiac reserve. Transient hypocalcemia caused by IV EDTA can bring on heart failure.

A drop in blood sugar may be a side effect of chelation therapy, resulting in *hypoglycemia*. The symptoms of hypoglycemia may be weakness, headache, hunger, problems with vision, loss of muscle coordination, anxiety or personality changes. The antidote is simple: taking a glass of fruit juice prevents or offsets the blood sugar reduction. The whole problem of hypoglycemia can be avoided if the patient will eat fruit, sandwiches or other foods during the course of taking chelation treatment.

Chapter Eight

THE PROTOCOL FOR ADMINISTERING EDTA CHELATION THERAPY— PART TWO

In San Antonio, Texas, naturopathic physician Diana J. Eaton, N.D., working under the supervision of Ronald Stogryn, M.D., had provided a few thousand patients with upwards of 20,000 intravenous infusions of ethylene diamine tetraacetic acid (EDTA) for chelation therapy. Because of its special attributes, occasionally Dr. Eaton added dimethyl sulfoxide (DMSO) as an adjunctive chelating agent. Primarily, however, she adhered to the official protocol for administering EDTA chelation therapy as approved by the American College for Advancement in Medicine (ACAM). In this second of two chapters devoted to chelation therapy's protocol, the actual ingredients and dosages making up the EDTA infusion solution will be described.

Dr. Eaton now works as an executive with Phyne Pharmaceuticals of Scottsdale, Arizona, an important supplier of chelation therapy materials for health professionals. She no longer renders direct patient care, but numbers of her former therapy recipients linger in her mind as unforgettable. One of them was Margaret Kleinfeld, a heavy-set, sixty-four-year-old maintenance person who cleaned clerical offices at night. The pulse waves in both of her feet were almost nonexistent as high as just above the ankle bones. Her dorsalis pedis and posterior tibial pulses, for instance, could not be found on palpation when skilled health professionals felt for them with their finger tips. Both of the patient's lower limbs had minimal blood circulation, if any, and some semblance of pulse beats only began high up her legs at her knees.

The dorsalis pedis pulse, from the artery of that name, can be felt on the top of the foot between and below the first and second toes. The posterior tibial pulse is felt on the ankle, just behind the bulge of the ankle bone.

Moreover, Mrs. Kleinfeld showed a slightly elevated blood pressure at 150/65. Periodic chest pain in the form of movement-stopping angina pectoris caused her to pop nitroglycerine tablets under her tongue as a means of finding heart muscle spasm relief.

When the patient first arrived in a wheel chair at Dr. Eaton's San Antonio clinic, she was already scheduled for right and left leg amputation. Even though the date of her two midcalf surgeries had been booked with the hospital and the operating room had been reserved, Mrs. Kleinfeld's peripheral vascular surgeon agreed to wait before performing them. At her request, the surgeon was giving his patient a chance to get another medical opinion, and this simple action saved both of her legs. She went searching for a medical practice that offered some medical/nutritional alternative to amputation.

Upon evaluating the patient's situation, Dr. Stogryn and Dr. Eaton agreed that the limbs could be saved if Mrs. Kleinfeld would undertake a couple of months of nutritional buildup not just with dietary correction and food supplementation but also by her taking intravenous infusions with megadose vitamins and minerals, plus DMSO and EDTA. She accepted their recommendation and arrived at the San Antonio clinic for infusion treatment every other day—a minimum of three times per week. As stated, today any leg amputation has been avoided, and she is walking on both limbs while performing her office maintenance work.

The patient began her combination IV injections on January 31, 1992. Deeply penetrating leg ulcers of the skin from insufficient dermal blood flow began healing right away. Then her pulses finally were felt not only with the oscillometer, vascular analyzer and other diagnostic instruments, but also through the less sensitive method of palpating with the fingers. By March 25, 1992, therefore, the impaired patient was walking unaided with good use of both feet and legs. Mrs. Kleinfeld discarded first, the wheel chair and then a pair of canes.

As mentioned earlier, when she entered Dr. Eaton's practice, Mrs.

Margaret Kleinfeld had been suffering with moderate angina pectoris of the heart muscle. She was also experiencing recurring intermittent claudication of both calf muscles. The two types of muscular spasms in which the contracting muscles cry out with pain from the inadequate blood flow were eliminated and to date have not returned. The woman is fully recovered and has kept her legs intact. She has resumed her occupation without any complications.

The Patient Evaluation Before Chelation Therapy

After going through a complete medical evaluation, including his or her full health history, laboratory testing and physical examination, the chelating physician decides whether a patient intent on undergoing EDTA chelation therapy is a candidate for the IV infusion. Some of the clinical items relevant to health that are checked by the doctor, physician's assistant or chelation technician invariably include (1) current medications the patient is taking, (2) allergies present, (3) quality of arterial pulses, (4) skin temperature of the extremities, (5) hair loss of the extremities, (6) abnormal (dystrophic) toenails, (7) patient's mental status and (8) any signs, symptoms or other indications of atherosclerosis.

As part of the patient's current clinical history, the physician also wants to record (1) an electrocardiogram, (2) noninvasive vascular studies, and (3) the segmental Doppler systolic blood pressure readings of the limbs. It's necessary to know (4) the patient's body weight and (5) blood pressure (both of which are taken upon the patient's entrance into the practice and before each EDTA infusion).

Numerous laboratory tests are recorded in order to have a baseline by which to determine progression or regression of the patient's health. Some of the tests include (1) a complete blood count with differential, (2) a panel of at least eighteen blood chemistries and the electrolytes, including sodium, potassium, chloride, blood sugar, blood-urea-nitrogen (BUN), creatinine, calcium, phosphorous, uric acid, total cholesterol and HDL cholesterol, (3) liver function tests including enzymes and serum proteins, (4) a complete urine analysis, (5) the thyroid function tests including T_4, T_3 and calculated T_7 and (6) the report of a prior chest X-ray film or the film itself. Also obtained are (7) a twenty-four-hour urinary creatinine clearance (CC) or Cockcroft–Gault computed creatinine clearance plus both (8) a urine analysis and (9) a hair analysis for trace and toxic elements. Provocative urine specimens for trace and toxic metal levels are collected immediately before and after the first EDTA infusion and periodically throughout treatment. Nutritional supplements containing minerals and trace elements are not allowed to be taken until all urine specimens have been collected. Urine testing for trace elements is more accurate if no EDTA has been administered for at least two weeks prior to testing.

The chelating physician screens his or her patient for abnormalities of carbohydrate metabolism and therefore performs additional appropriate testing such as (1) a blood glucose loading test, (2) a postprandial blood sugar test, and (3) the fructosamine or glycohemoglobin test.

At the doctor's option, more laboratory and clinical testing in individual cases may be called for, including (1) the noninvasive radioisotope blood flow and heart wall imaging studies, (2) plethysmography with pulse wave measurements of the extremities, (3) stress electrocardiography, (4) digital subtraction angiography, (5) computerized axial tomography (CT), (6) magnetic resonance imaging (MRI), (7) intravenous pyelography, (8) an echo- or phonocardiograph and (9) oculoplethysmography.

If time permits, surgery is better tolerated and less likely to cause complications when a presurgical course of chelation therapy is first taken. If chelation therapy fails, bypass surgery or angioplasty still remains available to the patient.

The Chelation Therapy Carrier Solution— Osmolarity

A variety of "appropriate" liquid vehicles or carrier solutions exist for transporting the EDTA and other IV ingredients into the patient's vein for accomplishing chelation therapy. In the past, the carriers have included any of the following: 0.5 percent normal saline, 5 percent glucose, 10 percent glucose, 10 percent fructose, 5 percent dextrose, 5 percent dextrose and normal saline, normal saline and 5 percent glucose, 0.45 percent sodium chloride with dextrose, lactated Ringer's solution, sterile water, and physiological saline (0.85 or 0.9 percent sodium chloride). Some of these vehicles are more appropriate than others; after experimentation, a few have turned out to be inappropriate.

Sterile distilled water by itself, for example, is absolutely wrong to use since it is hypo-osmolaric and causes erythrocyte (red blood cell) hemolysis or hemoglobinuria.[1] In *erythrocyte hemolysis,* the red blood cells break down and release hemoglobin. In *hemoglobinuria,* there is an abnormal presence in the urine of hemoglobin that is unattached to red blood cells.

Osmolarity (Os) of a solution is the concentration of solute (the dissolved substance) per liter of the particular solution. Osmolarity is measured in a unit termed an osmole. An osmole is the quantity of a substance in solution in the form of molecules, ions or both (usually expressed in grams) that has the same osmotic pressure as one mole of an ideal nonelectrolyte. A solution that's *hypo-osmolaric* is deficient or below normal in dissolved substance and has too low an osmole weight or gram formula weight (GFW) of ions of solute. The vehicle carrying ingredients for chelation therapy should be between 270 and 310 milli-osmoles (thousandths of an osmole). For instance, based on the fact that 1 osmole equals 1,000 millosmoles, a solution of physiological saline (0.85 percent sodium chloride) contains approximately 290 milli-osmoles per liter. The absolute osmotic pressure is the total pressure exerted by the ions in solution, and it is this pressure that affects the red blood cells. They will either swell and burst if the solution is hypo-osmolar, or they may become notched and shriveled (crenate) if the solution is hyper-osmolar (excessively osmolar). The total osmotic pressure is due to both metabolizable and nonmetabolizable substances in the infusion solution.

Dr. Diana Eaton advises, "What the chelating technician tries to do is keep the molecular weight of the infusion carrier solution just right so that there won't be any destruction to the red blood cells. If there is too heavy an amount or too much material in the carrier, using sodium chloride as an example, a hypertonic solution must result. Anything dissolved in the carrier solution has a milliosmole molecular weight, and the dissolved agent must be calculated in advance of infusion. Sterile water has no weight, and far more ingredients may be incorporated into that solution. For that reason, distilled sterile water cannot be injected alone, or the risk is so great that death could ensue from the injection. In contrast, D5W (water with a 5 percent dextrose added), normal saline, and Ringer's lactate can each be injected alone without the need to add more ingredients.

A close-to iso-osmolar solution of 250 to a maximum of 1,000 ml of carrier is normally infused. The infusion bottle is mixed individually for each patient, using sterile water Ringer's lactate, normal or one-half normal saline, or 5 percent glucose as the carrier, for intravenous use. The desired ingredients are added (see below for the full listing) in amounts calculated to produce the correct osmotic concentration (iso-osmolality). *Hyperosmolar infusions* normally don't cause problems, and their use is acceptable.

Ingredients Included in the Chelation Carrier Solution

Creation of the intravenous chelation solution follows the specific protocol recommended by ACAM, with variations made by individual chelating physicians. For example, one such solution, formulated by John Parks Trowbridge, M.D., of Humble, Texas, mostly follows the ACAM protocol and shows the typical formulation of ingredients and their dosages (see Table 8-1,). The various ingredients recommended for inclusion in the chelation carrier solution are as follows.

Ethylene diamine tetraacetic acid (EDTA) in a dose of 50 mg per kg of lean body weight is administered to patients with normal kidney function, to a maximum dose of 5 gm in an unusually large patient. If his or her creatinine clearance is less than 100 ml/min., the dose based on body weight is reduced by multiplying that dose by a fraction equal to creatinine clearance divided by ($\div$) 100. The standard average dose of EDTA is 3 gm per 500 cc of vehicle, but less may be given if the doctor judges that a patient is sensitive or reactive in any way.

Magnesium (Mg) in the form of an intravenous solution of magnesium chloride ($MgCl_2$) or magnesium sulfate ($MgSO_4$) to provide approximately 2000 mg of elemental Mg is added to each infusion bottle (10 ml of 20 percent $MgCl_2$ solution or 3 ml of 50 percent $MgSO_4$ solution). That amount of Mg converts the usual 3.0 gm of disodium EDTA to Mg-EDTA. Proportionately more Mg will be used for large patients, when more than 3.0 gm of EDTA is given. It's unnecessary to reduce the dose of Mg for lower doses of EDTA. Mg by itself is therapeutic by fulfilling two functions. First, it prevents pain from infusion of the EDTA, and second, it is beneficial for many conditions treated with EDTA. Most people who enter a program of EDTA chelation therapy infusions have suboptimal amounts of body Mg, and many others are deficient in the mineral.

Sodium bicarbonate buffer is added because of EDTA's unique characteristic. It releases hydrogen ions into solution when EDTA combines with Mg to form Mg-EDTA. The resulting acid pH of the infusion causes localized pain and inflammation at the site of infusion. A localized phlebitis may result. Sodium bicarbonate for intravenous use is added to the carrier in a ratio of approximately 10 mEq bicarbonate to 3 gm EDTA (1 mEq bicarbonate per 300 mg EDTA) to buffer the infusion solution to a physiological pH.

Local anesthetic in the form of lidocaine or procaine may be needed for the prevention of injection pain even with the use of Mg and bicarbonate buffer. This need occurs more commonly during the first few infusions. Allergic sensitivity to an anesthetic is less likely with lidocaine than procaine. Five to 10 ml of a 2 percent solution of either anesthetic agent (without epinephrine) is adequate. It's added directly into the infusion bottle in a dose not exceeding 20 ml of a 2 percent solution given over three hours.

Heparin, a naturally occurring substance that acts in the body to prevent clotting in the veins, is added to the infusion bottle in a dose of about 1,000 to 2,000 units. Heparin will be contraindicated for anyone with bleeding tendencies or for those who are already receiving full anticoagulating doses of warfarin. However, this small amount of added heparin is not enough to cause systemic anticoagulation of the blood.

Ascorbate (vitamin C), in a dose of 4 gm to 20 gm, sometimes is added to the infusion bottle to make a distilled water carrier solution that becomes iso-osmolar.[2] Ascorbate is also a weak chelating agent and is synergistic with EDTA. It enhances EDTA's ability to remove lead from the central nervous system, and it is also an antioxidant plus a free-radical scavenger. Yet, caution is taken with patients on strict sodium restriction because IV ascorbic acid is buffered to a physiological pH with sodium hydroxide (NaH_2O) and contains about 11 percent sodium (Na) by weight.

B-complex vitamins, including, B_1, B_6, B_{12}, and others, are sometimes added because they are synergistic with EDTA as antioxidant defenses. Moreover, since EDTA depletes vitamin B_6, this vitamin must be supplemented by mouth.

Potassium chloride (KCl) is added to the carrier for patients taking potassium-wasting diuretics or who are found by lab tests to need potassium. In general, nutritionists recognize that Americans and many Europeans are receiving insufficient amounts of potassium in their diets.

Table 8-1

A Basic Formula of Ingredients for Chelation Therapy in
500 ML of Sterile Water
(Developed by John Parks Trowbridge, M.D.)

Name of Constituent	in mg/ml Concentration	x X	ml Amount	= =	mg Total
Magnesium chloride (MgC12)	200 mg/ml		9 ml		1800 mg
Hydrochloric acid (HCl)	2 mg/ml		6 ml		12 mg
Potassium chloride (KCl)	40 mEq/ml		3 ml		120 mEq
Thiamin (vitamin B_1)	100 mg/ml		3 ml		300 mg
Niacinamide (vitamin B_3)	100 mg/ml		3 ml		300 mg
Pyridoxine (vitamin B_6)	100 mg/ml		3 ml		300 mg
Dexpanthenol (vitamin B_5)	250 mg/ml		3 ml		750 mg
Sodium thiosalicylate [a]	100 mg/ml		2 ml		200 mg
Cyanocobalamin (vitamin B_{12})	1,000 mg/ml		1 ml		1,000 mcg
Ascorbic acid (vitamin C)	500 mg/ml		50 ml		25,000 mg

The following ingredients may also be added to the carrier solution:

Lidocaine	20 mg/ml	6 ml		120 mg
Niacinamide (vitamin B_3)	100 mg/ml	3-6 ml		300-600 mg

(Usually, this extra niacinamide is optional and depends solely on the judgment of the chelating physician. It is added only for the treatment of peripheral vascular disease and becomes part of the formulation specifically at or after administration of the fourth IV. Since it's not part of the standard ACAM protocol, coauthor Dr. Hitendra H. Shah does not include this extra niacinamide for chelating his own patients.

Heparin	5,000 units	1 ml	5,000 units

MIC— the injectible vitamin formulation of Methionine 100 mg/ml; Inositol 100 mg/ ml; Choline 100 mg/ml; 6 ml of MIC = 600 mg of each vitamin; MIC is administered at every sixth intravenous chelation treatment.

EDTA—Ethylene diamine tetraacetic acid is incorporated at a standard dosage of 50 mg/kg of lean body weight. Note that the EDTA dosage also varies according to the patient's clinical condition and laboratory testing results.

Source: Trowbridge, J.P., Walker, M. *The Healing Powers of Chelation Therapy.* Stamford, CT: New Way of Life, 1988; [a]Current manufacturers are Phyne Pharmaceuticals, Inc., Scottsdale, Arizona; GY&N Nutriment Pharmacology, Carlsbad, California; and McGuff Co., Santa Ana, California.

Addendum to the ACAM Chelation Therapy Protocol

We've pointed out that the recommended doses of EDTA cited in the ACAM Protocol for the Safe and Effective Administration of EDTA Chelation Therapy is 50 mg per kg of lean body weight, administered over at least three hours and adjusted for lower than normal kidney function as determined by creatinine clearance. This yields an accepted safe rate of administration of 16.7 mg per kg per hour of EDTA within the carrier solution.

Some chelating physicians have found that a lower dose—as low as one-half of the above-cited dose—has been effective in the treatment of vascular disease. Therefore, a limited number of doctors have altered the protocol and administer this lower dose over a proportionately shorter time. In fact, no exact amount of EDTA has been determined to be the ideal for all patients. As a result, the protocol has been modified to allow for variation, depending on the judgment and experience of the chelating physician caring for the patient.

Still, the accepted rate of administration of EDTA for safety remains at 16.7 mg per kg per hour, adjusted for creatinine clearance. ACAM considers that infusion rates in excess of 16.7 mg/kg/hour do not have an established safety record as yet.

ACAM does not monitor its physician members who practice chelation therapy, and it is not in a position to approve or disapprove of their treatment methods or the management of their patients. Even so, the Board of Directors and the Scientific Advisory Committee of ACAM have not endorsed the safety or efficacy of any rate of administration of chelation therapy above 16.7 mg per kg per hour or any specific protocol dose. ACAM does not permit any physician to claim that his or her treatment method, if it differs from what has been written here, is approved by the Board of Directors of ACAM.[4]

Patient Evaluation After a Course of Chelation Therapy

The followup procedure for someone who has undergone a course of twenty, thirty, forty, or more chelation treatments for the relief or reversal of either atherosclerosis or toxic metal syndrome is variable. Recommendations from the official ACAM protocol suggest that the patient should return to the chelating physician at three-, six-, and twelve-month intervals for a reevaluation of his or her health status. Thereafter, annual consultations with the chelator is advised. Severely symptomatic patients should be evaluated more often, of course, as medically indicated.

Unfortunately, it's not unusual for a person, upon ridding oneself of the toxic metal or atherosclerotic health risk, to ignore the reconsultation requirement related to good health maintenance. That's only human nature! But is it proper human practice? Not if the individual needs a change in medications or an upgrading of nutrients to greater or lesser dosages.

Periodic urine and hair tests for trace and toxic elements must be performed to assure that there's been no return to the same circumstances that made an individual ill in the first place. The protocol advises, "Blood lipids (after a fourteen-hour fast) should be periodically monitored. Serum ferritin should also be checked and periodic phlebotomy (blood drawing) performed if iron levels pose a risk of free radical related disease. Additional laboratory testing should be performed, as indicated by the patient's medical history and the doctor's clinical findings."[5]

Additional Injectable Chelators Besides EDTA

EDTA is not the only chelating agent that may be injected. Some of the others include desferoxamine (DFO) but labeled "deferoxamine" in the United States, rhodotorulic acid and cholylhydroxamic acid.

According to life-extension expert Johan Bjorksten, Ph.D., of Houston, Texas, deferoxamine has the longest and best established clinical record.[6,7,8,9,10] It's produced by the mold *Streptomyces pilosus* and has been useful for the removal of excess iron associated with mass destruction of red blood cells following massive blood transfusions.

DFO is frequently administered to patients who have dementia of the Alzheimer's type, especially in Canada. In 1981, Donald R. McLaughlan, M.D., professor of physiology and medicine and director of the Centre for Research in Neurodegenerative Diseases at the University of Toronto, told the fall semiannual scientific convention of the American Academy of Medical Preventics (now the American College for Advancement in Medicine) that chelation therapy, using deferoxamine as the chelating agent, was helpful in treating Alzheimer's disease.[11] Dr. McLaughlan cited from numerous research papers that he had produced from 1972 to 1980, all on the connection of aluminum as a source of Alzheimer's disease and chelation therapy as its effective treatment.[12] (For the bibliographic listing of twenty-one published papers by Dr. McLaughlan in his use of DFO and other chelating agents for Alzheimer's disease, please see Chapter Twenty in the 1995 book published by Avery Publishing Group, *Toxic Metal Syndrome: How Metal Poisonings Can Affect Your Brain* by H. Richard Casdorph, M.D., Ph.D., and Morton Walker, D.P.M.)

The most usual dosage of DFO is by intramuscular (IM) injection of 500 mg dissolved in any aqueous isotonic medium such as Ringer's lactate.

Rhodotorulic acid, a naturally occurring iron chelator isolated from the supernatant of cultures of the wild yeast *Rhodotorula pilimanae*, is much less water soluble than deferoxamine. Thus, it is released very slowly following intramuscular injection. The blood level following an IM injection of rhodotorulic acid remains therapeutically active for several hours.[13]

A third chelating agent, cholylhydroxamic acid, is a synthetic product. An insignificant amount of information on it has been published in the medical literature, and cholylydroxamic acid has yet to be examined in depth.[14]

Chapter Nine

BLOOD VESSEL
DETOXIFICATION FROM
CHELATION THERAPY

Tears, urine, mucus, sweat, feces, sebum—all exemplify the products of natural body cleansing that we regard as normal expressions of our human physiology. The cleansing process is relatively simple to comprehend: when the organs of elimination (lungs, liver, kidneys, skin, oil glands, colon) become overwhelmed with impurities and toxins, these poisons may deposit themselves anywhere inside the cells, tissues, organs, glands, fat, bone, muscles and so on. In an attempt to maintain integrity, the body organizes a detoxification process, forcing out the accumulated poisons. But sometimes—too often for those people living in industrialized Western countries—the process becomes overwhelmed by the sheer massiveness of impurities (especially with the current popularity of junk foods) to which we subject ourselves. Then this natural cleansing course of action fails, and deterioration from degenerative disease begins to take over.[1]

Metallic Minerals as Body Toxins

Human beings around the world are adversely affected by metallic mineral toxicity. The poisonous metals consist especially of aluminum, mercury, lead, cadmium, tin, nickel, copper, manganese, iron, calcium and others deposited in the body as environmental pollutants in excess amounts.[2]

In 1941,[3] Johan Bjorksten, Ph.D., laboratory director of the Bjorksten Research Foundation of Madison, Wisconsin (and still doing research), revealed his remarkable theoretical concept of premature aging which connected this condition to metallic cross-linkages with protein molecules. Dr. Bjorksten particularly focused on aluminum and protein toxicity. Now, fifty-seven years later, his ideas have been proven with the finding that a combination of beta amyloid protein and aluminum is the underlying source for the formation of dementia of the Alzheimer's type (see *Toxic Metal Syndrome: How Metal Poisoning Can Affect Your Brain* by H. Richard Casdorph, M.D., Ph.D., and Morton walker, D.P.M., Avery Publishing Group, 1995). He went on to explain his theory in a detailed report published in 1942. Among Dr. Bjorksten's many findings was the following:

> The aging of living organisms I believe is due to the occasional formation of *tanning,* of bridges between protein molecules, which cannot be broken by the cell enzymes. Such irreparable tanning may be caused by tanning agents foreign to the organism or formed by unusual biological side reactions, or it may be due to the formation of a tanning bridge in some particular position in the protein molecules. In either event, the result is the cumulative tanning of body proteins which we know as old age.[4]

Today Dr. Bjorksten's theory is well accepted as fact by the scientific community, and the process he referred to as tanning is now called *cross-linkage.* Premature aging becomes established as a result of molecular cross-linkage. In the presence of toxic metal pollution, molecular chains of proteins, nucleic acids and polyvalent metals such as calcium, lead, aluminum and iron (which have more than one electrical charge in an atom) combine with other long protein molecules and form unnatural cross-links. Then the newly created, individual, giant, cross-linked protein is no longer able to function normally. It cannot be split or be hydrolyzed, as is usually done by enzymes present in the blood circulatory system Cross-linking produces free radicals that bring on pathology by preventing the usual splitting and hydrolization of proteins for use by the body. Thus, these free radicals from metallic minerals become highly destructive body toxins.[5]

One of the cross-linking metallic minerals, calcium (Ca), is particularly ubiquitous and plays a major role in chronic degenerative diseases.

It is largely responsible for the two common human pathological conditions, atherosclerosis and premature aging. Calcium is the most dominant mineral in the human body at about 14,000 parts per million (ppm).[6] Physiologists estimate the concentration of extracellular Ca to be 10^{-3} moles (M), whereas that in the cellular cytoplasm is about 10^{-6} to 10^{-7} M.

Ninety-nine percent of all calcium deposits in the body are in combination with phosphorus, which in chemistry is identified as *apatites*. These calcium-phosphorous complexes are tightly bound and are not usually available for physiological use. Calcium apatites are situated in the bones and teeth, primarily as hydroxyapatite which has the formula of $Ca_{10}(Po_4)_6(OH)_2$. As part of the hydroxyapatite complex, calcium can't be chelated.

EDTA chelation therapy does not remove the mineral from bones and is never or hardly ever a cause of osteoporosis. This statement is taken from proof furnished in a published clinical study of sixty-one chelation therapy patients provided by Charles J. Rudolph, D.O., Ph.D., Edward W. McDonagh, D.O., and D.G. Wussow, MSC, all of Gladstone, Missouri. They found that, regardless of the patient's sex, there was no decrease in bone density readings following EDTA chelation therapy. In fact, in those patients who had some degree of osteoporosis, there was a slight but statistically significant improvement in bone density readings. Results indicate that rather than a negative effect on bones, in some cases chelation therapy is probably beneficial to bone growth and stimulates an increase in bone density. When administered according to the guidelines outlined in Chapters Seven and Eight, intravenous infusion with EDTA does not cause or aggravate osteoporosis.[7]

In contrast, 60 percent of the body's highly usable calcium floats in the bloodstream and is known as *ionic calcium* (Ca++). The normal calcium range in blood serum is 9 to 11 milligrams (mg) per 100 milliliters (ml) of serum, the majority of which is loosely bound to blood proteins, with some small amount chelated by other substances such as the citrates. This usable ionic calcium is exceedingly important for the human physiology because it enters into immediate chemical reactions whenever the body requires a supply of the mineral. Ca++ is the specific mineral called upon, for example, to enter into blood coagulation, muscle contraction and relaxation, nerve impulse transmission, cell membrane permeability, heart pump contraction and many other vital body functions.[8]

Calcium Deposits as Disease Culprits

In lectures that coauthor Hitendra H. Shah, M.D. offers to his patients and in lectures to various civic health organizations, he states: "Degenerative cardiovascular disease is, simply put, caused by calcium deposits which occur on heart valves, the heart muscle, and artery walls. Calcium is always present in the bloodstream, for its necessary to sustain life. But under certain circumstances, calcium deposits form in the heart or arteries and interfere with blood flow."

"Any time body tissue is injured, calcium comes to the rescue. Calcium's job is to help bind the tissue, allowing it to mend. When an injury takes place, calcium moves from the bloodstream into the tissues where it is used as a healing agent," continues Dr. Shah. "If injuries are infrequent, this repair system functions well. However, when blood vessel walls, heart muscle or heart valves undergo chronic, repetitive injury, a dangerous situation exists. Then, each time the injury gets repeated, calcium floods into the damaged area, and after a series of such frequent injuries, the calcium builds up sufficiently to bring on arterial blockages."

"Moreover, fat and cholesterol compound the problem. They are the source of the initial injury to artery walls, and then they travel into the cells of the arterial walls with the calcium molecules at the site of injury. The mixture of calcium, fat, cholesterol and scar tissue from previous injuries hardens into athersclerotic plaque," Dr. Shah says.

"The body is equipped with a set of immune system components—the macrophages—designed to clear the fat and cholesterol from cells. Yet, recurrent injury arising from the eating of garbage-type fast foods such as fatty hamburgers tends to overburden the macrophages. They fail to perform their assigned task," says the physician. "If night after night, a person twenty to forty years old sits before the television set snacking on chips, pizza, fried chicken, and other unhealthy items, by the age of forty-five, he or she will have joined the majority of North Americans and Europeans with their rapid buildup of atherosclerotic plaque in the artery walls. Junk food eating accelerates the atherosclerotic process."

Why Calcium Deposits Are Dangerous

Explaining that protein–calcium complexes build up in the cardiovascular system, Dr. Shah lists the dangerous situations developing from them:

First, the arteries and valves become stiffened by calcium; they lose elasticity and can no longer function efficiently. When the calcium complexes accumulate in someone's arteries, the heart musculature with its heart valves can't pump blood at an acceptably healthy rate. As a result, cells in every body part are deprived of the required life-sustaining oxygen. When this happens, cells are damaged, malfunction and slowly die. The entire body deteriorates and eventually develops one of the more common (or uncommon) degenerative diseases such as arthritis, glaucoma, cancer, diabetes, coronary thrombosis, cataracts, parkinsonism, hypertension, stroke, gangrene or something else. (See Figure 9-1.)

Second, calcium deposits, combined with fat, cholesterol, and scar tissue, build up on the interior walls (the intima) of the arteries, and produce blockages around which the blood needs to flow, if it can. A stroke, for instance, arises from the blockage in a blood vessel to the brain. Blockages can also occur in the heart's main arterial feeder or in any other artery. Blood flow clogging within the heart's arteries is known as a *coronary thrombosis* or *heart attack.*

Figure 9-1 The progression of atherosclerotic involvement with advancement of age and the resulting common clinical complications.

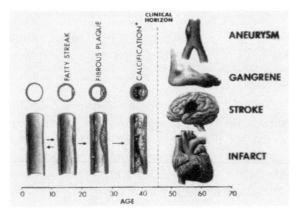

Source: Bruce W. Halstead *The Scientific Basis of EDTA Chelation Therapy* (Colton, Calif.: Golden Quill Publishers, 1979).

When doctors refer to "injury" within somebody's artery—along the walls of the arterial intima—they are describing something that is most likely different from what the ordinary person may imagine. Such damages are not bloody cuts or serious bruises caused by trauma such as happens in a fall or other physical accident. Rather, chronic blood vessel injuries are microscopic openings produced by constant irritation of the blood vessel lining. The cause of these mild but chronic injuries may be surprising to the average medical consumer. They include:

- Irritations from ingested toxic substances in drugs, foods, impure air, polluted water, cigarette smoke, engine exhausts and the like. Any of these substances can make the lining of your blood vessels sensitive. One of the most toxic culprits is dietary cholesterol present in a high-fat meal. For example, cholesterol oxide, a toxin causing microscopic arterial injuries, develops when oxygen combines with cholesterol within the body.
- Stress stimulates the release of hormones and other chemicals that act as irritants to injure the arterial tissues.
- Free-radical pathology is now considered a main cause of atherosclerosis and premature aging. In the normal course of living, electrons, which are negatively charged atomic particles, combine with positively charged particles. But when a molecule falls out of balance in that it acquires an unpaired electron, the imbalanced molecule turns into a free radical. In order to complete itself, the free radical will attack other homeostatic molecules that hold all the electrons they need. The free radical attacks homeostatic tissue molecules on the interlining of the walls of arteries. When this happens, microscopic injuries result on the intima, a process known in organic chemistry as *lipid peroxidation*. Among chelation therapists, lipid peroxidation is a recognized underlying source of atherosclerosis. (See Figure 9-2).

It becomes obvious that degenerative cardiovascular disease comes from the gradual buildup of atherosclerotic plaque on the arterial walls, with resulting oxygen deprivation at the cellular level. Atherosclerotic plaque is a combination of calcium complexed with fat, cholesterol, foreign proteins and other substances that pile on from chronic, repetitive microscopic injuries which started this pathology—probably at an early age.

For decades, the majority of conventional, allopathic medical profes-

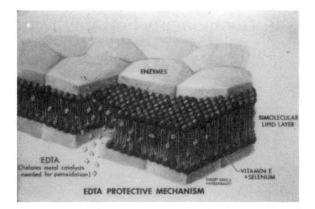

ENZYMES

BIMOLECULAR
LIPID LAYER

EDTA
(Chelates metal catalysts
needed for peroxidation)

VITAMIN E
+SELENUM

EDTA PROTECTIVE MECHANISM

Figure 9-2 EDTA assists in inhibiting lipid peroxidation of a lipid-containing cell membrane by removing metal ions such as iron and copper ions, which are required for the process of lipid peroxidation. Intravenously administered EDTA (chelation therapy) thereby helps maintain cellular homeostasis. (See also Figures 9-11 to 9-13)

sionals—with cardiologists chief among them—have stated erroneously that calcium has little or nothing to do with cardiovascular disease. It was long the party line of establishment medicine, as represented by the American Medical Association (AMA). The position thus held was wrong, but few physicians were predisposed to question it.

As far back as 1944, the AMA had ignored proof of calcium's culpability as the cause of atherosclerosis. Then, three pathologists, H. T. Blumenthal, M.D., A. I. Lansing, M.D., and P. A. Wheeler, M.D., published their autopsy findings in the *American Journal of Pathology* under the title "Calcification of the Media of the Human Aorta and Its Relation to Intimal Arteriosclerosis, Aging and Disease."[9] This study was followed up four years later with another published report.[10] Dozens more researchers named the calcium complexes forming with particular proteins as producing hardening of the arteries both in the cardiovascular system and in the peripheral vascular system (see the next section). They required detoxification by some form of chelating agent, but none became available until the advent of intravenous EDTA in 1952. Since then, EDTA chelation therapy has continued to be ignored as the primary means of eliminating calcium complexes.

Artery Wall Components Forming Ionic Calcium Complexes

Summarized here are the main chemical constituents of the arterial wall, cited by clinicians, pathologists, physiologists and other medical researchers during the past fifty-three years, which form complexes with ionic calcium (Ca++). These are the chief culprits that produce atherosclerosis. Using intravenous infusions of EDTA in a series of injections, such calcium complexes can be detoxified from the blood circulatory system.

Mucopolysaccharides **(MPCs),** a group of carbohydrates, contain chondroitin sulfate A, B and C; heparitin sulfate; heparin sulfate; amino acids and uronic acids. More recently, nutritionists have been referring to these MPDs as *glucosaminoglycans.* They are more concentrated within the intima and form complexes with ionic calcium, which definitely accelerates premature aging and atherogenesis.[11-19]

Elastin, which makes up 15 to 41 percent of the arterial wall's bulk, is a scleroprotein. During the pathological processes of atherosclerosis and premature aging, the elasticity of elastin progressively decreases by complexing with ionic calcium and then sclerosing.[20,21,22,23]

Collagen, an albuminoid protein, responds to decreased elastin flexibility by increasing in content in the arterial wall. It complexes with ionic calcium as well.[24]

The protein components normally combining chemically with fats circulating in the blood plasma are known as **lipoproteins.** Their usual function is to transport the combination of fatty acids and glycerol labeled as *glycerides* for storage in the liver, adipose tissue and muscle. There are "bad" **beta lipoproteins** and **pre-beta lipoproteins** which complex with calcium ions to produce atherosclerotic plaque and "good" *alpha lipoproteins* which offer a protective action against the formation of atherosclerotic plaque.

Low Density Lipoproteins **(LDLs)** are beta lipoproteins comprised of 35 percent cholesterol, 32 percent protein, 25 percent phospholipids and 7 percent triglycerides. The LDLs are atherogenic by readily forming calcium complexes to create the intima plaques which lead to hardening of the arteries.[25,26]

Very Low Density Lipoproteins **(VLDLs)** are pre-beta lipoproteins consisting of 64 to 80 percent triglycerides, 8 to 13 percent cholesterol, 5 to 15 percent phospholipids, and 2 to 13 percent proteins. The VLDLs transport liver triglycerides and form complexes with calcium ions to produce atherosclerosis.[27,28]

Chylomicrons, synthesized in the intestine, transport dietary glycerides from there through the thoracic duct to the blood plasma and on to various body parts where they are needed. The chylomicron lipoproteins are neither beta nor alpha but include 90 percent triglycerides, 6 percent cholesterol, 4 percent phospholipids and 0.5 percent protein.

High Density Lipoproteins (HDLs) are alpha lipoproteins comprised of 49 percent protein, 27 percent phospholipids, 17 percent cholesterol and 7 percent triglycerides. HDLs do not complex with ionic calcium but rather interfere with the formation of atherosclerotic plaques.

Very High Density Lipoproteins (VHDLs), although not so labeled, could be considered pre-alpha lipoproteins. They include 57 percent protein, 21 percent phospholipids, 17 percent cholesterol and 5 percent triglycerides. VHDLs do not complex with calcium ions.

Calcium Detoxification with EDTA Chelation Therapy

Conventional medical opinion is finally changing and is moving in the direction of holistic practitioners who use EDTA chelation therapy. During the past thirteen years, orthodox medicine has begun to accept the idea that calcium accumulation—not cholesterol deposition—is the major cause of atherosclerosis. This alteration in the AMA's thinking began to take shape in 1983, when the pharmaceutical industry capitalized on its billion-dollar new product investment and came out with calcium channel blockers. The AMA was then forced to respond to its pharmaceutical company sponsors, advertisers and financial backers. AMA physician/politicians recognized calcium as the main culprit responsible for the development of atherosclerosis. Vast amounts of advertising were poured into the new cardiovascular disease name-brand drugs, which continue to appear in clinical journals (including *The Journal of the American Medical Association*). Aron Fleckenstein, M.D., the clinician and researcher who discovered calcium channel blockers, stated before a policy-making medical meeting: "The single most important risk factor for the development of atherosclerosis at the age of sixty is the development of calcium deposits in the artery walls."

Calcium channel blockers are drugs that prevent calcium from entering smooth muscle cells, causing the smooth muscles to relax and reduce muscle spasms. Calcium channel blockers are used mainly to treat heart diseases marked by spasms in the arteries of the heart (angina pectoris). These drugs are also called *calcium antagonists* or *calcium blockers*. Still,

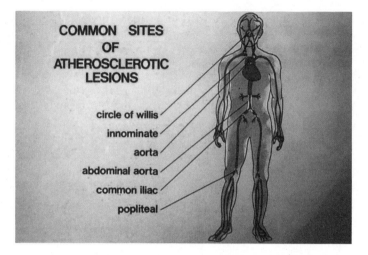

COMMON SITES
OF
ATHEROSCLEROTIC
LESIONS

circle of willis
innominate
aorta
abdominal aorta
common iliac
popliteal

Figure 9-3 shows the primary sites in the aging human body for the metastatic deposition of pathological calcium which brings on hardening of the arteries with subsequent cardiovascular and peripheral vascular diseases. The major affected arteries are shown.

because EDTA no longer holds patent protection for any pharmaceutical company sponsor, the AMA has never recognized that EDTA chelation therapy is the first and most effective calcium channel blocker.

Because of its ability to bind metals, especially those that are toxic, in 1958 the FDA approved the intravenous (IV) injection of EDTA for achieving chelation therapy. Now it serves as the primary medical technique for removing radiation toxicity, poison metallic molecules present in snake venom from snake bites, metallic poisons in Agent Orange affecting Vietnam War veterans, toxic metals such as aluminum and heavy metals such as lead from the bodies of children and adults. (Aluminum is not considered to be a heavy metal because it has a specific gravity of less than 5.)

As we have already described, the synthetic amino acid known as EDTA bonds with the bloodstream's ionic calcium that binds various components of junk material. The calcium and junk material are the components that form atherosclerotic plaque. The calcium-bound plaque attaches itself to the walls of blood vessels and blocks them from delivering sufficient quantities of blood nourishment to the cells and other tissues. Therefore, at the same time that an ill patient is being detoxified for heavy metal poisoning, he or she is having treatment to unclog the arteries—getting rid of atherosclerotic plaque. Together, toxic

metals and gluelike ionic calcium that complexes MCPs, elastin, collagen, LDLs, VLDLs and foreign proteins pass out of the body through
the patient's kidneys and bowel, thereby reversing hardening of the
arteries. Figures 9-3 to 9-15 show calcium deposits in various locations
in the body and the mechanisms of EDTA at the cellular level.

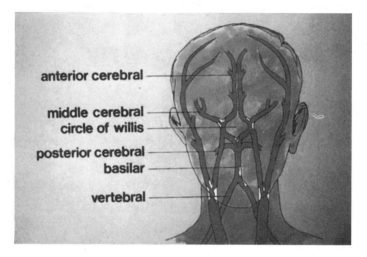

Figure 9-4 shows calcium deposits in the brain which impede blood flow and
cause brain cells to die, resulting in dementia, senility, Alzheimer's disease, and
other brain syndromes.

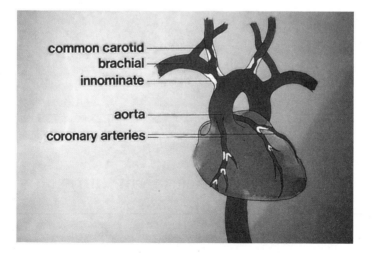

Figure 9-5 shows hardening of the arteries around the heart which produce
angina pectoris.

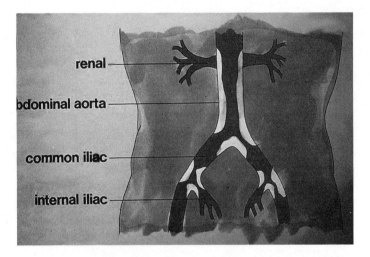

Figure 9-6 shows arteries calcified and subsequently blocked in their delivery of blood circulation to the internal organs and lower extremities.

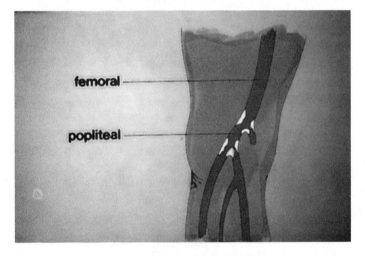

Figure 9-7 shows clogged arteries around the knee resulting in arthritis.

More Metallic Detoxification by Intravenous (IV) EDTA

In addition to calcium, toxic metals such as lead, tin, cadmium and nickel are removed by the intravenous (IV) infusion of EDTA from within cells and their cellular membranes. This removal of metals that result in pathology is advantageous, for it makes the cellular structures

stronger, allowing them to function homeostatically. This whole procedure of EDTA chelation is true cellular therapy. It has the overall effect
of cleansing nearly all body and brain cells, including the organelles
and the organelle membranes within the cells. The beneficial result is
a stimulation of the body's self-repair mechanism. (Organelles are the

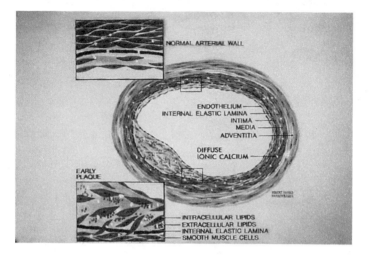

Figure 9-8 shows early atherosclerotic plaque depicted by the comparatively
small amount of diffuse ionic calcium. At this early state (when the person is
about fifteen years old) no calcium apatite is evident.

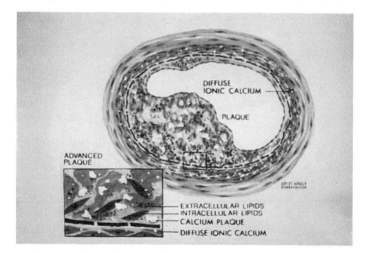

Figure 9-9 shows advanced atherosclerotic plaque depicted by the build-up of
ionic calcium and the laying down of calcium apatite (the actual plaque).

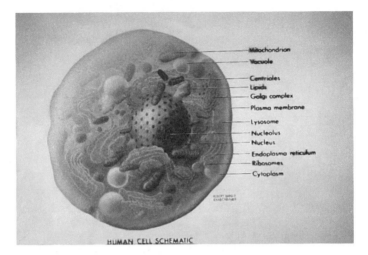

Figure 9-10 shows a typical human cell with its various subcellular components known as *organelles* (tiny chemical factories) which are involved with the various metabolic functions of each such cell.

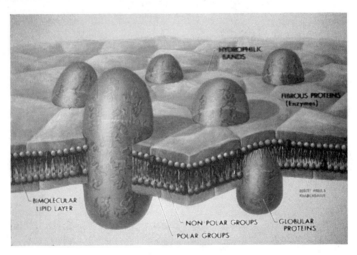

Figure 9-11 shows a modification of what is called the Singer-Nicholson model of a generalized biological cell membrane theoretically representative of all intracellular membranes. Scientific evidence suggests that extrinsic (projecting outside) and intrinsic (internal) proteins of these membranes float on a sea of lipids (fats). Many of the important biological communications between cells and their environment are conveyed by proteins intimately associated with such membranes. Alteration of these membranes can seriously affect the enzyme functions of any organelles with which they are associated.

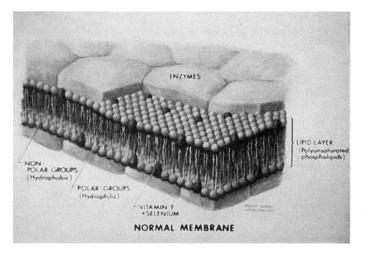

Figure 9-12 shows a more detailed view of the theoretical structure of a biologic membrane. Membrane proteins may interact with membrane lipids to launch biochemical reactions, evoking a series of chemical messengers to other membrane-bound structures within a cell. This results in a physiologic response. Located in the membranes are well-defined structural and functional sites, including ion pumps, antigens, neurohumeral receptors, intercellular junctions, immunoglobulins, etc. Damage of intracellular membranes can ultimately result in a biochemical disaster and terminate in a health catastrophe.

tiny but numerous different bits of living substances—actually like chemical factories—found within most of the brain's and body's cells. Typical organelles are the mitochondria, vacuoles, plasma membrane, ribosomes, lysosomes, nucleolous, endoplasma reticulum, the Golgi complex and the centrioles.)

Articles published in the spring/summer 1989 issue of the *Journal of Advancement in Medicine* by the laboratory personnel of Omegatech and AMNI Laboratory Services of Trout Dale, Virginia, attest to the efficacy of metallic detoxification by IV EDTA chelation therapy. Nineteen trace and toxic elements and minerals were measured in the urine of 104 chelation therapy patients, relative to urine creatinine, both before and immediately after they received intravenous infusions of magnesium disodium EDTA and vitamins.[29,30] EDTA was administered intravenously according to the protocol recommended by the American College for Advancement in Medicine, as described in Chapters Seven and Eight.

Note of clarification: Creatinine, a nitrogen substance common in blood, urine, and muscle tissue, combines with phosphorus to form

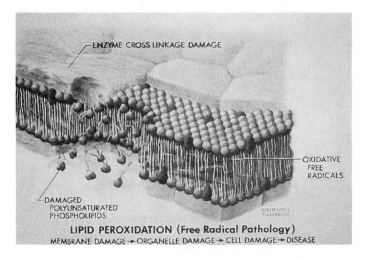

ENZYME CROSS LINKAGE DAMAGE

OXIDATIVE
FREE
RADICALS

DAMAGED
POLYUNSATURATED
PHOSPHOLIPIDS

LIPID PEROXIDATION (Free Radical Pathology)
MEMBRANE DAMAGE → ORGANELLE DAMAGE → CELL DAMAGE → DISEASE

Figure 9-13 shows free radicals adversely affecting cellular health by producing lipid peroxidation of intracellular membranes. Organelles such as mitochondria and lysosomes, which control cellular metabolism, are actually membrane-enclosed bags of enzymes. When these membranes are damaged, enzymes are lost and cellular homeostasis is altered, with resulting disease.

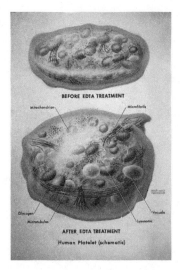

BEFORE EDTA TREATMENT

Mitochondrion   Microfibrils

Glycogen   Vacuole
Microtubules   Lysosome

AFTER EDTA TREATMENT
Human Platelet (schematic)

Figure 9-14 shows a blood platelet before and after it has come into contact with intravenous EDTA. With EDTA present, the platelet tends to become more rounded or globular in shape and is less "sticky" so that there is a reduced tendency toward coagulation. Such advantageous changes are due to the reduction of calcium ion by ethylene diamine tetraacetic acid.

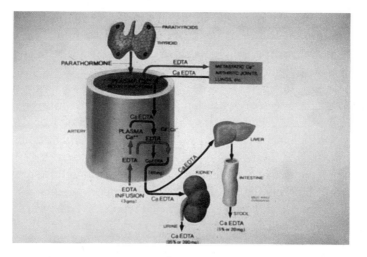

Figure 9-15 shows the movement of calcium as a result of EDTA intravenous infusion.

high-energy phosphate. Impairment of creatinine clearance by the kidneys indicates that they are malfunctioning, and such impairment could be considered a relative contraindication for the administration of IV EDTA (see Chapters Seven and Eight). Measurement of kidney function is best achieved by twenty-four-hour collection of the patient's urine or by use of the Cockcroft–Gault equation serum creatinine to provide a close approximation of the glomerular filtration rate (GFR). (The modified Cockcroft–Gault equation is shown in Table 7-1.)

In the Omegatech metallic detoxification and creatinine study referred to above, absolute and relative increases in urinary concentrations of the nineteen metallic elements as provoked by EDTA chelation therapy were computed. It was found that some metals have greater affinity for being grasped by EDTA than others. Their affinity is depicted in Table 9-1.[31]

IV EDTA is known to deplete essential nutritional trace elements, while it removes unwanted and toxic metals from the body. For exam-

All of Robert Harold Knabenbauer's artistic renditions (Drawings 9-1 to 9-15) are taken from the book *The Scientific Basis of EDTA Chelation Therapy*, authored by Bruce W. Halstead, M.D. (1979, Golden Quill Publishers, Inc., PO Box 1278, Colton, California 92324) in cooperation with the American Academy of Medical Preventics (the American College for Advancement in Medicine) and the Robert W. Bradford Foundation. They are reproduced here with permission of Dr. Bruce Halstead, Research Director of the World Life Research Institute of Colton, California.

ple, zinc, an essential trace element, is especially susceptible to depletion by chelation therapy. Consequently, before administering IV EDTA, the chelating physician routinely determines the patient's trace element status. This determination is made by recording a careful dietary history and by testing the patient's urine, hair and blood, as appropriate for adequacy of those essential nutrients.

Chelation therapy patients are routinely recommended or dispensed nutritional supplements that contain a balance of essential minerals and trace elements which are found to be lacking or removed by IV EDTA. This practice is part of the recognized protocol for administering chelation therapy. If chelating physicians find that their patients' nutritional status is poor, the patients are often placed on several weeks of oral replenishment of deficient nutrients. This may be done from the doctors' own dispensaries or by referral to health food stores, pharmacies, or mail order houses which provide such supplements. Such oral supplementation most likely begins several weeks before chelation therapy is administered. The option to take needed nutritional supplementation seldom lies with the patient; rather it is the province of the prescribing physician.

TABLE 9-1

URINARY EXCRETION FOLLOWING CHELATION THERAPY, NINETEEN METALS

Nineteen metals showing the highest to the lowest attraction and removal from the body in urinary excretion after provocative IV infusion of magnesium disodium EDTA are exhibited below with (1) being the highest EDTA attraction and removal rate and (19) being the lowest EDTA attraction and removal rate.

1. Sodium	11. Lead
2. Calcium	12. Selenium
3. Potassium	13. Cobalt
4. Magnesium	14. Nickel
5. Phosphorus	15. Lithium
6. Zinc	16. Cadmium
7. Iron	17. Molybdenum
8. Manganese	18. Copper
9. Aluminum	19. Chromium
10. Arsenic	

Chapter Ten

THE INTERNAL,
SELF-CHELATION
THERAPY EXERCISE

Would you want to know about a pleasurable exercise that induces a self-created, chelation therapy effect inside your body without the need for infusions, injections, nutritional supplements or other external assists?

Would you especially want to know that this exercise is easily performed at home, on the job, during business hours, in the office, at the factory, during days off, while vacationing, out-of-doors, in a hotel room or other place?

Would you be even more interested if you knew that this chelating exercise has other physiological attributes: it reduces body fat; firms arms, legs, thighs, hips and abdomen; increases agility; improves the sense of balance; strengthens muscle structure overall; provides aerobic outcomes for the heart; rejuvenates a fatigued body and mind; encourages sleep; conquers chronic insomnia; relieves nervous tension; dispels toxic wastes; and generally maintains health, homeostasis and fitness?

Would you particularly want more information upon learning that it requires you to do nothing more than bounce up and down on a resilient, shock-absorbing surface which offers more spring than a firm mattress but less hardness than a gym floor?

Well, here's some really good news: an internal self-chelation therapy exercise technique does exist. It's had people jumping for health for over twenty years and is fun to follow, too.

The Exercise That Self-Creates Internal Chelation Therapy

The exercise is called *rebounding*—aerobic bouncing movements performed on a device that looks like a small trampoline. The minitrampoline, called a *rebounder,* comes in round, rectangular, square or polygonal versions (see Photograph 10-1). For information on equipment, see Appendix D. Rebounders can also be modified so that they can be used by the elderly or people who need to sit while rebounding (see Photograph 10-2). This book's senior author (MW) owns five round rebounders, placed strategically in as many rooms of his home. Rebounding is a marvelous tool for producing medical articles and health books. It stimulates creative thinking and expansive functioning of the memory for stored facts and figures. It's never boring to rebound, because while jumping you can plan projects, watch television, talk on the telephone, go into a semimeditative state, think out some heavy problems, perform eye exercises by visualizing wall chart shapes or take other actions with your body and mind.

In addition, since the bouncing device is light in weight, you can travel on airplanes carrying a half-foldable, portable rebounder in its vinyl carrying case (with handle). When folded in this way, the minitrampoline fits in the airliner's overhead luggage compartment. We carry the rebounder along to use in a hotel room while on writing assignments and during the course of medical meetings, conventions and other conferences. The rebound movements are more effective for physical and mental conditioning than any equipment furnished in the fitness areas of those hotels which cater to business travelers.

Exercising on a minitrampoline for its beneficial rebounding result enables you to create chelation therapy within your body and brain. Rebounding is exercise with a bounce! It prevents heart attacks, drains the lymphatics, lowers elevated blood cholesterol, stimulates the metabolism, tones the endocrine and exocrine glands, keeps down excess body weight, enhances digestion, relaxes the mind, induces sleep, minimizes colds. In short, it promotes good health.

This self-created chelation therapy exercise is the finest form of aerobic action for detoxifying body cells ever to come out of the recreational sports field. Albert E. Carter, who first discussed the rebounding effect in the late 1970s, correctly identified rebounding when he described it as "the most efficient, most effective form of exercise yet devised by man."[1]

Figure 10-1. Shown is a rebounder on which an exerciser is jogging without feeling the jarring effect of landing on a pavement or a hardwood floor.

Figure 10-2. Seen here is a rebounder with a stabilizing bar attached. This bar offers those who are elderly or who feel unsteady on their feet a greater sense of security while rebounding. The bar also offers a handicapped person who must remain in a sitting position the opportunity to get rebound exercise.

Jumping for health in this way creates a cellular exercise and not just movement of the human skeleton with its various muscular attachments. Rebounding is different from other physical activities because it puts gravity to work in your favor. By subjecting each of the body's trillions of cells to greater gravitational pull (the G force), waste products are squeezed out of every cell and nutrition gets drawn in. The cells become cleansed, nourished, renewed, vitalized and more efficient in their functioning. Regular exposure to rebound exercise places your entire metabolism at the most homeostatic plateau of activity.

Bouncing up and down on the rebound unit creates a chelation effect. Your whole cardiovascular system becomes stronger even without increasing its heart rate. This happens because as you come down on the rebounding device you put greater gravitational force on the arteries, veins, capillaries and heart muscle. Any muscle automatically adjusts to its environment; in this case, heart muscle fibers grow in elasticity, stamina and strength. And all three muscle layers lodged within blood vessel walls expand with vitality, too.[2]

The Chelation Process of Rebounding

Rebounding causes a natural process of chelation therapy to proceed throughout the body. Through skeletal, articular, muscular, tendinous and ligamentous actions, rebound exercise produces lactic acid, a weak organic acid that chelates away toxic components within the cells. Lactic acid, which is normally present in body tissues, is copiously created by muscular action. A particular type of lactic acid present in muscle and blood is the product that comes from the transformation of carbohydrates, glucose and glycogen into energy during strenuous physical up-and-down bouncing.

Because natural lactic acid acts in the same way as does the medical intravenous infusion of the chelating amino acid, EDTA, the resulting responses from rebound movements produce numerous therapeutic effects, including the following.

- They dissolve atherosclerotic plaque attached to the intima (the innermost layer of arteries).
- They pull poisons out of the media layer of blood vessel walls.

- They trap the foreign proteins that occupy space between cell membranes.
- They remove these unwanted proteins for deposition as waste.
- They carry away the toxic type of proteins for processing through the kidneys as urine, through the liver as nitrogenous wastes, and then through the bowel as feces.

In fact, exercising on a rebounder does even more than cause a chelation effect. But rebounding also works better than any other single physical activity for optimal cardiovascular conditioning, greater peripheral vascular circulatory flow, improved tissue oxygenation, increased lymphatic system drainage and overall physiological detoxification. Let's look at several beneficial physiological effects that regular performance of rebound exercises has on cardiovascular and peripheral vascular systems.

Cardiovascular/Peripheral Vascular Benefits from Rebounding

Between twenty and twenty-five years ago when rebounding was first recognized as a therapeutic series of movements, exercise therapists evaluated a group of hospitalized patients in Sweden. The patients were surveyed for symptoms and altogether, the clinical researchers named 150 different ailments from which their patients were suffering. Chief among their difficulties were palpitations of the heart, breathlessness from cardiovascular inadequacy, peripheral vascular insufficiency indicated by cold hands and feet, dizziness, headaches and deep sighing. Each patient averaged 5.4 symptoms.

This hospitalized group was given an exercise program that included rebounding for approximately one hour per day, several times weekly. At the program's end, their symptoms were surveyed again and the results were recorded: 44 ailments had vanished; 68 had diminished; only 21 persisted. The average number of symptoms per patient had dropped from 5.4 to 1.1. The research clinicians at the Karolinska Institute who had been conducting this investigation therefore concluded that rebound exercise protects and strengthens the cardiovascular and peripheral vascular systems, and offsets any potential harm caused by catecholamines released in the body's effort to combat stress.[3]

Catecholamines are chemicals that work physiologically as important nerve transmitters. Their main job is to prepare the body to act—the "flight or fight" syndrome—which includes increased blood pressure, faster heart beat, faster breathing and other aspects of vascular alertness. The three most significant catecholamines are dopamine, epinephrine (adrenaline) and norepinephrine. Norepinephrine and epinephrine are made by the adrenal medulla glands. Epinephrine opens up blood vessels that serve muscles, whereas norepinephrine slightly closes down these blood vessels. Both compounds excite the heart. Dopamine is found mainly in certain types of nerve tissue in the brain (the basal ganglia).

For a sick person who is able to rebound even in the midst of illness, rebounding serves as a physiological antidote to norepinephrine, epinephrine, dopamine and other catecholamines that act as internal stressors. Besides cellular detoxification and nourishment, rebounding produces a kind of cellular sedative that gives any damaged or sick cells the opportunity to heal themselves.

Rebounding has been identified by exercise physiologists such as James R. White, Ph.D., who teaches rebounding as an aerobic exercise in the department of physical education at the University of California, San Diego. Dr. White maintains that rebound exercise offers cardiovascular enhancement, increased aerobic capacity, the training effect, improved stamina, endurance and improved wind. He points out that the specific aerobic rhythmical exercises consist of jogging, running, bicycling, swimming, skating and cross-country skiing, and he particularly cites rebounding.

"Aerobic exercises use large muscles repeatedly, during which you maintain a designated exercise heart rate and sustain an even pace for many minutes. This submaximal-comfortable-steady-pace allows improved circulation in the working muscles but is not so strenuous that it produces undue fatigue and early exhaustion," Dr. White writes.[4]

With regard to the expected benefits of a rebound exercise program, Dr. White lists the following cardiovascular effects:

1. Increased strength and size of the left ventricle of the heart.
2. Increased diameter of the heart.
3. Increased diameter of the arteries of the heart.
4. Increased number of latent arteries used for distributing blood to the heart and the rest of the body.
5. Slowdown of the heart rate.
6. Decreased amount of oxygen needed by the heart.[5]

Rebounding causes peripheral vascular improvement of occlusive disease by encouraging blood clots in the limbs to dissolve. A series of studies performed at Duke University and published in the May 1, 1980 issue of the *New England Journal of Medicine* reports that regular, vigorous exercise such as rebounding improves a person's ability to have blood clots disappear. This clot-dissolving ability, known as *fibrinolytic activity,* is called into play when a clot closes off a blood vessel. The greater the fibrinolytic response, the faster the clot is dissolved, reducing the chances of some serious medical consequences from blood vessel blockage.[6]

By the fourth or fifth decade of life, when atherosclerosis (hardening of the arteries) begins to manifest symptoms, especially in men and women in industrialized Western countries, raised focal fibro-fatty plaques develop as streaks along the intima (inner wall) of arteries. The fatty streaks possess cores of mainly cholesterol lipid (fat), usually complexed to proteins and cholesterol esters which cover fibrous caps. Complicating these fatty streaks is the combination of calcification, internal hemorrhages, ulceration through the arterial wall (endothelium) with discharge of emboli into the bloodstream and overlying thrombus formations on the surfaces of the plaques.

If a victim of such atheromata formations were to rebound regularly, lactic acid's chelating effect would be stimulated from smooth muscle tissue that makes up the inner and middle layers of blood vessels with each rebounding session. Theoretically, the intimal and medial smooth muscle cells would tend to dissolve the calcifications that bind together these various complicating factors. Lipid accumulation might begin to diminish, and possibly less atheromata would develop. Calcium-complexed lesions which involve most of the major chemical constituents of the atheromatous pathology would eventually disappear if one could sufficiently rebound them away.[7,8,9,10]

Oxygenation Exercise for the Heart/Lung System

If you have a resting heart rate of less than sixty beats a minute, don't smoke, don't have chest pain presently, never experienced angina pectoris, live a generally healthful lifestyle and engage in rebounding for forty minutes or more each day, at least five days a week, theoretically you'll most likely never develop a heart problem if you have none now.[11]

Rebounding is a heart/lung endurance exercise that provides optimal oxygenation for the entire network of blood vessels and muscle fibers in the cardiopulmonary system. In-place running on your rebounding device for uninterrupted periods in excess of five minutes (more than ten minutes is better) builds up cardiopulmonary endurance and ensures saturation of the blood with oxygen molecules.

Exercise physiologist H. C. Carlson, Ph.D., in experiments at the University of Pittsburgh, developed the following method for achieving cardiovascular-pulmonary conditioning: Run on the rebounder for ten seconds and count the number of single foot contacts. Rest for ten seconds. Try to increase the number of single foot contacts by at least one each time you do another interval of rebound running. Rest for ten seconds between each run. Keep this up for five (or ten) minutes, all the while raising your feet high with each bounce. The higher you lift your feet, the harder the effort but the greater will be its aerobic effect.[12]

Rebound exercise improves the tone and quality of the heart muscle and increases the coordination of the heart's muscle fibers as they wring blood out of its chambers during each beat. The overall aerobic effect while you are rebound-running equals and often surpasses that of regular running, but rebounding helps you avoid the jarring effect of hitting a hard surface.

As indicated, your rate of jumping will vary, depending on how vigorously you bounce and how high you lift your feet off the mat. Rebound exercise will give you the ideal cardiopulmonary aerobic effect with almost any rate of performance, because it fills all the requisites of an oxygenating exercise.[13]

Through synergistic cooperation between the heart and lungs, the body enjoys homeostasis of this cardiopulmonary combination system. But there's another system that's all-important—lymphatic drainage— and it, too, is enhanced thanks to the self-created internal chelation therapy effect of rebound exercise.

How Lymphatics Work with the Heart and Lungs

In discussing the chelating benefits of rebounding aerobics with his patients, coauthor Hitendra H. Shah, M.D., explains, "The lymphatic drainage system of the body is an amazingly complex structure. It works hand in hand with the blood circulatory system and the pulmonary system. In the circulatory system, newly oxygenated blood from the lungs moves from the heart along smaller and smaller arteries until it reaches the tiniest vessels called *capillaries*. It is in these microscopic tubules that the blood exchanges oxygen and nutrients for cellular waste products with surrounding body cells. The capillaries then gradually become larger and form veins through which the unoxygenated, waste-carrying blood returns back to the lungs and then to the heart to be recirculated time and time again.

"Much of the fluid accompanying the blood and large protein molecules leak from these capillaries. Additional fluids and waste products are expelled from every cell in the body. These fluids accumulate in the small spaces between the cells," Dr. Shah says. "If all of this material weren't somehow removed, we would begin to swell like toads and die within a matter of twenty-four hours. Fortunately, we have a completely separate circulation system, called the lymphatic system, that is able to absorb and remove these fluids, proteins, and waste materials. With the exception of the brain, where these proteins transfer directly into the fluid that surrounds them, the extensive lymphatic network has hundreds of miles of tubules that cover the entire body. Through these tubules, all of the material is returned to the blood so it can be utilized or eliminated from the body. (There is no pathway, other than the lymphatic system, which trapped excess protein molecules can use to return to the circulatory system.)

"Several problems occur when the lymph drainage slows and fluids begin to accumulate around the cells. First, the individual cells are forced further away from the capillaries. The amount of oxygen and nourishment they receive is decreased. Under exertion or stress some cells may die," adds Dr. Shah. "Cells are forced to survive in their own waste and toxic byproducts. Such a situation can eventually lead to the degeneration and destruction of organs. For example, poor lymphatic drainage of the extremities can lead to tissue damage and then to poor blood circulation with swelling and pain. Besides occurring in the limbs, similar problems can happen in any other organs of the body.

"A good analogy would be if you are confined in one room of your house," continues Dr. Shah. "Someone may bring you food and water, but possibly not remove any of your waste products. This being the case, eventually you would have difficulty remaining healthy in such an environment. As your waste accumulated, not only would you become sick, those around you would begin to experience the same fate. It is the same for each cell; in addition to nourishment and oxygen, the removal of waste products is essential for continued health of all the organs and ultimately the entire body."

Dr. Shah strongly recommends rebound exercise as one of the two main ways to improve lymphatic flow and toxin drainage. Rebounding, he emphasizes, must be part of any chelation/detoxification program for reaping the optimal advantages of intravenous EDTA chelation therapy.

The Lymphatic Drainage Effect of Rebounding

Earlier we mentioned the deleterious consequences of foreign proteins trapped in the spaces between the cellular membranes that separate cells from one another. Now we must emphasize that these trapped proteins create numerous forms of pathology. They bring harm to the whole body's functioning by

- Attracting excess sodium to the tissues.
- Blocking the fluid circulation within tissue spaces.
- Producing nutritional deficiencies inside the cells.
- Causing unhealthy and swollen cells to develop.
- Increasing the pressure of the interstitial fluid (between cells).
- Bringing on local tissue pain from lack of oxygen.
- Decreasing the ability of the lymphatic system to neutralize and destroy the poisons produced by cellular waste.
- Short-circuiting the body's electrical system by allowing the accumulation of nerve poisons.
- Draining the body's cells of energy.
- Placing a continual strain on the liver, kidneys, lungs and skin to excrete accumulating wastes.
- Reducing the efficient functioning of body organs in proportion to the amount of excess protein concentration they possess.
- Blocking blood flow to the muscles and allowing bones (especially vertebrae of the spinal column) to be pulled out of place by muscular spasm.
- Leading to illness and eventual death of the entire human organism.[14]

As we've implied, the lymphatic system is responsible for eliminating trapped harmful proteins from the body, for it's the metabolic garbage can for each of us. It rids us of toxins, nitrogenous wastes, fat, infectious microorganisms, heavy metals, dead cells, cancerous cells and other assorted junk cast of by the cells' metabolism. The movement performed in rebounding provides the stimulus for a free-flowing lymphatic drainage of all this metabolic junk.

Unlike the blood circulatory system, the lymphatic drainage system does not have its own pump such as a heart muscle to move the fluid around through the lymph vessels. Lymphatic flow requires three natural activities for drainage: (1) muscular contraction from exercise and movement, (2) gravitational pressure, and (3) internal massage to the valves of the lymph ducts. Rebounding supplies all three of these methods of removing protein waste products from the cells and from the body. The bouncing motion effectively moves and recycles the lymph and the entire blood supply through the circulatory system many times during the course of the rebounding session.

Rebounding is a lymphatic drainage exercise which has the same effect on one's body as jumping rope, but without any jarring to the joints that comes from hitting the gym floor or ground. Better than rope jumping or jogging, however, the lymphatic channels are placed under hydraulic pressure to move fluids containing waste products of metabolism around and out of the body through the left subclavian vein.[15]

Rebound exercise conforms to the many ramifications of body cleansing and detoxification which were described in the last chapter. It's a true chelation therapy exercise.

Exercises That Can Be Done on the Rebounder

Rebound exercise has its "ups and downs" accomplished by a series of thirty-three bouncing techniques performed on the small trampoline. Your option is to utilize only the motions which become your favorites. One precaution to take, however, is to start rebounding gradually with the simplest of movements. Your up-and-down motion compresses and decompresses the flesh and fluids of the whole body, all its tissues, organs, and systems so that wastes will be sucked out of the cells quickly and efficiently. Causing this to happen before your cells are conditioned to receive so much detoxification may unload more toxins into your bloodstream than you're used to. Too much of the sophisticated movements of rebounding at the start can actually cause lethargy and fatigue from the escape of your own stored cellular poisons. Take it slow and get rid of them *gradually*. For an illustrated book of re-bounding exercise that includes the following exercises, see Appendix D.

Rebounding Exercises Several exercises can be done on a rebounder. Photograph 10-1 shows an exerciser jogging without feeling the jarring effect of landing on a pavement or a hardwood floor. As shown in photograph 10-2, a stabilizing bar offers those who are elderly or who feel unsteady on their feet a great sense of security while rebounding. The bar offers a handicapped person who must remain in a sitting position the opportunity to get rebound exercise.

The "health bounce" is a good warm-up movement and creates a self-induced, internal chelation therapy effect the same as do other more vigorous rebound exercises. To accomplish the health bounce, in the center of the rebounder, move up and down by using the toes and calf muscles only. Your feet should not leave the mat.

To do jumping jacks, stand in the center of the rebounder with your feet together, hands at your sides. Jump to a position of feet apart, simultaneously swinging arms to the side and up over your head. Keep arms straight. Return to the starting position and repeat.

To perform running in place, in the center of the rebounder, start a walking, jogging or running motion. Lift your knees high in front of you. Don't wait for the rebounder to bounce your leg up; instead, run at your own speed.

Another exercise is the high bounce. To do the high bounce, stand in the middle of the rebounder and use your toes and calves with force. Bend your knees to bounce off the mat from four to ten inches vertically so that you land in the center of the rebounder.

The twist is another good rebound exercise. To perform this exercise, begin in the middle of the rebounder and bounce so that your hips and legs turn to the left and your chest and shoulders turn to the right. On the next bounce turn hips and legs to the right and chest and shoulders to the left. On the next bounce, reverse again. Keep up the exercise for a good workout.

Chapter Eleven

THE HEALING POTENTIAL OF ORAL CHELATION THERAPY

Beset by some serious cardiovascular problems, fifty-one-year-old Marvin Angstrom of Upper Darby, Pennsylvania, was forced to retire in 1991 from his managerial position with United Parcel Service. All of his working life after graduation from high school, Mr. Angsrom worked as a UPS employee and had seen his authority increase steadily with the package delivery organization. He started at the bottom and after seven years of driving one of those big brown UPS trucks, for another ten years he sat at a desk dispatching overseas shipments. Then he moved to the UPS management level at which he set policy, negotiated contracts, hired and fired, and thoroughly enjoyed his role as an operating executive.

His enjoyment ended when working under conditions of stress, he experienced a myocardial infarction (MI) to the left side of his heart. The heart attack occurred on a sunny summer Sunday at home while cooking well-marbelized steaks outdoors for his family. All of the Angstroms—his wife, daughter, two married sons, two daughters-in-law and himself—were active meat eaters. Even his two grandchildren enjoyed gnawing on chops or cuts of steak. It was part of the Angstrom family's lifestyle.

Myocardial infarction is the blockage of a main heart artery caused by atherosclerosis (hardening of the arteries) arising from a blood clot. The MI results in a dead tissue area (necrosis) within the heart muscle, which in Mr. Angstrom's case struck inside of the heart's left ventricle.

As typically happens, the MI began with crushing, viselike chest pain, which then moved to his left arm, neck and upper abdomen. At first he thought it was indigestion, but this pain was so persistent and penetrating that he finally concluded it must be much more. Seeing her husband become ashen in color, clammy with cold sweat, short of breath, anxious and then fall in a faint, his wife panicked, screamed and fainted as well. It was his oldest son who called for an ambulance, while his other son, Arnold, administered whatever first aid he knew how to give.

Death was near as his heart beat sped along too rapidly and irregularly, his blood pressure dropped and his body temperature rose. Arnold could barely feel any pulse at the wrists and neck. The young man was attempting to give his father mouth-to-mouth resuscitation when the emergency medical technicians arrived. They expertly used cardiopulmonary resuscitation (CPR) equipment before the patient was taken to an intensive cardiac care unit (CCU) at the nearest hospital. In the CCU, staff members administered oxygen, heart drugs, anticoagulants, painkillers and sleeping pills. Marvin Angstrom's life was saved, but he had sustained heart muscle damage. Catheterization for an angiogram at the CCU showed blockage in his coronary arteries.

"I underwent an angioplasty. That's where the surgeon sticks a balloon into the artery and presses junk material that was causing. my arterial clogging to squash against the blood vessel walls," the patient explained. Actually, as described in the case of Lindley M. Camp who discussed his own weakened heart situation in our introductory chapter, an angioplasty of the percutaneous transluminal type is an operation for enlarging a narrowed arterial lumen by peripheral introduction of a balloon-tip catheter and dilating the lumen on withdrawal of the inflated catheter tip.

"Afterward I took a great number of medicines for my heart," continued Marvin Angstrom. "For four years I swallowed eighteen pills a day—different types of heart drugs. The pills didn't seem to be doing me any good either; none of them made me feel any better. Often they had me feeling worse, in fact, because upon taking them I would get this numbness all over. My cardiologist said it couldn't be from the pills, but after taking his medicines is the only time I would have this numb feeling."

During his long period of recovery, the patient experienced another serious heart involvement, mitral valve prolapse. With this condition there's a sticking out of both small cusps (flaps) of the mitral valve back into the upper chamber (left atrium) of the heart during narrowing of the lower chamber (left ventricle). The mitral valve is one of the four valves of the heart located between the left atrium and the left ventricle. It's the only valve with those two small cusps, and its job is to allow blood to flow from the left atrium into the left ventricle. Normally, this valve stops blood from flowing back into the atrium. Narrowing of the ventricle forces the blood up against the mitral valve which closes the cusps so that the flow of blood is moved from the ventricle into the main artery of the body, the aorta. With prolapse, the valve fails to close properly and a flow of blood back into the atrium results. The condition leads to swelling of the left side of the heart resulting in symptoms consisting of some chest pain, an irregular heart rate, a feeling of generalized weakness and breathing difficulty.

Healthplex Medical Center in Marshalls Creek, Pennsylvania

Four years of unsatisfactory doctoring finally led this patient to the Healthplex Medical Center in Marshalls Creek, Pennsylvania. Healthplex is a health care facility specializing in alternative and preventive medicine that treats the entire person and not just a symptom or an individual body part. Under the administrative supervision of chiropractic internist and certified clinical nutritionist Michael Jude Loquasto, D.C., Ph.D.[c] (candidate), C.C.N., Healthplex Medical Center offers the services of a staff of doctors who practice allopathic medicine, holistic medicine, oriental medicine, massage therapy, nutritional therapy, reflexology, sports medicine, physical therapy and physical rehabilitation.

The medical center offers intravenous chelation therapy with EDTA as a procedure, but Marvin Angstrom was not predisposed to receive it. The reason was strictly financial. While his health insurance carrier would cover chelation therapy when administered for toxic metal syndrome, it refused reimbursement for the treatment's application to reverse atherosclerosis or other types of cardiovascular disease. Therefore, the patient took chelation treatment in another form. He participated in a program of oral chelation therapy which employs nutritional supplements as the means to reverse hardening of his arteries.

"I'm off the heart medicines and onto the oral chelating agents. And I feel like a brand new man," Marvin Angstrom affirmed. "I visit Dr. Loquasto once a week for his supervision of my oral chelation therapy, the new vegetarian diet that he has me eating, the exercise therapy in which I'm engaged, and to receive chiropractic adjustments to relieve my hiatal hernia and to improve blood supply to my heart. I use the skills and knowledge provided by many of the staff members working in this Healthplex medical complex.

"Through the week a lot of questions arise with vegetarianism for somebody like me who once ate meat at every meal. Normally these days I breakfast on oatmeal or corn flakes without milk. I used to drink nearly two quarts of milk and eight cups of coffee with heavy cream each day. Now I don't need any dairy products or coffee. While formerly I drank hardly any water at all, bottled water is my usual beverage from here-on. I drink almost a gallon of water daily. And I've cut down my sugar consumption by more than 90 percent," Mr. Angstrom assured. "My new normal diet includes only vegetables, salads, fruits, soups, cereals and grains. I used to eat massive amounts of ice cream, but no more. Probably the last time I had ice cream was a small cone three months ago just before my entering Dr. Loquasto's practice.

"As you can understand, I've changed my approach to food consumption entirely. My eating habits are altogether different because I don't want another heart attack. After working for twelve hours most days at UPS, taking a food break for me had involved stopping for lunch and then dinner to eat steak and eggs, fast food cheeseburgers, hot dogs, pizza pies with much cheese, bacon and french fries, quarts of ice cream, and other artery-clogging stuff," Marvin Angstrom said. "For a lot of years, I was the biggest eater of fatty meats, luncheon meats like smoked sausage, corned beef, salami or bologna, chicken, lamb, and veal. I don't miss eating those foods anymore. I know what they did to me. I destroyed my own body, and now I'm on the verge of getting it back to where it should be. It took coming close to dying from a heart attack to have me live healthfully. I do want to live!

"So I take oral chelation therapy rather than drugs every day. Chelation is really helping me feel well. Now when I get up in the morning, it's a joy to face what life has to offer. In contrast, three months ago, just before I started on the oral chelating agents, rising from bed was almost torture. I didn't want to do it because I felt as tired in the morning as when I went to bed the night before," the patient stated. "It's difficult to believe that I could feel as well as I do in such a short time. That's definitely because of my new lifestyle and treatment program: weekly spinal adjustments, exercise therapy, a vegetarian diet, and most of all because of the oral chelation therapy that I'm giving to myself at home, but under medical supervision."

What Oral Chelation Therapy Is and Does

Oral chelation therapy calls into play a natural chelation mechanism that's built into human physiology. A very complicated biochemistry is involved, which we will attempt to simplify.

The chelation mechanism is a chemical process in nature and in living organisms. Plants and animals at all levels use the process to live and thrive. Chelation usually involves a heterocyclic ring compound (a compound containing more than one kind of atom in its ring structure) which encircles or "captures" some metallic ion. The process of chelation has taken place when the ring compound binds to or contains at least one metal cation (a positively charged atom) in the ring. The metallic ion is then considered to be chelated.

Organic compounds in which atoms form more than one coordinate bonding (a shared pair of electrons forms the bond between two atoms) with metals in solution often are chelating agents. The chelating agents for people which are edibles such as garlic, onions, chives, scallions and other food stuffs may be swallowed to produce a slow chelation effect in the blood which carries over to all of the body's parts, including its whole systems, organs, tissues, cells and organelles.

The various oral chelating agents are body part detoxifiers and blood purifiers. Part of the definition of oral chelation therapy is that it's *a prolonged process of chemical detoxification of the most inner recesses of one's physiology.*

We learned in the previous chapter that rebounding is a chelating exercise because rebound movement causes the muscles to release lactic acid, a chelating agent. And rebounding stimulates action of the lymphatic system, the body's overall waste accumulator; thus, chelation therapy given to oneself by intravenous infusion, rebound exercise, nutritional supplementation and other ways are marvelous means of detoxifying all areas of the body.

Oral chelation therapy involves the use of particular foods, supplemental nutrients, orthomolecular cofactors, small-dose toximolecular drugs and such other items taken by mouth to create a therapeutic response in the human physiology. The most common benefit derived from oral chelation therapy is the quenching of free radicals, which otherwise are destined to bring about pathological changes in the body or brain.

Furthermore, gerontologists tell us that as aging increases, immunity decreases. One of the main elements of the aging process is the lowered effectiveness of the immune function.[1,2,3]

The immune system is also impaired by environmental factors such as radiation, insecticides, food preservatives and pharmaceuticals. Physical and emotional stress and intense physical exercise also affect immunity adversely.[4] It is well documented that healthy athletes frequently suffer from influenza or pneumonia following heavy periods of intense exercise. The same immunosuppression is observed in people like Marvin Angstrom with stress-related diseases such as coronary heart disease. Under these influences, the number of macrophages available in the blood as immune defenses are reduced and unable to participate in the immune cascade. In turn, this macrophage reduction causes an even deeper immunosuppression for the stressed individual. Oral chelation therapy has proven itself both to lower the aging effect of free radicals and to stimulate or activate macrophage cells which efficiently counter these negative body reactions.[5,6,7]

The most effective oral chelating agents are weak organic acids such as citric acid, lactic acid, acetic acid and ascorbic acid. Since many food substances have the ability to seize and "sequester" metal atoms such as calcium ions just like EDTA and other chelating drugs, these foods offer a promising foundation for the development of a group of food chelators for the enhancement of health and the prolongation of life. Orthomolecular nutritionists point out that food chelators are the obvious rational and exciting nutritional pharmacology selections for the future. Although we cannot hope to get as rapid or dramatic effects as we see when the chelator is directly introduced into the bloodstream as an intravenous (IV) solution, we can easily keep up the oral program for a long time and achieve great advantages. Measurements by chelating physicians indicate that IV chelation therapy does work well eventually. How fast? It depends on the extent of impairment of your body. Our advice is "just be patient!" Take your oral chelating agents the rest of your life to live healthfully and die feeling young at a very old age.

As a mechanism in plant and animal biology and chemistry, the chelation reaction has been recognized for over forty-five years by medical scientists. It is a vital biochemical process that is fundamental in[8]

1. Food digestion.
2. Nutrient assimilation.
3. The formation of numerous enzymes.
4. The functions of enzyme systems.
5. The synthesis of many hormones.
6. The detoxification of certain poisonous chemicals.

7. The detoxification of toxic metal syndrome involving lead, arsenic, mercury, aluminum, nickel, copper, iron, cadmium, manganese and more heavy metals.
8. The movement of vitamins, minerals, hormones, enzymes and other nutrients across membranes of body tissues as part of transport systems.

Are Chelated Minerals from Health Food Stores Useful?

Chelation is an integral part of human physiology. The process is associated with many familiar substances in nature and in the body. Health food store purchases that provide you with iron and other minerals often are labeled as being "chelated" or amino-acid-complexed. Such a label refers to a laboratory process that, if properly performed, is slightly different from the physiological process occurring in the body. Yet, the artificial laboratory chelation method can accomplish the same desired effect—markedly enhanced absorption and utilization by the body of the inorganic mineral.

Chelated minerals are powerful nutrients that are comprised of a mineral complexed or bonded with a ligand such as an amino acid. Ascorbic acid or aspartic acid can be used as such a ligand, too. A chemical conversion takes place between the ligand and minerals. The newly formed chelated complex helps the body utilize the nutrients in the metabolic processes.

The body's self-chelation of iron may be used as an example. In ordinary metabolism, before inorganic iron such as iron sulfate can be absorbed, the body must remove the iron from the sulfate. To do this, it ionizes the iron. Then the body must take protein and hydrolize it into amino acids. Finally, through its own chelating processes, the body chelates some of the iron with those amino acids and carries the mineral into the intestinal wall. Through this natural chelation process your body generally absorbs less than 5 percent of originally nonchelated iron. Once the small amount of iron has entered the intestinal wall, your body combines ferric hydroxide-phosphate compound to form *ferritin,* which is the first stage in the absorption of iron.

This resulting iron amino acid chelate carries the iron across the intestinal cells of the bloodstream. The iron is released in the bloodstream and is rechelated a third time with a beta-globulin, which is similar to hemoglobin, from the blood. The new chelate, called *trans-ferrin*, moves the iron to the required body stores, such as the liver or the marrow of the bones.[9,10]

Because the body does not have to make significant changes in the mineral presented in the properly chelated form, independent laboratory tests have shown that absorption and retention of properly chelated minerals are much higher than for nonchelated minerals.[11]

Industrial Companies Employ Chelation in Their Products

Knowing that drug effects must take place in a manner adaptable to the human physiology, nearly all pharmaceutical companies employ oral chelation therapy. The chelation process is partly responsible for the activity of many of the drugs used in medicine to treat disease, including aspirin, terramycin, cortisone, adrenaline, penicillin and a host of others. Without this oral chelation mechanism, drugs could not act as effectively and react easily with the body's metabolism. For example, most of the cytotoxic agents used in chemotherapy against cancer accomplish cellular poisoning through their ability to chelate biochemical components within the cancer cells. Chelation removes those components so that the cancer cells must die.

Ringer's lactate, an acceptable vehicle for following the protocol for administering IV chelation therapy and for intravenous feedings, contains a natural chelator. Lactic acid in the Ringer's solution accounts for an unappreciated therapeutic effect in patients who receive this fluid. Ringer's lactate actually lowers the serum calcium exactly like EDTA. Other pharmaceutical chelates not mentioned previously are penicillamine, streptomycin, bacitracin, oxytetracycline, polymyxin, ammonia, cyanide ion, glycine, oxine, dipyridyl, tetraethyllithuram, isonizid, aminosalicyclic acid and many other common generic drugs.

Each chelating agent has a varying affinity for a variety of cations, depending on the various spatial arrangements of the bound-up molecule. There are many additional chemical and physical factors such as the pH or acidity of the solution which determine the efficacy of an oral chelating agent.

Some of the most basic and yet complex chemical reactions found in nature and in humans are encompassed by the chelation process. Industrial processes utilizing the chemistry of chelation are numerous. To understand its application in commerce, look at the softening of water. Certain ion exchange materials, such as zeolite that's used to soften water, are chelates. Zeolite is a complex sodium compound. When it comes in contact with hard water, it exchanges sodium for calcium and magnesium, which are the two minerals that make water hard. No lather forms when soap is added to hard water; a scummy precipitate drops out instead. Zeolite chemically forms sodium carbonates and sulfates to provide a softened water exactly the way that intravenous EDTA and other chelating agents work in the human body.

Chelation forms the basis for the action of detergents in getting clothes clean and dishes washed. Just as the chelating physician does for patients, a modern homemaker employs the principle of chelation when she gets out stains from her husband's shirts and cleans off the dinner dishes. Detergents form soluble chelates with calcium and magnesium that are readily washed out by water rinsing. No scum builds up as a ring around the dishwashing machine, bathtub or washbasin because of the chelation chemical actions. These same actions take place inside the body—the gastrointestinal tract, the blood vessels, the urinary track and other body systems—because of a person's swallowing nutritional supplements. Oral chelation therapy begins in the mouth and continues physiologically from there all the way to the anus.

Oral Chelation Therapy Makes Our Planet Healthier

Taking IV chelation therapy with EDTA is preferable to the singular use of oral chelation therapy, but medical supervision of the IV procedure by a skilled health professional who has received training in its administration is mandatory. Sometimes IV injections with EDTA are not financially feasible as was the case for Marvin Angstrom when his health insurance would not reimburse him for chelation therapy to unclog blocked arteries. In another situation, EDTA delivered intravenously may become impossible when traveling long distances to a chelating physician's office is necessary. Alternatively, there may be some IV EDTA contraindication for the patient, or there may be dangerous side effects. Whatever the reason for not receiving the more effective infusions of EDTA, oral chelation therapy can be a viable—if slower—beneficial substitute for intravenous chelation treatment. That being the situation, a number of practical oral chelating agents are available for home use.

Oral Chelation Agents to Use for Yourself at Home

If people everywhere would ingest nutritional agents which provide oral chelation therapy, our planet's populations—especially those in the Western industrialized countries—would be healthier and richer in all regards.

Do you know that preventable illness accounts for 70 percent of all expenditures paid out for health care in the United States?

Are you aware that 35 million Americans suffer from hypertension, a major cause of the 500,000 strokes and 1.25 million heart attacks that occur each year?

Does it surprise you to learn that one in every three Americans will get cancer before age 74 and that by the turn of this new century the number will increase to one in two?

Are you conscious of how little we spend for disease prevention in this country—only four cents out of every medical care dollar?

Do you wonder why Americans rate only seventeenth in the average life expectancy of occupants of industrialized nations?

Are you outraged to learn that $23 billion of American taxpayer money has been spent to fight the so-called war on cancer since 1971 but that during this period the overall rate of cancer has risen in the United States by 18 percent?

None of these questions would have validity if all of us consumed oral chelating agents. Therefore, we will provide you with a listing of nutrients to which we have added knowledge about an excellent nutritional formulation (Vita Chel Plus™). These nutrients, readily available from health food stores or by mail order from holistic health clinics and nutrition supply houses, are highly useful oral chelating agents that unclog blocked, spasmotic or otherwise malfunctioning cardiovascular/ peripheral vascular blood circulatory systems. See **Table 11-1** for the full listing of individual nutrients which act as oral chelating agents.

Every nutrient on our list is approved as a food or food supplement by the FDA. Most of them are generally recognized as safe (on the GRAS list posted by the FDA) and may be acquired over the counter and without prescription. Taken in sufficient dosage, these agents provide oral chelation therapy. Orthomolecular psychiatrists frequently use them for the treatment of mental illnesses as part of their orthomolecular nutrition programs.

TABLE 11-1

NUTRITIONAL SUPPLEMENTS WHICH ARE ORAL CHELATING AGENTS[12]

Ascorbic acid (vitamin C)	Protomorphogens
Pyridoxine (vitamin B_6)	Supplemental green drink powders
D(dextro) alpha tocopherol (vitamin E)	(Greens+® and Pure Synergy™)
Bioflavonoids (vitamin P)	Niacin (vitaminB_3)
Aspartates	Dimethylglycine
Aged garlic extract (Kyolic®)	B-complex vitamins
Papain	Magnesium
High-fiber foods	Orotates
Proanthocyanidines (Pro-N-50+®)	Bromelain
Glutathione peroxidase	Onions
Methionine reductase	CoEnzyme Q_{10}
Superoxide dismutase	L-Carnitine
Omega-6 essential fatty acids	Pycnogenol®
from evening primrose	Catalase
oil/black current oil	Gingko biloba
Omega-3 essential fatty acids	Chromium picolinate
from fish oils, flax, soy,	Zinc
and seeds	Selenium
Potassium	Glycine
Bee pollen	L-Cysteine
Vanadium	Glutamine
Silicon	Lecithin
The Dr. Rinse Formula®	Mucopolysaccharides
Chondroitin sulphate-4	Probiotics
Alginate	
Pectin (modified citrus pectin as	
Pecta-sol™)	

Oral Chelation Formulations

Throughout this chapter, we have followed the case history of one patient, Marvin Angstrom of Upper Darby, Pennsylvania.

After sustaining a myocardial infarction which brought him close to death, followed by an angioplasty operation to open some passage for blood flow through his coronary arteries, to which were added eighteen separate cardiac medications that he needed to take daily, and a subsequent mitral valve prolapse because the heart remedies were not working, Marvin Angstrom finally found the ultimate life-preserver. Oral chelation therapy is sustaining his heart action, keeping open his partially clogged arteries, and making him feel marvelous once again. The patient routinely takes his oral chelation formulation at home under the once-a-week supervision of its clinician/inventor, Dr. Michael Jude Loquasto.

Dr. Loquasto's oral chelation formula has been used by Mr. Angstrom and a few thousand other informed people who, since 1984 have taken it prophylactically or as therapy. It prevents and reverses atherosclerosis in several ways; by eliminating free radicals, by stimulating the immune system's macrophages, by stopping the formation of atherosclerotic plaque from attaching itself to the interior walls of blood vessels and by slowing down the aging process. **Table 11-2** lists the nutrients, antioxidants, glandulars, free-radical scavengers and the dosages of these components in the formulation.

Dr. Loquasto has declared: "This oral chelation formula has been worked on, tested, refined, and retested, and is currently being used with great success in treating patients with cardiovascular disease and peripheral vascular disease." The nutrients in the formulation work in the following way: Plaque attaches itself to the arterial wall after it has been roughened by free-radical attack. If the immune system is up to par, it will prevent these free radicals from damaging tiny muscle cells in the arterial lining. Atherosclerosis may be prevented and reversed by eliminating free radicals and by keeping the immune system healthy, which is done through the use of proper diet, chiropractic care and oral chelation therapy. Some examples of sources that cause the formation of free radicals are smoking, chemical food additives and radiation.[13]

"In approximately 96 percent of all North Americans over fifty years of age, circulatory problems occur to some degree. I believe that the nutritional formula created by me, taken in proper dosages and under the care of a qualified doctor, will dramatically reduce and prevent those blood flow difficulties," Dr. Loquasto added. For further information about the formulation, see Appendix D.

"Here are two examples of results obtained from its use: One of my patients, a fifty-three-year-old school teacher who was scheduled for a coronary artery bypass operation, is now 80 percent corrected in her blood flow to the heart after having taken the formula every day for four months. She no longer needs the open-heart surgery," said Dr. Loquasto.

"A forty-three-year-old factory worker who suffered from chronic hypertension had been treated for over two years with impotence-producing medication. He experienced minimal results. Then, two months ago he started on my formula, and his blood pressure has come down exceedingly well," concluded Dr. Loquasto. "His medical doctor took him off the blood pressure drugs and his sex life has returned to normal."

The nutritional ingredients and the dosages in the formulation are indicated in **Table 11-2.**

Brief Descriptions of Dr. Loquasto's Formula

As a result of the oral chelating attributes of the ingredients, Dr. Michael Jude Loquasto's formula acts to prevent, reduce or reverse atherosclerosis. The following information offers a very brief explanation of what the ingredients do for the physiology of someone who is taking them:

Vitamin A (retinol) promotes cellular growth, repairs damaged cell membranes and heals mucous membranes.

Vitamin D (calciferol) enhances the metabolism of calcium and phosphorus and assimilates vitamin A.

Vitamin E (tocopherol) prevents oxidation of fat compounds as well as that of vitamin A, selenium and vitamin C. It's an important vasodilator and anticoagulant.

Vitamin C (ascorbic acid) is an antioxidant and helps form collagen.

Vitamin B-1 (thiamin) neutralizes free radicals with the other B vitamins, and improves circulation and blood formation.

Vitamin B-2 (riboflavin) neutralizes free radicals and aids cellular growth and cellular reproduction.

Vitamin B-3 (niacin) neutralizes free radicals and increases blood flow and lowers serum LDL cholesterol.

Vitamin B-6 (pyridoxine) is involved in more bodily functions than any other single nutrient and promotes red blood cell formation.

Vitamin B-12 (cyanocobalamin) aids in cell formation, cellular longevity and nutritional metabolism.

Pantothenic acid helps produce adrenal hormones, antibodies and adrenal steroids.

Folic acid is needed for energy production and the formation of red blood cells.

Table 11-2

Dr. Loquasto's

Oral Chelation Therapy Formula

Vita Chel Plus™

Contents: Six Tablets Contain:

Vitamin A (Natural)	20,000 I.U.
Vitamin D (Natural)	280 I.U.
Vitamin E (Natural)	400 I.U.
Vitamin C (Rose Hips)	1,600 mg
Vitamin B-1	80 mg
Vitamin B-2	8 mg
Vitamin B-6	100 mg
Niacin/Niacinamide	40 mg
Pantothenic acid	200 mg
Vitamin B-12	400 mg
Folic acid	160 mg
Choline	400 mg
Biotin	40 mg
Inositol	60 mg
Lecithin	80 mg
PABA	200 mg
Calcium (chelated)	200 mg
Magnesium (chelated)	200 mg
Potassium (chelated)	200 mg
Zinc (chelated)	40 mg
Iron	4 mg
Iodine	60 mcg
Copper	1.5 mcg
Chromium	40 mcg
Selenium	100 mcg
Manganese	8 mg
Adrenal	40 mg
Thymus	40 mg
Pituitary	14 mg
L-Cysteine	300 mg
Methionine	80 mg
Rice bran	160 mg
Pectin	40 mg
Flax powder	20 mg
Bromelain	40 mg
Garlic	40 mg

Choline is needed for nerve transmission, gallbladder regulation, liver function and lecithin formation.

Inositol generally prevents hardening of the arteries and removes fats from the liver.

Lecithin, needed by every living cell, prevents the sclerosing of cell membranes and protects them from oxidation.

PABA (para-aminobenzoic acid) is an antioxidant and acts in the breakdown and utilization of protein.

Calcium regulates the heart beat, blood clotting and blood pressure.

Magnesium assists in calcium and potassium uptake, and protects the arterial lining from stress.

Potassium regulates heart rhythm, prevents stroke, aids in muscle contraction and controls water balance.

Zinc helps synthesize protein and collagen, and promotes immunity.

Iron is needed for production of hemoglobin and the oxygenation of red blood cells.

Iodine assists metabolization of excess fat and prevents goiter.

Copper is needed to help form bone, hemoglobin, elastin and red blood cells.

Chromium is needed for energy and functions in the synthesis of cholesterol, fats and protein. It stabilizes blood sugar levels.

Selenium, a vital antioxidant, combines with vitamin E to prevent the formation of free radicals.

Manganese is needed for protein and fat metabolism, blood sugar regulation, healthy nerves and immunity.

Adrenal, a protomorphogen, as are all the glandulars used for oral chelation therapy, promotes the functioning of adrenal glands.

Thymus promotes thymus gland function.

Pituitary promotes pituitary gland function.

L-Cysteine, an amino acid, detoxifies harmful toxins and preserves the cells. It's one of the best free-radical destroyers and protects against radiation toxicity, alcohol imbibing and cigarette smoke damage.

L-Methionine, an amino acid, is not synthesized in the body and must be obtained from food or dietary supplements. It helps break down fats, preventing their buildup in the liver and arteries, which otherwise would obstruct blood flow to the brain, heart and kidneys.

Rice bran, the broken seed coat of cereal grain, lowers serum cholesterol.

Pectin, a fiber, removes unwanted metals and toxins, lowers cholesterol, reduces heart disease and protects against radiation.

Flax powder from flax seed provides omega-3 fatty acids (linoleic and linolenic acids) for healthy homeostasis.

Garlic, among the most valuable of earth's foods, lowers elevated
blood pressure, thins the blood by inhibiting platelet aggregation,
reduces blood clots, prevents heart attacks, lowers serum cholesterol, stimulates the immune system and aids digestion.

The Oral Chelation Formula Utilized by Dr. Shah

Each chelating physician makes use of his or her own groups of favorite
nutritional ingredients to accomplish oral chelation therapy for patients
who are undergoing IV EDTA. And such formulations usually are taken
routinely for purposes of health maintenance after the patients' comple-
tion of the chelation treatment. Other informed consumers take oral
chelation formulas as medical preventive food supplements. For instance, coauthor Dr. Hitendra H. Shah utilizes just such an oral chelation formula (shown in **Table 11-3**). For more information see
Appendix D.

Essential fatty acids (EFAs) as well as the vitamins B_{12}, B_6, folic acid,
C and E have been purposely left out of the formulation used by Dr.
Shah due to the desire of most health care professionals to adjust these
nutrients according to their patients' individual needs. A good multivitamin and multimineral formula containing antioxidants such as beta carotene, vitamin C and vitamin E should be seriously considered as an
addition to the diet along with this oral chelation therapy formula. Since
most patients take various kinds of multivitamins, chelating physicians
do not want to duplicate this dose.

Supplementing one's diet with EFAs may also help to lower the level
of homocysteine, the known free-radical generator that's capable of oxi-
dizing cholesterol, and is one of the major contributing factors in heart
disease. Omega-3 essential fatty acids are confirmed as useful in reducing high LDL cholesterol levels. They prevent heart attacks by eliminating clotting and arterial damage. Omega-6 EFAs have been shown to
decrease the aggregation or stickiness of platelets, allowing them to pass
through the arteries without danger of clotting. Dr. Shah advises his
patients to use Omega-3 EFA from salmon oil or for vegetarians to
supplement their food intake by utilizing flax seed oil or borage oil or
black currant oil. Most important, recent studies have proven that the
three B-vitamins B_6, B_{12} and folic acid do dramatically lower homocysteine blood levels.

TABLE 11-3

DR. SHAH'S

ORAL CHELATION THERAPY FORMULA

Contents: Six Tablets Contain:

L-Taurine	600 mg
Magnesium (rice amino acid chelate)	300 mg
Magnesium aspartate	20 mg
Potassium (chloride)	290 mg
Potassium aspartate	20 mg
Calcium (rice amino acid chelate)	150 mg
Calcium aspartate	10 mg
Raw heart concentrate	150 mg
Hawthorne berries (*Crateagus oxycantha*)	250 mg
Gentian (*Gentiana lutea*)	50 mg
Selenium aspartate	100 mcg
Chromium picolinate	200 mcg
L-Carnitine	150 mg
Chondroitin sulphate-A	50 mg
CoEnzyme Q_{10}	150 mg
Bromelain	100 mg
Thyroid	150 mg
Choline bitartrate	250 mg
Inositol	125 mg
L-Methionine	30 mg
L-Tyrosine	500 mg

Collectively, all of the nutrients listed in the above two formulas, Dr. Loquasto's and the one used by Dr. Shah, offer synergistic actions for preventive oral chelation therapy. If a person is symptomatically ill with cardiovascular or peripheral vascular disorders or other degenerative diseases, however, it must be emphasized (and it is so emphatically articulated by every health professional knowledgeable about the intravenous form of chelation therapy) that *oral chelation therapy is no substitute for intravenous chelation therapy to completely correct diseases.* Sometimes it takes months or years to accomplish desired beneficial effects from taking oral chelation therapy, whereas intravenous chelation therapy often is able to achieve these same benefits in days or weeks.

Chapter Twelve

THE COST FOR CHELATION THERAPY

There is no greater reward in our profession than the knowledge that God has entrusted us with the physical care of His people. The Almighty has reserved for Himself the power to create life but He has assigned to a few of us the responsibility of keeping in good repair their bodies in which this life is sustained.

—ELMER HESS, M.D. past president, AMA
American Weekly, April 24, 1955

Chelating Physicians Take Treatment Themselves

Yiwen Y. Tang, M.D., of Reno, Nevada told the ad hoc committee of the Scientific Advisory Board of the California Medical Association (CMA) in 1976, "I was born in 1922. I have had one hundred thirty-eight treatments with chelation therapy—not in the expectation to cure any disease, but because I just wanted to do something preventic so that I may remain in the state of health I am now."

Dr. Farr Gave His Mother Chelation Therapy

Charles H. Farr, M.D., Ph.D., of Oklahoma City, Oklahoma, supplied for publication the case history and photographs of his mother, Mrs.

W. E. (Myrtle) Farr of Oklahoma City, Oklahoma, who at the time of her arteriosclerotic problem was seventy-two years old. Myrtle Farr was a registered nurse, but she had discontinued working at her profession the previous year because of the onset of senility. Months were going by while she did nothing much more than live from day to day. Most days she could hardly drag herself from bed.

Dr. Farr said. "I was becoming concerned because my mother was confused, forgetful and had lost all interest in life in general and herself in particular. She suffered with all the classical signs of *senile dementia,* or chronic brain syndrome, which is a result of cerebral arteriosclerosis. I started her on chelation therapy as soon as I could talk my father into taking the treatment, too. She refused to take it by herself.

"My mother was treated quite satisfactorily as you can see from the two photographs [Photograph 12-1] I have supplied. One picture was

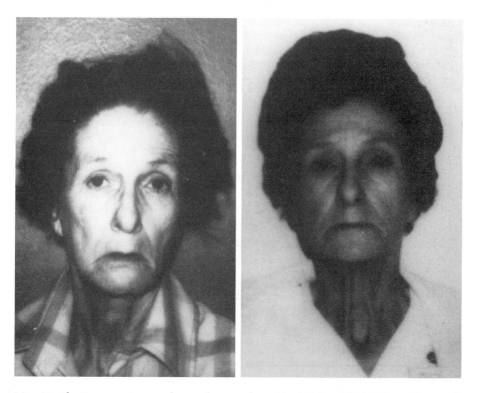

Mrs. Myrtle Farr was in an advanced state of senility in May 1974, when *Photograph 12-1* (left) was taken. Four months later, the 73-year-old nurse was able to return to her profession (*Photograph 13-2*, right), after a series of chelation treatments.

taken May 21, 1974 before I gave my mother chelation therapy. The other picture was taken August 29, 1974 after she received a series of treatments. It indicates her change back to her former status as a very proud and alert person. In this late photograph she was seventy-three years of age and returned to private duty nursing working full eight-hour shifts. The picture shows her wearing her nurse's uniform."

Dr. Farr said that, when dealing with cerebral arteriosclerosis, a chelating physician cannot predict the outcome of treatment. His own experience with administering EDTA infusion to approximately three thousand senile patients has shown him that significant improvement occurs in about 50 percent of these elderly people. He believes that a 50 percent chance of improvement is worth the investment of time and money in chelation therapy. His experience shows that while chelation is not a cure-all, it is far better than abandoning patients to a hopelessly impaired senile state.

Dr. Harper Persuades His Mother

"After starting to practice chelation therapy," said the now deceased Harold W. Harper, M.D., of Los Angeles, "I encouraged my mother for almost three years to take treatment from me. She was sixty-eight years old and had severe arthritis at the time. I saw the terrible condition she was in, limping and hardly able to walk. She was overweight and had high blood pressure. Finally her pain became so great she decided to try anything—even treatment from her son. When she arrived by plane for chelation, she could not put one foot in front of the other without stumbling from stiffness and pain.

"I did a diagnostic workup on my mother and began the EDTA infusion. Between the fifth and seventh treatment she walked without a limp and had more energy than she'd shown in ten years. By the time she had taken the tenth treatment she was walking more than a mile a day and couldn't be held back because of her excess energy. There was no arthritic pain anymore, and her blood pressure completely returned to normal," said Dr. Harper.

Physicians who employ chelation therapy for vascular occlusive conditions and other diseases find there is the return of a patient's function, in addition to relief of symptoms, as Dr. Harper had found. The rate of patient success is in the area of 80 percent.[1] Noninvasive tests easily remonitor improvement, and if regression has occurred, the patient's entire lifestyle can be reviewed and more chelation therapy given.

Alternatively, if response to chelation has been inadequate and a surgical approach seems warranted, the patient will withstand surgery much better because of the EDTA intravenous injections. General circulation can be improved by receiving the EDTA infusions. Even specific presenting conditions are often relieved by the nonspecific generalized chelation effects.

Invasive radiologic techniques, such as transluminal dilation[2,3] (the passage of light through dilated blood vessels), make chelation more efficacious by allowing better flow to the most obstructed areas. This will reduce the total number of chelation treatments required. There is no limitation as to who should be a recipient of the therapy. It is quite safe and almost riskless. Repeatedly, angina symptoms have been relieved entirely even after the failure of two coronary bypass operations in the same patient.

The Financial Costs of Chelation Therapy

The cash required to finance chelation therapy varies around the country from a low of $60 per treatment to a high of $110. On the West Coast of the United States it tends toward the higher range. The fee along the Eastern seaboard averages about $90 per treatment. Some of these "price" differences relate not so much to the actual chelation infusion but to the adjunctive measures that are employed as well. Each treatment, for instance, may require you to take megadoses of vitamins and minerals because your body is deficient in these nutrients. The costs quoted sometimes include these adjunctive measures.

All the chelating physicians invariably request blood, hair, urine or saliva and feces tests in order to determine vitamin and mineral deficiencies. They do a diet analysis, too, so that you may receive the correct orthomolecular nutrition program specific for your need. The diet analysis forms are among the most thorough investigatory questionnaires. Results are returned to you from a computer. The computer printout tells you what food deficiencies you have and how you may alter your nutritional lifestyle.

Twenty chelation treatments is a usual series. However, twenty treatments are considered the *minimum course* for altering artery pathology that is *mild*. If given for medical *prevention* rather than as a corrective therapy, the number of infusions administered in a series may be less.

Certainly, twenty treatments is not enough to *reverse* a condition of hardening of the arteries that is *severe,* but the series can produce markedly improved functional changes throughout the circulatory system. Most persons' hearts do function better with a series of twenty EDTA infusions taken over seven to fourteen weeks. For the more severe occlusive arterial problems, probably thirty or forty treatments will be recommended for a single series of chelations. With various tests and examinations included, the initial total cost is likely to approach $3,000.

The Time Costs of Chelation Therapy

Among the larger problems faced by people who want EDTA chelation for preventive or therapeutic purposes is the expenditure of time. Cost alone is not the whole obstacle. An individual will ask himself, "How can I visit the doctor's office twice a week and remain there for four to six hours each visit? Can I afford the time? Won't I lose money? Who will run my business? How can I explain it to my boss?"

Most physicians find it difficult to get people to invest time in themselves. The motivation must come from within the individual. A person has to reorder his priorities if preventive medicine and prolonged life is part of his major desires.

On the other hand, heart pain that strikes an individual cannot be argued with. Days, weeks and months will be found for bed confinement to recuperate from a heart attack. If circulatory distress has turned a leg gangrenous, somehow a person finds the time to have the amputation that will save his life.

"I was no different," said Warren M. Levin, M.D., of New York City. "I decided I was going to take chelation twenty years ago, and I just never got around to it because I thought I couldn't afford the time. Finally, I told myself that I've just got to do it! I managed to arrange for the therapy at the end of my full working day. I ate dinner, relaxed a little, then got into bed, put the needle into my own vein and went to sleep. A registered nurse, whom I had hired at regular nursing rates, sat by my bedside all night for a full-eight-hour shift to keep the intravenous drip going at the correct speed. She made sure the chelate did not infiltrate into surrounding tissues. The financial cost to me actually was greater than it is to one of my patients. I was paying a nurse's wages for all those hours that I slept."

Individual treatment times vary for patients, but on the average EDTA administration takes four hours. It will be shorter—as little as two and a half hours—if the patient can tolerate a faster drip. It will be longer—as long as six hours—if the patient has a medical problem such as congestive heart failure and is sensitive to the components in the EDTA solution.

From one to three treatments per week is a usual number, two per week being most common. This will be the schedule except in those instances where the patient has traveled far for a short stay in a hospital facility or doctor's clinic. Then treatment will be given for five days in a row with a two-day pause and five days consecutively again. This consecutive treatment also is administered when the patient is in danger of imminent death and radical measures are required. This daily frequency has been safely applied to thousands of people for over forty years. The thinking by chelating physicians is changing, however. Current medical malpractice conditions and other legal considerations are causing many physicians today to opt for the ultraconservative program of one, two or maybe three treatments per week. As more doctors adopt chelation in more cities, it may someday be possible to avoid lodging and meal costs altogether.

Many doctors give a mini-drip for working people who lack time. They use a half dose of EDTA for 1½ hours. Many patients take the EDTA mini-drip during their lunch breaks. The results may be equally effective as the regular four-hour treatment.

The Cost in Skill and Training

The actual technique of chelation administration does not take much skill on the part of medical professionals. Almost anyone can give it— like delivering a baby—even paraprofessionals perform the technique well. That is one of the aspects of this treatment that upsets organized medicine; no extra special training is required. Any physician anywhere can give it to his patient. Medical service monopoly is taken from the hands of super specialists, such as cardiologists, internists, vascular surgeons, chest surgeons, anesthesiologists and various maintainers of sophisticated hospital facilities. The rendering of medical series is handed back to the general practitioner when he or she administers chelation therapy.

The generally trained medical practitioner or his nurse can take on the responsibility of administration, and that is the key here—*responsibility*. A medical professional has to be able to react responsibly to the patient's possible discomfort during administration or to any side effects afterward. This means simply that the doctor should be knowledgeable of the technique. He or she must attend medical meetings oriented to chelation therapy. He or she also might tour the facilities of other chelating physicians and, of course, the doctor who chelates has to do a *lot* of reading on the subject.

Then you might wonder why, if the treatment is so easy and so simple to administer, the cash costs should be relatively high. There are several pertinent reasons to explain the charges.

First, you must be in the doctor's office for so many hours. During that time the doctor and his staff are responsible for your well-being. Patients pay the physician to take that responsibility.

Second, chelation physicians usually require larger offices and more employees to accommodate the huge amount of traffic that moves in and out. This results in significantly larger overhead to pay.

Next, the physician who chelates must take the time from his practice to attend the required expensive conventions.

Finally, the chelating physician usually has to retain several competent attorneys. Why? Because patients, you and I, have to pay for the doctor's legal risk and the peer pressure he gets from organized medicine. Several chapters that follow tell of the politics involved in chelation therapy. You will read about the intra- and interprofessional stress that physicians face for daring to offer EDTA chelation to their patients.

The Cost of a Singular Chelation Case

Illustrative of the costs in time, money and anxiety connected with chelation therapy is the singular case of George Kavic of West Mifflin, Pennsylvania. He is a retired foreman on permanent disability from United States Steel Corporation. Living on a pension, Kavic did not have the "cash on the barrelhead" required for extensive chelation therapy. Nor did he have the time to earn the cash by taking odd jobs, because he was told by his doctors, "George, don't make any definite plans. You have only three to six months to live!"

Kavic suffered constant pains and burning sensations because three-fourths of his myocardium had been damaged by a series of heart attacks. The angina he felt was so great it took him five minutes to move just ten yards across a room. In addition, his right leg was so circulatorily deficient, it turned blue and claudicated with any weight bearing. His doctors said that they hoped the leg would not have to be amputated because the patient would never survive the operation.

During our interview, George Kavic said, "My cardiologist told me the results of my angiogram. He said that bypass surgery wasn't possible even though I needed it in both my leg and my chest. I had blockage of two coronary arteries that narrowed their openings by 80 percent and 90 percent. The risk that I would die on the operating table was too great.

"I asked the cardiologist what he thought about my taking chelation therapy, and he said that I was nuts to consider it! He also said, 'If you are still living a year from now, then make an appointment with me. You may make it that long, but you have a very tough case.' So I was left waiting to die, but while waiting I had terrible and unbearable pain in my right leg," Kavic said. "I didn't tell my wife because it would frighten her to death. It was blue up to the ankle, and I couldn't walk at all."

Out of desperation, and over his cardiologist's objections, the patient telephoned Dr. H. Ray Evers of Cottonwood, Alabama, to inquire about the chelation treatment. Learning the therapy's cost, Kavic knew that such funds were out of his grasp. But he knew, too, that no alternative lay open, whereas chelation therapy did offer some possibility of relieving his condition at least a little. He hoped he could squeeze another year of life out of having the treatment. Therefore, George Kavic borrowed money from loving friends and relatives. He knew from Dr. Evers' telephone estimate that about thirty chelations were required to be given daily with a pause on the weekends. That would be five or six weeks of hospitalization that he had to finance, besides the airfare south to the hospital where Dr. Evers administered the treatment.

The trip south had Kavic almost exhausted. He experienced feelings of tremendous anxiety. "I was scared," Kavic confessed. "I wondered if this trip was worth it."

The patient took thirty-two chelation treatments. Physical improvement began for him on about the fourth treatment day. After one week he telephoned home to report that he was able to walk a mile without feeling chest pains or leg pains. After five weeks Kavic's pedometer showed that he walked six miles a day without any difficulty.

George Kavic told us, "I haven't had the return of symptoms. I have no family doctor anymore. I don't take any medication, except with each meal I add five food supplements that I buy at a health food store. I swallow these vitamins with my food, and I feel like a million dollars. I walk regularly four, five and six miles a day because that's part of my rehabilitation program—regular exercise. I returned for a recheck of my laboratory tests about ten months after the chelation treatment. The readouts were magnificent. Dr. Evers exhibited me that my triglycerides, cholesterol and other tests all showed improvement over the first time. Then I had five more bottles of the EDTA solution too, for a total of thirty-seven treatments."

George Kavic looked like a classic example of good health. He was energetic and forceful—so much so that occasionally he pushed himself to the point of heart pain. Those pains remind him that once he was told he had less than six months to live. It is now eleven years since George told us this story, and the man is still doing well.

Chapter Thirteen

HEALTH INSURANCE COVERAGE FOR INTRAVENOUS CHELATION THERAPY

The private insurance companies have been a massive success in selling health insurance, but they have been an equally massive failure in providing cost control and effective health coverage. The companies are so preoccupied with writing up new policies that they have written off any responsibility for the health system. The insurance industry works for profit. To the insurance companies, people are the enemy, because every private claim is a threat to corporate profit.

—U.S. SENATOR EDWARD M. KENNEDY,
The American Legion Magazine, July 1971

The Cure of Mr. Aubrey Is Not Usual and Customary

Alfred Aubrey of San Diego, California, was sixty-eight years old and an eligible Medicare recipient. He appreciated the Social Security benefits he received when he got them. Mr. Aubrey had been relieved of the symptoms of coronary artery heart disease. He was saved from having another heart attack, too. But since the treatment this Medicare recipient received was something other than open-heart surgery, the Social Security Administration refused to pay his doctor's bill.

"Regardless of the desperateness of Mr. Aubrey's health situation, and regardless of the effectiveness of the treatment, there is no coverage," ruled the Medicare hearing officer. The federal government in effect decided how the patient could be treated and how he could use his body. Why? Why should the Medicare insurance carrier and the government's hearing officer deny payment for chelation therapy to save a life? Because "this was not the *usual and customary* treatment for the conditions diagnosed," said Clyde H. Burgardt, the hearing officer.

Alfred Aubrey received intravenous chelation therapy for angina pains, diabetes and postcardiovascular accident. He had been suffering from acute atherosclerosis of the coronary arteries and was in immediate danger of being struck down by a second heart attack. Nevertheless, the involved insurance carrier for Medicare, Occidental Life Insurance Company of California, which was obligated to pay 80 percent of the patient's $515 medical bill, reimbursed him only $8.50—even though he was a worthy Medicare recipient. Sounds silly—downright ridiculous—doesn't it Shrugging your shoulders you might say, "Well I don't know Medicare's side of the story." OK! I'll lay out the facts, and you be the judge.

The following information comes directly from Hearing Officer Burgardt's decision document. Mr. Burgardt was an independent licensed insurance claim adjuster of San Gabriel, California. He was called upon to conduct a "Fair Hearing" in San Diego to decide on benefits the insurance recipient deserved under Part B of the Medicare Program.

A Brief Explanation of Medicare

Medicare is a program of medical insurance under the Social Security Act passed into law in 1965. The program offers people over age sixty-five health insurance and consists of two parts.

Part A, *hospital insurance,* is basic and is financed out of compulsory contributions paid by employers and workers in their working years. It tends to be more liberally administered in that it pays for therapies that are not "usual and customary."

Part B, *medical insurance,* is supplementary and optional. It helps to pay "allowable charges" for doctors' and surgeons' fees and other medical services and items not included under hospital insurance. Persons over age sixty-five voluntarily pay a monthly premium for Part B, and the federal government matches the sum. Also the participant pays the first $100 of expenses for covered services in a calendar year and 20 percent of the annual costs above $100.

Unlike the hospitals which are direct payment recipients, claimants of Part B must request their own reimbursements by filling out forms and sending them to the appropriate insurance carrier office. The claimants may offer assignment of benefits to servicing doctors if the doctors will accept them. Otherwise, claimants must pay the medical bills and attempt to be reimbursed from the carrier.

Part B medical insurance covers: (1) Physicians' and surgeons' services; (2) home health services ordered by a doctor up to 100 visits a year, even if the patient has not been in a hospital; (3) other health and medical equipment, surgical dressings and splints, and diagnostic tests.[1,2]

Millions of Part B Medicare dollars are spent annually by health insurance carriers. The insurance companies are paid administrative fees to spend participants' and U.S. taxpayers' money (channeled through the Social Security Administration). Every payment request usually is subjected to rigid scrutiny under insurance regulations over which we, the medical consumers, have no control. Because insurance home office people seem to assume in advance that all claims are fraudulent or excessive, the claimant is treated as if he is a crook. This is the usual insurance company practice, as the chapter opening quote by Senator Edward Kennedy says: "To the insurance companies, people are the enemy . . ." If health insurance companies can "save" money for Uncle Sam's health programs, more of the funds may become available for "administrative purposes"—that is, home office wages, salary increases and bonuses. Wherever the insurance company employees can, they "save."

The Shocking Case of Alfred Aubrey

Alfred Aubrey was a Medicare Part B participant, and, for the second time in his life, his heart was seized with pain. The angina was so knifelike that he was unable to perform any substantial physical activity. He could not even carry on as a church usher. The slightest exertion—including slow walking—brought on severe chest pains. A surgeon to whom he went for help advised Mr. Aubrey that he was in dire danger of death. His need, he was told, was to have open-heart surgery to correct his angina. But the heart surgeon warned also that the mortality risk for him in such a surgery was 50 percent. He had a 50–50 chance of dying from the operation.

Despite the threat of death, the patient consented to the operation anyway. Subsequent hospital tests then showed Mr. Aubrey was not eligible—not a fit candidate—for open-heart surgery. In effect, he was refused the operation and left to die.

The hopeless man turned to William J. Saccoman, M.D., of El Cajon, California, who is a specialist in family practice. The patient appealed to Dr. Saccoman for any possible solution to his several health problems. Mr. Aubrey left it to the physician to choose the type of treatment, and he paid for the various services that were rendered.

After receiving a course of chelation care from Dr. Saccoman, the patient's chest pains disappeared. Clyde Burgardt wrote: "He was able to resume normal physical activities, without bringing on a return of the angina," a direct quote from the Fair Hearing officer's record. "His blood pressure returned to well within normal limits, and his heart action has been good subsequent to and as a result of the services performed by Dr. Saccoman," Mr. Burgardt continued.

Aubrey testified at the Medicare Fair Hearing that now he walks four miles daily, before breakfast, and this he was able to do shortly after being treated with EDTA chelation. Also his blood sugar level, which had been elevated from diabetes, returned to normal.

Aubrey, now a *former* heart victim, visited another physician, Dr. Cooper. The patient went strictly for his personal gratification in order to get a medical checkup by an impartial observer. Dr. Cooper pronounced the man's heart good and his lungs clear. He could no longer be considered a cardiac patient.

Was it reasonable and necessary for Alfred Aubrey to seek help from Dr. Saccoman? Is it something you would have done to save your own life? Do you believe Medicare, Part B, should have compensated this retired person for payment of the physician's bill in the amount of $364? The sum due for reimbursement consists of 80 percent of the bill for which the carrier was responsible, but the carrier paid only $8.50.

Regulation 405.310, as set forth in the Hearing Officers Handbook, states that Medicare, Part B, shall make no payment for services "which are not reasonable and necessary for the diagnosis or treatment of illness or injury." Occidental Life Insurance Company of California disallowed the expense of Aubrey's chelation therapy. The carrier had labeled the treatment "experimental and not tested, as to treatment of arteriosclerotic heart disease" and "is not considered the usual and customary treatment."

The hearing officer ruled only on the question of what was "reasonable and necessary." The decision he rendered said, "The controlling thing here is that the Law, Regulations and Guidelines do provide coverage *only* for usual and customary treatment for the conditions diagnosed. The greater weight of evidence here is that this treatment was not the usual and customary treatment for the conditions diagnosed. Therefore, regardless of the desperateness of Mr. Aubrey's health situation, and regardless of the effectiveness of the treatment, there is no coverage."

If the patient had been accepted as a candidate for open-heart surgery, Occidental Life Insurance Company of California, representing Medicare, Parts B and A, would have paid the whole $50,000 coronary bypass surgical fee, plus the accompanying hospital costs—about $25,000 more, less the small amount for which the patient was responsible. And with that $25,000 expenditure, Mr. Aubrey was told his chance of *survival* was only 50 percent! Nevertheless, the carrier refused to reimburse for chemical endarterectomy with EDTA, a safe and life-preserving procedure. And its refusal was upheld by this "Fair Hearing."

Following such a "Fair Hearing," elderly citizens supposedly covered by Part B Medicare, but denied the benefits owed them, are informed that they have *no* recourse to the courts—and they do not! There is no appeal from the hearing officer's decision.

Medicare, Part B, Also Refuses Payment for Pre-Chelation Tests

It has been reported that 20 percent of vein grafts put in place as substitutes for occluded portions of coronary arteries become occluded themselves within one year of surgery. Vein grafts, in fact, have been shown as accelerators of disease in the very same arteries that receive the grafts. Not infrequently, a new total occlusion occurs on either side of the graft.[3-6]

New occlusion *did* take place in the arteries of Walter W. Watson of San Francisco after he had been subjected to two previous heart attacks and had undergone two bypass operations, performed one after the other. Both heart surgeries were covered by medical and hospital insurance to the tune of $50,000 per procedure. The reoccurrence of occlusions of his coronary arteries affected Mr. Watson two years later. The slightest physical effort, even slow walking, caused him tremendous chest pain. A third heart operation seemed a certainty, but he was not anxious to face bypass surgery again.

Walter Watson brought his health problem to Garry F. Gordon, M.D., then the director of the Sacramento (California) Medical Preventics Clinic, who administered chelation therapy to him. The patient realized great therapeutic benefit with complete elimination of his discomfort.

Watson paid his $1,393.75 bill to Dr. Gordon for medical services rendered and, since he was a Medicare beneficiary, submitted the bill for reimbursement to Blue Shield of California, the responsible Part B Medicare carrier. But Blue Shield of California allowed only $10 of the total billed. It was an allowance for just one office visit. Payment for the remainder of the services was refused on the grounds that the Social Security Administration has specifically stated that the services and tests connected with chelation therapy are not a benefit of the Medicare program.

A Fair Hearing was requested by the Sacramento Medical Preventics Clinic on behalf of Mr. Watson. The hearing was held in the Sacramento, California, Social Security Administration office.

In attendance at the hearing were Dr. Gordon, Robert Wolfe, M.D., a Blue Shield of California medical advisor, and Elizabeth Rossi, an administrative representative of the carrier. C. W. Lemming of San Francisco was the Medicare hearing officer.

Mrs. Rossi quoted from the Medicare Carriers' Manual, Part 3, Section 2050.4 (D)(1)(b), which states, "Endrate (EDTA) may be considered a benefit of the Medicare program only for the emergency treatment of hypercalcemia, and or control of ventricular arrhythmias and heart block associated with digitalis toxicity." Walter Watson was *not* a victim of these conditions.

Dr. Wolfe said, "Chelation is not a benefit, and when a service is not a benefit the tests done to monitor it, such as in this case: the quantitative urine, the biofeedback, the thermography (and the plethysmography), also are deleted. These tests are not payable. This is a specific regulation. Now we could discuss this matter until doomsday, but it is not in our jurisdiction. This is up to the Bureau of Health Insurance and the FDA [Food and Drug Administration] to make the decision. When they have it they will put it down in [Medicare] regulations and then we can pay it. Until then our hands are tied."

Dr. Gordon asked, "Would you agree that if I did an electrocardiogram [EKG], and it comes back showing ischemic heart disease then my judgment must have been correct to have done the procedure?"

Dr. Wolfe replied, "An EKG is payable as part of the standard physical examination on a patient with cardiac symptoms."

Dr. Gordon said, "OK! Then a patient who has symptoms of vascular disease and is unable to walk [such as Mr. Watson] and has loss of memory, central nervous system symptoms, probably carotid artery disease, and whose study comes back positive, would have to be paid because it is obvious that an EKG is no more accepted a procedure then plethysmography or thermography (when performed prior to chelation therapy)."

Dr. Wolfe said, "This, again, is beyond our jurisdiction because the level of the screening test is something that regulations dictate and not us."

Dr. Gordon said, "Dr. Wolfe, are you going to state that this man, who came to me unable to walk, with two previous heart attacks, is being *screened* for arteriosclerosis when I do these tests on him?"

Dr. Wolfe answered meekly, "No, I'm not."

Dr. Gordon said, "Then let's get that clear! I have checked with Cedars of Lebanon Hospital in Los Angeles prior to coming to this meeting. Hal Ross, D.Sc., of the hospital's Non-invasive Vascular Laboratory advised me that they charge exactly twice what I charge for plethysmography and thermography, and they get paid for outpatient care by Southern California Medicare every single day. Just because my physician reviewer [who is the same Dr. Wolfe in Northern California] is not knowledgeable about these areas [diagnostic techniques] doesn't mean it is not accepted by medical experts around the country such as at Harvard University Medical School and the University of Vermont Medical Center."

Dr. Wolfe and Mrs. Rossi then admitted that they specifically do not make Medicare payments for diagnostic tests to determine the feasibility of using *chelation therapy* on a patient because chelation therapy is considered "investigational" and "experimental."

Once again the specter of closed minds among Medicare bureaucrats was causing these people to deny reimbursement even for diagnostic tests connected with heart disease prior to chelation. Yet, every reputable journal that physicians read regarding *bypass surgery* says it remains a controversial procedure. Famous heart surgeon Denton Cooley told a medical convention that the surgical bypass procedure should probably be stopped. But Medicare, Part A and B, does pay all costs less the usual deductibles for the bypass operation.

Still, in the opinion of Mr. Lemming, the Fair Hearing officer, the clinical and laboratory tests and treatments received by Walter W. Watson were not considered a benefit of the Medicare program. The patient was refused reimbursement of his medical bill, even for the diagnostic tests.

The irony and injustice of this ruling against Mr. Watson is that the diagnostic tests were performed to measure accurately the extent of his vascular disease. These same test costs would have been paid if they had been performed by any other facility besides a clinic where chelation therapy is carried out. This is true by Medicare's own rulings. The tests should have been paid when done by Dr. Gordon's clinic. But organized medicine today steadfastly refuses to recognize the value of chelation, possibly because it is not really understood. And organized medicine in large measure determines what health insurance benefits will and will not be paid.

A Private Group Health Insurance Carrier Will Not Cover Chelation

Typical of this sort of violation of a patient's health insurance rights was another nonpayment ruling after the patient applied to a private group health insurance carrier to fulfill contract obligations for which the policy holder paid premiums. The violation was experienced by John Michaels of Woodenville, Washington.

At age forty-five, Mr. Michaels developed disabling angina pectoris. His visit to a cardiologist for an exercise tolerance test with electrocardiogram showed that he was the victim of severe ischemia of the heart muscle. He suffered with 2 millimeters of S-T segment depression on his electrocardiogram. This degree of depression indicated an impaired coronary blood flow.

Mr. Michaels was stunned by the realization that he was now unable to fulfill his longtime dream to become a gentleman farmer. The farm he had just purchased was useless to him. He could not pick up a spade-load of dirt without being incapacitated by angina pain. His cardiologist recommended the coronary bypass operation as the *only* option available. Michaels wasn't convinced, however, and he pondered his decision.

Another doctor, Leo J. Bolles, M.D., of Bellevue, Washington, had been the Michaels' family physician for a while. "John Michaels came to visit me to discuss whether or not he should have the coronary bypass surgery done," said Dr. Bolles. "I pointed out that there really was an alternative, and the patient elected not to have the operation performed but to try chelation therapy first.

"I administered ten chelation treatments to him," Dr. Bolles said. "I then cautiously performed a two-step electrocardiograph which turned out to be positive, although it was not as bad as had been his previous readings.

"I administered another ten chelations to the patient and exercised him again on a two-step test. He was still slightly positive but by this time had absolutely no anginal pain symptoms. He could work seven hours a day doing hard manual labor on his farm.

"I gave him a third series of ten chelations and then decided to send Mr. Michaels back to the cardiologist to have a new cardiological evaluation."

With a smile Dr. Bolles said, "This cardiologist exercised him very vigorously for about five minutes. He walked the patient up and down the two-step for the whole time, but the doctor could not produce any symptoms of coronary ischemia. Mr. Michaels no longer showed any S-T segment depression on his electrocardiograph. The cardiologist sent me a copy of the tracing but didn't interpret it. And the patient has been asymptomatic since."

Although at the outset of treatment Michaels had been told by Dr. Bolles that health insurance refuses to pay for chelation therapy, the recovered patient submitted a claim anyway. His logic was that if he had acceded to the orthodox medical option—heart surgery—his private policy would have paid the bills without a murmur. The same health insurance should then cover the tests and treatments he did choose, Michaels reasoned. But it did not.

The Prudential Life Insurance Company was the private carrier for group health insurance issued by the Teamsters' Union in Seattle. Michaels was a holder of that union's insurance plan. That private carrier was literally making a decision for John Michaels as to how he must treat his body. The insurance company was determining his treatment for him, according to the dictates of its policy clauses and by its payment or nonpayment of his health-connected bills.

Michaels and Correll Confront the Health Insurance Carrier

Michaels became angry when the reply to his claim stated that the therapy he had selected was not "usual and necessary." "Usual, chelation treatment may not be," the patient said, "but *necessary* for me, it sure as hell was!"

He went directly to the insurance company offices to demand a hearing. Surprising as it may sound, the hearing was not granted until two years later. William D. Correll, who was Dr. Bolles' business manager, accompanied the patient at this time and attended a two-hour meeting with Prudential Insurance Company representatives. Mr. Correll also was executive director of the Northwestern Academy of Preventive Medicine at the time.

"I sat down at the table with the chief Prudential representative," said William Correll. "He opened a folder and stated, 'We are following chelation very closely across the country.' "

Correll replied, "Let's get to the facts in the case at hand. Mr. Michaels was suffering angina. He could not work at all. He suffered with intermittent claudication and a host of other health problems. Today his condition is altogether improved. He's working eight hours a day plus running this large farm. He has no angina. The pain left him during the course of treatment and has not returned to this point which is two years afterward. The patient is well. Those are the facts!"

At that meeting, Michaels and Correll met with narrow minds and rule book regulations as if they had struck against a stone wall. The stock insurance industry phase, "this is not usual and customary procedure," was heard over and over.

Correll said, "That insurance representative told me, 'It really doesn't matter to us whether the patient got well or died. What matters to us is that the doctor did not use usual and customary procedure.' For John Michaels, what was usual and customary might possibly have killed him," concluded William Correll.

Medicare, Part A, Is Forced to Pay for Chelation Care

If both kinds of carriers, the private health insurance companies and the carriers that administer Medicare, Part B, deny reimbursement to policy holders who take chelation care, is any chelation insurance available? Yes, Medicare, Part A, the hospital protection for U.S. citizens sixty-five years old and older, provides reimbursement for payment of therapeutic EDTA chelation bills. The payment will be made if service is rendered in a hospital. Medicare, Part A, has been forced by legal precedent to pay hospitals for the costs involved with chelation. Be advised, however, that each case is judged individually.

The precedent was set in the case of Mr. D. D. Dominey, Sr., of Atlanta, Georgia, who was sixty-nine years old at the time of his admission to Columbia General Hospital, Andalusia, Alabama, from November 29 to December 11, 1970. That was the practice location of H. Ray Evers, M.D., before he moved to Montgomery, Alabama and then on to Cottonwood, Alabama.

Mr. Dominey had been the head of three corporations, but then he found himself becoming senile and unable to function. He withdrew as corporate chief.

Dominey had a fifteen-year history of heart and angina attacks and had suffered a cerebral vascular accident (stroke) with some apparent hemorrhage into the cerebral tissue. He was experiencing numbness in his right arm and hand, a cough and chest pain upon exertion, severe pain in his legs at night, weakness, anxiety, tension and severe precordial pain. Despite his medications, which were nitroglycerine and cardilate, his condition was becoming worse. His ophthalmologist testified that after he had examined Dominey's eyes and had seen the terrible condition of his blood vessels, he advised the patient to be hospitalized or his health problem could be fatal.

Upon the patient's admission to Columbia General Hospital, Dr. Evers administered extensive diagnostic tests to him. The result was a diagnosis of coronary heart disease, arteriosclerotic heart disease, and moderately severe generalized arteriosclerosis. Dr. Evers decided on chelation therapy as the method of treatment. Dominey received ten intravenous infusions of Endrate®, daily myoflex treatments (a form of physical therapy), medications and a special diet. His condition was closely monitored to make certain that any essential minerals lost during chelation were replaced. He improved steadily and was discharged greatly improved, although he was still feeling numbness in his arm and hand.

Chelation Therapy Makes Dominey a New Man

Within a few weeks of treatment, Dominey found he was able to discontinue his cardilate and seldom had to take a nitroglycerine pill. The ophthalmologist, upon a reexamination of the patient's eyes, was amazed to observe that he was like a new person after chelation therapy.

In fact, Dominey *felt* like a new person. His angina had gone away altogether and he could walk all he wanted. He was subject to absolutely no intermittent claudication, no night pain, no chest pain, and once again he found himself sexually potent where he had not been so before EDTA chelation. He got married. He again took over total control of the three corporations in which he held stock.

Dominey paid the hospital's $3,500 bill for the chelation therapy he had received and then filed for Medicare, Part A, reimbursement for which he was qualified. Medicare refused the reimbursement.

Having considerable independent wealth, and with a long history behind him of having paid large federal taxes, and having made Social Security payments for himself and his employees, Mr. Dominey decided to demand the Medicare money to which he was entitled. He sued the Social Security Administration for hospital insurance benefits under Title XVIII of the Social Security Act, as amended.

Now you should be made aware of the unique system under which Social Security is administered. For instance, the Social Security System has its own court system. The legal administrators, judges and hearing officers are all hired and paid salaries by the Social Security Administration. In other words, they are dependent for their paychecks upon a system that they are asked to rule for or against. They make rulings in areas where they have a conflict of interests which would likely favor their employer.

There is an arbitration level in the Social Security System to which a plaintiff applies before he sues. Dominey made application for arbitration and then won his case at that level. The system's arbitrator had ruled against the Social Security Administration, who was his own boss, since the facts spoke for themselves. The Dominey case was that strong.

However, the Social Security Administration did not accept the arbitrator's ruling. It had a lot to lose if it did. Just how much is at stake if Medicare must pay for chelation therapy, I shall disclose more fully in Chapter Fifteen.

Dominey Wins Case After Case

The Dominey case progressed up the line with multiple appeals. The first appeal was heard on October 12, 1973 by Judge Cutler, who also found for the claimant and ruled that Medicare should reimburse him. The Social Security Administration, realizing that this might set a precedent for payments to a hundred thousand other patients, appealed the case to the next higher administrative Social Security Court.

Dominey's case did not come up again for about a year and a half. By that time Judge Cutler, who had heard the first appeal, had become a higher appeals court judge in the administrative law system. He reheard the appeal himself on February 24, 1975. Social Security Courts are not legal courts but are administrative only, and it was legitimate for the judge to reassess his own prior decision.

To collect $3,500 in paid medical expenses Dominey was spending upwards of $15,000 in legal fees and other expenses. Medical experts flew to Atlanta, where the appeals hearings were held. Additional costs amounting to $10,000 were paid out by physician witnesses themselves in travel expenses, lost wages and lost time. Expert witnesses included Drs. Bruce Halstead, H. Ray Evers, Harold W. Harper, Norman Clarke, Sr., and others. Dominey again won his case.

The Social Security Administration brought a motion for review to the Appeals Council in Atlanta, presided over by council members Marshall C. Gardner and Irwin Friedenberg. More money was spent for more witnesses to appear. Dominey persisted with his claim and dipped into his pocket again. Finally he won! The Appeals Council's opinion was that "the claimant's twelve-day hospital stay was *reasonable and necessary.*" Dominey's win was a benefit for every Medicare, Part A, recipient—within limitations.

Among other findings in Mr. Dominey's favor, the two Appeals Council members wrote: "It was *reasonable and necessary* that the extensive diagnostic testing be given the claimant on an in-patient basis because he was severely ill.

"When chelation therapy was decided as the proper course of treatment, it was *reasonable and necessary* that these treatments be given the claimant on an in-patient basis so that his condition could be properly monitored.

"The Claimant received services which were *reasonable and necessary* to be given by professional medical personnel on an in-patient basis for treatment of his illnesses.

"It is the decision of the Appeals Council that payment may be made on the claimant's behalf under Part A of Title XVIII of the Social Security Act for the services furnished him by Columbia General Hospital from November 29 to December 11, 1970. The decision of the administration law judge is hereby affirmed."

The decision was handed down on December 1, 1975 and Dominey collected his reimbursement soon after that. In that way, Medicare, Part A, was forced to pay for chelation care, but it still fights each recipient's payment request on an individual basis.

The Health Insurance Conspiracy Against Us

It is obvious to anyone who reads the signs that the health insurance industry has conspired and is conspiring to avoid paying patients' claims wherever it can get away with it. Insurance carriers are in subtle conspiracy in part by their abrogation of our freedom of choice to select the therapy we require and the therapy our physicians recommend. Being of sound mind, having complete information and feeling full confidence in our physicians, we are owed the right to seek various medical alternatives besides what the medical profession establishment dictates is "usual and customary" and what the health insurance industry decides is "necessary and reasonable."

Breach of contract is being perpetrated on every person who holds a health insurance policy. *"Premium Payer Be Damned"* is the overriding motto of health insurance industry leaders when it comes to chelation therapy. They use political agitation to intensify what best fits their own industrial health and not the public's physical and mental health. A strong insurance lobby in Washington attempts to supplant the law in taxation. It nets the insurance companies tax-free buildings and other tax-free properties. If they are able to alter the tax laws in their favor, isn't it logical that they would attempt the manipulation of therapies, too? They have made exactly that attempt and have been exceedingly successful.

The insurance industry, which is supposed to furnish underwriting guarantees and protection of the nation's health, is able to suppress therapy through local medical societies that are uninformed or misinformed. As a result, the *only* procedures they recommend just happen to be horribly expensive, require the services of many highly trained (and costly) specialists, involve lengthy hospital stays—and are only marginally successful!

Bypass surgery is among these silver pocket-lining procedures foisted on the unknowing American public by medical pressure groups (as we shall see in the next chapter). Another way organized medicine lines its pockets with health insurance company silver is with drug therapy for which health insurance policies pay. Drug therapy supports many medical functions, such as the publication of medical journals, the running of conventions and other physician activities related to health. The physician members of organized medicine often carry investment portfolios filled with drug stocks and various business-health enterprises.

In fact, many practicing physicians in the medical mainstream sit on the boards of directors of these health-related enterprises. More often than not, they are the very physicians who influence health insurance company decisions. The health insurance industry responds to the medical care industry. They conspire jointly.

Chapter Fourteen

BYPASS SURGERY: THE CONTROVERSIAL ANTAGONIST TO CHELATION THERAPY

Surgery is always second best. If you can do something else, it's better.
Surgery is limited. It is operating on someone who has no place else to go.

—JOHN KIRLIN, M.D., heart surgeon,
Mayo Clinic, *Time*, May 3, 1963

Don't Get Chest Pains in Spokane

"Get chest pains in Spokane, Washington, and ninety minutes later you'll be on the operating table with your sternum split open having a triple bypass," said Harold W. Harper, M.D. On a number of occasions, in interviews and from the public speaking platform before groups of holistic physicians, Dr. Harper told the story of the marvelous efficiency of Spokane chest surgeons.

Public and private ambulance companies in Spokane speed any person complaining of chest pains to a particular hospital emergency room. As the ambulance dashes through crowded streets, the driver radios ahead, and the surgical team assembles in readiness. No time is wasted in case a cardiopulmonary bypass surgery is needed.

Bypass surgery is a shunting operation in which a vascular prosthesis is used between the aorta femoral artery to relieve obstruction of the lower abdominal aorta, its bifurcation and the proximal iliac branches (the aortoiliac bypass); or another operation to shunt blood through vein grafts or other conduits from the aorta to branches of the coronary arteries, in order to increase the flow beyond the local obstruction (the coronary bypass); or a third operation in which a vascular prosthesis is used to bypass an obstruction in the femoral artery where the graft may be synthetic material such as Dacron, or autologous tissue such as bovine carotid artery (the femoropopliteal bypass).

The coronary bypass is the most popular chest surgery done today. It takes tremendous skill, much training and a large investment in the surgeon's education, along with some highly sophisticated and costly equipment supplied by the hospital involved. The whole procedure must go quickly and cleanly with great efficiency of motion and time. Every health professional involved works as part of the team.

Dr. Harper described the Spokane hospital operation as among the most efficient. "First you receive an arteriogram [angiogram]; then a shave and cleaning of the chest. The anesthesiologist arrives and the operation begins," said Dr. Harper. "The surgeon's first cut is made before an hour and a half has passed."

Medical specialists shunt your blood to oxygenate it while your heart lies exposed. This is *the cardiopulmonary bypass,* a method of maintaining extracorporeal circulation by diversion of the blood flow away from the heart; blood is passed through a pump oxygenator (heart–lung machine) and then returned to the arterial side of the circulation.

Consider what might have happened to you just a few hours before. Luckily, the pain struck when your family was there and someone called for help. The ambulance with red light flashing and siren screaming rushed you to the big sterile building. At the hospital they didn't even ask what was wrong but wheeled you directly to the cardiopulmonary laboratory. There, some masked and white-coated doctor cut into your arm or leg under a local anesthetic and pushed a catheter through the vein into your heart. A technician took X-ray pictures as dye traveled through. The films were developed.

"Just sit there," you were told as they went into the hallway to speak with the little woman.

Your wife stands there wringing her hands and being brave.

"Your husband has had a heart attack," said the doctor. "He shows an abnormal angiogram. Come right in here and we'll show you the pictures. There! See how this artery is blocked and that artery is blocked? Your husband must have surgery immediately! Here is the operating permit to sign; he's not capable of signing."

In shock, the little woman asks, "Well, what if . . . what if he doesn't have the surgery?"

"He'll die! Your husband won't have enough oxygen to his heart tissue to live until morning."

She signs and you undergo a $50,000 operation within the next ninety minutes.

Hazards and Risks of Coronary Angiography

According to Dr. Harper, open-heart surgery in Spokane, Washington, is not predicated on the various enzyme studies which are usually employed and which are counted on to show abnormalities twelve to twenty-four hours after a heart attack occurs. And all cardiac attacks don't record on the EKG (electrocardiogram), so that even if your EKG is normal you may be operated on. The operation's sole criterion to be performed in Spokane is the angiogram—even though chest pain can come from pleurisy, pneumonia, muscle spasm or even anxiety. There are many causes other than coronary occlusion. Have a chest complaint and get an angiogram!

Coronary angiography, also known as *arteriography,* involves passing a catheter into the heart under fluoroscopic control and injecting radiopaque contrast material through the catheter into the coronary arteries. Films of the dye flowing through the coronary arteries can demonstrate narrowing or complete obstruction.

The technique has been extremely beneficial for diagnosis in the hands of a highly skilled physician-technologist. It has its hazards when the technician is not so skilled. Angiography is used to determine whether coronary artery surgery is indicated, especially in those people who suffer with severe disabling angina pectoris unresponsive to medical therapy. It may also be useful as a diagnostic determinant for preoperative evaluation for valvular surgery and only *occasionally* for patients with recent myocardial infarction. A primary rule in the use of angiography is that the benefit of its use must outweigh its risks.[1]

Invasive Searches for Blocked Arteries Are Unneeded

Most modern-day cardiologists, internists and family medicine specialists place a great deal of trust in the angiogram. If you experience angina pectoris, a cramping pain in the chest caused most often by a shortage of oxygen to the heart (myocardial anoxia) often linked with hardening of the arteries (atherosclerosis), the physician most likely will urge you to get an angiogram. The angina pain usually travels down the inside of the left arm and occurs with a feeling of suffocation and impending death. It's frightening! Your physician may tell you: "Look, you are a walking time bomb. Unless we do this angiogram to find the blockages to your heart and do something about them, you could have a fatal heart attack any time." Such terrifying words keep heart surgeons very busy.

Patients submit to angiographic procedures under assumptions that the combination dye and X-ray film search for heart artery blockage is necessary for them to receive adequate treatment. As medical director of the Institute of Holistic Medicine in Grand Terrace, California, coauthor Hitendra H. Shah, M.D., is of the firm opinion that such assumptions are simply untrue. The angiogram is too often misused in order to facilitate the business of coronary bypass surgery and angioplasty. Since 1985, "business" has gotten steadily better. Today, over a million angiograms are performed each year for a total patient payout of over $10 billion.

Not all cardiologists are persuaded of the need to use this aggressive cardiac catheterization approach. A renowned cardiologist from Harvard Medical School, Thomas Graboys, M.D., has published the results from several studies which suggest successful alternatives to the "let's catheterize" approach. In his most recent study published in the November 11, 1992 issue of the *Journal of the American Medical Association,* Dr. Graboys reported on 168 patients who had been told that they needed to undergo cardiac catheterization to determine the degree of arterial blockage they were experiencing and consequent need for additional therapy.

These patients then consulted Dr. Graboys for a second opinion. He used noninvasive, less expensive clinical tests to check on the angiogram recommendation. This cardiologist's examinations included an exercise stress test; the echocardiogram, which uses sound waves to assess the function of the heart; and the Holter heart monitor, worn by the patient for twenty-four hours. Dr. Graboys determined that 134 patients (80 percent) did not need to undergo the catheterization. For the remaining 20 percent, he recommended a change in medication or treatment and observation for two months. At the end of those two months, he concluded that the majority of these heart patients did not need catheterization. In all, out of 168 patients, Dr. Graboys recommended that six patients (less than 4 percent) required catheterization.

Contrary to the doom-and-gloom proclamations of the original referring cardiologists, these 168 patients experienced an annual fatal heart attack rate of only 1.1 percent over a five-year period. This rate is much lower than the mortality rates associated with either coronary artery bypass surgery (5 to 10 percent) or angioplasty (1 to 2 percent). Dr. Graboys concluded that "in a large fraction of medically stable patients with coronary disease who are urged to undergo coronary angiography (heart catheterization), the procedure can be safely deferred."[2]

Dr. Graboys demonstrated to the medical world that an invasive diagnostic procedure such as the angiogram to determine whether bypass surgery or angioplasty is required is unneeded. Noninvasive testing to determine the functional state of the heart is far more important in determining the type of therapy that is required than the invasive search for blocked arteries. Only if the heart is not functioning well is the angiogram needed to see if surgery should be done.

Dr. Shah affirms that if your physician recommends you to have a coronary angiogram (catheterization), the chances are eight out of ten that you do not need it. The critical factor in determining whether you do require one is how well your left ventricular pump is working. It doesn't have to do with the degree of cardiovascular blockage or the number of arteries affected. Rather, it's related to the ejection fraction, the amount of blood pumped out by the heart with each beat.

The *ejection fraction* tells us how the heart is performing its function as a pump and is one of the most important factors in determining the outcome of treatment. Please realize that it's not so much the degree of blockage or the number of arteries blocked that is vital, but rather the amount of blood ejected with each heart beat.

Medical scientists know that a generally healthy heart will show an ejection fraction of 50 percent or greater, but the heart may be filled with 100 milliliters (ml) of blood; if it pumps out 50 ml with each beat, the ejection fraction is recorded at 50 percent. If your heart only pumps out 40 ml, its ejection fraction is 40 percent.

The bottom line is that most aggressive "replumbing" techniques for the heart and its arteries have been found irrelevant to the typical course of the disease; blockages found by an angiogram are usually not relevant to the patient's risk of heart attack. The most sophisticated study of coronary artery bypass surgery, the Coronary Artery Surgery Study (CASS), demonstrated that healthy-hearted patients with one, two or all three of the major heart blood vessels blocked did surprisingly well without undergoing cardiac surgery. Regardless of the number or severity of the patients' blockages, each group had the same very low fatality rate of 1.6 percent a year; their survival rate was 98.4 percent. That same year of the CASS (1984), the average fatality rate from coronary artery bypass surgery was 10.1 percent, averaging about one death per ten operations. Thus, a lot of mortality surrounds this operation, yet it remains popular as a heart-corrective procedure.[3]

Some clinicians use arteriography to diagnose or exclude coronary artery disease in patients unlikely to be considered for surgery, while others consider the procedure too hazardous for such "routine" diagnostic use.[4] Most physicians, however, will employ the procedure for patients only when surgery is contemplated, since it is relatively hazardous.

The death rate for angiography varies from 0.1 percent to 1.0 percent, depending on who the doctor is, how old and healthy the patient is, and whether the mortality statistic takes into account the patient's death at the time of procedure or six months later from an embolism sustained when the angiogram was performed. At any rate, the procedure may result in death, myocardial infarction, stroke, cerebral emboli, arrhythmias, thrombosis, arterial tear and dissection at the site of arterial puncture.[5]

"The procedure is hazardous," says *The Medical Letter,* and warns against its overuse as a diagnostic test.[4] *The Medical Letter* offers information about drugs and therapeutics. It provides no-holds-barred commentary about the newest in medicine. Written by a bevy of renowned medical experts in many fields, it is sent to subscribing physicians.

Using arteriography, or angiography, as the sole criterion for determining surgical correction of coronary artery lesions seems unsound. Besides, the X-ray films are sometimes difficult to read, particularly when the patient is obese, and even experienced cardiologists and radiologists may differ in their interpretations.[6] In addition, perfect human specimens at age forty who run five miles every morning and can conquer treadmill tests of 185 heart beats a minute will still frequently show documented abnormal angiograms (as much as 50 percent of healthy volunteers in a study), with 50 percent narrowing of the arterial lumen at age forty. Even so, the last thing the patient may need is dangerous heart surgery.

The Established Medical-Surgical Fad

Just as there are medical differences of opinion about the benefits and risks of coronary arteriography, the same situation exists for that other potentially more dangerous vascular procedure, surgical bypass. *Coronary artery surgery,* also known as *bypass surgery,* is supposed to improve coronary circulation. It is a controversial, expensive and extensive operation which remains unproven. Possibly coronary artery surgery has some value for relieving severe heart pain, but for only a limited number of patients with a narrow range of coronary conditions. Or possibly it might be used for relief of severe heart pain which fails to respond to medical therapy, including chelation therapy. Nevertheless, 800,000 people a year in more than 500 hospitals are undergoing open heart surgery. Introduced in the late 1960s, it has become an established medical-surgical fad for supposed repair of coronary arteries. The reason? Most of those undergoing surgery are told there are no alternatives. Do it or die!

James O. Stallings, M.D., a plastic surgeon of Des Moines, Iowa, told us, "The scar of open-heart surgery has become a kind of status symbol." In the minds of upward climbers, he said, a scar on the chest seems to have become a sign of social standing and the ultimate consequence of a life of hard work. It supposedly shows sacrifice to one's job and disregard of one's person for the building of a business.

Patients Take High Risks

The past decade has seen a proliferation of both bypass surgery and angioplasty, in spite of strong scientific evidence that neither may be helpful in the long run for the overwhelming majority of patients. "The only reason for the current 800,000 bypass and angioplasty surgeries performed each year is the high number of working cardiologists and surgeons in the medical community," says Julian Whitaker, M.D., author of the monthly newsletter, *Health and Healing.* "If there is no difference in heart attack rate in patients with one vessel blocked, compared to those with all three vessels blocked, the significance of any blockages found on the cardiac catheterization is not much. This possibly unnecessary operation, supposedly to save your life, is about five to ten times more deadly than the disease!"

Why? Because blockages are not any kind of accurate estimate of the reduction of blood flow in the artery. According to another study published in the *New England Journal of Medicine* in 1984, researchers at the University of Iowa measured blood flow in over forty-four blockages and demonstrated them by angiogram in thirty-nine patients. Much to their surprise, the researchers found no correlation between blood flow and the severity of the heart artery blockage. In other words, the angiogram was worthless.

The authors of this study further concluded that the blockages found on the heart catheterization simply do not correlate with blood flow restriction. They commented that "the results of these studies should be profoundly disturbing on the coronary arteriogram." With regard to angiograms, they further added that needed information "cannot be determined accurately by conventional angiographic approaches." If blockages aren't designated a source of interrupted blood flow, why would anyone require coronary artery bypass?

Increasing numbers of patients without anginal pain or any other coronary symptoms are having clogged arteries bypassed in the hope of delaying a fatal heart attack. Yet there is virtually no evidence at all to support this hope. Patients accept high risks. They take as high as a 12 percent chance of inducing a heart attack due to the surgery—during or immediately after the operation. The 20 to 30 percent reclusion rate of their graft in the next two years also must be considered.

The explosive growth in the last twenty years of open-heart surgical facilities has raised serious questions about the adequacy of health care planning and controls in the way doctors are creating a demand for this possibly unnecessary surgery. The underlying reason for the surgery's overuse is its profitability. Are the doctors offering reasonable disclosures of the risks and the alternatives? In her book, *The Unkindest Cut,* Marcia Millman declares that they are not.[7]

Chelation therapy aside, critics of the bypass procedure say that many individuals may have their angina relieved by proper medication, weight loss and a cessation of smoking. The National Heart, Lung and Blood Institute reported that many patients with unstable angina responded well to drug treatment and had fewer heart attacks after therapy than those who underwent bypass surgery. And angina accounts for more than 75 percent of the bypass operations performed.

Henry D. McIntosh, M.D., of the Methodist Hospital in Houston, Texas, said at a symposium of the American Heart Association in Miami Beach that bypass surgery should be reserved for patients with *crippling* angina who did not respond to more conservative treatment. "I do not believe that surgery is indicated for the asymptomatic patient," Dr. McIntosh said.[8] His comments are totally supported by the National Institutes of Health study.

Open-Heart Surgery Is Enormously Profitable

"Every time a surgeon does a heart bypass," suggests a health care delivery analyst, "he takes home a luxury sports car." The busy cardiac surgeon can easily earn over one million dollars a year doing bypass procedures. By 2001, if enthusiasts of the operation have their way, hospitals and doctors will collect $100 billion a year doing just this one type of surgery.[5] American taxpayers will be responsible for making most of those payments. We already have paid our $5 billion in charges for open heart surgery performed just in 1996. Medicare picks up the tab on those over age sixty-five. The operations cost about $20,000 apiece for surgeons fees and $20,000 to $30,000 each for hospital expense.

"Yes, it's expensive," admitted heart surgeon W. Gerald Austen, M.D., of Massachusetts General Hospital in Boston. Then he sounded a warning, "We have to be careful of overly expanding its use."

Opponents say many of the operations are needless, that doctors are cashing in on a lucrative practice, which in turn encourages too many hospitals to invest in facilities that drive up health costs. Greater numbers of smaller hospitals throughout the country which seek more prestige in their communities are developing the extensive and expensive laboratory and surgical facilities and the medical teams needed to do coronary bypass surgery. Then, to justify the expenditures, keep beds filled, and maintain an appropriate level of staff skill, the hospitals must do several hundred such operations a year. The result is that they go looking for more patients. Knowing this, you can better understand why you should not get chest pains in a place like Spokane, Washington.

Tremendous financial outlays in surgical facilities are likely to create prejudice in favor of using them. This could inadvertently represent a powerful vested interest group among physicians who might feel threatened by an office procedure (chelation treatment) that avoids the need for up to 90 percent of these surgeries. Such situations involving conflicts of interest do exist.

Teamwork and Attention Are Required

The key to technical excellence for the bypass procedure, as mentioned previously, is expert medical teamwork and careful anesthesia. The operation takes an average of three hours. Sections of the saphenous vein in the leg are removed and sewn to the aorta at one end and coronary arteries at the other end. These attachments bypass parts of coronary arteries that are severely or totally obstructed, which ordinarily would supply the heart muscle with oxygen that it needs to pump effectively. During the operation, the patient's circulation is temporarily taken over by a heart–lung machine.

Before surgery, the status of the patient's coronary blood vessels must be evaluated by angiogram. As already stated, this involves injecting a dye and inserting a catheter in the vessels to determine which arteries are blocked and to what extent. About two patients in every 1,000 die as a result of the evaluation procedure itself. Others are disabled by resulting complications with about an overall 1 percent complication incidence. Those are very real hazards of angiography, which usually must be done before bypass surgery.

The individual's survival after surgical bypass also depends largely on astute postoperative nursing in a coronary care unit, where potentially fatal complications can be detected and treated.

This type of teamwork and attention before, during and after surgery calls for big money paid by the patient or his health insurance carrier. It would not be such a terribly high price to pay if coronary artery bypass really cured heart disease or prolonged life at least a little. It does neither. What does the surgery accomplish? It temporarily relieves chest pain symptoms—maybe—if the operation doesn't first kill the patient.

Medical Authorities Confirm That Bypass Does Not Cure

It was 1967 when Rene Favalarro, M.D., a cardiac surgeon from the Cleveland Clinic, successfully performed the first coronary artery bypass surgery. Because of its high-tech appeal, this operative procedure grew so rapidly that no one stopped to question the benefits. In fact, hardly any benefits are to be found. Over a ten-year period when compared with medical management, heart bypass surgery did not prolong life or increase the number of patients free of chest pain or reduce the number of heart attacks suffered or increase the employment rate for people who had the procedure done or improve the overall quality of life. Certainly, it did not cure.

Thomas A. Preston, professor of medicine at the University of Washington in Seattle, concluded: "It's particularly dramatic and expensive surgery and scandalously overused. Many—perhaps half—of the bypass operations performed in the United States are unjustifiable. It's not so much the public's health as the medical profession's wealth that dictates the use of this expensive, risky and often unjustifiable operation."

Robert J. Hall, M.D., clinical professor of medicine at Baylor College of Medicine in Dallas, Texas, states: "Bypass surgery is not curing the disease. It is modifying it with a piece of pipe. Not only is the disease not cured, it almost inevitably returns."

Norman Ratlif, M.D., at the Cleveland Clinic in Cleveland confirms Dr. Hall's remarks. Dr. Ratlif says, "One bypass surgery procedure inevitably leads to the need for another."

There are only limited occurrences when heart bypass surgery is helpful: (1) when the left main coronary artery is blocked, (2) when the patient has severe anginal pain that remains unresponsive to all forms of therapy, and (3) when there is evidence of three or more blockages of the main coronary arteries and the ejection fraction shows up as less than 40 percent. Based on these criteria, it is estimated that greater than 90 percent of all bypass procedures are unnecessary. If this surgery were to be performed only on appropriate candidates, the heart surgery industry would probably suffer significant financial losses.

Complications of Coronary Bypass Surgery

The purpose of coronary artery surgery is to improve the coronary circulation by graft insertion, but 5 to 25 percent of the grafts become occluded within a year.[9,10] And up to 30 percent reocclude in two years. Whether or not the grafts become occluded, after months or years pain may recur with progression of atherosclerosis, reports Paul L. Tecklenberg, M.D., of Stanford University School of Medicine.[11] Some patients are advised to undergo a second coronary artery operation when angina pain returns.[12] Usually the *patient* meekly assumes the blame for failure of the surgery. He knows that he did not alter his style of living after the surgery, which he thought had made him "safe." Therefore, the surgeon is seldom blamed for those treatment failures, says author Marcia Millman.[7] Her book, *The Unkindest Cut,* is an indictment of medical cupidity in exploitation of patients. The coronary artery bypass procedure is one of the methods of that exploitation, she says.

Coronary artery bypass operations sometimes done as an emergency in patients with myocardial infarction can produce operative mortality rates as high as 30 percent.[13] The death rate from the operation varies, however with the number of procedures performed at a given facility. For example, Thomas Chalmers, M.D., of the Mount Sinai Medical Center in New York City pointed out that surgical reports indicate a mortality rate of 12 percent for hospitals that perform 100 or fewer operations annually; reports of 100 to 200 cases performed annually at a facility indicate a 9 percent death rate; when 200 or more cases are operated in the same surgical facility by its "team," the average mortality rate for the year drops to 4.5 percent.

In addition, operative mortality for patients with congestive heart failure may be as high as 23 percent.[14] When the very severe complication known as *cardiogenic shock* strikes, the coronary artery surgical bypass patient death rate approaches 70 percent.[15.]

All of this mortality connected with coronary artery bypass surgery certainly makes the opponents of chelation therapy sound downright silly. They dwell on the less than ten deaths over forty-five years in which chelation therapy *may* be implicated, out of tens of thousands of patients who have been helped, while no one stops to mention the thousands of deaths directly and unequivocally due to unproven bypass surgery.

A nonfatal complication of surgical bypass includes *perioperative infarction,* which is a reocclusion around the operative sites where the graft splices were made. This happens in as many as 20 percent of patients.[16,17] Some patients also experience arrhythmias, persistent post-operative bleeding, pulmonary complications and infection. A major reason for complication with reinfarction to take place among coronary bypassed patients is that the same conditions exist in their bodies after the surgery, as prevailed before.

Another nonfatal complication of coronary artery bypass surgery was reported in the December 19, 1996 issue of the *New England Journal of Medicine* (*NEJM*). Each year, approximately 25,000 Americans, about 6.1 percent of those patients undergoing heart bypass procedures, end up with serious, lingering brain damage, a condition simulating dementia of the Alzheimer's type.

The study described in the *NEJM* reported that 129 of the 2,108 heart surgery "participants suffered new and severe neurological complications, including stroke or substantial deterioration of memory, concentration or other intellectual function similar to Alzheimer's disease. Of these, eight participants died from strokes." Those who were mentally normal before the surgery were left confused and agitated, unable to recall phone numbers, focus on conversations or do many of the things that had come easily to them before undergoing their chest operations.

"People who were once great bridge players can't win a game anymore." said Katherine Marschall, M.D., of New York University.

A stroke specialist not involved in the study, Philip A. Wolf, M.D., of Boston University, called the degree of brain injury seen in the research surprisingly high. "And you know it's a gross underestimation, because these people were not seen systematically by a neurologist. It must be the tip of the iceberg," Dr. Wolf said.

Among the most common post–bypass problems observed were the following: Eight patients died of brain injury, fifty-five suffered nonfatal strokes, fifty-five experienced significant loss of intellectual ability that was still apparent when they were released from the hospital, and eight had seizures. These complications occurred in twenty-four of the United States' most experienced and prestigious surgical facilities dedicated to coronary artery surgery, including operating facilities and hospitals affiliated with New York University, New York Hospital–Cornell Medical Center, Harvard University, Stanford University and Yale University. The twenty-four surgical centers investigated perform more than 10 percent of all such chest surgeries carried out in this country. Adverse outcomes for the patients' brain function ranged from 1 percent to 13.8 percent among the institutions.

Assisted by six investigators who independently reviewed details of the participants, the study so reported in the *NEJM* was written and submitted for publication by Dennis T. Mangano, M.D., an anesthesiologist at the University of California at San Francisco. Dr. Mangano did not provide a breakdown of his findings by individual medical centers because, he said, "We were lifting up the rock" in looking for neurological complications. "If each center could be exposed, none of them would have participated."

The surgical bypass patient's brain is so affected because bits of fatty deposits in the arteries as well as pieces of blood clots and even air bubbles produced by the heart–lung machine (an apparatus that circulates the blood during surgery) dislodge. Such debris blocks tiny blood vessels in the brain, starving it of oxygen. Plaques that break off from the type of blockages being operated on can lead to strokes and other brain damage.

"The basic reasons for these people to have arteriosclerosis in the first place still persist," says Yiwen Y. Tang, M.D., chelation therapist of Reno, Nevada. "Even one of the first heart transplant patients, a dentist named Philip Bleiberg, operated on by South African heart surgeon Dr. Christian N. Barnard in 1967, was reported to have died of coronary thrombosis after eighteen months. In other words, the patient received a new, young heart but became sick and died of used, old arteries. Not his doctor or anybody else bothered to help him change his lifestyle."

Coronary Bypass Fails to Prolong Life

What Dr. Tang has pointed out may explain the lack of prolonged life for heart transplant patients and coronary bypass patients.

According to the Organ Transplant Registry of the National Institutes of Health, only about 20 percent of human heart transplant patients survive longer than one year. And patients treated with coronary bypass surgery, compared to those treated with drugs, showed no evidence of increased survival or lowered risk of heart attack as a result of the surgery.[18,19]

One randomized trial involving forty patients with acute coronary insufficiency of various coronary vessels compared medical with surgical management; patients who had operations had higher functional capacity four months later, but differences in mortality were higher from them.[20]

More extensive controlled clinical trails comparing medical and surgical therapy have been underway. They were carefully designed by experts and are sponsored by the Veterans Administration and the National Heart, Lung and Blood Institute.[22,23] The studies, though welcomed by medical researchers, were described by some as too slow, especially in view of the enthusiasm that has surrounded bypass surgery since it was first described in the medical literature in 1970.

Life's Quality After Surgical Bypass Is Questionable

Famous talk show host Joan Rivers discussed her husband's suicide with Phil Donahue on the former "Phil Donahue Show." The man took his own life just a short time after he underwent a coronary artery bypass operation. Joan Rivers explained about her husband, "He was never the same after his bypass. Before surgery nothing ever got him down. He was ready to do battle anytime and place . . . and then one day he committed suicide just like that!"

To reverse her own atherosclerosis, Joan Rivers has taken a series of chelation treatments.

Every kind of question has arisen about the quality of life after coronary artery surgical bypass. A previous surgery for heart disease called *the Internal Mammary Artery Ligation* was abandoned after it was conclusively demonstrated that the operation's relief of angina was all "placebo effect." Some physicians suspect that same placebo effect is partially responsible for the "benefits' of today's popular bypass surgery.

"Many patients do receive pain relief, but the relief is likely to come from the death of the symptomatic area from the heart attack induced at the time of the surgery with subsequent replacement of the area by a scar," Harold W. Harper, M.D., suggested.

"There is also an interruption of the nerve bundle that passes to the affected area of the heart. The pain receptor nerves are severed. As a result, no warning pain is present to signal when the heart is ischemic," he said.

Lucien Campeau, M.D., former chief of cardiology at the Montreal Heart Institute, Montreal, Quebec, Canada, studied 235 patients angiographically one year after their coronary artery bypass operations. He split them into two groups. Dr. Campeau found the patient's graft opening had improved from 60 percent to 80 percent. But three years after surgery half of those same patients again studied by Dr. Campeau had no grafts remaining open. Even so, many of the closed-graft patients reported being improved or angina-free.[24]

"This unexpected pain relief may be the result of a 'pain-denial placebo effect,' " Dr. Campeau said. He confirmed what we implied earlier: The mere knowledge that they had undergone such a risky and expensive operation may be why the patient denies the sensation of pain, even if it actually is still present.

There are other explanations for the lack of pain. Dr. Campeau said, "These patients may be getting better medical therapy. They're encouraged to stop smoking and lose weight. Many do not resume the same activity after surgery, and many are less anxious because of the operation."

Dr. Campeau cautions that there are serious implications for patients for not feeling pain. Just as Dr. Harper mentioned, Dr. Campeau said, "Not having pain and yet having ischemia might jeopardize patients because they have lost the alarm of pain and might lead too active a life. If they have a positive stress test and still say that they are angina-free," he advises, "they should be watched more closely."

Thus, the quality of life after coronary bypass surgery *seems* to improve when in reality this does not mean the patient has been *truly* benefited. The patient may only think he is restored to health and is lured to his death through overexercise, suggested Ara G. Tilkian, M.D., of the Palo Alto, California, Veterans Administration Hospital. Without the chest pain, Dr. Tilkian said, a person can sometimes overexercise himself into new problems.

Exercise which is too severe can cause bypass surgical patients to develop arrhythmias, or irregular heart beats. "In our studies, one man got a lethal level of arrhythmias," said Dr. Tilkian. The absence of the chest pain removes a natural limiting factor.

Why Coronary Bypass Gets Heavy Referrals

We pointed out earlier that the surgical bypass for coronary arteries costs $50,000, more or less, including hospitalization, anesthesiologists' fees, surgeons' fees, and other expenses. It has a high mortality rate. It may reduce the incidence of chest pain but fails to prolong a person's life. The surgery does not cure atherosclerosis, which is a chronic progressive disease. It only grafts a substitute blood vessel which is a vein or an artery, as a replacement for an occluded artery. Thus, the substitute blood vessel is thinner and more prone to develop disease. Furthermore, this treatment covers only a small arterial segment. All the rest of the arterial system is affected by the same problems. Toxic materials remain present in the bloodstream and vessels, but they are left untreated. The latest treatment is use of calcium channel blockers.

Nonetheless, with all of these disadvantages, hazards and risks connected with coronary artery bypass, a lot of physicians recommend their patients have this operation. Why? Why are doctors willing to put their patients' lives in jeopardy for so little lasting benefit? We know of at least two major reasons.

Heavy referrals come from some physicians who have been led to believe that not much can be done for angina victims. They try arterial dilating agents first, such as nitroglycerine, papaverine, propanolol and perhaps a hundred other drugs of this type that are medically marketed. Then the doctors may give up on the vasodilators and move to blood thinners such as coumadin and other medications. One of the marks in medicine of a therapy being ineffective is that there are so many different drugs to treat the same problem. If drugs were specific and effective, there would be a need for only one.

The arterial dilating agents in general cannot work. They cannot stretch, or make larger, a blood vessel that has a calcium-lined wall. The arterial wall is hardened, diseased and scarred. The dilators will work only on those arterial segments that are undiseased. Their action, therefore, may be primarily psychological. They have a placebo effect for the patient and give the physician a little soothing for his own conscience by his trying to accomplish something—anything—for an otherwise hopeless disease. Sadly most physicians finally realize that they are unable to do very much for their arteriosclerotic patients. This realization is very hard on the average doctor's ego, for it reminds him of how impotent he really is.

Consequently, even those physicians who are conscientious and empathetic have the compulsion to get the hopeless patients with severe angina off their hands. Also, many doctors don't know the true statistics of failure for bypass surgery. They treat severe heart cases with standard drugs that are extremely limited. Such frustrated physicians are forced finally to sweep these personally discomforting patients under the therapeutic rug—out of their practices and into the hands of vascular surgeons or chest surgeons or others who perform open-heart surgery.

The second major reason for heavy referrals to open-heart surgeons is the better financial return for referring cardiologists. They collect larger and more frequent fees to carry out preoperative and postoperative procedures on surgical in-hospital patients than to manage strictly medical therapy. Also, health insurance carriers seem to more readily pay on policies to cardiologists when chest surgery is involved.

Surgical Bypass Is Controversial

If physicians were more selective about their referrals and sent only the sickest patients for surgical repair, the bypass procedure would not be so controversial. But the heart surgeons are careful to take only healthy candidates, such as forty-year-olds with a little chest pain and a slightly irregular electrocardiogram. They will not take on a desperate patient who might increase an individual surgeon's death score. That kind of seriously ill patient is denied surgery and seldom is informed of the chelation alternative. The only answer is a shrug of the shoulders by the surgeon and his admonition, "You are not a surgical bypass candidate." The really desperate patient is left to wait and wonder and. . . .[25-32]

Even someone who has had heart surgery is often refused for later repeated bypass attempts, no matter how seriously ill that person is now. The heart surgeons guard their patient mortality rates against expansion but not necessarily out of humanitarian motives.

We see than that selection of patients is biased in favor of good surgical results. Not just anybody can have a coronary bypass. The heart surgeons prefer not to add onto their mortality scores. They accept only those people they believe will have a high survival rate. Worst of all, many patients are even encouraged to have chest surgery "prophylactically." This is wonderful for the surgeon, since these have the best survival rates and keep his or her mortality statistics looking good. It is a big money maker in medicine with elaborate facilities and highly trained personnel that have to be kept hard at work. The huge investment won't permit otherwise.

Angioplasty: The Other Surgical Folly

During the 1980s, when it appeared that coronary artery bypass surgery was not doing the job, another procedure emerged as an alternative. Percutaneous transluminal angioplasty (PTCA) was developed. PTCA makes use of a balloon inflated inside the coronary artery to compress the atherosclerotic plaque against the walls of the affected blood vessel. As we learned at the start of this book in the case of Lindley Camp, angioplasties often must be redone because they don't entirely work. Thirty to 40 percent of all angioplasties result in a reclosure of the operated artery. Half of the repeat procedures must be done a third time. And 20 percent of all the angioplasty patients must have the more serious coronary artery bypass surgery because of failure or complications connected with the initial or repeat angioplasty.

Angioplasty is a surgical folly which needs to be shunned by any thinking individual, whether it be patient or doctor. Still, cardiologists praise it enthusiastically.

How do you think the surgical establishment responded to these dismal statistics enumerating failure? The cardiologists and heart surgeons have not abandoned their moneymaking procedure but have only refined the technique. Now the operators insert a wire basket—a stint—into the affected artery to prevent the atherosclerotic plaque from closing back onto itself. According to the October/November 1996 *Health Naturally* Magazine (pages 4 to 6), however, this wire stint procedure is not better than the previous angioplasty method.

In summarizing the open-heart surgical procedures being performed, former heart surgeon Robert D. Willix, Jr., M.D., puts it best: "After performing more than a thousand bypass operations, I was beginning to find that a great many of my patients were back on the operating table within three to five years. Many of the others were dead. Heart surgery didn't cure them. It just prolonged their death."

Then Dr. Willix admitted, "I haven't picked up the scalpel since 1981, but I have saved more lives than I did as a surgeon. I have taught that if lifestyle is the cause of heart disease, then isn't the treatment lifestyle changes? The answer to the heart disease phenomenon is reversing already existing plaque and preventing heart disease from developing."

The Chelation Therapy Contrast

Arteriosclerotic vascular disease is not a segmental disease. Medical science has shown in repeated studies that the condition does not affect only individual arteries, such as the coronaries around the heart, the carotids leading to the brain or the aorta and femorals leading to the legs. It affects the entire body everywhere, particularly wherever there is an arterial bifurcation (a division or offshoot of the artery).

Unlike surgery which cannot be done on the smaller and frequently inaccessible blood vessels, the arterioles and the capillaries, chelation therapy does reach the tiny occluded segments along with the larger occluded ones. The entire arterial system and all the cells of the body have toxic minerals removed by EDTA infusion. Basic causes are thus treated. The load on the heart is reduced by lowering the resistance to blood flow. Anytime flow resistance in the arterial system is reduced, the heart is required to work less hard to accomplish the same job. Other problem areas improve, including a lowering of insulin requirements for diabetics, a decrease in elevated blood pressure, a fall in excess serum cholesterol and triglycerides, reduced senility, more mobility for arthritic joints and many other improvements.

Bypass surgery performed in the limbs, the heart or anywhere in the body comes nowhere near providing the beneficial effects of EDTA chelation therapy. Chelation apparently does prolong life and does heighten the quality of life. Its cost is usually less than 10 percent of the expense of bypass surgery.

Finally, despite the heart surgeon's common claim that he has never heard of the treatment or that it could not help, chelation therapy has often come to the aid of those whom the surgeons failed to help. Or it has provided new life to people who were so far advanced in their disease they decided against even trying surgery. In fact, numbers of cardiac surgeons and cardiologists have undergone chelation therapy to save their own lives.

Chapter Fifteen

PROFESSIONAL BIAS AND GOVERNMENTAL ERROR IN JUDGING EDTA CHELATION

After forty years as a student and practitioner of medicine I have reluctantly concluded that much of what I have done has been a waste of time. The world is little better off and may soon be worse off than in my student days. I believe this is so because medicine—by which I mean the whole art and science of improving and preserving health, and not just that part of it performed by doctors of medicine—is on the wrong track. . . . We are heading for disaster if we keep on. That is my view.

—SAM McCLATCHIE, M.D.,
Misdirected Medicine, 1973

Modern Medicine Is Headed in the Wrong Direction

As director of the World Life Research Institute, which is an international reference center in marine biotoxicology for the World Heath Organization, Bruce W. Halstead, M.D., of Grand Terrace, California, was at the pinnacle of his career in 1972. Dr. Halstead, however, found himself with a serious and irreconcilable personal problem. He could not earn a living devoting himself exclusively to the investigation of the world's environmental resources and economic development. His own resources were in jeopardy. The Nixon Administration had cut off bio-medical research grants and contracts on which the medical scientist depended. Although he was then and still is a world renowned scientific researcher, an author of textbooks in toxicology and a former medical school professor for twelve years, the scientist lacked sufficient financial resources to support his family. Consequently, he broadened his activities and entered the field of clinical medicine.

After extensive evaluation of basic biochemical data and clinical investigational information, Dr. Halstead began to use EDTA chelation therapy. He also adopted the program recommended by the Longevity Research Institute then in Santa Monica, California (now known as the Pritikin Institute).

Using these two main therapeutic regimens, the diet and chelation, and hyperbaric oxygen therapy as well, Dr. Halstead managed a dramatic reversal of hardening of the arteries for his patients. He had startling success with them. High blood pressure came down, exercise tolerance increased and a variety of symptoms connected with the artery-narrowing process disappeared. Overall, the physician's patients thrived, and other seemingly unrelated diseases, such as diabetes and arthritis, also improved. As a result of Dr. Halstead's reduction of patients' disease symptoms, his practice grew and people flocked to his offices.

Drastically ill patients entered the physician's practice. They were people from all over the United States who had previously gone from doctor to doctor seeking some solution to their arteriosclerotic problems. Some of them had seemingly insurmountable illnesses. They were senile or had already undergone bypass surgery. In many cases, surgeons had told them there was nothing more to be done. Patients arrived ready to have their legs amputated but praying that "something" could be found to save them. Diabetics came with well-established complications, such as blindness or ulcerations of the skin, and they hoped for a miracle, too. Some people were deaf because of apparent difficulties they had with excessive calcification buildup on their vestibular mechanism in the ears. Patients arrived hardly able to stand—dizzy and falling. Many already had sustained heart attacks, and most knew that heart attacks were a very likely prospect. Some patients brought angiogram records that showed constricted blood vessels. The lineup of the halt, the lame and the blind was amazing to behold.

As with other physicians who care for patients near the terminus of illness, Dr. Halstead should have been hospitalizing ten or fifteen people every day from his practice. He did not! It is a fact that although he was on the staff of three hospitals, he found it unnecessary to admit more than one person every three months to any hospital at all. He had his patients walking, running, jogging, jumping, swimming and going through a variety of other exercises. His patients should have been dropping like flies sprayed with insecticide, but they did not. Their lives were prolonged and given a renewed quality. Dr. Halstead's patients worked at preserving themselves by using all of the different therapies he recommended.

"Today, on the admission of the National Heart, Lung and Blood Institute of our own Department of Health and Human Services, modern medicine is heading in the wrong direction," said the scientist turned clinician. "We have spent billions of dollars for the wrong research and lost millions of lives in the interval. We are faced with a plague of hardening of the arteries that literally threatens the whole of the Western world. The trend is getting progressively worse, with an annual increase in the disease of 6 to 9 percent *each year!* Still, American medicine generally ignores chelation therapy and condemns anyone who uses it. There is something wrong with the organized arm of a profession that consistently refuses to examine the clinical and biochemical facts."

Professional Bias Delayed EDTA Chelation for Years

The summary of an article published in July 1961 in *The American Journal of the Medical Sciences,* "The Long Term Use, Side Effects, and Toxicity of Disodium Ethylene Diamine Tetraacetic Acid (EDTA)," contained the statement:

> Two thousand consecutive infusions of disodium EDTA were given to 81 subjects in a study of the effectiveness of this therapy in coronary artery disease during a 2-year-period. *We have found no serious side effects or toxicity with the use of disodium EDTA when administered as a 3-gm. dose and infused as a 0.5% solution over 2½ to 3 hours. It is, therefore, our opinion that the drug can be used without danger over prolonged periods.*
> *The most serious side effect ascribed to this agent has been nephrotoxicity, but with the administration methods described here there has been no evidence of such damage* [emphasis ours].

The authors of that article were Lawrence E. Meltzer, M.D., J. Roderick Kitchell, M.D., who was then head of the Department of Cardiology at the Presbyterian Hospital, Philadelphia, and Florentino Palmon, Jr., M.D.[1]

Then in March 1963, *Medical World News* published an interview that quoted Dr. Kitchell as saying: "Peripheral vascular occlusive disease of the smaller blood vessels shows remarkable changes following treatment with EDTA. Candidates for below-the-knee amputations have lost their gangrene, and one ended up walking seven miles when he could not walk a block before."[2]

Dr. Meltzer was interviewed by that same medical magazine's reporter. He said, "Eleven of twelve patients with vascular disease secondary to diabetes have improved, and considering the absence of any valuable method for treating diabetic vascular disease, chelation therapy assumes great importance."[2] Dr. Meltzer expressed the additional hope that chelation treatment would avoid many of the amputations currently required because of gangrene.

One month after the *Medical World News* article was published, however, the same two authors had another article published in the *American Journal of Cardiology*. Its title was "Treatment of Coronary Artery Disease with EDTA—A Reappraisal."[3] Amazingly, these two research physicians who had for years been writing articles that sang the praises of EDTA chelation, suddenly pulled a giant reversal on the therapy. Even as the medical news reporter was interviewing them, the physicians had a directly opposite viewpoint in the press. It was a superficially negative article—the only negative one published on the subject—which had a devastating effect on the entire therapeutic concept of EDTA chelation. That 1963 "reappraisal" article changed all orthodox medical thinking about the therapy, so much so that it has yet to recover from the effect.

Busy clinicians, it seems, relied on the conclusion of this negative 1963 article by Kitchell and Meltzer. Until now, traditional physicians have not taken the time to carefully read every word in the article. Such a careful reading would have strongly suggested that the conclusion was not statistically valid. They would have learned that "below-the-knee' artery circulation was improved, for instance. Doctors need to reevaluate chelation therapy in light of all the new developments in the field. Then they would learn that the Kitchell and Meltzer article's significance is totally neutralized by a comprehensive review of the literature. This literature includes publication of at least twenty clinical articles about the benefit of EDTA in vascular disease in particular and another 7000 articles on the general subject of chelation for other medical uses. In addition, about 6,000 science articles have been published describing the chelation action in nature.

Garry F. Gordon, M.D., explained to us the events that occurred after publication of the Kitchell–Metzer "reappraisal." Dr. Gordon said, "The negative reappraisal by Kitchell and Meltzer virtually stopped all chelation progress in this country for twelve years. Yet, I have talked to Dr. Meltzer on the telephone for hours, and he has admitted to me that he had been pressured extensively by National Blue Cross and Blue Shield to come out against chelation. He told me confidentially over the phone during 1976 that he believes chelation therapy may be the most beneficial of treatments known to humankind, but until we can tell our medical colleagues exactly how it is working we should not broadly promote it.

"And as for Kitchell," Dr. Gordon continued emphatically, "his last published work,[4] two years later, in 1965, still cites the beneficial results of chelation in vascular disease and diabetes, and he has never published again. I ask you—or anyone—is the negative reappraisal valid at all? Kitchell has published no other article. His total scientific writing before his EDTA assertions were several articles supporting the use of internal mammary ligation which turned out to be only a placebo effect."

The internal mammary artery ligation for alleviation of angina pectoris has been abandoned by chest surgeons. This operation was shown to provide only a "wished-for" effect—an imagined effect—on patients.

"One day I will blow this whole 'reappraisal' article on chelation wide open! It calls for some very astute investigative reporting of the most fascinating kind," Dr. Gordon said.

"Funding for the Kitchell and Meltzer EDTA research was from the John A. Hartford Research Foundation. The Foundation gave them $1,000,000, and they ostensibly set out to attempt to duplicate the clinical results of Dr.. Norman E. Clarke[5,6] that he had published in 1956 and 1960. When the anticipated clinical improvement did not occur immediately after treatment, Kitchell and Meltzer were almost ready to abandon the project.[7] Then research was continued because their review of the protocol required reevaluation of the patients after three months; otherwise the researchers might have lost their grant-in-aid. Surprising to Kitchell and Meltzer, they found the angina of their patients was much improved—on the order of 90 percent. They therefore went ahead with further investigation," said the ACAM past president.

"A coauthor with Drs. Kitchell and Meltzer on chelation research was Marvin J. Seven, M.D.," Dr. Gordon continued. "He was a brilliant researcher who, unfortunately, committed suicide at age thirty-one in 1961 during the period of the Kitchell and Meltzer research and publications on chelation. His death virtually terminated any major interest in chelation treatment for several years. Dr. Seven had devoted great energy to the development of EDTA chelation therapy and helped arrange the first two major symposiums on chelation which were held in 1959 and 1960.[8,9] Those symposiums were attended by scientists and clinicians from many of the leading medical centers and research facilities throughout the United States, including such research centers as Stanford University, Brookhaven National Laboratories, Cardiovascular Research Laboratories, Baltimore City Hospital, the California School of Medicine, the Dow Chemical Company and many others."

Dr. Gordon showed us a textbook edited by Marvin Seven called *Metal Binding in Medicine*.[8] It contained the entire proceedings of the first symposium. Apparently, owing to Dr. Seven's death, the second chelation symposium, held in September 1960, which he had helped to organize, did not appear as a published book. Rather, it is listed in the medical library in the form of a periodical entitled: "Proceedings of a Conference on Biological Aspects of Metal Binding."[9] The series of such setbacks help to explain the uphill battle for chelation, until now.

At these two symposiums on "metal binding" and EDTA chelation, scientists of multiple disciplines sat down together and exchanged information. They agreed that during the ten years since EDTA had been introduced in this country fantastic therapeutic results were already being recorded. Clinicians talked to pharmacologists and to biochemists. That year, 1960, many exciting reports about the therapeutic effects of EDTA chelation therapy were presented, but the journal that carried this important information never came to the attention of the general medical community.

Then, as now, almost half of all deaths were related to hardening of the arteries. The field of chelation therapy was just beginning to attract general medical interest around the world and was starting to take hold in the United States. But Marvin J. Seven, the young and dynamic leader who was sparking the chelation therapy movement, killed himself. The people who looked on his work with admiration asked, Why? There was speculation of all kinds. But no one in the United States moved to carry on Dr. Seven's work and, therefore, it was left for investigators in other countries to develop further the chelation concept. Clearly beneficial results in arteriosclerosis have been reported in Germany, Russia and the former Czechoslovakia.[10,11,12] The agent is employed to reverse hardening of the arteries in those countries. And those foreign physicians give full credit in their references to the early American physicians who discovered this use of EDTA.

The Erroneous National Research Council Report

The combined efforts of Drs. Seven, Kitchell, Meltzer, et al. have had far-reaching effects on all our lives and pocketbooks. In general, physicians themselves never have read the complete articles, but they have responded to the few article excerpts reported in medical journals and textbooks. Most of these have focused on seemingly negative comments contained in the one article labeled "A Reappraisal." Even government agencies prefer this one negative article. The U.S. government has issued statements based on a clearly erroneous report predicated on the Kitchell et al. research paper, particularly their reappraisal.[3]

This 1963 article was picked up, and the five other plainly positive studies performed by those authors were ignored. Government agencies concentrated on the negative aspects, which in reality were really *neutral* conclusions in the article. The medical bureaucrats failed to acknowledge the openly favorable aspects contained in the same report!

The Panel on Cardiovascular Drugs of the National Research Council (NRC) of the National Academy of Sciences was asked to consider the use of Endrate (EDTA) in vascular occlusive disorders. The FDA made that request and a report resulted. This vital report was written to record, once and for all, the erroneous work of Kitchell and Meltzer. But several major errors were made in the report!

In one error, the NRC mistakenly attributes a negative conclusion to the researchers' 1960 paper, when that particular publication was extremely positive. The authors had been highly impressed with the potential of chelation treatment, and clearly stated so, although their haphazard and inadequate testing methods could well have resulted in total failure. That original 1960 study reported on ten patients who were initially disabled with severe persistent angina pectoris. The patients' conditions could not be controlled by other known therapies at that time, so they were treated with disodium EDTA. The bare adequacy of

Kitchell and Meltzer's treatment programs caused essentially no improvement to be noted by either patients or investigators after the first series of treatments,[13] and they planned to abandon the experiment, as Dr. Gordon has described.

The doctors had not counted, however, on one of the most important characteristics of the chelation treatment. The loss of pathologic calcium and removal of cholesterol and other fatty debris from the interior arterial walls apparently continues long after the conclusion of a course of EDTA therapy. Reports of improvement began coming back from the chelated patients, and the doctors reevaluated all ten of them three months after they had completed their initial series of chelation treatments.

Unforeseen by the researchers, three months after the beginning of their experiment, nine of the ten patients were showing reduced frequency and severity of anginal attacks. They had a reduced requirement for nitroglycerine. They had increased their exercise tolerance. Of the nine who originally had abnormal electrocardiograms, five now showed improved ECGs. Most impressive of all, the three patients who had first indicated enlarged heart size when viewed by X ray now showed reduced heart size. The investigators declared these positive results a direct effect of the EDTA chelation. This was exactly as Dr. Clarke had described in his 1956 article! This positive response caused Kitchell et al. to continue their chelation research on more patients, none of whom was ever given nutritional therapy or a program of exercises. In short, the patients did not change their lifestyles. Thus, even though chelation gave good symptomatic relief to many patients, it did not seem to significantly extend the life expectancy of those who were treated, simply because the patients continued with their atherosclerotic way of life.

Then the 1963 "Reappraisal" hit![3] No one has been able to explain the turnabout on any logical basis, and the authors kept contradicting themselves. They ran a foolishly designed study that anyone can read about in that second article. A medical scientist will immediately see the inadequacies of its design. Kitchell and Meltzer failed to establish an adequate or comprehensive therapy. Instead, they attempted to treat a polygenic (an interaction from many variations) with only one active therapeutic agent that actually increased the chances for complications from arteriosclerosis to later occur. How? Because of the mineral deficiencies they knew they induced—but did not treat. The two researchers also tried a double-blind crossover investigation which was doomed to failure, and they arrived at conclusions that were not at all justified by the data.

Most ridiculous of all, Kitchell and Meltzer claimed that the chelation therapeutic effects were "not lasting." But consider this: diabetics who would quickly die without their daily injections of insulin have been known to live full and vigorous lives for decades, and nobody criticizes insulin injections because they are *not lasting*. Why then do Kitchell and Meltzer condemn intravenous injections of EDTA on that basis as "not a useful clinical tool"? A conclusion like that for insulin would be recognized as idiocy, and it is idiotic to say the same for EDTA. This is particularly true since zinc and chromium are recognized as involved in arteriosclerosis. As a physician, you would not leave patients deficient in these essential trace minerals and expect their EDTA injections to keep them alive and free of past disease. That would be stupid and medically negligent as well.

The National Research Council Makes Its Awful Error

A reportedly responsible quasigovernmental agency that supposedly checks its facts first, the National Research Council (NRC) has accepted such illogical conclusions despite five other positive reports from the same authors. The NRC has made an awful mistake by this silly acceptance and created additional havoc in the bargain. It is an error that cannot readily be forgiven by the families and friends of those who have died from being denied EDTA chelation because of publication of the NRC report. Everyone in the United States, directly or indirectly, relied on that NRC report—but it was not checked for accuracy. In addition, the error was compounded and made worse.

Another error, one that shows outright dishonesty or utter indolence, is that the NRC purports to quote verbatim from the Kitchell and Meltzer positive paper, of 1960 when it, in fact, actually must have been quoting from their 1963 reappraisal article. Then, *they erroneously claimed that both studies were negative.*[13] The National Research Council's medical consultants and bureaucrats obviously did not read that 1960 paper all the way through. Certainly, they did not quote from it verbatim. It is incredible to realize that these authors actually wrote five favorable reports and one somewhat unfavorable one as we have pointed out, and the NRC report concludes that all of their studies are negative.

In our research of the literature, uncovering this tragic error had us in shock. It indicates the height of laxity by scientists in the highest seats of office.

A third error is the NRC statement that says, "Investigations by other authors are little more than testimonials." *Frustration* is another word that best describes these medical journalists' feelings, when we hold in our hands twenty additional, plainly valid, published studies by other clinical investigators.

Why has the National Research Council selected the flawed, inadequate, self-contradictory and illogical writing of the single Kitchell and Meltzer 1963 "Reappraisal" paper? Such a selection reminds one that, prior to the Wright brothers' flight at Kitty Hawk, expert scientists examined the failures and supported the dictum that man would never be able to build a machine that could fly. Even to this day, the NRC report leads the federal government and the medical establishment to insist on remaining earthbound by shackling themselves down with oversight, stubbornness and error. Thus, the patients who would want chelation therapy—and their physicians who would offer it—apparently must be deprived of a most effective anti-atherosclerosis treatment because they do not know what it is, or they think its benefits will not endure.

We, the people, are the big losers by this completely incorrect NRC report. It shades the opinion of any doctor who would use it as a legitimate reference on EDTA chelation. Any medical researcher or clinician who relies on its erroneous finding will receive a seriously distorted picture. Worse still, the effects of this wrong NRC report continue to this day. For example, Medicare continues to refuse to pay for chelation, citing a 1969 decision that relies on this faulty NRC report.

A near-final note: If, in fact, Kitchell and Metlzer had found negative results initially, which had stayed negative throughout their studies regarding the effectiveness of chelation treatment, that would have been a solid case against the therapy. Rather, Kitchell and Meltzer coauthored five articles before the 1963 one, which favorably discussed chelation therapy. Still the unexplainable professional bias as manifested by their "reappraisal" article, combined with the awful governmental errors, have set back the use of chelation therapy in the United States for decades. It seems obvious to us that Kitchell and Meltzer were pressured into a change of heart.

Chapter Sixteen

GOVERNMENT HARASSMENT OF A CHELATING PHYSICIAN

Sometime ago I suggested in a memo that it was not fanciful to suspect that the ethics which we saw at work during the Watergate affair had not been confined to politics. . . . We know from our own experience in Washington that high federal officials have countenanced dubious behavior as regards our work. . . . It is unlikely that so important an activity as science can be apolitical: apart from anything else its politics impinge upon it so heavily, that it is the duty of scientists to insure that its morals and ethics are not eroded.

—A memo from Humphrey Osmond,
M.B., M.R.C.P., F.R.C. Phych. to
Abram Hoffer. Ph.D., M.D., F.A.O.P.,
F.R.C.P. (C), March 27, 1975

Eugene Carlson Avoids Triple Coronary Bypass

"The first signs of my heart trouble started in the summer of 1975," said Eugene Carlson, an automobile mechanic of McKeesport, Pennsylvania. We spoke with Mr. Carlson after we arrived in Pittsburgh on January 21, 1977 to attend a meeting of the National Health Federation. Mr. and Mrs. Carlson were among the audience attendees who were anticipating the appearance of H. Ray Evers, M.D., of Montgomery, Alabama, the scheduled speaker. We too expected to listen to that famous chelator and then interview Dr. Evers for the first edition of this book. This physician, one of chelation therapy's foremost pioneers, never did arrive to address that meeting, because he was being watched day and night by the U.S. government. Agents were waiting for Dr. Evers to make some medical mistake—anything at all—so they could take away his professional license, get him sued, put him in jail or worse. They have attempted all these things already. We will tell you the whole story about the man's experiences shortly.

In the meantime, Mr. Carlson agreed to be interviewed, as a substitute for the missing speaker. He described how EDTA chelation had eliminated the need for his having to undergo a triple coronary artery bypass operation. Mr. Carlson's medical tale took on rather dramatic form, as do most of these experiences connected with chelation therapy. Those who come to use the treatment often do so as a last resort, when it should be their *first* resort.

"I got short of breath while cutting grass one day. I just did not seem to have the energy to do the daily and weekend jobs around the house that I had always done," Carlson told us. "I let the chores go more and more. During the winter, shoveling snow in a cold wind bothered me very much, too. After a while, I felt a crawling sensation along the chest that did not go away, and I became even more short of breath. Then I felt pains in my left arm.

"In April 1976, I went to my family doctor to have a complete physical examination. The doctor said that my blood pressure, triglycerides and cholesterol readings were very high and my heart was skipping every third beat. He gave me blood pressure and heart pills and made an appointment for me to see a cardiac specialist in Pittsburgh.

"The specialist put me in St. Francis Hospital in May for a heart catherization [an arteriogram]. When he read the results, this heart surgeon said I needed three or four coronary artery bypasses. 'But Gene,' he said, 'I might get you on the operating table, cut you open, and sew you right up again without doing much of anything because there would be too much occlusion.' I realized then that I really was a sick man and I sure needed help," Carlson said.

While talking to us Carlson shook his head from side to side, and beads of perspiration formed on his forehead as he recalled the doctor's diagnosis. Mrs. Carlson stood nearby and shook her head also, in confirmation. He said that he thought seriously about accepting the risks of open-heart surgery, even though the operation might net him nothing.

"I was talking to my dentist about my possible chances of coming out alive from the operation," Carlson said. "He told me of his friend, Max Weiss of White Oak, Pennsylvania, who had gone through a similar problem but solved it by going to Belle Chasse, Louisiana, for chelation treatment. I didn't know where the place was or what the treatment was.

"I visited Mr. Weiss over at White Oak and talked to him. He described his experience and referred me to others who had gone through the treatment. I talked to many of the people that he mentioned. They included Nick Jurich and many of the folks who have attended tonight's National Health Federation meeting," Carlson pointed out. "After that, I felt I'd rather chance the medical treatment with chelation than undergo any heart operation."

Mrs. Carlson recalled the tension-filled weeks they lived through. She said that they spent many anxiety-ridden nights talking over the prospects of Eugene's life-or-death situation.

Carlson said, "I called Dr. Evers and told him of my problem and asked if he thought he could help. He made no claims of curing, but he said he felt that chelation would help my arteries get cleaned out and then with the aid of the correct nutritional program such as diet, vitamins and minerals, I could keep myself in much better health."

Smiling broadly, Carlson said, "he has been so right. I feel better today than I have in a long time. The only work time I lost was while I stayed in the Meadowbrook Hospital in Belle Chasse. Then I took off just two more weeks after I got home. I do a lot of vigorous work on my job in the garage.

"I went to my family physician in December 1976 and had myself checked again. My blood pressure, triglycerides, cholesterol, and electro-cardiogram readings were all very good—normal, the doctor said. And my heart no longer skips a beat. I had taken treatment from Dr. Evers in July 1976. I took twenty-five chelations then. After the first week at his hospital I quit taking the heart pills that I brought from home, and to this day I haven't needed them. I know I'll never have to take heart medicine again—that's how well I feel."

The Big Worry Always in the Forefront

Eugene Carlson had one worry though—that Dr. Evers, or any other physician in this country, may not be allowed to continue giving EDTA chelation. Mr. Carlson's alarm came sharply into focus while he was a patient at Dr. Evers' Meadowbrook Hospital. During his stay, he and his fellow patients felt compelled to circulate petitions that asked the state of Louisiana and the U.S. government to stop the harassment of Dr. Evers. The patients asked the authorities to remove the pressure they were putting on the hospital staff and to keep open the hospital's doors. (The hospital was about to be forced to stop its activities. In fact, it was shut down soon after Carlson had his treatment.)

In an effort to stop Dr. Evers from using EDTA for treatment of circulatory diseases, on two occasions in 1975 the FDA designated his chelation drugs as misbranded and seized them. This was totally without precedent, as the FDA had always insisted that it had no control over the private practice of medicine. Nevertheless, government officials marched into the hospital supply room and removed the bottles of synthetic amino acid solution from its shelves. The FDA had gotten a court order permitting it to do that.

In our later talk with Dr. Evers, he said: "The judge said that I had misbranded the article for arteriosclerosis and used it for treatment of this disease, which is not listed on the drug insert. Therefore, the judge said, I misbranded it because it was shipped in interstate commerce."

As described earlier, we were present at the Pittsburgh meeting Dr. Evers was to address. In an open-line telephone conversation broadcast to the audience, he explained that this very evening the FDA and the Alabama State Licensing Board of Medical Examiners were watching him closely at his newly relocated clinic in Montgomery, Alabama.

The Remarkable Medical Wanderings of H. Ray Evers, M.D.

H. Ray Evers, M.D., a Southern gentleman and Presbyterian Sunday School teacher, learned about EDTA chelation in 1965 from the late Carlos P. Lamar, M.D., of Miami, Florida. The two physicians gained national reputations among those familiar with chelation therapy. They developed large medical practices. Some 400 physicians scattered throughout the country took their chelation training from Dr. Evers. Approximately 1,000 practicing physicians today actively use chelation therapy in some form. Dr. Evers had been known as the treatment's most prominent living exponent. The sixty-six-year-old physician gave chelation treatment to over 20,000 patients.

The Columbia General Hospital of Andalusia, where Dr. Evers began to practice chelation therapy in 1965, had a sixty-bed capacity which he had built from his general practice income. Treatment with EDTA infusions then started to expand tremendously. People began arriving daily from all over the United States. They wanted to avoid dying of hardening of the arteries or becoming part of the 10 or 12 percent (or more!) patients who died attempting bypass surgery.

The chelating doctor needed more beds to accommodate the large number of patients for whom he had no room. They clamored for him to save their lives, their limbs, or their loved ones. The word spread throughout Alabama, and sick people arrived with or without appointments to receive this mysterious treatment that they had heard created "miracles." This Southern country doctor rose to the demand; he expanded the hospital. Still, more people kept coming to Andalusia, a sleepy little town in the deep South.

Having a lot of land, Dr. Evers just continued to build on new hospital wings and hire more staff. He increased his hospital's capacity to 160 beds. Then the physician discovered that he had been earning too much money too fast. He developed a federal tax problem. The hospital bookkeeping records had been sorely neglected, because Dr. Evers was kept busy as the medical director, hospital administrator, nursing supervisor, purchasing agent and other duties all rolled into one. With financial records such a terrible mess, he hired a certified public accountant to correct things.

The tax matters were finally straightened out. His accountant recommended that the best thing Dr. Evers could do was to purchase an insurance policy that would pay him a million dollars when he was sixty years old and to donate the whole hospital with its land, equipment, medical supplies and various sundries to the Presbyterian church as a tax writeoff. He followed the accountant's advice and gave the hospital to the church in which he taught Sunday School. Dr. Evers' office remained located within the hospital.

As the years passed, the patients kept arriving in droves. They came from foreign countries as well as from around the United States. The church elders, the physician's old cronies who were the Columbia General Hospital's Board of Directors, began to drop off the board, one by one. Either they died or moved away or were replaced with alternate members.

Up to then, he had taken no notice of his loss of board control. But suddenly one day Dr. Evers found himself facing an entirely new hospital board. They handed down uncomfortable new restrictions. First, the board members charged him office rent, where there had been none before. Then they levied telephone charges for his intercommunication to the hospital. The Board of Directors realized that if something happened to Dr. Evers, their hospital would be in trouble, since 75 percent of all its patients belonged to him. It was usual for the chelating physician to have ninety people hospitalized at one time. He was too powerful, the board believed; the hospital could use some other medical leadership, said the murmurings.

This new board heard in hysterical language how new physician leaders on the Board of Directors described chelation treatment as unethical and unorthodox. "The hospital will get sued," they were warned. "Just think of the bad publicity. Evers isn't practicing traditional medicine like everyone else. It's out of the medical mainstream! Chelation treatment isn't even mentioned in medical school! It's poisonous, dangerous, murderous! How can we be a party to murder?"

The hospital board agreed to pass a resolution stating that as of February 1 of the following year no more chelation therapy could be given at Columbia General Hospital. Dr. Evers was told to cease chelation treatment at once and dispense orthodox medical care, or prepare to leave the hospital—the hospital he personally had started!

In January, as the Board's antichelation deadline approached, Dr. Evers arranged to take up medical practice and accept hospital privileges in Atlanta, Georgia. The Atlanta Eye Hospital, owned and administered by one of his physician friends, offered to rent him an empty wing. Dr. Evers moved like a whirlwind to transfer all of his patients by ambulance and airplane to the new facility. He had acquired a temporary license in Georgia. He practically emptied the Columbia General Hospital of all of its patients.

Dr. Evers Moves Again

A falling out soon developed between Dr. Evers and the Atlanta Eye Hospital owner. They were, unluckily, two very strong-minded and stubborn men who differed about how much the Alabamian should pay the Georgian to buy the facility.

Dr. Evers then accepted another invitation, one offered by the Seventh Day Adventists. They invited the physician to use their new $20 million facility in the Georgia capital. The Atlanta West Hospital had multiple floors, one of which was offered entirely for his use to administer whatever treatment he deemed necessary. Dr. Evers could conveniently have his personal office on the same floor. Again he moved his patients.

The Atlanta operation ran smoothly for a short time, until spite and jealousy broke through the dignified veneer of other medical professionals. Envy consumed some as they saw the accommodations and consideration given to the new physician. Several doctors complained that their recently arrived hospital colleague had not applied for staff privileges through the usual channels. Collectively, doctors and nurses charged bias in Dr. Evers' favor. The staff asked for a meeting to air their complaints openly, and Dr. Evers was not allowed to attend.

A clause in his contract gave the Atlanta West Hospital's Board of Trustees the singular right to rule on Dr. Evers' staff privileges. His patients had been moved to the Atlanta West Hospital, in part because he would not need to go through the rigmarole invariably involved with gaining hospital staff privileges. Besides, the Alabamian lacked the time to wait for rules, regulations and protocol connected with a big city hospital. Still, staff members sided against him and refused to acknowledge the unusual circumstances of his arrival.

The entire medical staff began a boycott of their 450-bed hospital. General services were reduced. Patients were left largely unattended. The media picked up the story and ran with it for many days. Pressure built on Dr. Evers from all quarters. Finally, he was forced to withdraw from the Atlanta West Hospital and from the state of Georgia as a whole.

Big City Publicity Hits a Little Louisiana Town

The physician concluded that to conduct his hospital practice successfully he must control administrative policy. Consequently, Dr. Evers began to search for a facility that he could buy outright. He finally found one reasonably priced in Belle Chasse, Louisiana, a town of 13,500 population outside of New Orleans. Even before the physician held a permanent license to practice medicine in the state of Louisiana, he took possession of the Meadowbrook Hospital.

What do you think is going to happen when a small, dusty, antebellum sort of Southern town, slumbering in nonactivity, suddenly is swamped by people from the North and other places, who are looking for Lourdes-like cures against sickness and death?

Referred patients from far and near descended on the unprepared Belle Chasse populace. Each desperate and disabled person was ready to hang up crutches, wheel chairs, sacks of medicines and other impedimenta of invalids on the town walls. It was a medical nightmare—a sociological bane to the once somnambulant community.

The town folk of Belle Chasse experienced culture shock similar to the citizens of Plains, Georgia, when Jimmy Carter first became president of the United States. Churches were shaken by the schism. Local politics was polarized. Taxes increased along with the appreciation of real estate. And day after day, week after week, scores of cars with out-of-town tags rolled slowly into town looking for the Meadowbrook Hospital. Coincidental with the arrival of patients, news reporters and feature writers descended on the town. The press gave the rural community more publicity than it wanted.

A Belle Chasse Patient's Story

Joseph Gaudio, a forty-seven-year-old bachelor from Palm Desert, California, was one of those patients who spoke to the press. "I am grateful beyond words. I was directed by God to go there," he said, for what he believed was a life-saving treatment.

A treadmill test and angiocardiogram taken at Eisenhower Medical Center in California indicated that without heart surgery Mr. Gaudio might have but two more years to live. Two of his major coronary arteries were 95 percent clogged with fatty plaque, and a third major artery was 70 percent blocked.

Gaudio explained that at Cedars of Lebanon Hospital in Los Angeles, a heart specialist told him "I'd die in two years if I didn't have the surgery, a three-way bypass . . . my appointment was with a doctor in Pacific Palisades who . . . told me that statistically, the surgery was 'not all it's made out to be in the long range'—they don't get at the cause," said Gaudio.

"I asked him what the alternatives were and he said, 'None. I wouldn't make any long-term investments, you're sitting on a powder keg, you could go any moment,'" the former patient repeated.

Then Joe Gaudio learned about Dr. Evers from Betty Lee Morales, a contributing editor of *Let's Live* magazine. He telephoned the physician to learn about the treatment given, and he rechecked with three other physicians because the patient was fearful of "quackery." While the chelation theory "seemed to make sense" he still was undecided, he said. The three doctors told him, "if chelation were any good, we would be using it."

After six more telephone calls to Dr. Evers in Louisiana and weeks of indecision—"mental torture, believe me!"—Gaudio finally boarded a plane for Belle Chasse. He remained at Meadowbrook Hospital from August 6 to September 28, 1974, staying two more weeks than was considered necessary because, he said, "I wanted to be sure everything was okay." The treatment made him feel like a new person because of a resurgence of energy he experienced—"something I hadn't had for years. Bang! I felt like a million dollars!"

Some time after his return from Meadowbrook Hospital, Gaudio arranged to take a treadmill test at Loma Linda Community Hospital. He did not reveal his history to the medical intern there. The usual stress test exercise was given with the stress set at 173 heart beats per minute. "I hit 170, and he told me there was no indication of any problem. I asked if he would let me run on it for a bit; he said it wasn't necessary, but agreed since I was persistent. He set the stress at the starting point, and I ran for ninety seconds, reading a stress point of 175. I couldn't have done that last year," said Joseph Gaudio.[1]

Many other dramatic testimonials like Gaudio's were ballyhooed around Louisiana, and this sort of publicity turned neighboring physicians against Dr. Evers. In addition, some people in surrounding communities left their physicians or transferred themselves out of hometown hospitals and into Meadowbrook Hospital. Local physicians did not care for that very much, either.

Attack from the Louisiana Medical Board

Roman law was the basis of legal procedures in Louisiana under both the French and Spanish regimes. After admission to the Union in 1812, the state made many attempts to establish a legal basis similar to that of the other states. The result has been the development of a legal system that rests on the French and Spanish codes in the area of civil law and largely on English legal precedents in criminal law.[2] As a result, it is remarkably easy to become licensed to practice medicine or most other professions in the state of Louisiana.

Using his credentials from medical school and reciprocity from licensure in other states, Dr. Evers had been granted a temporary license to practice medicine until the Louisiana Board of Medical Examiners met again in three months. Then he was sure to receive a permanent license. He had accepted his three-month permit and leased the Meadowbrook Hospital in Belle Chasse with the privilege to buy. Dr. Evers took possession of the facility even before the temporary license came through.

A growing backlog of patients were literally camped on the hospital's doorstep waiting for Dr. Evers to take possession. Some had very little time left to live. They begged for treatment. A few of the ones who were viable, and could undergo heart or artery surgery, probably did so during the physician's practice hiatus from Atlanta to Belle Chasse. Others who wished to become his patients may have died while they waited for the hospital to open.

From investigations we have done to uncover facts about H. Ray Evers, one major criticism is accepted even by his fellow chelating physicians. They say that he lacks the ability to say no. He won't tell a hopeless victim, "I won't give you chelation treatment because your physical condition is beyond hope."

Dr. Evers gave care to whoever felt they needed it. Even recognizing that a person is just days away from death, he would tell the patient's family confidentially, "The condition is impossible and past hope, but I'll try to do something anyway." Humanitarian reasons aside, that is medical misjudgment, his colleagues said. Dr. Evers countered with "remember the oath of Hippocrates!" But the professional criticism had been leveled and had validity in the minds of his critics, friends and admiring colleagues alike.

As a result of this physician's attitude over the years, some of the most severe cases of hardening of the arteries in the whole country— perhaps in the world—came under Dr. Evers' care. Patients had been brought to him who were critically close to death. A few thousand people had had their lives saved and health restored, but a few dozen others, indeed, had died just as predicted.

Several physicians, even fellow ACAM members with whom we spoke, faulted him for recognizing but not accepting patient risk factors that were obviously too great. They shook their heads and said almost in unison, "Dr. Evers had put himself and chelation therapy in jeopardy. He had taken any patient who crawled to his door. That's taking too hazardous a risk with one's reputation and with the validity of the treatment. Why didn't he consider the rest of us who are chelating physicians? Sometimes we have to defend the therapy because of patients about to die but given chelation treatment anyway. Look at the heart and artery bypass surgeons! They operate only on those patients who are the healthiest. They won't accept just *anyone* for heart surgery. The vascular surgeons make sure to keep their mortality statistics as low as they possibly can."

When several cases—without hope but treated by Dr. Evers anyway—did die, the news was picked up by the New Orleans television stations. Histrionic human interest stories broke in the newspapers nationally about patient deaths. Some were wire services stories. One news story we found in the *Salt Lake Tribune* for August 22, 1976 reads: "The FDA reported ten deaths at the hospital associated with chelation agents as well as several patients who required dialysis."[3] What the various national news reports neglected to mention was that in most cases these people died from terminal cancer, *not* from any side effects of chelation therapy. Dr. Evers had given the therapy in response to pleadings by family members as a last resort, to hold a little longer to the thread of a loved one's life. But as a consequence of the news stories, when the Louisiana Board of Medical Examiners met to consider making Dr. Evers' license permanent, his request was denied. The medical examiners predicated their decision strictly on the press reports of the ten deaths with which he was connected.

Louisiana Troubles Had Just Begun for H. Ray Evers

Being denied a permanent Louisiana medical license was just the start of more legal and governmental troubles for Ray Evers. Here was a physician in possession of a hospital, with hundreds of patients pounding at its doors to get in, yet he remained without a license for a year. In the meantime, Dr. Evers hired John R. Potter, M.D., to be his chief of staff at the hospital. Dr. Evers took on the role of hospital administrator, which did not require a medical license.

On January 14, 1976, he filed a new motion for permission to present additional evidence to the medical examiners. This was granted, and the Board held a hearing. Witnesses flew in from various parts of the country in support of Dr. Evers. Joseph Gaudio was one of a hundred patients who offered to testify in the physician's behalf, and he was granted the privilege.

"Dr. Evers brought my 'before and after' reports to the hearing—those from California showing the condition I was in when I went to Meadowbrook, and then the treadmill and circulation report from Meadowbrook. About eight doctors were at the hearing. [Five of them sat on the Board of Medical Examiners.] One asked how I felt," said Mr. Gaudio, "and I told him 'great'—like a nineteen-year-old. I thought of course they would examine the reports on my case, but no—they didn't bother to look at them."

The Board again denied Dr. Evers a license to practice medicine in the state of Louisiana, and obtained a temporary restraining order against him as well. They declared him incompetent. And, because he charged for treatment, they also accused him of defrauding the public. The chairman of the board openly stated that he would see that Dr. Evers never got a Louisiana medical license.

As he had for the previous year, Dr. Evers continued to permit chelation therapy to be administered at his hospital despite the restraining order. He was subsequently arrested. The Medical Board of Examiners had made its move. He was sentenced to ten days in jail on a contempt charge. Later the Appeals Court voided the sentence.

While the matter of Dr. Evers' license remained on appeal, a group of patients and friends joined together and formed the National Educational Society for Natural Healing, 1717 Homer Street, Metairie, Louisiana 70005. Under the leadership of Fred J. Doughty-Beck, D.C., this group won a civil class action suit on June 20, 1975. Under its new president, Herbert Stahl, Sr., the National Educational Society for Natural Healing expanded its membership to thirty-seven states. The class action suit that it won caused the Parish Court to issue an order to enjoin the Louisiana State Medical Board of Examiners from depriving Dr. Evers of his license to practice. As we shall soon see, however, this was only a temporary victory.

Meadowbrook Hospital Also Under Attack

To stay out of jail on further conviction of contempt, Dr. Evers avoided all direct patient care and acted strictly as administrator of Meadowbrook Hospital. His skills and talents of more than thirty-eight years were totally denied to patients. Medical services were rendered by a staff of qualified professionals under Dr. Potter's medical direction.

Then, Meadowbrook Hospital also came under attack. Its license renewal was delayed by the State Board on Hospitals. The excuse given was that it had no surgical department, which was true. This institution specialized in preventive medicine and the medical care of degenerative diseases. It referred patients for surgery to other institutions when absolutely necessary. Dr. Evers' attorney, Kirkpatrick W. Dilling, filed for a hospital review hearing.

A grand jury hearing subpoenaed all of Dr. Evers' hospital records on two separate occasions, without doing anything with them except to make copies. Recordkeeping, in truth, is another critical fault of Dr. Evers, as friendly fellow physicians had told us. They admit he was notoriously weak in this record-writing area.

"He didn't document well enough," one of his supporters said. "Several of our ACAM (American Academy of Medical Preventics) members had gone very deeply into this inadequate documentation with him. In most ways Evers was far ahead of other physicians in practicing preventive medicine—except in documenting what he did in practice. There he remained just a country doctor." Dr. Evers himself admitted the same thing to us.

The grand jury looked over Dr. Evers' records as a prelude to possibly filing criminal–civil charges against him. Although his recordkeeping no doubt could have used much improvement then, nothing in Dr. Evers' actions was criminal or negligent. He received a clean, impartial ruling, and the grand jury ended its interest.

Inadequate documentation of case histories was a minor weapon used by both Medicare and Blue Cross to blitzkrieg Meadowbrook Hospital. Their major complaints also were that the hospital lacked twenty-four-hour operating room service and did not do major surgery. They joined together in a decision not to pay any of the hospital's charges to patients. These two main hospital insurance coverages in the United States were denied to that institution. Thus, patients received no hospital benefits. Chelation care was not covered, patients were told, and either they paid the hospital charges out of their own pockets when they expected the bills to be paid by health insurance or the hospital did not get paid at all.

A Federal Appeals Council had ruled, you may recall from Chapter Thirteen, that such payments must be made, as in the December 1, 1975 decision of J. J. Dominey, Sr. But Medicare and Blue Cross have carried that issue further. Each case must be adjudicated on its own merits by a series of suits and appeals. Few patients will take the time or spend the legal fees involved. In fact, even Alabama Blue Cross and Medicare still owe Dr. Evers' estate a large amount of money from his practice in Andalusia, Alabama, years before.

Persecution by the FDA and IRS

The Federal Food and Drug Administration, in an entirely unprecedented action, entered the antichelation attack on Dr. Evers, as we have mentioned previously. The FDA seized Meadowbrook Hospital's inventory of disodium edetate on grounds that it was misbranded. The governmental agency charged, "EDTA labeling not only carries no recommendations for its use in circulatory disease (*USA vs DISO-Tate*, DC La) but even states that 'chelation therapy is contraindicated in generalized arteriosclerosis associated with aging' [circulatory problems]."

Dr. Evers counterattacked with a civil rights action in federal court. A patients' civil class action was filed in Louisiana's Plaquemines Parish Court asking for a restraining order. An injunction was issued against the FDA. The physician's countercharge stated that this FDA action was a vicious invasion of a physician's rights to prescribe medication for patients. But the bureaucrats still were not through with him. Then the Internal Revenue Service stepped in.

The IRS Charges Evers with a Felony

Dr. Evers was behind in paying his 1974 income tax and was assessed a penalty and a fine by the Internal Revenue Service. By May 1976, he had scraped together $25,000 and paid the back taxes, with just the penalty and fine remaining.

About two weeks after his tax payment, an IRS officer arrived at Dr. Evers' office door to impound his automobile. The IRS agent had no bill of charges and gave no prior warning. He demanded the car, he said, because the government wanted the automobile as collateral for approximately $2,500 the physician still owed.

Dr. Evers was enraged and used strong language in reply. He explained that the tax principal was paid and that the penalty and fine soon would be paid. Meanwhile, he was paying the government its usual interest. The IRS agent still wanted his car keys. Dr. Evers shouted that the IRS's demand for his car was illegal, since a doctor's vehicle is a tool of his trade, needed to make house calls and to get to and from the hospital. He refused to give up his car. The IRS agent finally left.

In response, the government tried to indict him for a felony, claiming that he attempted to run down the IRS agent. If a physician was found guilty of such a charge, he probably would never be able to acquire or retain a medical license anywhere in the United States. In that way the IRS was offering a sister governmental agency, the FDA, a little extra assistance. Luckily, no indictment could be made to stick. In between, however, there was a lot of legal hassling and warding off of the police.

Dr. Potter and the Meadowbrook Hospital staff went on obtaining and administering EDTA to patients with arteriosclerosis. Again the FDA took legal recourse. It obtained its own unprecedented injunction ordering the hospital to stop stocking the chelation drug. The requested injunction was granted on grounds that without such restraints the government agency would be forced to resort to daily seizures to enforce the removal of the "misbranded" drugs from interstate commerce. The injunction also required notification to patients that the hospital was forbidden to hold or use the drugs.

Then the State Medical Board of Louisiana induced the Orleans medical parish to badger and pressure Meadowbrook Hospital's chief medical officer. Dr. Potter had been a member of the staff since the hospital opened in 1974. He was the licensed Louisiana physician that ran Meadowbrook, but because of horrendous vilification he experienced from fellow physicians and the medical examining board, he finally was harassed into resigning. Dr. Evers now had no licensed physician supervisor to take legal responsibility for patients.

Dr. Evers Abandons the Louisiana Fight

During the FDA trial in the summer of 1975 in New Orleans, the FDA attorney, Guy Pffifer from Washington, D.C., admitted before Judge Gordon that Dr. Evers was being singled out for individual prosecution and destruction. It was said that if the federal government could prevent him from practicing medicine, any other physician who attempted to employ EDTA chelation therapy could be shown Dr. Evers as an example of the consequences of such a misdeed. He was, after all, the chief teacher and leading proponent for the intravenous treatment. "Get Evers and you'll stop them all," was the word circulating in the Department of Health and Human Services.

In twenty-six months of legal battles, Dr. Evers spent $142,000 in legal fees. He remained without a license to practice medicine in the state of Louisiana, and he could furnish no other licensed physician on the hospital staff. He was warned, "If you are caught even taking a person's blood pressure, you will be put in jail for a year and receive a stiff fine."

Bureaucrats told him to get out of town within thirty days or be hit with the next harassment. When news came to him that other governmental agencies were ready to move in, he finally closed his hospital and left Louisiana.

Dr. Evers Moves to Montgomery, Alabama

Dr. Evers next leased a forty-bed clinic in which he offered chelation therapy in a new technical form—The Ra-Mar Clinic in Montgomery, Alabama. The FDA followed Dr. Evers to Montgomery and filed a suit, civil action 78–93–N (*United States of America vs. H. Ray Evers, M.D.*) in the United States District Court for the Middle District of Alabama, Northern Division. The FDA tried to stop him from doing chelation therapy of any kind—not just with EDTA. In June 1978, it filed for an injunction for him to "cease and desist." It was a test case for every physician in America. If Dr. Evers had lost the case, the judgment against him would have affected the medical practice of every U.S. doctor. He or she would have lost the right to deviate in any way from the instructions on the package insert of a drug.

"No doctor could give penicillin for an abscess tooth because the package insert doesn't recommend penicillin for this purpose," explained Dr. Evers. "The judge asked the FDA lawyer, 'You mean if I went out and played golf and sprained my ankle and I called my doctor, the doctor couldn't suggest I take aspirin because it's not recommended for ankle sprain?' 'That's correct your honor,' said the lawyer.

"I had two hundred witnesses—patients—at court ready to testify about what was done for them. The judge heard ten of them testify in my behalf. The time was getting lengthy, and the judge turned to the FDA lawyer and asked, 'Will you stipulate that these other one hundred and ninety witnesses will tell similar stories? If you don't we'll be sitting here a whole week just listening to them.' Some of the witnesses were other lawyers, physicians, and one was a Supreme Court judge from the state of North Carolina. They finally came to an agreement to stipulate that the whole two hundred witnesses would say something beneficial in my behalf," said Dr. Evers.

United States District Judge Robert H. Varner ruled in 1978 that the government, or anyone else, has no right to determine how a physician must practice. "The FDA in trying to get an injunction for chelating of any kind would have stopped me from using aspirin, penicillin, or other drugs because they all act by the process of chelation," Dr. Evers pointed out. "However, the judge ruled that I was doing nothing wrong and as a doctor I had the right to choose the method of treatment. No one could interfere with my right to practice medicine. This ruling protected the medical practice rights of every physician in the United States."

The Ra-Mar clinic operated unhindered, successfully administering chelation therapy until April 1979. But Dr. Evers was harassed professionally and financially until 1989. At that time, he and a partner established the International Medical Center in Juarez, Mexico (see Appendix D). The Center, despite Dr. Evers's death, continues to follow his protocol, including use of the chelating solution that he had invented.

Herbert Ray Evers, M.D., was the most bureaucratically harassed physician in the history of medicine. After what he went through in order to practice holistic medicine, it's a wonder that any doctors are left to pursue the healing of patients in an honest, open, insightful and natural manner.

Louis Pasteur said, "Let me tell you the secret that has led me to my goal. My only strength lies in my tenacity." H. Ray Evers, M.D. was tenacious to the end.

Chelation therapy is still under the gun in the United States. A not-so-subtle conspiracy seems to be afoot in the land. Led by a variety of special interests, mostly in conflict with the needs of the medical consumer, it has reached into the agencies of government. More doctors who use ethylene diamine teteraacetic acid (EDTA) in the treatment of arteriosclerosis are being tracked down and oppressed by commercial and political interests. The treatment has practically been made illegal except for human elimination of another mineral poisoning—lead rather than calcium. Don't you wonder why? If it is recommended by the government in the lead detoxification of children, why cannot EDTA chelation be used to prolong the lives of adults that are young, old, healthy, sick, enthusiastically alive, or on the threshold of death? In the next chapter, we shall present you with some answers to this puzzle.

Chapter Seventeen

THE CONSPIRACY AGAINST CHELATION THERAPY

For the sick and diseased, the restoration of health is the overriding concern of their lives. For the healthy, the threat of illness and disease, while less immediate, remains a "brooding omnipresence." While good health and the absence of disease is always a central private concern, it is only in the last few decades that it has emerged as a central public concern. Yet two hundred years ago we pledged our society to safeguarding "life, liberty and the pursuit of happiness." Is there any human condition which more directly and poignantly denies to us those inalienable rights than dread disease and inadequate health care? A government which does not direct its energies to the eradication of disease or injury and does not provide its citizens with basic health care is as derelict as that government was from which we declared our independence almost 200 years ago.

—U.S. SENATOR WARREN G. MAGNUSON,
How Much for Health, 1974

A Conspiracy That Could Kill

A former violinist with the Cleveland orchestra, Bert Arenson of Cleveland, Ohio, underwent double coronary artery bypass surgery in late spring 1973. The operation was only partially effective. In less than a year, Mr. Arenson experienced coronary insufficiency almost as severe as before the procedure. He quickly realized that his health situation was absolutely unendurable.

Arenson found himself unable even to stand for more than five minutes without angina. Pain pierced his chest with any exertion. Walking for the man was confined to his home—going from room to room—slowly and infrequently. In fact, any effort led to irregular heart rhythm and immediate chest discomfort. He could not tolerate cold temperatures; even stepping out of his house brought on heart symptoms. "My whole problem was getting worse and deteriorating rapidly. It became quite clear—I did not have too much longer to live," Arenson said.

His cardiac condition made reconsideration of further bypass surgery seem foolish. The patient had blockages downstream from his vein-artery grafts, in the small arteries beyond the bypassed main branches. Surgery could not reach them, and except from EDTA chelation, there is at present no effective treatment for this occlusive arteriolar condition in the heart. After the obvious failure of the first operation, the cardiac patient could foresee no benefit from additional open-heart surgery.

Fortunately, Arenson watched a television documentary on chelation therapy. He became curious but held his enthusiasm in check until he could learn more. His wife Sylvia investigated this potentially life-saving treatment. She made long-distance telephone inquiries, studied clinical journals at the medical library and spoke with people about the procedure. The therapy was then unavailable in their home city of Cleveland or in any of the nearby states. Within a month Sylvia embarked with her husband for Miami, Florida, so he could receive chelation from Carlos P. Lamar, M.D.

By the end of six months of travel back and forth to Miami and forty-five EDTA infusions, Arenson was walking briskly two and a half miles daily, even in freezing weather, which ordinarily is not possible for angina patients.

Half a year later, the heart patient had finally located a Pittsburgh physician who would administer the therapy. But he was struck down by acute cardiac insufficiency and was hospitalized the evening before he was to begin another course of chelation. The appointment came too late to prevent his latest heart seizure.

His emergency cardiologist at the Pittsburgh hospital held out no hope that the man would get better following his heart attack.

"The picture was terribly gloomy," Bert Arenson told us. "But then the hospital authorities allowed something unprecedented and really unusual. They permitted me to travel by ambulance daily to the office of Howard T. Lewis, Jr., M.D., of Pittsburgh for five days of chelation therapy during my second week in the hospital."

Improvement of the patient was so obvious and rapid that in a few days the hospital's doctors and nurses and even the cleaning women looked at him in wonderment. His skin color changed from sallow to normal, appetite returned, and he could walk without feeling chest pain or gasping for a breath, as he did before the chelation. Arenson left the hospital and continued with twenty more infusions which he received from Dr. Lewis.

Since that time of cardiac crisis, the patient has taken additional chelations regularly. He eventually received a total of 205 treatments. Now they are administered to him by a family practitioner in Cleveland, James P. Frackelton, M.D., who became interested in providing this treatment. Dr. Frackelton became president of the American College for Advancement in Medicine and is a member of its board of directors.

The Conspiracy Against Chelation Therapy

Some powerful, established institutions feel threatened by EDTA chelation therapy. They are the driving force behind an unspoken, unacknowledged, but powerful movement to illegitamize magnesium disodium-EDTA treatment. They want chelation therapy eliminated from the American scene. Even now, only a few courageous physicians have the temerity to use magnesium disodium ethylene diamine tetraacetic acid (EDTA) in their clinical practices.

Why is *anyone* against intravenous EDTA? Why do certain special-interest groups fight so hard against the treatment being made generally available? Why are there, in fact, vested interests cooperating in a possible conspiracy against the therapy? Who are the conspirators? What do they have to gain? We know the answers to these questions, and by the time you have completed reading this chapter, you will know them, too. Then perhaps together we can begin actions that will force our government to permit us to use this basic health care to reverse hardening of the arteries.

Three powerful interest groups are apparently conspiring to keep chelation therapy away from the American people. One group has evolved from the collective efforts of vascular surgeons, heart surgeons, chest surgeons, anesthesiologists, the administrators of hospitals with bypass surgical facilities, cardiologists, internists, other physicians and self-serving politicians from the American Medical Association. These specialized groups collectively claim that the EDTA chelating agent is dangerous and unproven. They point to the lack of double-blind research studies. Yet, these same physicians permit and even encourage *more dangerous and unproven* bypass surgery to go on, with a known 10 percent mortality rate.

Pharmaceutical companies combine to prevent EDTA from coming on the market, and they comprise a third conspiring group. Theirs is a kind of economic boycott, which is markedly unfair to the medical consumer in its effect. This counter-consumer attitude is motivated by a few factors which I shall describe, but all of them are tied to money.

The health insurance industry is committed, as much as possible, to preventing health insurance policy holders from being reimbursed for chelation treatment. They seem to fear that although eventually it would save them much money which today is wasted on surgery, too many people would take the treatment who now take nothing to prevent or reverse hardening of the arteries. Or perhaps they are simply responding to pressure put on them by the medical and political establishments. For whatever reason, the health insurance companies act as a third conspiratorial group to block the acceptance and widespread use of chelation therapy.

The American Medical Conspirators

As it becomes more widespread, the effects of chelation therapy on the American medical profession, particularly the specialists of internal medicine, cardiology, heart surgery, chest surgery, vascular surgery and anesthesiology, will certainly be devastating. Fewer patients will seek out these medical professionals to receive their services. The high prices they have been commanding will have to drop precipitously. Expensive equipment will go unused. A tremendous reduction in the utilization of hospital operating rooms, hospital beds, nursing homes and medical clinics will be another result.

We have said that cardiovascular disease is the largest single cause of disability and death in the United States. Our statement is supported by the American Heart Association, which estimates that heart disease alone presently costs the American public more than $150 billion a year. And the AHA projects that the figure will go much higher.

As an industry, the sale of medical services for just cardiovascular disease is not far behind the automobile industry. American medical traditionalists are not known to waste all of their builtup hospital facilities and the investments they have made in bypass surgical equipment. Certain highly trained specialists are not going to sacrifice their cardiac surgical skills to become just good samaritans and exist on the 5 to 10 percent of patients who may still have some form of vasculary surgery performed after they have received chelation therapy. The loss of various securities and endowments would be too great.[1-3]

Something is quite wrong with the present orthodox medical system that requires more and more bypass surgical patients to keep expensive equipment operating. An excess of catheter-trained cardiologists are disgorged into the health ranks each year. There is an overabundance of cardiovascular surgeons.[4] The shift from primary-care physician to specialist has caused an excessive use of invasive cardiologic techniques.[5] Our country has become overly oriented toward vascular surgery. Still, the medical investments have been made and organized medicine is attempting to make these investments pay off.

Administration of chelation therapy does not require the supervision of a medical specialist. No extra technical training is required. The approximately one thousand doctors now providing EDTA infusion around the United States are mostly general practitioners, who often are less vulnerable to the constraints imposed by medical specialty boards than the specialist. The treatment is usually given in a physician's office with extremely effective results. General practitioners soon discover that they hardly need to refer their patients to other medical specialists at all. And they seldom require hospital facilities for their patients.

EDTA chelation is highly effective—simply too effective—for the medical profession. That is the reason disciplinary actions in obvious open restraint of trade are being taken against chelating physicians.

Medical Pressure Against Another Chelating Physician

The case of Robert J. Rogers, M.D., of Melbourne, Florida, is typical of how organized medicine is attempting to thwart the use of chelation therapy. He is a physician we described in Chapter One. In November 1975, the Brevard County Medical Society expelled Dr. Rogers and ordered him to stop giving chelation treatment, which he had used since 1970.

The medical society held a hearing on Dr. Rogers after Dorothy M. Shamp, of Port Angeles, Washington, wrote to complain, saying her mother had received EDTA chelation from the physician in 1974. Mrs. Shamp said that over a three-month period her mother, Ruth Norris, spent between $1,500 and $2,000 for treatments and examinations— "nearly half of the equity she received from the sale of her home."[6,7] Dr. Rogers' records, however, show that Mrs. Norris paid $884 for all treatments and examinations over a six-month period in 1974.

Mrs. Shamp admitted in a January 1977 telephone interview that while her mother praised the treatments, she, Mrs. Shamp, was suspicious of them simply because she had never before heard of chelation.

At the medical society hearing, Dr. Rogers was not allowed to present objective medical evidence, such as the tests on his patients, which proved the effectiveness of the treatment. Nor were his patients permitted to testify about the benefits they had received, or that chelation was *their* preferred treatment.

Since Dr. Rogers would not agree to stop using chelation, he was expelled from the Brevard County Medical Society, which also brought the matter to the attention of the Florida State Board of Medical Examiners. Dr. Rogers' license to practice medicine in the state was in jeopardy.

His hearing before the state board was held in Orlando, Florida, September 10, 1976. He was represented by Attorney Andrew Graham, who raised serious legal questions, including one regarding the qualifications of the board's medical witness, Waldo Fisher, M.D., a medical researcher at the University of Florida who disputed Dr. Rogers' claims for chelation. Dr. Fisher was not an "expert" on chelation, for he had no professional expertise with EDTA or chelation therapy, said Attorney Graham.

Despite this, the board gave the previously written recommendation of Robert C. Palmer, M.D., of Pensacola, Florida full ratification. Dr. Palmer represented the Brevard County Medical Society. He wrote, after hearing testimony from Dr. Fisher and Dr. Rogers, "The use of such method of treatment by a private practitioner in a manner that must be categorized as haphazard and flippant . . . fails to conform to the standards of acceptable and prevailing medical practice."

The Florida Board of Examiners ruled on January 21, 1977 that Dr. Rogers be put on one-year probation, with the stipulation that his license be revoked if he continued to use chelation therapy.

With assistance from the American Academy of Medical Preventics (now the American College for Advancement in Medicine) Dr. Rogers filed an appeal against the Florida Board of Medical Examiners' order with the District Court of Appeal, First District State of Florida. The case (R. 1324–1326) took two years and the expenditure of about $20,000 by the physician. Furthermore, the board's action had an adverse effect on his practice, of which only 20 percent involved chelation. In conversations with Dr. Rogers, he told me, "People were reticent to come to me for care. It cost me considerable in time, money and distress."

Then, on January 11, 1979 a three-judge panel ruled strongly against the medical board—both the Florida Board of Medical Examiners and the Brevard County Medical Society had their actions criticized. Acting Judge Tyrie A. Boyer in the First District Court of Appeal ruled that the medical board had no authority to deprive a doctor's patients from therapy they want, unless it can prove "unlawfulness, harm, fraud, coercion or misrepresentation."

Just because most of the medical profession rejects a certain method of treatment, the court ruled, does not give the state medical board authority to punish a doctor for using it. Then, in a moment of philosphical musing, Judge Boyer wrote, "History teaches us that virtually all progress in science and medicine has been accomplished as a result of the courageous efforts of those members of the profession willing to pursue their theories in the face of tremendous odds despite the criticism of fellow practitioners." He compared Dr. Rogers to Copernicus, Pasteur and Freud as an innovator in science and medicine. He said those scientists were first ridiculed and then lionized for their unorthodox ideas. But how many other physicians in Florida, witnessing such persecution of a fellow M.D. by his peers, would have the courage and convictions of Dr. Rogers? How many were cowed into silence—and ignorance—about chelation by the medical establishment?

Pharmaceutical Companies Are a Conspiring Group

EDTA, used for intravenous injection, has been in the public domain for a long time. We previously pointed out that its patents had expired, and, unfortunately, there is no real profit for most pharmaceutical companies in making and distributing it. They are therefore not willing to invest any money in EDTA to prove through research its use in preventing or reversing hardening of the arteries.

The pharmaceutical companies might not want to disseminate general information about EDTA, even if they could, because the substance's latent potential is to compete for sales with their current, fully invested and highly profitable drug products. These products number in the thousands and include such items as drugs for hypertension and angina, vasodilators for arteriosclerosis, and others for problems resulting from impaired blood circulation. Intravenous EDTA therapy might eliminate the need for all of them.

To adequately document the therapeutic effects of EDTA on hardening of the arteries, a large, expensive study has to be undertaken. To satisfy the purists in science, the study theoretically should be a double-blind controlled investigation that would cost millions of dollars. A pharmaceutical company with faith in its patented product ordinarily underwrites this sort of study. Understandably, with no clear-cut patent to protect its financial interests, no pharmaceutical company is going to foot the bill for an extensive double-blind investigation, even though the government offers some "label protection" on drugs which can no longer be patented. Pharmaceutical industry executives are not altruists. They are businesspeople, often with stockholders to report to, and they must have a return from investment.

But the pharmaceutical industry can be severely faulted as a group conspiring against chelation therapy in another way. In 1978, the pharmaceutical package insert that described the effects of EDTA injection listed calcified arterial disease as a viable use (that is, "possibly effective"). That listing has been removed. Melting under the heat of FDA demands, Abbott Laboratories and other EDTA manufacturers have taken a negative step away from preserving the nation's life and health. By agreeing to the removal of the indication for occlusive vascular disease from the package insert, the pharmaceutical companies have, in effect, affirmed their own disapproval of the use of EDTA chelation for hardening of the arteries. This action has left physicians with a previous warning against use of the drug in "generalized arteriosclerosis associated with aging" to explain to their potential or actual medical malpractice claimants. That statement made some sense when above it the package insert recommended the product in angina and other blood vessel conditions. Now without those possible indications the chelating physicians have an additional legal obstacle in using EDTA for their patients. Even the FDA is unable to explain why the negative statement about its use in arteriosclerosis prevails. Why was it put there in the first place? No one offers an answer.

On its own, the ACAM researched how to get EDTA moved from "possibly effective" to "proven effective" for purposes of FDA regulations. The FDA referred ACAM officers and directors to Abbott Laboratories, which had already done the basic new drug application on EDTA many years before. ACAM contacted Abbott Laboratories for assistance in completing the necessary paperwork for its application. The ACAM physicians proposed that they would append their physician-sponsored investigational new drug application to Abbott's basic NDA. This procedure would incorporate the data the physicians had accumulated on EDTA to make a meaningful application for FDA purposes. It would be no extra trouble for the pharmaceutical company.

To finance the additional research they intended, and to do it without help from the pharmaceutical industry or the U.S. government, all the ACAM physicians assessed themselves $600 each. Suddenly, in response to pressure from representatives of organized medicine who are chelation opponents, Abbott Laboratories cut off the friendly relationship it had developed with ACAM members. Perhaps Abbott did that as protection against FDA or organized medicine reprisals. Without Abbott's co-operation, the executive committee of ACAM decided to temporarily postpone the research project on EDTA and vascular disease which the physicians had planned to accomplish. Then the ACAM physicians found they had to spend their research funds to fight organized medicine to maintain their physician rights to offer EDTA treatment to their own patients. The battle is being fought continuously. The research funds set aside by ACAM must be wasted in defense of those doctors to practice medicine in the way they know best will help their patients.

We Need Double-Blind Studies

The Department of Health and Human Services' chief spokespersons on chelation demand that double-blind studies be performed to prove chelation therapy is a low-risk therapeutic procedure. But no one will do them—and the medical establishment and political bureaucracy stop anyone who wishes to try. Clearly, it is time these studies be carried out, under federal or private foundation sponsorship, with funds allocated for full-blown medical research of EDTA.

Yet bypass surgery is done daily in the United States without the "appropriate controls" asked of EDTA chelation physicians. As noted earlier, studies were done in the evaluation of the Mammary Artery Ligation Operation, and it was determined that this surgical procedure, quite popular in the 1960s, was apparently producing primarily a "placebo effect." In other instances, some double-blind studies attempted in psychiatry have also shown serious deficiencies with this form of medical care.

Some chelation opponents feel that the EDTA infusion therapy may be a placebo. They are certainly welcome to that opinion. Nonetheless, as long as 80 percent of chelating physicians' patients stop having angina and leg cramps, recover their memories, do not need any amputation of gangrenous legs and toes, and find vision returning, it should be considered a useful therapy, placebo effect or not. Currently, none of the chelated patients dies as a result of this safe, effective, nonsurgical approach.

The pharmaceutical industry, as we have noted, has a tremendous investment in cardiovascular and ancillary drugs. But it must also invest in drug advertising to get any single product sold. No pharmaceutical firm is going to spend additional millions of dollars to clear EDTA through the FDA for cardiovascular disease and then more millions to promote the drug. Why? The reason is that they could not protect their investment. Anyone can make EDTA. Other drug companies would get a free ride. They could make and sell the same substance, although they might not be allowed to state the same claims on the package insert for a period of time. In the meantime, the investing company might never recover its costs.

Promotion for a drug is necessary in American medicine. No practicing physician adhering to the AMA line would have the temerity to use any drug that the drug industry does not heavily promote in medical journals. A physician puts his career on the line recommending *any* treatment other than the usual, reasonable and customary one. Drugs promoted in medical journals are considered usual, reasonable and customary. The drug companies are forced to spend many millions in drug promotion; otherwise, a physician will refuse to use the nonpromoted product.

The Role of Health Insurance Companies in the Conspiracy

We have pointed out that widespread use of alternative cardiovascular therapies will have a considerable effect on medical practice. There is now no generally effective treatment for patients who suffer from vascular occlusive disease. The medical profession's response has been to provide little treatment other than simply to observe the course of the patient's arteries as they are undergoing their hardening. When the patient's condition becomes severe, either he dies or he becomes a candidate for vascular surgery. Simply put, in most cases the nonholistic-type orthodox practice abandons the patient. Palliative segmental surgery is sometimes carried out—for a disease that is not at all segmental. Vascular surgeons may attempt to repair your heart or your legs, but arteries in your head still remain diseased. And this medical neglect is aided and abetted in a not-so-subtle manner by the health insurance industry.

Health insurance companies refuse to deal with treatment of a person's entire arterial system. Instead their health insurance policy payout is biased in favor of crisis-oriented medicine. Health insurance is like fire insurance. The house has to catch fire before a fire insurance company will pay on its policy. The same goes for your health—or loss of it. "Health" insurance should be called "sickness" insurance, since you must be sick before you can receive reimbursement on your policy. The only way we as medical consumers can collect third-party compensation is to undergo some emergency or crisis medical care, such as surgical bypass. Diseases must be well established before there is any financial assistance from our carrier. We receive no preventive treatment, or very little, that is reimbursed by health insurance.

We do not even get compensation for comprehensive medical checkups because we feel some chest pain. With no diagnosis, there is no reimbursement. In other words, the health insurance industry pays us to be sick and ignores us if we remain well. It is the ultimate in negative living—reimbursement only if we get sick.

If chelation therapy were to become an accepted modality, it soon would be in widespread use. The net result might be an upset in the immediate financial balance of many insurance carriers. They are not projecting long-term savings through the diminished need for intensive-care procedures, high-priced surgery, prolonged hospitalization and other medical expenses. Insurance executives seem to see only the initial costs of treating 115 million potentially arteriosclerotic patients among our populace in the first few years that chelation therapy becomes popularly accepted. They don't want to pay for this sort of preventive medicine.

Yes, it is clear that preventive care may cost more initially. But the long-term savings to the carriers could be tremendous, if only the new diagnostic methods were put to use in a concentrated preventive medical program. The procedures already exist. New sensitive tests, such as treadmill cardiology, noninvasive laboratory techniques, plethysmography, systolic ejection times, high-speed retinal vessel photography, omnicardiography, Doppler ultrasound, hair analysis and early stroke-risk detection with thermography, have come into more common use. These techniques, instruments and machines diagnose disease processes at an earlier stage.

Thus, more and more patients who now receive only watchful observation as treatment could request or receive EDTA chelation. This would let them live longer without disability. Costs to insurance carriers for health maintenance of policy holders might be formidable at first. Insurance company executives certainly recognize this. Some patients who know of chelation treatment have accepted bypass surgery of the arteries, simply because it was covered by their insurance policies and EDTA chelation therapy was not.

The health insurance companies' opposition to chelation therapy comes down finally to that secret motivating word—*money*. Even though chelation treatments for policy holders represent significant long-range financial savings to the insurance carriers, they opt instead for crisis medicine and emergency intervention. Actuaries have shown insurance executives that with continued encouragement for the practice of crisis medicine only a few patients survive to reach major medical centers where they receive very expensive medical care. Or, many patients refuse surgery, preferring to let events take their natural course instead. The health insurance companies can thus get off the hook early in a cardiovascular patient's illness. He soon dies!

Immediate implementation of a program of EDTA intravenous treatment to potentially 115 million policy holders at a cost of $2,000 to $3,000 each would possibly bankrupt all the health insurance companies several times over—up to $345 billion worth! Obviously, that seems to be a present fear of carriers. Of course, this would not happen in one year, but the payout might occur over a ten- to fifteen-year period. People would live a lot longer and be a lot healthier.

The evil tentacles of the health insurance industry conspiracy reach into every chelating physician's practice. The importance of insurance carrier reimbursement to a physician's patients for the financial well-being of a professional practice is clear. Patients rely on their health insurance to pay for the majority of major medical expenses. Many patients who do not get paid are forced to limit the medical services they seek or go elsewhere for their care. Chelation therapy is sacrificed, and its preventive approach cannot be instituted. Crisis medicine then must continue as an individual patient's ongoing illness program. Until now, health insurance carriers have not encouraged Americans to remain healthy.

Why Not Try Chelation Therapy Before Surgery?

An extremely important part of the conspiratorial suppression of chelation therapy is the refusal of Medicare, Blue Shield and other third-party payers to compensate or reimburse for the treatment. The economic interests of medical orthodoxy are, of course, the most basic underpinning of this refusal. If chelation therapy was paid for by third-party insurance, who would undertake vascular surgery without first trying chelation? Many of the heart surgeons and peripheral vascular surgeons would probably have to change their specialties.

More unfortunate than any other factor in this whole conspiracy, however, is that our own government is aiding the advancement of those medical financial interests above the interests of ordinary citizens. The financial drain on the average person can become quite serious. For patients without financial resources, it could mean denial of treatment and death.

How crazy the system is! Medicare is willing to pay ten to twenty-five times as much for bypass surgery as chelation therapy might cost. Nevertheless, the patient is directed toward surgery and away from chelation.

If chelation therapy hadn't faced this longtime, effective and ruthless conspiracy, there would be more data, more experience, perhaps several double-blind studies and a much greater background of research on the subject. There would be more facilities, more chelating physicians and undoubtedly much lower costs. This would make the treatment more effective because it could be better tailored to the needs of us all as individual patients, with the development of more data. Our individual needs vary, but what never varies is our right to select the means by which we may preserve our bodies. That is our medical right! Should we be denied our medical right to take chelation therapy if we want it?

Chapter Eighteen

OUR MEDICAL RIGHT TO CHELATION THERAPY

Decisions about accepting/rejecting, withholding/withdrawing treatment are decisions (to be distinguished from diagnosis and prognosis) that whenever possible belong to the patient or, when the patient is incompetent, to those who presumably have the best interests of the patient at heart—saving right of appeal. This can easily be forgotten in a highly technological health-care system.

> —Statement by ANDRE E. HELLEGERS, M.D., LeRoy Walters, James Childress, Rabbi Seymour Siegel, Richard A. McCormick, S.J., Roy Branson, Thomas Beauchamp, Seymour Perlin, M.D., and Joseph A. LaBarge (all members of the Kennedy Institute for the Study of Human Reproduction and Bioethics at Georgetown University), *The New York Times,* May 18, 1977

The Near-Death of Ophelia Clementino

For thirty years Palma C. Seders and her husband Amos have lived either with or close by Palma's parents in Temple City, California. Palma watched gratefully as her mom and dad grew older gracefully together. Although they had their little illnesses, the old folks had many more ups than downs—until, that is, a few days after the mother, Ophelia Clementino, celebrated her seventy-ninth birthday.

"My first indication of her illness," said Palma, "was when Momma came into the laundry room. On this particular morning I noted that she was incapable of operating the clothes washer. She seemed confused. The laundry was not properly sorted, and I had to help her with the task."

Palma observed her mother during the next few days and became alarmed at her incoherence and the obvious hallucinations she was experiencing. Then Palma made an appointment with Mrs. Clementino's personal physician in Pasadena, California. The doctor told them the problem was simply "old age."

This seemed an unsatisfactory diagnosis to the daughter, but she gave her mother the prescribed medication anyway. Severe and frequent headaches soon affected the patient.

Mrs. Clementino awoke one night with a severe headache. She looked pale, was upset, spoke incoherently and acted unstable. Her doctor again examined her in the afternoon and decided that Mrs. Clementino had suffered a serious cerebrovascular accident (stroke). He recommended calling in a general practitioner who was located conveniently closer to the family's home. The second doctor confirmed the diagnosis and admitted the patient to the San Gabriel Valley Hospital.

Laboratory tests showed a blood clot had developed on the right side of the woman's head. It was causing some brain damage. Mrs. Clementino remained in the hospital and received treatment until she was allowed to return to Palma's home ten days later. There she was nursed by her daughter and a few other members of their large and loving family.

"Between May and September Momma suffered three more major strokes and several minor ones," Mrs. Seders related. "Each one left her more unstable and incoherent. By mid-October she had undergone a drastic change that was heartbreaking to see. She was no longer able to walk alone or write her name. Even her eating habits became abnormal. She ate with her fingers because she could not distinguish the silverware or was unable to hold it.

"It was twenty-four hours around the clock for dad and me watching my mother. She had to be pushed in the wheel chair because she couldn't comprehend how to operate it. She could not sleep without medication and remained awake much of the time. Her mind was fuzzy, which prevented her from realizing she couldn't stand alone, so she fell down at night when she attempted to go to the bathroom by herself.

"The afternoon that we had an appointment to see her new doctor," Mrs. Seders continued, "my mother was struck again with a severe headache. I saw her color change, lips turned blue, and she trembled. The doctor said she was having another stroke. He injected Talwin (a pain killer) and sent me home with her to put her to bed. She remained there for two days except for the time she fell again and cut open her hand while attempting to go to the bathroom. A surgeon was called to stitch it.

"Then she had still another stroke. I recognized the signs, since her body turned limp and her skin became sallow, cold and clammy. She had no eyeball movement under the lids. She drifted into what appeared to be a coma. The doctor arrived many hours later and said Momma must be hospitalized as she had already begun to retain a lot of fluid and would soon develop pneumonia."

Mrs. Clementino was hospitalized for a second time in the San Gabriel Valley Hospital, where she was nursed by two of her daughters and other family members around the clock.

Ten days later the patient went home, but there she experienced another very serious stroke. This one contorted the right side of her face. It prevented her from swallowing even water without choking. The patient was paralyzed along her entire right side, including the throat muscles. Mrs. Seders tried to reach the doctor again by telephone.

"I explained to him what had happened and asked what more I could do for mother," she said. "He explained there was nothing he could tell me to do. He suggested that we should keep on making her as comfortable as possible and she would slowly slip away.

"As I replaced the receiver I sat there and wondered how long must this poor tortured soul go on like this—dying such a slow death? I would rather see my mother dead when I went back to her room than to have her suffer this way."

Dr. Harper Meets Mrs. Clementino

But Ophelia Clementino hung on to life for another three weeks. The whole family—her sons, daughters, daughters-in-law, sons-in-law and husband—took turns nursing her. They gave her physical therapy three times a day. They fed her carefully by letting fluid trickle down the left side of her throat. Her throat muscles were too paralyzed for the use of a straw. They changed her diapers regularly, since she was incontinent and had lost control of her bowel sphincters. The matriarch was mindless—had no idea of where or who she was—and at times she thought Palma was her own mother.

Mrs. Clementino lost weight until she looked like the picture of death. She continued to suffer small strokes. For those who loved her, it was a heartbreaking time—a nightmare, they said. And even as the children worked to keep their mother alive, they agreed it would be better for Momma if she were already dead.

Al Clementino, Palma's younger brother, arrived with news about a doctor in Alabama who was having success treating patients for this same condition. Al telephoned Dr. Evers in Andalusia at the Columbia General Hospital. Dr. Evers listened to Al's description of his mother and determined that she was not strong enough for a flight to Alabama. He referred the family to Harold W. Harper, M.D., director of the Harper Metabology and Nutrition Group in Los Angeles, California.

Dr. Harper returned the family's frantic call and consented to travel the thirty-eight miles from his office to Mrs. Seders' home, where the patient was being cared for. Dr. Harper asked that her medical and hospital records be acquired so that he could read them when he examined her. Four days later Palma had all of her mother's medical records. The physician arrived to examine his new patient.

"I'll always remember Mrs. Clementino," Dr. Harper said. "Her ankles were swollen and fluid was in the base of her lungs. She was paralyzed on the right side; there was an absence of neurological responses on the right side—an absence of pulses also. Babinski reflex was negative; deep tendon reflexes were absent and she could not swallow; she could not hear. She could not speak or understand words either in English or Italian. The patient had no control of bowel movements; was semi-comatose—lapsing in and out of sleep. The condition of her skin indicated a dehydrated condition. There was arrhythmia of the heart, overflowing medical evidence in all the parameters of the presence of arteriosclerotic disease; congestive heart failure with a free flux (swelling) of the lower extremities. My judgment was that Mrs. Clementino literally could have dropped dead at any moment."

Dr. Harper asked all the adult Clementino family members to gather together in the living room. "As we sat down I was sure he was thinking the same as were all of us—that it was almost too late for my mother," Palma Seders said. "Then for almost an hour he explained to us about chelation therapy—its meaning and purpose and the risks involved, since Mamma was so far gone. We knew that the American medical profession did not approve of the procedure. Dr. Harper told us that.

This meant that Medicare would not accept the financial burden. The treatment would probably be at our expense, without reimbursement from insurance. Therefore, it would incur much medical cost on our part. Momma would have to be hospitalized so there would be the risk of transporting her to the hospital by ambulance. There was the risk of losing her with the first treatment. She was so critical!"

"Yes, we discussed the dire emergency of the patient's condition," Dr. Harper later told me. "There was very little hope for her survival, no matter what modality she was treated with. One of the family members asked, 'Is there anything whatsoever that can be used to treat Momma?' In my medical opinion there was no therapy that would possibly give the patient even a chance, other than chelation therapy. Even with chelation, as I told the family that night, the patient might die before we could get her into the hospital. She might die after receiving the first chelation bottle, or the second. She might die in the middle of getting the treatment, or even at the end of it—because of her dire physical condition."

Silence lay heavy in that room. Seconds ticked by. The patient's children sat thinking. Then one of them said, "Neither one of her other doctors had any recommendations. They sent her home to die, and we can't accept that. Will you try to help her?"

Dr. Harper repeated his warnings about the closeness of death. He told them to think it over some more, and if they wished to have their mother treated, yes, he would try to help.

That was a Friday night. The family telephoned the physician the following Sunday with the news that Momma Clementino had suffered her ninth stroke on Saturday morning. They thought surely she would die then, but this tenacious old lady still held onto life. What a will to live she possessed! She lingered through Sunday morning, and her children and husband decided they had to give her at least a fighting chance. The family begged the doctor to give her chelation treatment on Monday—if she survived until then.

The patient was transferred by ambulance from the Seders' home to St. Joseph's Hospital in Burbank, California, where Dr. Harper had provisional staff privileges. He was supervised by a medical staff advisor. In the hospital the physician's careful reexamination of Mrs. Clementino took much of Monday morning. She had been comatose now for several days. He ordered a full laboratory workup and medications for her. She also received oxygen.

In the afternoon Dr. Harper returned to read the patient's X-ray studies and to evaluate some of her laboratory test results. He did more of the same Tuesday and prescribed digitalis and diuretics to relieve her congestive heart failure and pulmonary edema. All of the various laboratory tests were completed by Friday morning.

Since the patient had remained in a stable condition, Dr. Harper ordered the first chelation treatment be given. He left complete written and oral instructions with the nurses on duty. The nursing staff members knew exactly how the solution was to be mixed—how much and the drops per minute. Dr. Harper had given unmistakable orders of what was to be done and how.

Mrs. Clementino Is Refused Chelation Therapy

Dr. Harper told the Clementino family that the first bottle of EDTA was going to be infused that day. "I wanted somebody from the family in attendance twenty-four hours a day," Dr. Harper said. "The lady needed full attention, and the hospital couldn't spare around-the-clock nurses. The Clementinos were a very close-knit and loving family. They were anxious to help. Two of her children agreed to stay with the patient all the time."

Dr. Harper went back to see his patient and to make rounds Friday afternoon. Then he returned again after office hours Friday evening.

"I asked the two family members present what time the hospital staff had finished giving their mother the treatment," Dr. Harper explained. "And they said, 'Well they didn't bring anything in at all, doctor!' I was shocked! I said, 'What? Do you mean they didn't start the IV yet?'

" 'There's no IV, doctor. They haven't given her anything!'

"Well, I flew out of that hospital room like a shot," said Dr. Harper, "and went to the nursing station and shouted, 'why weren't my orders followed?' One of the nurses said, 'To find out, you'll have to see the nursing director!'

"I hunted her down," said the physician. "The nursing director told me she had been instructed not to follow my orders by the head of the experimental medicine committee of the hospital, who is a cardiologist. She told me I had to talk with him."

The chairman of Experimental Medicine told Dr. Harper, "St. Joseph's Hospital really doesn't care what you give to your patients, doctor. If you want to take a tablet of arsenic and personally put it into the patient's mouth and wash it down with a glass of water because that's your way of practicing medicine, well—OK—you may poison anyone you wish as long as you take the entire responsibility. However, the nursing staff of St. Joseph's Hospital will not administer any of your poisons or other medications, because that implies that we approve of what you're doing, and we don't.

"You're new here, Dr. Harper—on provisional staff," continued the committee chief. "If you wish to give chelation therapy, you will have to sit there as every drop goes in; otherwise, it ·cannot be given in this hospital. We don't believe in that therapy or what you are doing with it."

Dr. Harper pointed out that it would take six hours or more for this particular patient to receive intravenous EDTA chelation for just one treatment. "I'll be happy to mix the solution and start the I.V. if I can save someone's life," he said, "but the family cannot afford to have me sit there for the whole time."

The hospital's experimental medicine committee chief remained unrelenting and refused any compromise. Dr. Harper was left dangling with his problem.

Palma Seders said, "The next thing for consideration was finding a place where this therapy could be administered. Dr. Harper was able to find a convalescent hospital where they agreed to permit chelation therapy. It was the best he could do. On the next day Mom was discharged from St. Joseph's Hospital and transferred by ambulance to the Victory Convalescent Home in North Hollywood, California."

Palma Seders described how she and the family members approached the situation. She wrote in a long letter that the place was old and awful. The first thing the daughters did was to strip the bed, wash it with disinfectant, and order fresh linen. They cleaned the room and disinfected the furniture, too. The daughters agreed they were glad their mother was so incoherent and confused that she did not see the surroundings or understand what was taking place. Nevertheless, this was the only health facility available where anyone from the medical establishment would allow chelation therapy to be administered to the patient.

Unknown to the parties at that time, there was a single legal consequence of the patient's confinement in the convalescent home that would deprive Ophelia Clementino of Medicare reimbursement of her medical expenses. The reason was that she was not a patient in a certified hospital when Dr. Harper finally was able to administer EDTA to her.

The Patient Finally Receives Intravenous Chelation

"That North Hollywood convalescent home did not have a staff able to start the I.V.s, so I went there and mixed the solution and started the drip," Dr. Harper said. "The family members watched it go in and then told the nurses when it had finished. The nurses would enter the room and remove the IV needle and tubing. My plan was for a series of twenty-one chelation treatments administered every other day."

Palma Seders discussed the changes that started to take place. "It was after the third treatment that Momma started to recognize my sister Mary, Dad, and me," she told me. "She could swallow, too—not just liquids but solids."

"By the fifth treatment day," Dr. Harper related, "her neurological responses had begun to return to the right side. The Babinski reflex now became normal. By the sixth treatment day movement was noticed on the right side."

"He asked her to squeeze his hand," Palma said. "At first Momma refused for fear of hurting him. I told her to show Dr. Harper how strong she was by squeezing his hand. She did, and there was enough force in that weak little grip for the doctor to know she was responding. I could tell how pleased he was by the expression on his face. Mary, Dad and I were in tears. It was the first sign she had reflexes. Now we felt some hope. To think that after all she had been through, perhaps now there would be a chance!"

Dr. Harper said, "She began active movement of the right side of the body and was swallowing well by the eighth treatment day. She began to hold onto the bedside rail with her right hand and actively use it. I could communicate with her at that point very well."

Palma Seders added, "During the next four weeks Momma continued to make progress. Her improvement was remarkable. I took about 200 pictures of her during this time. By January fourth she looked great. The paralysis was completely gone. By January eleventh (the tenth chelation) she was able to use bedside facilities, brush her teeth and eat by herself. It was amazing to watch how she took a cup of coffee and brought it to her mouth with her right hand. On January 14, with our assistance she maneuvered herself to sit at the edge of the bed. Then we got her up in the wheel chair twice a day. Momma was doing so well that Dr. Harper felt we should try to get her on her feet, even if only to stand, to prepare her to relearn to walk.

This she did with the aid of a walking device. She was quite proud of herself."

On the twelfth treatment day, the physician removed the indwelling catheter from Mrs. Clementino's bladder. She was continent and able to control her urinary flow. Her bowel movements had been controlled by the tenth treatment. By the sixteenth treatment the patient walked 150 yards by herself while using the walker. She doubled the distance by the eighteenth treatment, and finally she walked out of the home after the twenty-first treatment.

Two weeks after her discharge from the convalescent home, Ophelia Clementino prepared to keep an appointment to see her physician. She anticipated it with excitement. A new hairdo was in order, she insisted, even for an eighty-year-old lady. Ophelia refused use of the walker because she wanted to walk into the doctor's office unaided on her own two feet. Her husband, her daughter Palma and Palma's husband Amos held their emotions in check as the elderly woman made her way through Dr. Harper's reception room door.

Palma told of the events of that day: "Now came what was to be one of the greatest days of my Mom's life, February 18. She had a very restful night; she looked wonderful this morning; quite excited about getting to Dr. Harper's office. He hadn't seen her since she was discharged two weeks ago, and she had improved considerably.

"After breakfast I got her ready early so as to give us enough time to travel. We were to be at his office at 1:00 P.M. My husband stayed home from work that day to help me. He placed her wheel chair in the car and gave her the walker to help her outside. To my surprise she insisted she didn't need it anymore. She wanted to walk alone! We helped her into the car. I think we all tried to hold back our emotions. She looked just beautiful, and I took some snapshots of her as I always wanted to remember this moment.

"We arrived at the office at 12:30 P.M. I signed Mom in and told the doctor's receptionist that we were here. As we waited, Dr. Amy (Dr. Harper's associate) came out to the business office and noticed us seated in the waiting room. She had been at the convalescent hospital several times to give Mom some of her treatments. She rushed out into the waiting room to greet us and kissed my mother gently. Immediately she left the waiting room to tell Dr. Harper that we were here.

"Suddenly we looked up and out comes Dr. Harper! This was one of his very rare occasions to come out into the reception room. He put his strong arms around my Mom and kissed her tenderly. We could not hide our emotions.

"By now, everyone in the office knew who we were, even the patients who were waiting to see the doctor.

"As he examined her it was very obvious that he was quite pleased to see how much Mom had progressed in the past two weeks. He was rather surprised to hear that she walked without the use of the walker. We were to see him again on March 18.

"It was 5:00 P.M. when we left the doctor's office. I knew she was getting hungry, since we had eaten an early lunch. I told her we would be home soon and I would get our dinner ready. She turned to me and said I must be crazy to want to prepare dinner on such a wonderful day. My Mom wouldn't take no for an answer, so we ended up going out to dinner at her favorite coffee shop. She ate very well. We arrived home two hours later, and I was more tired out than my Mom was."

Following her original twenty-one chelations, Mrs. Clementino took five more treatments six months later and five further treatments six months after that. Nine months then passed without treatment, and she began showing signs of the return of her paralysis. Consequently, Dr. Harper administered ten additional chelation treatments—her last to date. The chelation therapy kept the patient well and functional.

Mrs. Clementino is now well and carrying on a productive life. She vacuums, washes dishes, cooks, gardens and is generally active in other ways in her own home. Her hearing has returned, and her appetite is so good the family says she eats anything put in front of her, including Italian wine and sausage!

Ophelia Clementino's family refused to abandon their mother and give up her right to live with dignity. They rejected the medical establishment's advice to let her simply slip quietly into death. The woman owned a body, mind and spirit, and Palma, Frank, Mary, Al, Amos, Vickie, Joe, Dad and other family members did everything in their power to restore all three.

Every human being has that right. As long as a certain medical method exists that can be clinically applied to make a sick person function more normally, he or she, you or I, deserves the opportunity to receive that particular method. Regardless of cost or risk or criticism from orthodox organized medicine, we must demand our medical rights. Even if treatment has to be rendered in a motel, the back room of a pool hall, or in a broken-down convalescent home, as in Mrs. Clementino's case, it is our legal, moral, and ethical right to use our bodies as we see fit. It is also our constitutional right.

Ignorance of Treatment Is Malpractice

Alfred Soffer, M.D., former executive director of the American College of Chest Surgeons, says, "Unbridled therapeutic accessibility is not a service to the physician or patient, and the medical profession does not consider that unnecessary restrictions have been placed on it when worthless compounds are prohibited from sale and distribution."[1]

This is where Dr. Soffer's interpretation of the scientific method is in disagreement with the holistic concept of whole-person medical management.

George W. Kell, J.D., an attorney who practiced law in Modesto, California, represented Ophelia Clementino in her fight for a Fair Hearing pursuant to Part B of the Medicare Act, after the carrier, Occident Life Insurance Company of California, turned down her request for reimbursement of her medical bills. In his post-hearing brief, Attorney Kell wrote, "Had EDTA chelation therapy not been administered to the claimant, she could not have survived more than a few days or at the outside, two to four weeks. EDTA chelation therapy was responsible for her recovery."[2]

According to Dr. Soffer's line of thinking, Mrs. Clementino should have been allowed to die. This attitude was also reflected by the second doctor Palma Seders called, who recommended that she should make her mother "as comfortable as possible and she would slowly slip away." Dr. Soffer's kind of thinking is also represented by the administration at St. Joseph's Hospital, which refused to permit hospital personnel to administer life-saving treatment. The various parties who represented the medical establishment condemned the patient to death, simply because they did not have knowledge of the treatment or did not like the therapy proposed.

In fact, both of Mrs. Clementino's former physicians, and St. Joseph's Hospital as well, had professional liability in her case. A court decision in California holds that every physician or hospital facility must explain *all* therapeutic alternatives. The California Supreme Court handed down that decision in the case of *Cobbs vs. Grant* (8 Cal 3d 229, 240; 104 C.R. 505, 513). The court said that every doctor owed the "duty of reasonable disclosure of the available choices with respect to proposed therapy and of the dangers inherently and potentially involved in each" to his patient.

The doctor or hospital that fails to deliver the best product for the patient, or withholds a therapy offering less danger to the patient, which the doctor or hospital has power to provide, may be held guilty of medical malpractice.

Cobbs vs. Grant further holds that a person of adult years and in sound mind, or his responsible agent, has the right, in the exercise of control over his own body, to determine his own course of treatment.

Ignorance of the treatment is also tantamount to malpractice, the court ruled. If the doctor or hospital *knew* of the alternative treatment and did not tell the patient, or her family, they, under the *Cobbs vs. Grant* informed-consent doctrine, would have every reason to sue. If the doctor or hospital did *not* know about chelation therapy, their ignorance of the method won't protect them if it is shown that, because of their ignorance, the patient has been deprived of treatment alternatives.

The Physician's Right to Practice Nontoxic Medicine

"Nontoxic drugs can be deadly because their use may cause delay in instituting correct therapy," Dr. Soffer also said.[1] But no other life-saving therapy had been instituted or even suggested for the dying patient. The administration of EDTA therapy was absolutely necessary and reasonable, Attorney Kell argued. Mrs. Clementino would not be alive otherwise. It is the role of the physician to extend life if possible, and to make what remains of life more comfortable. The reason this patient did not die was because of chelation therapy alone, the attorney said, and for no other reason.

Mr. Kell also argued that under the case of *People vs. Montecino* (66 Cal App 2d 85; 152 P 2d 5; 10 ALR 1137), a doctor is potentially subject to criminal liability if he fails to administer a curative substance, resulting in the death or injury of the patient. As to his patient, Ophelia Clementino, Dr. Harper testified, "This woman would have undoubtedly died if the therapy had been withheld."

As was noted above, under *Cobbs vs. Grant,* a doctor is required under penalty of being found guilty of malpractice to inform his patient of all available modalities of treatment. The patient then has the right to make an informed decision as to which therapy the patient will elect to receive. Dr. Harper acted honorably and so informed the Clementino family, the patient's representatives. The family made its decision, and the physician then had no alternative except to comply with the family members' choice of treatment. Had he failed to provide chelation therapy, or had he failed to advise the family of its availability, the doctor would have been guilty of malpractice under that rule of law. Had Dr. Harper failed to provide the therapy, it would have meant the abandonment of the woman.

Thus Mr. Kell advised, "A physician who is following his conscience must use whatever modality is necessary in order to sustain the life of the patient in as comfortable and as functional a way as possible. This would include chelation therapy or anything else, regardless of whether the therapy is generally recognized or not."

Attorney Kell told the Fair Hearing officer, Attorney Curtis L. Klahs of Glendale, California, that with respect to the use of drugs authorized for *one* purpose, and under some conditions used for *another* purpose, "there is no medical prohibition against such use by a practicing and qualified physician."

The drug's package insert only sets up guidelines for use of the medication, not parameters, he argued. Attorney Kell cited Valium as an example. "Valium is licensed as a tranquilizer, but is often prescribed as a sedative," he said. "Several hundred drugs are commonly used in this way in American medical practice, although the use is not specifically listed on the drug enclosure."[2] That was the common practice in Dr. Harper's community, as it is in the communities of most physicians around the country. In addition, this practice has the sanction of the FDA itself. The FDA had sent letters to that effect to H. Ray Evers, M.D.

One more thing regarding the physician's right to practice medicine according to his conscience: the doctor has the right and duty to treat any patient who is suffering from morbidity, lack of appetite, weight loss, pain, the potential of imminent death or other malfunctions. He must use his best judgment in doing so to accomplish the purpose for which he is employed. How does the doctor justify himself or protect himself from incrimination by medical colleagues, health insurance carriers, governmental agencies and other involved parties when—even though he has been able to bring about the alleviation or cure of various conditions—he is attacked by his colleagues because he has treated with a medication that is frowned upon or disapproved? Must he face going to jail, or be threatened with forfeiture of his license, as happened to Dr. H. Ray Evers of Montgomery, Alabama, in the first instance, or Dr. Robert J. Rogers of Melbourne, Florida, in the second?

The Federal Ruling Against Mrs. Clementino

Elderly Mrs. Clementino did not succeed in her pursuit of a "Fair Hearing." Attorney George Kell pointed to the evidence that overwhelmingly established the reasonableness and necessity of chelation therapy in her case at her "Fair Hearing." That was all that the Medicare recipient was allowed under part B.

Mr. Kell said, "Ophelia Clementino would have been dead within hours or days at the most, and as additional treatments were administered she continued to prosper in her health, from day to day and from week to week. Thus, to hold that she should have been denied the benefit of this treatment because it does not, in the opinion of some experts, constitute a 'specific or effective treatment for the particular condition' from which she was suffering, would amount to a denial of her right to life."[3]

Mr. Kell argued into a vacuum, for Hearing Officer Klahs denied the beneficiary's claim under Part B of Medicare. And she could not collect under Part A because her treatment was given in a convalescent home and not in a regular hospital. Remember, she had to be moved out of St. Joseph's Hospital in order to receive the treatment of her doctor's choice.

Attorney Klahs wrote: "It has been found by this Hearing Office that chelation therapy with endate [sic] disodium (EDTA) is not *reasonable and necessary* in treating the beneficiary's diagnosed condition. Therefore, this treatment is not covered under the Medicare program and was properly disallowed by the Carrier [emphasis added].

"It has further been found by this Hearing Officer that the diagnostic procedures relating to the chelation therapy treatment were not *reasonable and necessary* and therefore were not covered under the Medicare program and properly disallowed by the Carrier."[4]

Strangely enough, the Medicare Act, Part B, provides that there shall be no appeal from this "Fair Hearing" decision, although under Part A of the Act an appeal is allowed for the identical services. In a Part A appeal from a Hearing Officer's prior decision denying payment for a chelation hospital confinement, D. D. Dominey won his appeal. Attorney Kell cited the Dominey case in his brief. He argued that it should be followed in Mrs. Clementino's Part B case because the facts were identical. If Mr. Dominey was entitled to relief under Part A so was Mrs. Clementino entitled to relief under Part B of the Medicare Act. But the argument was ignored by Mr. Klahs. The technicality of the Victory Convalescent Hospital not being a regular hospital may have been a factor here, but Mr. Klahs did not state that one way or another. He just ignored the Dominey precedent.

This adverse ruling for the Medicare, Part B, recipient occurred despite the enactment of guidelines under Section 2050.1 of the *Hearing Officer's Coverage and Limitations Handbook*. These guidelines have no standing as a statute and tell only of procedures to be followed. These guidelines can be changed to fit the case, but Mr. Klahs offered a deaf ear, a blind eye and a closed mind.

Section 2050.1 states:

> Endrate *(Chelating Agent)*—Based on the Food and Drug Administration's evaluation, the intravenous injection of disodium edetate is indicated in selected patients for the emergency treatment of *hypercalcemia* and *for the control of ventricular arrhythmias and heart block associated with digitalis toxicity*.

A guideline is, by definition, no more than a guideline. Mr. Kell quoted from Webster's Dictionary as follows:

> A line by which one is guided, as: (a) a cord or rope to aid a passer over a difficult point or to permit retracing a course; (b) an *indication* or *outline* (as by a government) of policy or conduct. [emphasis added]

Interpreting that definition, the attorney's brief suggested that the guideline provided an "indication" but was not conclusively determinative of an issue. Thus, Mr. Kell argued, Klahs should have ruled according to the circumstances, under which the beneficiary had been barely surviving *before* she received chelation therapy and the undisputed fact that this treatment had saved her life. But no, Hearing Officer Klahs did not see fit to vary from the strict letter of the medical establishment's guideline.[3]

Another portion of Section 2050.1 states:

> *Injections Not Specifically Indicated.*—Payment should not be made for injections which are not considered by accepted standards of medical practice to be indicated as a specific or effective treatment for the particular condition for which they are given (although the injection may be accepted treatment for another illness). . . .

The key word in this guideline, obviously, is *should*. If the guideline were intended to have the force and effect of law it would necessarily provide that "payment *shall* not be made . . ." Thus we see that, by its own terms, the guideline itself is not conclusive as to its application, but is only meant to provide a serviceable guide for use in the absence of substantial evidence to the contrary. Mr. Kell's brief argued that this guideline conforms to congressional intent by permitting the hearing officer to award payment in those cases wherein injections are in fact shown to be "reasonable or necessary for the diagnosis or treatment of illness or injury," as provided by Section 1862 (a) of the Medicare Act (Title XVIII of the Social Security Act). But the point was simply ignored by Klahs' decision, which ritualistically cited the "hypercalcemia/ventricular arrhythmias and heart block" formula as its basis for denial.

Nonpayment for Chelation by Medicare Denies Due Process

Ophelia Clementino is an example of but one more U.S. citizen and beneficiary of the Medicare Act who was denied the right of due process. The medical rights of chelated patients have been abrogated illegally. The federal officials or private carriers who decided against payment of bills for chelation therapy are taking upon themselves the control over what kind of medicine the patient should receive.

Under Section 1801 of the Medicare Act, it is provided that:

> Nothing in this Title shall be construed to authorize any Federal officer or employee to exercise any supervision or control over the practice of medicine or the manner in which medical services are provided . . ."

Where Section 2050.1 of the Hearing Officer's guidelines attempts to declare ineffective that which is *shown* to have been effective, as in the particular patients whom I have described, the guideline amounts to nothing less than a covert attempt by federal agents to exercise the forbidden supervision or control over the practice of medicine, and the method of practice of that profession. For these reasons the guideline, where it is preferred by a hearing officer over the provisions of the Act requiring payment for reasonable and necessary services, constitutes a denial of the right of due process for all these patients. What possible compelling governmental interest exists, for example, to justify the denial of EDTA therapy in the case of Ophelia Clementino?

As indicated, the Hearing Officer's guidelines say: "disodium edetate is indicated in selected patients for the emergency treatment of hypercalcemia and . . . ventricular arrhythmias and heart block associated with digitalis toxicity."

In his testimony about Mrs. Clementino's condition, Dr. Harper said that arteriosclerosis is caused by deposits of mineral and arterial plaques in the arteries and veins of the patient. Chelation therapy was given to her in order to cause a chelate to form between the mineral deposit on the arterial wall and the chelating agent itself, and thus improve her vascular circulation. The calcium deposits in this lady's arteries and veins, and throughout the cells of her body, were abnormal. Such an abnormality is a hypercalcemic condition. It was this abnormality which resulted in her arteriosclerotic disease.

"As a physician, I am not able to prevent the EDTA from affecting the arteriosclerosis in the process of chelating for excess minerals, such as calcium," said Dr. Harper. "Hypercalcemia is a *laboratory finding,* rather than a disease."

"The removal of excess calcium deposits by the EDTA chelation therapy," said Attorney Kell, "was the specific which preserved this patient's life. There could not be anything more specific or effective." (There is one other effective chelating drug marketed in the Orient, but it is not available in the West. It is called *anginen,* an oral tablet produced by the Japanese.)

Therefore, the argument that chelation therapy is not compensable because of the provision of the guidelines which allow for its use only in cases of "hypercalcemia" and digitalis intoxication is shown to be in error. (*Digitalis intoxication* is a poisoning of the patient caused by too large a dose.) Furthermore, since its use for hypercalcemia is allowed, and since arteriosclerosis consists of excessive plaques containing calcium, other minerals, waste products and fat deposits, then it must be clear that the use of EDTA infusion for the removal of the calcium deposits constitutes a proper treatment.

Why is chelation therapy authorized for the treatment of a laboratory finding, *hypercalcemia,* and not for the related disease process, *atherosclerosis?* Proper interpretation of the guidelines would be that chelation therapy is authorized for the removal of excessive calcium deposits where these, alone or in conjunction with other material, threaten the health and well-being of a patient. Atherosclerosis happens to be an associated finding and, in fact, is an integral part of the disease. Thus we see that, even under the existing guidelines, the treatment with EDTA chelation must be authorized. Those patients denied this authorization are having their medical rights nullified. This is a violation of human rights that is now occurring regularly in this country.

Medical Rights Groups Form

Realizing that vested interests are attempting to take away the patient's right to receive, or the physician's right to administer, chelation therapy, a number of medical rights groups have formed. For example, Hugo Loseke of Sebastian, Florida, doesn't think the government has any business telling him whether he can or cannot take the therapy. Loseke, age seventy-four, owns a construction firm. He organized the National Association for Freedom of Medical Choice. Along with other members of this Brevard County group, Loseke believes he has a constitutional right to receive any medical treatment he or his fellow members and their physicians agree on.

"We're scared to death we won't be able to get chelation," said Loseke, who has arteriosclerosis. "It just boils down to one fact. If my physician and I decide on a treatment, nobody else should have a say in it."

In Hartford, Connecticut, in the fall of 1978, the Association for Cardiovascular Therapies, Inc. was formed, with Audrey Goldman as secretary-treasurer, Alvin Kavaler as vice president and myself as president. Our intent was to perform a public service by furnishing information on chelating physicians in local areas. The office is now closed, and the Association has been discontinued.

Since current medical practice does not subscribe to the chelation therapeutic technique, we created the Association for Cardiovascular Therapies (ACT) to encourage this and other more holistic approaches. ACT suggested that medical attention should be rendered to the whole person and take into account his body, mind, spirit and emotions. It endorsed the finding of an improved delivery system for the preservation of human life and health. It encouraged two facets of improvement: first, the individual must take responsibility for personal health; and second, every available therapy, including alternatives to traditional treatments, should be tried. Chelation therapy is among those alternatives.

ACT endeavored to protect the physician/patient relationship against government or other outside intervention. It also attempted to increase reimbursement and expand coverage by third-party health insurance for alternative therapies. ACT members paid $25 annual dues and worked to educate legislators and other government officials about the many techniques useful to alter cardiovascular degeneration—reverse hardening of the arteries—among the populace. We conducted seminars and published a quarterly newsletter describing advances in cardiovascular care, preventive medicine, diagnosis and treatment.

The Connecticut contingent of ACT was patterned after the Association for Chelation Therapy, created twenty-seven years ago by Mrs. Collie Green of San Gabriel, California. The California Association for Chelation Therapy (ACT) was a tax-exempt corporation that disseminated information about chelation therapy. It, too, has gone out of business because of lack of public participation.

ACT was helping to defend physicians against the legal, financial and peer pressures of the medical establishment. The Association successfully defended Donald E. Medaris, M.D., of Pasadena, California. Dr. Medaris practiced internal medicine and specialized in cardiovascular diseases for which he used chelation therapy. He had been harassed by the California State Board of Medical Examiners for his patient treatment with intravenous infusion of EDTA.

Mrs. Greene had close personal knowledge of chelation therapy's value, and that is when she formed ACT. She wished to help others avoid the harrowing events that she and her husband had undergone before turning to chelation therapy.

He Had No Alternative

At 6:30 A.M. on February 3, 1973, forty-eight-year-old Robert E. Greene of San Gabriel, California was rushed by firemen to his community's coronary care unit (CCU). Doctors there diagnosed his chest pain as acute myocardial infarction. He was treated and his life saved. After he returned home from three weeks of hospitalization, Dr. Greene's heart did not seem much better, though, and this caused him to worry. His overriding questions were, "Where do I go from here? Will there be any kind of life for me? How do I avoid having a heart attack again?"

For answers, the patient's cardiologist recommended the standard course for heart attack victims, a full cardiac study, including coronary arteriography. The evaluation and his arteriogram were carried out at the Rancho Los Amigos Hospital, the University of Southern California Medical Center in Downey, California.

Dr. Greene and his wife Collie listened to findings afterward which left them stunned. The patient had triple blood vessel involvement. Two of his coronary arteries were totally occluded, and another artery was 80 percent occluded. Forty percent of the man's left heart ventricle had turned to scar tissue, due to the massive heart attack. Severe damage caused the blood that nourished the heart to have slowed to a trickle.[5]

"The panel of doctors who studied my husband explained that he could not live in this condition," said Collie Greene. "They said his only hope of survival was surgery. They would do a resectioning of the heart and a double bypass. They thought it would also be absolutely necessary to remove the damaged tissue from the heart muscle. Essentially, this was two different heart operations.

"We asked about the success of such an operation," the wife recalled. "But the doctors had no information to give on this type of surgery because it had only been done at their major hospital for three years. We did talk at length about the risks involved. They said there would be a 30 percent chance of death for my husband with such an operation. When asked about being able to return to his present position [as a corporate personnel director], the doctors were in doubt. They felt that the load my husband was carrying—recruiting, lecturing and meetings that went with his full-time job—would be too much for him after such a delicate operation." Mrs. Greene added, "To us the recommendations seemed more like an omen of death rather than a hope of survival.

"We asked for alternatives. It being a research center, we thought the panel of Rancho Los Amigos doctors would have some answers for us. We were told that there were no alternatives. No alternatives? We were shaken! Then we started to beg—we pleaded—and we were told again, 'There are *no* alternatives!'

"It was the middle of May, and the panel suggested that if Bob were still alive we should return to Rancho Los Amigos Hospital again in September to discuss further the question of surgery. We felt such hopelessness, such despair and very much alone," she shuddered.

"As we left the room almost stumbling in a daze, a doctor walked out with us. He advised us to face reality. 'Go home, make your will and put your house in order. No matter what you do, the situation is a dismal one,' he said. We went home and took this doctor's advice.

We set out to put our affairs in order. It was an ordeal for the whole family to tend to these necessary tasks," Mrs. Green remembered. "Then we decided to look for alternatives on our own. After two weeks of searching, we found out about chelation therapy."

The entire Greene family and many of their friends had put in what seemed like endless telephone calls to all parts of the United States. They were looking for *some* kind of alternative to open-heart surgery, where the risk of death for Robert Greene would not be so high. They found an alternative in the little-known intravenous EDTA chelation procedure. The patient took the therapy.

"In about four months my husband returned to work full time, to the same position. He is responsible for two thousand people. He is able to do all the traveling, lecturing, and everything necessary to fulfill his job. He has been able to take all the stress and strain that this type of work entails," said Mrs. Greene.

"He has made a total commitment to the full treatment regimen that goes with chelation, as his doctors repeatedly request it of patients. He had to change his lifestyle and especially his eating patterns. This has been stressed over and over again," she said.

"My husband walks nearly four miles an hour now. He rides his bicycle twelve miles in an hour. He enjoys all the sports, and he enjoys being able to go back to sailing." Mrs. Greene smiled, "Bob keeps telling us that sailing takes very little effort, and according to his pulse rate, it really does."

Robert Greene joined a cardiac rehabilitation program at Ranchos Los Amigos Hospital in December 1973 and routinely played three games of vigorous volleyball. By April 1980, he had taken almost eighty chelation treatments in a regular maintenance program. He enjoyed seven active, happy and fulfilling years from the time his imminent death was forecast in 1973. His only legacy of that time is a massive scar in his heart— and some unhappy memories of orthodox medicine's stubborn refusal to sanction chelation therapy.

Collie Greene founded and was the director of the Association for Chelation Therapy, because the treatment is hardly known in the United States, even among physicians—to say nothing of the public. It is the only alternative to progressive arterial degeneration—the *one* proven means by which a person can prevent or quickly reverse hardening of the arteries. Her organization was formed to educate the public and the doctors that atherosclerosis can be reversed through chelation therapy.

Collie Greene founded and was the director of the Association for

Chelation Therapy, because the treatment is hardly known in the United States, even among physicians—to say nothing of the public. It is the only alternative to progressive arterial degeneration—the *one* proven means by which a person can prevent or quickly reverse hardening of the arteries. Her organization was formed to educate the public and the doctors that atherosclerosis can be reversed through chelation therapy.

Mrs. Greene added, "We are really pleased that we did not accept the surgery. We are very fortunate to have found chelation. We feel this therapy has, indeed, given my husband a new life."

In our last contact with Collie Green before we finalized this chapter, she said, "As I reflect on our experiences, I still shudder at the thought that we almost made the vital decision for Bob to have open-heart surgery when we were in such total ignorance and fear. I keep asking myself, why did we have to live a nightmare that way? Why were we not informed of alternatives when we begged for them? The doctors said, 'There are no alternatives.' But they lied! If a physician does not know of treatment alternatives, why in the world doesn't he seek them out for the sake of his patient? If he does know about them, then he must tell you what else you can do before undergoing something so hazardous as open-heart surgery or other surgery. Perhaps with publication of your book everyone in the country—in the world—will know that hardening of the arteries can be reversed by chelation therapy. Now there will be no excuse not to be informed."

Mrs. Greene concluded: "What keeps going through my mind is that the patient has the right to be informed of any alternatives, regardless of the personal opinion of the physician toward those alternatives. This is the right of the patient, and he must not be denied this right."

Now, It Is Up to You

This is the right of the patient, and he must not be denied this right. Those words by Collie Green summarize our own feelings regarding chelation therapy. We know that, today, virtually all of our friends and family— in fact, virtually every American adult—suffers from some hardening of the arteries. This disease will kill more than 1.25 million Americans this year; millions more will face restricted lifestyles, heavy medical bills, and even costly and dangerous surgery because of this epidemic disease.

And yet, as we have learned, hardening of the arteries *can be prevented or reversed.* A safe, simple and inexpensive treatment called chelation therapy could perform medical miracles in this country, if only it were understood, accepted and properly promoted. We would live longer, healthier, happier lives.

There are powerful forces at work in our country to suppress this important medical discovery. For many different reasons—united only by a combination of ignorance, arrogance and greed—the medical establishment, the political establishment, drug companies and the health insurance industry have combined to deny this treatment to you and your loved ones.

A few courageous physicians have defied the powers-that-be to promote chelation therapy. Thousands of desperate patients have proven to themselves the lifesaving benefits of this treatment. It is up to us to make certain that more Americans learn of it. It is for this reason that we have written this book. Now, it is up to you.

NOTES

Introduction

1. Berkow, R., and Fletcher, A. J., eds. *The Merck Manual of Diagnosis and Therapy* Rahway, N.J.: Merck and Co., 1992, pp. 406, 507.
2. Sifton, D., ed., *Physicians' Desk Reference*. Montvale, N.J.: Medical Economics Data Production Co., 1994, pp. 2514–2516.
3. Whitaker, J. "Who determines what is 'allowed'?" *Dr. Julian Whitaker's Health & Healing™: Tomorrow's Medicine Today*, 2 (Sept. 1991), 8.

Chapter One

1. Clark, Matt, and Greenberg, Peter S. "Riddled by isotopes." *Newsweek*, Mar. 21, 1977.
2. Wolinsky, Howard: "Area man: treatment restored vision." *Today*, Jan. 9, 1977.
3. Ibid.

Chapter Three

1. Alsleben, H. Rudolph, and Shute, Wilfrid E.: *How to Survive the New Health Catastrophes*. Anaheim, Calif.: Survival Publications, 1973.

Chapter Four

1. Gordon, T.; Kannel, W. B.; and Sorlie, P. D. "The Framingham Study." National Institutes of Health, May 1971.
2. Holling, N. E. *Peripheral Vascular Diseases*. Philadelphia: J. B. Lippincott Co., 1972.
3. Keys, A. "Coronary heart disease in seven countries." *Circulation 41* (1970), 1.
4. Keys, A., et al. "Probability of middle-aged men developing coronary heart disease in five years." *Circulation 45* (1972), 815.

5. Enos, W. F.; Beyer, J. C.; and Holmes, R. H. "Pathogenesis of coronary disease in American soldiers killed in Korea." *JAMA 158* (1955), 912–914.

6. McNamara, J. J., et al. "Coronary artery disease in combat casualties in Vietnam." *JAMA 216* (1971), 1185–1187.

7. Brucknerova, O., and Tulacek, J. "Chelates in the treatment of occlusive atherosclerosis." *Vnitr. Lek. 18* (1972), 729.

8. Kurliandchikov, V. N. "Treatment of patients with coronary arteriosclerosis with Unithiol in combination with decamevit." *Vrach. Delo. 6* (1973), 8.

9. Ohno, T. "Clinical and experimental studies of arteriosclerosis." *Excerpta Medica: Intern. Med. 17* (1963), 8.

10. Seven, M. J. (ed.). *Metal Binding in Medicine.* Philadelphia: J. B. Lippincott Co., 1960.

11. Soffer, A. *Chelation Therapy.* Springfield, Ill.: Charles C. Thomas, Publisher, 1964.

12. Spencer, H. "Studies on the effects of chelating agents in man." *Ann. N.Y. Acad. Sci. 88* (1960), 435.

13. Clarke, N. E.; Clarke, C. N.; and Mosher, R. E. "Treatment of angina pectoris with disodium ethylene diamine tetraacetic acid." *Am. J. Med. Sc. 232* (1956), 654–666.

14. Kitchell, J. R., et al. "The treatment of coronary artery disease with disodium EDTA—A reappraisal." *Am. J. Cardiol. 11* (1963), 501–506.

15. Lamar, C. P. "Calcium chelation of atherosclerosis—nine years' clinical experience." Fourteenth Annual Meeting, American College of Angiology, 1968.

16. Meltzer, L. E.; Urol, M. E.; and Kitchell, J. R. "The treatment of coronary artery disease with disodium EDTA." In M. J. Seven, ed. *Metal Binding in Medicine.* Philadelphia: J. B. Lippincott Co., 1960, pp. 132–136.

17. Boyle, A. J., et al. "Studies in human and induced atherosclerosis." *J. Am. Geriatr. Soc. 14* (1966), 272.

18. Lamar, C. P. "Chelation endarterectomy for occlusive atherosclerosis." *J. Am. Geriatr. Soc. 14* (1966), 272.

19. Lamar, C. P. "Chelation therapy of occlusive arteriosclerosis in diabetic patients." *Angiology 15* (1965), 379.

20. Nikitina, E. K., et al. "Treatment of atherosclerosis with trilon B. (EDTA)." *Kardiologiia 12* (1972), 137.

21. Olwin, J. H., and Koppel, J. L. "Reduction of elevated plasma lipid levels in atherosclerosis following EDTA therapy." *Proc. Soc. Exp. Biol. Med. 128* (1968), 1137–1139.

22. Klevay, L. M. "Coronary heart disease: zinc/copper hypothesis." *Am. J. Clin. Nutr. 28* (1975), 764–774.

23. Zapadnick, V. I., et al. "Pharmacological activity of Unithiol and its use in clinical practice." *Vrach. Delo. 8* (1973), 122.

24. Soffer, A. "Chelation therapy for arteriosclerosis." *JAMA 233* (1975).

25. Craven, P. C., and Morelli, H. F. "Chelation therapy." *West. J. Med. 122* (1975), 277–278.

26. "CMA warns against chelation." *CMA News* 20: 13, Sept. 12, 1975, p. 3.

27. Pullman, T. N., et al. "Synthetic chelating agents in clinical medicine." In A. D. DeGraff, ed. *Annual Review of Medicine,* Annuals Reviews, 1963.

28. James, T. N. "Selective experimental chelation of calcium in the sinus mode." *J. Mol. Cell. Cardiol. 6* (1975), 493–504.

29. Isaacs, J. P., and Lamb, J. C. "Trace metals, vitamins, and hormones in ten-year treatment of coronary atherosclerotic heart disease." Library of Congress Catalog Card Number 74–82883, as delivered at the Texas Heart Institute Symposium on Coronary Artery Medicine and Surgery, Houston, Tex. Feb. 21, 1974.

30. Soffer, A.; Toribara, T.; and Sayman, A. "Myocardial responses to chelation." *Br. Heart J. 23* (1961), 690–694.

31. Soffer, A., et al. "Clinical applications and untoward reactions of chelation in cardiac arrhythmia." *Arch. Intern. Med. 106* (1960), 824–834.

32. Popovic, A., et al. "Experimental control of serum calcium levels *in vivo.*" Georgetown University Medical Center. *Proc. Soc. Exp. Biol. med. 74* (1950), 415–417.

33. Rubin, M. "Fifth Conference on Metabolic Interrelations." *Biologic Action of Chelating Agents.* Macy Foundation, 1954, pp. 344–358.

34. Hastings, A. B. "Studies on the effect of alteration of calcium in circulating fluids on the mobility of calcium." *Trans. Macy Conf. Metabolic Interrelations 3* (1951), 38–50.

35. Friedman, H. "The significance of Mg/Ca ratio." Ph.D. thesis, Graduate Department of Chemistry, Georgetown University, 1952.

Chapter Five

1. Gordon, Garry F., and Vance, Robert B. "EDTA chelation therapy for arteriosclerosis: history and mechanisms of action." *Osteopathic Annals 4:* 38–62, Feb. 1976.

2. Demesy, F., "On the mechanism of papaverine action on the control of vascular smooth muscle contractile activity by extracellular calcium." *J. Pharm. Pharmacol, 23* (1971), 712, 713.

3. Triner, L., et al. "Cyclic phosphodiestasterase activity and the action of papaverine." *Biochem. Biophys. Res. Commun. 40* (1970), 64–69.

4. Greengard, P., et al. *Advances in Cyclic Nucleotide Research,* Volume 1. New York: Raven Press, 1972, pp. 195–211.

5. Sivjakov, K. I. "The treatment of acute selenium, cadmium and tungsten intoxication in rats with calcium disodium ethylene diamine tetraacetate." *Toxicol. Appl. Pharmacol. 1* (1959), 602–608.

6. Tessinger, J. "Biochemical responses to provocative chelation by edatate disodium calcium." *Arch. Environ. Health 23* (1971), 280.

7. Klevay, L. M. "Coronary heart disease: zinc/copper hypotheses." *Am. J. Clin. Nutr. 28* (1975), 764–774.

8. Schroeder, H. A. *The Poisons Around Us.* Bloomington, Ind.: Indiana University Press, 1974.

9. Freemen, R. "Reversible myocarditis due to chronic lead poisoning in childhood." *Arch. Dis. Child. 40* (1965), 389–393.

10. Price, J. M. "Some effects of chelating agents on tryptophan metabolism in man." *Fed. Proc.* (Suppl. 10, 1961), 223–226.

11. Petersdorf, R. G. "Internal medicine in family practice." *N. Engl. J. Med. 293* (1975), 326.

12. Malmstron, B. G. "Role of metal binding in enzymic reactions." *Fed. Proc.* (Suppl. 10, 1961), 60–69.

13. Zelis, R., et al. "Effects of hyperlipoproteinemias and their treatment on the peripheral circulation." *J. Clin. Invest. 49* (1970), 1007.

14. Sincock, A. "Life extension in the rotifer by application of chelating agents." *J. Gerontol. 30* (1975), 289–293.

15. Blankenhorn, D. H., and Bolwick, L. E. "A quantitive study of coronary arterial calcification." *Am. J. Pathol. 39* (1961), 511.

16. Schroeder, H. A., and Perry, H. M., Jr. "Antihypertensive effects of binding agents." *J. Lab. Clin. Med. 46* (1955), 416.

17. Shin, Yeh Yu. "Cross-linking of elastin in human atherosclerotic aertas." *Lab. Invest. 25* (1971), 121.

18. Hall, D. A. "Coordinately bound calcium as a cross-linking agent in elastin and as an activator of elastolysis." *Gerontologia 16* (1970), 325–339.

19. Wilder, D. A. "Mobilization of atherosclerotic plaque calcium with EDTA utilizing the isolation-persusion principle." *Surgery 52* (1962), 5.

20. Schreiber, G. "*In vivo* thinning of thickened capillary basement membranes by rapid chelation." (unpublished manuscript).

21. Boyle, A. J.; Mosher, R. E.; and McCann, D. S. "Some vivo effects of chelation. 1: Rheumatoid arthritis." *J. Chronic Dis. 16* (1963), 325–328.

22. Leipzig, L. H.; Boyle, A. J.; and McCann, D. S. "Case histories of rheumatoid arthritis treated with sodium or magnesium EDTA." *J. Chronic Dis. 22* (1970), 553–563.

23. Uhl, H. S. M., et al. "Effect of EDTA on cholesterol metabolism in rabbits." *Am. J. Clin. Pathol. 23* (1953), 1226–1233.

24. Jacob, H. S. "Pathologic states of erythrocyte membrane." University of Minnesota. *Hospital Practice,* December 1974, 47–49.

25. Soffer, A.; Toribara, T.; and Sayman, A. "Myocardial response to chelation." *Br. Heart J. 23* (1961), 690–694.

26. Soffer, A., et al. "Clinical applications and untoward reactions of chelation in cardiac arrhythmias." *Arch. Intern. Med. 166* (1960), 824–834.

27. Perry, H. M., Jr. "Hypertension and the geochemical environment." *Ann. N.Y. Acad. Sci. 199* (1972), 202–228.

28. Popvic, A., et al. "Experimental control of serum calcium levels *in vivo.*" Georgetown University Medical Center. *Proc. Soc. Exp. Biol. Med. 74* (1950), 415–417.

29. Lamar, C. P. "Calcium chelation of atherosclerosis—nine years; clinical experience." Fourteenth Annual Meeting, American College of Angiology, 1968.

30. Meltzer, L. E.; Urol, M. E.; and Kitchell, J. R. "The treatment of coronary artery disease with disodium EDTA." In M. J. Seven, ed. *Metal Binding in Medicine*. Philadelphia: J. B. Lippincott Co., 1960, pp. 132–136.

31. Meltzer, L. E., et al. "The urinary excretion pattern of trace metals in diabetes mellitus." *Am. J. Med. Sci.* 244 (1962), 282–289.

32. Kitchell, J. R.; Meltzer, L. E.; and Seven, M. J. "Potential uses of chelation methods in the treatment of cardiovascular diseases." *Prog. Cardiovasc. Dis.* 19 (1961), 798.

33. Bjorksten, J. "Crosslinking and the aging process." In M. Rockstein, ed. *Theoretical Aspects of Aging*. New York: Academic Press, 1974.

34. Koen, A.; McCann, D. S.; and Boyle, A. J. "Some *in vivo* effects of chelation. II: Animal experimentation." *J. Chronic Dis.* 16 (1963), 329–333.

35. Kitchell, J. R.; Meltzer, L. E.; and Rutman, E. "Effects of ions on *in vitro* gluconeogenesis in rat kidney cortex slices." *Am. J. Physiol.* 208 (1965), 841–846.

36. Strain, W. H., et al. eds. *Clinical Application of Zinc Metabolism*. Springfield, Ill.: Charles C. Thomas, Publisher, 1974.

37. Friedman, M. *Pathogenesis of Coronary Artery Disease*. San Francisco: McGraw-Hill, 1969.

38. Zohman, B. "Emotional factors in coronary disease." *Geriatrics* 28 (1973), 110.

39. Miller, In Strain, W. H., et al., eds.: *Clinical Application of Zinc Metabolism*. Springfield, Ill.: Charles C. Thomas, 1974.

40. Peters, H. A. "Trace minerals, chelating agents and the porphyrias," *Fed. Proc.* (Suppl. 10, 1961), 227–234.

41. Timmerman, A., and Kallistatos, G. "Modern aspects of chemical dissolution of human renal calculi by irrigation." *J. Urol.* 95 (1966), 469–475.

42. Birk, R. E., and Rupe, C. E. "The treatment of systemic sclerosis with EDTA, pyridoxine and resperpine." *Henry Ford Med. Bull.* 14 (June 1966), 109–118.

43. Chisholm, J., Jr. "Chelation therapy in children with subclinical plumbism." *Pediatrics* 53 (1974), 441.

44. Gordon, G., and Harper, H. Studies submitted to Food and Drug Administration, July, 1974. American Academy of Medical Preventics, North Hollywood, Calif.

45. Lamar, C. P. "Chelation therapy of occlusive arteriosclerosis in diabetic patients." *Angiology* 15 (1964), 379.

Chapter Six

1. Schroeder, H. A. *The Poisons Around Us*. Bloomington, Ind.: Indiana University Press, 1974.

2. Kopito, L., Brilet, A. M. and Schwachman, H. "Chronic plumbism in children: Diagnosis by hair analysis." *JAMA* 209 (1969), 243–248.

3. Vitale, L. P., et al. "Blood lead—An inadequate measure of occupational exposure." *J. Occup. Med.* 17:3 (1975), 155.

4. Seppalainen, A. M., et al. "Subclinical neuropathy at 'safe' levels of exposure." *Arch Environ. Health* (1975).

5. Graham, A., and Graham, F. "Lead poisoning and the suburban child." *Today's Health,* Mar. 1974.

6. Caprio, R. J.; Margulis, H. I.; and Joselow, M. "Lead absorption in children and its relationship to urban traffic densities." *Arch. Environ. Health 28* (1975), 195–197.

7. Freeman, R. "Reversible myocarditis due to chronic lead poisoning in childhood." *Arch. Dis. Child. 40* (1965) 389–393.

8. Strain, W. H., et al., eds. *Clinical Application of Zinc Metabolism.* Springfield, Ill.: Charles C. Thomas, Publisher, 1974.

9. Isaacs. J. P., and Lamb, J. C. "Trace metals, vitamins, and hormones in ten-year treatment of coronary atherosclerotic heart disease." Library of Congress Catalog Card Number 74–82882, as delivered at the Texas Heart Institute Symposium on Coronary Artery Medicine and Surgery, Houston, Feb. 21, 1974.

10. Marsh, L. and Fraser, F. C. "Chelating agents and teratogenesis." *Lancet* (1973), 846.

11. Perry, H. M., Jr., and Schroeder, H. A. "Lesions resembling vitamin B-complex deficiency and urinary loss of zinc produced by EDTA." *Am. J. Med. 22* (1957), 168–172.

12. Foreman, H. "Toxic side effects of EDTA." *J. Chron. Dis. 16* (1963), 319–323.

13. Perry, H. M., Jr. and Perry, E. F, "Normal concentrations of some trace metals in human urine, changes produced by EDTA." *J. Clin. Invest. 38* (1959), 1452.

14. Tidball, C. S. "Nonspecificity of cation depletion when using chelators in biological systems." *Gastroenterology 60* (1971), 481.

15. Davies, J. T. *The Clinical Significance of the Essential Biological Metals.* Springfield, Ill.: Charles C. Thomas, Publisher, 1972.

16. Schettler, G., and Weizel, A., eds. *Atherosclerosis. 111: Proceedings of the Third International Symposium.* New York, Heidelberg, Berlin: Springer Verlag, 1974.

17. Baumslag, N., et al. "Hair-metal binding." *Environ. Health Perspec. 8* (1974), 191–199.

18. Hinners, T. A., et al. "Trace element nutriture and metabolism through head hair analysis." Department of Surgery, Case Western Reserve University School of Medicine, Cleveland.

19. Hammer, D. I., et al. "Trace metals in human hair as a simple epidemio-

logic monitor of environmental exposure." National Environmental Research Center, Environmental Protection Agency, Research Triangle Park, N.C.

20. Hoekstra, W. G., and Suttie, J. W., eds. *Trace Element Metabolism in Animals, II.* University Park Press, 1974.

21. Kurliandchikov, V. N. "Treatment of patients with coronary arteriosclerosis with Unithiol in combination with decamevit." *Vrach. Delo.* 6 (1974), 8.

22. Zapadnick, V. I., et al. "Pharmacological activity of Unithiol and its use in clinical practice." *Vrach. Delo.* 8 (1973), 122.

23. Brucknerova, O., and Tulacek, J. "Chelates in the treatment of occlusive atherosclerosis." *Unitr. Lek.* 18 (1972), 729.

24. Levy, R. I., et al. "Dietary and drug treatment of primary hyperlipoproteinemia." *Ann. Intern. Med* 77 (1972), 267.

25. Popovici, A., et al. "Experimental control of serum calcium levels *in vivo.*" Georgetown University Medical Center. *Proc. Soc. Ex. Biol. & Med.* 74 (1950), 415–417.

26. Rostenberg, A., Jr., and Perkins, A. J. "Nickel and cobalt dermatitis." *J. Allergy* 22 (1951), 466.

27. Proescher, F. "Anticoagulant Properties of Ethylene-diamine tetra-acetic acid." *Proc. Soc. Exper. Biol. & Med.* 76 (1951), 619.

28. Clarke, N. E.; Clarke, C. N.; and Mosher, R. D. "The in vivo dissolution of metastatic calcium: an approach to atherosclerosis." *Am. J. M. So.* 229 (1955), 142.

29. Clarke, N. E.; Clarke, C. N.; and Mosher, R. E. "Treatment of angina pectoris with disodium-ethylene diamine tetraacetic acid." *Am. J. Med. Sci.* 232 (1956), 654–666.

30. Lamar, C. P. "Chelation therapy of occlusive arteriosclerosis in diabetic patients." *Angiology* 15 (1964), 379.

31. Lamar, C. P. "Calcium chelation of atherosclerosis—nine years' clinical experience." Fourteenth Annual Meeting, American College of Angiology, 1968.

32. Oser, B., et al. "Safety evaluation studies of calcium EDTA." *Toxicol. Appl. Pharmacol.* 5 (1963), 142–162.

33. Doolan, P. D., et al. "An evaluation of the nephrotoxicity of ethylene diamine tetraacetate and diethylene triamine pentaacetate in the rat." *Toxicol. Appl. Pharmacol.* 10 (1967), 481–500.

34. Schwartz, S. L.; Johnson, C. B.; and Doolan, P. D. "Study of the mechanism of renal vacuologenesis induced in the rat by EDTA." *Mol. Pharmacol.* 6 (1970), 54–60.

35. Schwartz, S., et al. "Subcellular localization of EDTA in the proximal tubular cell of the rat kidney." *Biochem. Pharmacol.* 16 (1967), 2413–2419.

36. Seven, M. J. "Observations on the dosage of I.V. chelating agents." *Antibiot. MED.* 5 (1958), 251.

Chapter Seven

1. Cornfield, J., and Mitchell, S. "Selected risk factors in coronary disease." *Arch. Environ. Health 19* (1969), 382–294.
2. Vavrik, M. "High risk factors and atherosclerotic cardiovascular diseases in the aged." *J. Am. Geriatr. Soc. 22* (1974), 203.
3. Malmros, H. "Primary dietary prevention of atherosclerosis." *Biol. Nutr. Dieta 19* (1973), 108.
4. McGandy, R., et al. "Dietary fats, carbohydrates and atherosclerotic vascular disease." *N. Engl. J. Med. 277* (1967), 186.
5. Moses, C. *Atherosclerosis: Mechanisms as a Guide to Prevention.* Philadelphia: Lea and Febiger, 1963.
6. National Academy of Sciences, National Research Council. *Dietary Fat and Human Health,* Publ. No. 1147, 1966.
7. Larsen, O. A., and Lassen, N. A. "Effects of daily muscular exercise in patients with intermittent claudication." *Lancet 2* (1966), 1093.
8. Goodman, L. S., and Gilman, A. *The Pharmacological Basis of Therapeutics.* 4th ed. New York: Macmillan Co., 1975, p. 1785.
9. Cranton, E. M. "Introduction." In: *A Textbook on EDTA Chelation Therapy.* New York: Human Sciences Press, 1989, pp. 9, 10.
10. Meltzer, L. E.; Palmon, F., and Kitchell, J. R. "Long term use, side effects, and toxicity of disodium EDTA." *Am. J. Med. Sci. 242* (1961), 51–57.
11. Foreman, H. "Toxic side effects of EDTA." *J. Chron. Dis. 16* (1963), 319–323.
12. Perry, H. M., Jr., and Perry, E. F. "Normal concentrations of some trace metals in human urine, changes produced by EDTA." *J. Clin. Invest. 38* (1959), 1452.
13. Tidball, C. S. "Nonspecificity of cation depletion when using chelators in biological systems." *Gastroenterology 60* (1971), 481.
14. Perry, H. M., Jr., and Schroeder, H. A. "Lesions resembling vitamin B-complex deficiency and urinary loss of zinc produced by EDTA." *Am. J. Med. 22* (1957), 168–172.
15. Marsh, L., and Fraser, F. C. "Chelating agents and teratogenesis." *Lancet* (1973), 846.
16. Matthew, H. *Side Effects of Drugs,* Volume VII. Amsterdam: *Excerpta Medica,* pp. 326–329.
17. Foreman, H.; Finnegan, C.; and Lushbaugh, C. C. "Nephrotoxic hazard from uncontrolled EDTA calcium-disodium therapy." *JAMA 160* (1956), 1042–1046.
18. Dudley, H. R., and Ritchie, A. C. "Pathologic changes associated with the use of sodium EDTA in treatment of hypocalcemia." *N. Engl. J. Med. 252* (1955), 331–337.
19. Seven, M. J. "Observations on the dosage of I. V. chelating agents," *Antibiot Med 5* (1958), 251.

20. Doolan, P. D., et al. "An evaluation of the nephrotoxicity of ethylene diamine tetraacetate and diethylene triamine pentaacetate in the rat." *Toxicol. Appl. Pharmacol. 10* (1967), 481–500.

21. Schwartz, S. L.; Johnson, C. B.;; and Doolan, P. D. "Study of the mechanism of renal vacuologenesis induced in the rate by EDTA." *Mol. Pharmacol.* 6 (1970), 54–60.

22. Schwartz, S. L., et al. "Subcellular localization of EDTA in the proximal tubular cell of the rat kidney." *Biochem. Pharmacol. 16* (1967), 2413–2419.

23. Oser, B., et al. "Safety evaluation studies of calcium EDTA." *Toxicol. Appl. Pharmacol.* 5 (1963), 142–162.

24. Sincock, A. "Life extension in the rotifer by application of chelating agents." *J. Gerontol. 30* (1975), 289–293.

25. Cranton, E. M. "Kidney effects of ethylene diamine tetraacetic acid (EDTA): A literature review." *J. Holistic Med.* 4 (1982), 152–157.

26. Oliver, L. D.; Mehta, R.; and Sarle, H. E. "Acute renal failure following administration of ethylenediamenine-tetraacetic acid (EDTA)." *Tex. Med. 80* (1984), 40–41.

27. Doolan, P. D.; Schwartz, S. L.; Hayes, J. R.; Mulleln, J. C.; and Cummings, N. B. "An evaluation of the nephrotoxicity of ethylenediaminetetraacetate and diethylenetriaminepentacetate in the rat." *Toxic. Appl. Pharm. 10,* (1967), 481–500.

28. Payne, R. B. "Creatinine clearance: A redundant clinical investigation." *Ann. Clin. Biochem. 23,* (1986), 243–250.

29. Cockcroft, D. W., and Gault, M. H. "Prediction of creatinine clearance from serum creatinine." *Nephron 16,* (1976), 31–41.

30. Reidenberg, M. M. "Kidney function and drug action." *New England J. Med. 313* (1985), 816–817.

31. Frackelton, J. P. "Monitoring renal function during EDTA chelation therapy." *J. Holistic Med. 8,* (1986), 33–35.

32. McDonagh, E. W.; Rudolph, C. J.; and Cheraskin, E. "The effect of EDTA chelation therapy plus supportive multivitamin-trace mineral supplementation upon renal function: A study in serum creatinine. *J. Holistic Med. 4* (1982), 146–151.

33. McDonagh, E. W.; Rudolph, C. J.; Cheraskin, E. "The effect of EDTA chelation therapy plus supportive multivitamin-trace mineral supplementation upon renal function: A study in blood urea nitrogen (BUN)." *J. Holistic Med. 4* (1983), 163–171.

34. Sehnert, K. W.; Clague, A. F.; and Cheraskin, E. "The improvement in renal function following EDTA chelation and multivitamin-trace mineral therapy: A study in creatinine clearance." *Med. Hypothesis 15,* 3 (1984), 307–310.

35. Doolan et al., 1967.

36. Schwartz, S. L.; Johnson, C. B.; Hayes, J. R.; and Doolan, P. D. "Subcellular localization of EDTA in the proximal tubular cell of the rat kidney." *Biochem. and Pharm. 16* (1967), 2413–2419.

37. Schwartz, S. L.; Johnson, C. B.; and Doolan, P.D. "Study of the mechanism of renal vacuologenesis induced in the rat by ethylenediamine tetraacetate." *Molec. Pharm.* 6 (1970), 54–60.

Chapter Eight

1. Rudolph, C. J., and McDonagh, E. W. "The Chelation carrier solutions: An analysis of osmolarity and sodium content." *J. Int. Acad. Prev. Med.* 8, 1 (1983), 26–34.
2. Ibid.
3. This formulation is taken from Trowbridge, J. P., and Walker, M. *The Healing Powers of Chelation Therapy.* Stamford, Conn: New Way of Life, 1988, p. 17.
4. Addendum. *Special Issue of the J. Advancement in Medicine: A Textbook on EDTA Chelation Therapy.* E. M. Cranton, ed. New York: Human Sciences Press, Aug. 1, 1993.
5. Cranton, E. M. *Protocol of the American College of Advancement in Medicine for the Safe and Effective Administration of EDTA Chelation Therapy.* Laguna Hills, Calif.: ACAM, 1989, p. 12.
6. Meyer-Brunot, H. G., and Keberle, H. "The metabolism of deferoxamine and ferioxamine B." *Bull. of Biochem. and Pharmacol.* 16 (1967), 527.
7. Bothwell, T., and Finch, C. *Iron Metabolism.* Boston: Little, Brown, 1962–1963, p. 351.
8. Propper, R. D.; Churin, S. B.; and Nathan, D. G. "Reassessment of deferioxamine B in iron overload." *New Eng. J. Med.* 294 (1976), 1421.
9. Hershko, D.; Grady, R. W.; and Cerami, A. "Mechanism of iron chelation in the hyper-transfused rat: Definition of two alternate pathways of iron mobilization." *J. Lab. and Clin. Med.* 92, 2 (1978), 144.
10. Fairbanks, V. F. "Chronic iron overload: new chelators and new strategies (Editorial). *J. Lab. and Clin. Med.* 92, 2 (1978), 141.
11. Crapper-McLaghlan, D. R. "Aluminum toxicity in senile dementia—implications for treatment." Presented to the Fall 1981 meeting of AAMP.
12. Casdorph, H. R., and Walker, M. *Toxic Metal Syndrome: How Metal Poisonings Can Affect Your Brain.* Garden City Park, N.Y.: Avery Publishing Group, 1995, p. 267.
13. Grady, R. W.; Graziano, J. H.; Akers, H. A.; and Cerami, A. "The development of new iron chelating drugs." *J. Pharm. Exper. Therapeutics 196* (1976), 478.
14. Grady, R. W.; Graziano, J. H.; White, G. P.; Jacobs, A.; and Cerami, A. "The development of new iron chelating drugs." *J. Pharm. Exp. Therapeutics 205,* 3 (1978), 757.

Chapter Nine

1. Gates, D., and Schatz, L. *The Body Ecology Diet: Recovering Your Health and Rebuilding Your Immunity.* Atlanta, Ga.: B.E.D. Publications, 1993, pp. 41–43.
2. Casdorph, H. R. and Walker, M. *Toxic Metal Syndrome: How Metal Poisonings Can Affect Your Brain.* Garden City Park, N.Y.: Avery Publishing Group, 1995, p. 73.
3. Bjorksten, J. "Recent developments in protein chemistry." *Chem. Ind. 48* (June 1941), 746–775.
4. Bjorksten, J. "Chemistry of duplication." *Chem. Ind. 50* (Jan. 1942), 68–72.
5. Casdorph and Walker, pp. 112, 113.
6. Schroeder, H. A. *Trace Elements and Man.* Old Greenwich, Conn.: Devin-Adair Co., 1973, pp. 34–37.
7. Rudolph, C. J.; McDonagh, E. W.; and Wussow, D. G. "The effect of intravenous disodium ethylenediaminetetraacetic acid (EDTA) upon bone density levels." *J. Adv. in Med. 1*, 2 (Summer 1988), 79–85.
8. Halstead, B. W. *The Scientific Basis of EDTA Chelation Therapy.* Colton, Calif.: Golden Quill Publishers, 1979, pp. 29–33.
9. Blumenthal, H. T.; Lansng, A. I.; and Wheeler, P. A. "Calcification of the media of the human aorta and its relation to intimal arteriosclerosis, aging and disease." *Amer. J. Path. 20* (1944), 665.
10. Lansing, A. I.; Blumenthal, H. T.; and Gray, S. H. "Aging and calcification of the human coronary artery." *J. Geront. 3* (1948), 87.
11. Amenta, J. S., and Waters, L. L. "The precipitation of serum lipoproteins by mucopolysaccharides extracted from aortic tissue." *Yale J. Biol. Med. 33,* (Oct. 1960), 112–121.
12. Gero, S.; Gergely, J.; Devenyi, T.; Virag, S.; Szekely, J.; and Jakab, L. "Inhibitory effect of some mucopolysaccharides on the lipolytic activity of the aorta of animals." *Nature 194* (June 1962), 1181–1182.
13. Hall, D. A. *International Review of Connective Tissue Research.* New York: Academic Press, 1963, p. 401.
14. Bihari-Varga, M. "Precipitation complexes formed from mucopolysaccharides and serum-beta-lipoprotein with the introduction of metal ions." *Acta. Chim. Hungarian Tomus 45* (1964), 219–230.
15. Srinivasan, S. R.; Lopez-S, A.; Radhakrishnamurthy, B.; and Berenson, G. S. "Complexing of serum pre-beta- and beta-lipoproteins and acid mucopoysaccharides." *Atherosclerosis 12* (1970), 321–334.
16. Berenson, G. S.; Srinivasan, S. R.; Dolan, P. J.; and Radhakrishnamurthy, B. "Lipoprotein-acid mucopolysaccharide complexes from fatty streaks of human aorta." *Circulation, Suppl. 11,* 6, (1971), 43–44.
17. Srinivasan, S. R.; Dolan, P.; Radhakrishnamurthy, B.; and Berenson, G. S. "Isolation of lipoprotein-acid mucopolysaccharide complexes from fatty streaks of human aortas." *Atherosclerosis 16* (1972), 95–104.

18. Morrison, L. M., and Schjeide, O. A. *Coronary heart disease and the muco-polysaccharides (glycosaminoglycans)*. Springfield, Ohio: Charles C. Thomas, 1974, p. 251.

19. Srinvasan, S. R.; Dolan, P.; Radhakrishnamurthy, B.; Pargaonkar, P. S.; and Berenson, G. S. "Lipoprotein-acid mucoplysaccharide complexes of human atherosclerotic lesions." *Biochem.-Biophys*. 388 (1975), 58–70.

20. Blumenthal, et al., 1944.

21. Lancing, et al., 1948.

22. Hall, 1963.

23. Partridge, S. M., and Keeley, F. W. "Age-related and atherosclerotic changes in aortic elastin." In: W. D. Wagner and T. B. Clarkson, *Arterial Mesenchyme and Arteriosclerosis*. New York: Plenum Press, 1974, pp. 173–191.

24. Fels, I. G. "Radioautographic study of aortic plaque formation." *Circulation Research* 7 (1959), 693–699.

25. Bihari-Varga, 1964.

26. Srinivasan, et al. 1972.

27. Berenson, et al., 1971.

28. Berenson, G. S.; Srinivasan, S. R.; Radhakrishnamurthy, B.; and Dalferes, E. R. "Mucopolysaccharide-lipoprotein complexes in atherosclerosis." In: W. D. Wagner and T. B. Clarkson, eds., *Arterial Mesenchyme and Arterio-sclerosis*. New York: Plenum Press, 1974, pp. 141–159.

29. Cranton, E. M.; Liu, Z. X.; and Smith, I. M. "Urinary trace and toxic elements and minerals in untimed urine specimens relative to urine creati-nine, Part I: provoked increase in excretion following intravenous EDTA." *J. Ad. in Med.* 2, 1/2 (Spring/Summer 1989), 331–349.

30. Cranton, E. M.; Liu, Z. X.; and Smith, I. M. "Urinary trace and toxic elements and minerals in untimed urine specimens relative to urine creati-nine, Part II: provoked increase in excretion following intravenous EDTA." *J. Adv. in Med.* 2, 1/2 (Spring/Summer 1989), 351–397.

31. Cranton, Part II, 1989.

Chapter Ten

1. Carter, A. E. *The Miracles of Rebound Exercise*. Edmonds, Wash.: National Institute of Reboundoloy and Health, 1979, p. 44.

2. Walker, M. *Jumping for Health*. Garden City Park, N.Y.: Avery Publishing Group, 1989, p. vii.

3. Mitchell, C. *The Perfect Exercise: The Hop, Skip and Jump Way to Health*. New York: Pocket Books, 1976, p. 178.

4. White, J. R. *Jump for Joy*. La Jolla, Calif.: USSD Press, 1981, p. 7.

5. Ibid., p. 9.

6. Walker, 1989, pp. 28, 29.

7. Jones, R. J. *Evolution of the Atherosclerotic Plaque.* Chicago: University of Chicago Press, 1963, p. 360.

8. Hall, D. A. *International Review of Connective Tissue Research, Volume 1.* New York: Academic Press, 1963, p. 401.

9. Department of Health, Education and Welfare. *Arteriosclerosis.* National Institutes of Health, DHEW Publication No. (NIH) 72–219 (1971), 1–365.

10. Wissler, R. W. "Development of the atherosclerotic plaque." In: E. Braunwald, ed. *The Myocardium: Failure and Infarction.* New York: H. P. Publishing Co., 1974, pp. 155–166.

11. Walker, M. "Bounce your way to health and fitness." *Townsend Letter for Doctors 103/104* (Feb./Mar. 1992), 126–128.

12. Ricci, B. *Physical and Physiological Conditioning for Men.* Dubuque, Iowa: Wm. C. Brown, 1972, p. 51.

13. Walker, 1992, p. 126.

14. Walker, M. "Jumping for Health." *Townsend Letter for Doctors 144* (July 1995), 42–48.

15. Walker, 1989, pp. 69–70.

Chapter 11

1. Inamuzu, T.; Chang, M. P.; and Makinodan, T. "Influence of age on the production and regulation of interleukin-1 in mice." *Immun.* 55 (1985), 447.

2. Price, G. B., and Makinodan, T. "Immunologic deficiencies in senescence." *J. Immun. 108,* 2 (1972), 403–412.

3. Carrow, D. J. "Beta-1,3-glucan as a primary immune activator." *Townsend Letter for Doctors & Patients, no. 155* (June 1996), 86–91.

4. Kohut, M. L.; Davis, J. M.; et al. "Effect of exercise on macrophage antiviral function in the lung." *J. Amer. Coll. Sports Med. 26* (1994), 33 (Abstract).

5. DiLuzio, N. F. "Immunopharmacology of glucan: a broad spectrum enhancer of host defense mechanisms." *Trends in Pharm. Sci. 4* (1983), 344–347.

6. Seljelid, R. "Macrophage activation." *Scand. J. Rheum. Suppl. 76* (1988), 67–72.

7. "Beta-1,3-glucan activity in mice: Intraperitoneal and oral applicatons." *Research Summary,* Baylor College of Medicine, 1989.

8. Walker, M. *The Chelation Answer.* New York: M. Evans and Co., 1992, p. 114.

9. Guthrie, H. A. *Introductory Nutrition.* St. Louis: C. V. Mosby Co., 1975, pp. 11–12.

10. Ashmead, H., et al. *J. Applied Nutr. 26* (Summer 1974), 5.

11. Ashmead, H. "Mineral chelation means better health." *Let's Live,* 1975.

12. Walker, M. *The Chelation Way.* Garden City Park, N.Y.: Avery Publishing Group, 1990, pp. 151–245.

13. Loquasto, M. J. "Adjunctive procedures: How is their circulation? Oral chelation." *The American Chiropractor* (January 1985), 16, 48.

Chapter Thirteen

1. *Encyclopedia Americana* 25:186m, New York: Americana Corp., 1966.
2. *Pension Plan Guide, 1976 Social Security and Medicare Explained.* Chicago: Commerce Clearing House, 1976.
3. Geha, A. S., et al. *J. Thorac. Cardiovasc. Surg.* 70 (1975), 414.
4. Loop, F. D., et al. *Am. J. Cardiol* 37 (May 1976), 890.
5. Tecklenberg, P. L., et al. *Circulation 52*, Suppl. I, (1975), 98.
6. Winkle, R. A., et al. *Circulation 52,* Suppl. I (1975), 61.

Chapter Fourteen

1. Mundth, E. D., and Austen, W. G. *N. Engl. J. Med. 293* (1975), *13, 75, 124.*
2. *Graboys, T. D.,* et al. "Results of a second opinion program for coronary artery bypass surgery." *JAMA 258* (1992), 2537–2540.
3. CASS principal Investigators and their associates. "Myocardial infarction and mortality in the coronary artery surgery study (CASS) randomized trial." *New Engl. J. Med. 310* (1984), 750–758.
4. "Coronary arteriography and coronary artery surgery." *The Medical Letter 18* (issue 456), July 2, 1976, p. 14.
5. Adams, D. F., et al. *Circulation 48* (1973), 609.
6. Zir, L. M., et al. *Circulation 53* (April 1976), 627.
7. Millman, Marcia. *The Unkindest Cut: Life in the Backrooms of Medicine.* New York: William Morrow, 1977.
8. Brody, Jane E. "Doctors query bypass surgery as aid to heart." *The New York Times.* Nov. 22, 1976.
9. Geha, A. S., et al. *J. Thorac. Cardiovasc. Surg. 70* (1975), 414.
10. Loop, F. D., et al. *Am. J. Cardiol. 37* (May 1976), 890.
11. Tecklenberg P. L., et al. *Circulation 52, Suppl 1* (1975), 61.
12. Winkle, R. A., et al. *Circulation, 52, Suppl 1* (1975), 61.
13. Berg, Jr., R., et al. *J. Thorac. Cardiovasc. Surg. 70* (1975), 432.
14. Winterscherd, L. C., et al. *Amer. Surg. 41* (Sept. 1975), 520.
15. Keon, W. J., et al. *Can. Med. Assoc, J. 114* (Feb. 21, 1976), 312.
16. Alderman, E. L., et al. *N. Engl. J. Med. 288* (1973), 535.
17. Bassan, M. M., et al. *N. Engl. J. Med. 290* (1974), 349.
18. Cohen, M. V., and Gorlin, R. *Circulation 52* (1975), 275.
19. Takan, T., et al. *Circulation 52, Suppl. II* (1975), 143.
20. Selden, R., et al. *N. Engl. J. Med. 293,* (1975), 1329.
21. Mathur, V. S., and Guinin, G. A. *Circulation, 52, Suppl. I* (1975), 133.
22. Kloster, F., et al. *Circulation, 52, Suppl. II* (1975), 90.

23. Russell, R. D., et al. *Am. J. Cardiol.* 37 (May, 1976), 896.
24. "Bypass blocked—but still no angina." *Medical World News,* Aug. 9, 1976, p. 68.
25. "Comparing treatments for angina." *Medical World News,* Apr. 7, 1975.
26. Kansal, S., et al. "Ischemic myocardial injury following aortocoronary bypass surgery." *Chest* 67 (1975), 20–26.
27. Kouchoukas, N. T., et al. "An appraisal of coronary bypass grafting." *Circulation* 50 (1974), 11.
28. Kouchoukas, N. T. "Operative therapy for femoropopliteal arterial occlusive disease—A comparison of therapeutic methods." *Circulation (Suppls.)* 35 (1967), 1–178, 36 (1967), 1–182.
29. Thompson, J. E. "Acute peripheral arterial occlusions." *N. Engl. J. Med.* 290 (1974), 950.
30. Segal, B. L., et al. "Saphenous vein bypass surgery for coronary artery disease." *Am. J. Cardiol.* 32 (1973), 1010–1013.
31. Mundth, E. D., and Austen, W. G. "Surgical Measures for coronary heart disease." *N. Engl. J. Med.* 293 (1975), 124–129.
32. Fulton, R. L., and Blakely, W. R., "Lumbar sympathectomy: A procedure of questionable value in the treatment of arteriosclerosis obliteraus of the legs." *Am. J. Surg.* 116 (1968), 735.

Chapter Fifteen

1. Meltzer, L. E.; Palmon, F.; and Kitchell, J. R. "Long term use, side effects, and toxicity of disodium EDTA." *Am. J. Med. Sci.* 242 (1961), 51–57.
2. "Peripheral flow opened up." *Medical World News,* Mar. 15, 1963, pp. 37–39.
3. Kitchell, J. R., et al. "The treatment of coronary artery disease with disodium EDTA—A reappraisal." *Am. J. Cardiol.* 11 (1963), 501–506.
4. Kitchell, J. R.; Meltzer, L. E.; and Rutman, E. "Effects of ions on *in vitro* gluconeogenesis in rat kidney cortex slices." *Am. J. Physiol.* 208 (1965), 841–846.
5. Clarke, N. E.; Clarke, C. N.; and Mosher, R. E. "Treatment of angina pectoris with disodium ethylene diamine tetraacetic acid." *Am. J. Med. Sci.* 232 (1965), 654–666.
6. Clarke, N. E., Sr., Clarke, N. E., Jr., and Moser, R. E. "Treatment of occlusive vascular disease with disodium ethylene diamine tetraacetic acid (EDTA)." *Am. J. Med. Sci.* 239 (1960), 732–744.
7. Kitchell, J. R.; Meltzer, L. E.; and Seven, M. J. "Potential uses of chelation methods in the treatment of cardiovascular disease." *Prog. Cardiovasc. Dis.* 19 (1961), 798.
8. Seven, M. J., ed. *Metal Binding in Medicine.* Philadelphia: J. B. Lippincott Co., 1960.

9. Seven, M.J., and Johnson, L. "Proceedings of a conference on biological aspects of metal binding." *Fed. Proc.* (Suppl. 10, 1961).
10. Brucknerova, O., and Tulacek, J. "Chelates in the treatment of occlusive atherosclerosis," *Vnitr. Lek. 18* (1972), 729.
11. Kurliandchikov, V. N. "Treatments of patients with coronary arteriosclerosis with Unithiol in combination with Decamevit." *Vrach, Delo. 6.* (1973), 8.
12. Ohno, T. "Clinical and experimental studies of arteriosclerosis." *Excerpta Medica: Intern, Med. 17* (1963), 8.
13. Meltzer, L. E.; Urol, M. E.; and Kitchell, J. R. "The treatment of coronary artery disease with disodium EDTA." In M. J. Seven, ed. *Metal Binding in Medicine*. Philadelphia: J. B. Lippincott Co., 1960, pp. 132–136.

Chapter Sixteen

1. "Palm Desert Man Tells Meadowbrook Experience." *National Health Federation Bulletin 21* (Oct. 1975), 6–9.
2. "Louisiana." *Encyclopedia Americana* 17:784, New York: Americana Corporation, 1966.
3. "New Warning on Therapy." *Salt Lake Tribune*, Aug. 22, 1976.

Chapter Seventeen

1. Soffer, A. "Chelation treatment for arteriosclerosis." *JAMA 233* (1975).
2. Craven, P. C., and Morelli, H. F. "Chelation therapy." *West. J. Med. 122* (1975), 277–278.
3. "CMA warns against chelation." *CMA News 20*: 13, Sept. 12, 1975, p. 3.
4. Kannel, W. "Long-term value of coronary bypass disputed." *Family Practice News 6*:1.
5. Petersdorf, R. G. "Internal medicine in family practice." *N. Engl. J. Med. 293* (1975), 326.
6. Kaegor, Bill. "Probation urged for physician." *Today*, Dec. 18, 1976.
7. Wolinsky, Howard. "Treatment under attack." *Today*, Jan. 10, 1977.

Chapter Eighteen

1. Soffer, Al. "Chihuahuas and laetrile, chelation therapy, and honey from Boulder, Colo." *Arch. Intern. Med 136* (Aug. 1976), 865, 866.
2. Kell, G. W. Brief filed with Curtis L. Klahs in the matter of Ophelia Clementino, Sept. 9, 1976.
3. Kell, G. W. Brief filed with Curtis L. Klahs in the matter of Ophelia Clementino, Sept. 3, 1976.
4. In the Matter of Ophelia V. Clementino, HIC #236–03–7068–B, "Decision

of Hearing Officer." *Proceedings before the Occidental Life Insurance Company of California,* Sept. 13, 1976.

5. Turk, Randall. "San Gabriel man is living, active testament to alternative therapy." *Star-News,* Pasadena, Calif., June 21, 1976.

Appendix A

1. Nikitina, E. K. "Treatment of arterosclerosis with Trilon B (EDTA)." *Kardiologia 12,* 11 (Nov. 1972), 137.
2. Zapadnick, V. I., et al. "Pharmacological activity of Unithiol and its use in clinical practice." *Vrach Delo.* 8 (1973), 122.
3. Kurliandchikov, V. N. "Treatment of patients with coronary arteriosclerosis with Unithiol in combination with Decamevit." *Vrach. Delo.* 6, (1973), 8.

Appendix C

1. Foreman, H. "Toxic side effects of EDTA." *J. Chron. Dis.* 16 (1963), 319–323.
2. Oser, B., et al. "Safety evaluation studies of calcium EDTA." *Toxicol. Appl. Pharmacol.* 5 (1963), 142–162.
3. Doolan, P. D., et al. "An evaluation of the nephrotoxicity of ethylene diamine tetraacetate and diethylene triamine pentaacetate in the rat." *Toxicol. Appl. Pharmacol.* 10 (1967), 481–500.
4. Schwartz, S. L.; Johnson, C. B.; and Doolan, P. D. "Study of the mechanism of renal vacuologenesis induced in the rat by EDTA." *Mol. Pharmacol.* 6 (1970), 54–60.

THE MEDICAL CONTROVERSY OVER EDTA CHELATION THERAPY

The medical mystique has its own rules and regulations. Many have a compelling logic and are judiciously applied. But some of them ought to be questioned. The central question is whether the rules are used to promote the therapeutic aspects of the medical mystique, or whether they are employed to reinforce the mystique's authoritarian aspects. . . . Hippocrates, in his oath, speaks not just of taking care of patients, but of the obligations of all new members to their teachers. And Fellows. Most lay people think of the Hippocratic Oath as a dedication to the patient. But the oath also clearly defines what a doctor's obligations are to other members of the profession.

—MARVIN S. BELSKY, M.D. and
Leonard Gross, *How to Choose and Use Your Doctor*, 1975

The Antichelation CMA Resolution 151–75

Reference Committee D-1 of the California Medical Association House of Delegates met February 23, 1975 to consider Resolution 151–75 on chelation therapy, as part of its studies on "Scientific and Educational Activities." Resolution 151–75, introduced by Wayne B. Bigelow, M.D., of Turlock, California, representing the Stanislaus County Medical Society, declared:

WHEREAS, Chelation has been demonstrated by the FDA to be dangerous and

WHEREAS, its effectiveness has not been established in arteriosclerotic disease, be it

RESOLVED: that the use of Chelation be limited to research centers until further data is available.

Communications consultant Phil Townsend Hanna, a legislative advocate for the Committee for Medical Freedom, 1127 Eleventh St., Suite 501, Sacramento, California, was an observer at the committee meeting. Mr. Hanna reported that Dr. Bigelow, who assists in doing coronary artery bypass surgery, stated he was "unfamiliar with the general aspects of chelation therapy except for its use to remove heavy metals." Dr. Bigelow had introduced his antichelation resolution on his own, without first clearing it with the Scientific Committee of the California Medical Association (CMA). Then he agreed that his resolution should be rewritten to exclude this use in heavy-metal poisoning. Dr. Bigelow said he knew of several clinics which were formed or were being formed to deal exclusively in chelation therapy for arteriosclerotic diseases. He complained to the reference committee that patients were being charged "high fees" for this unproved treatment, and that the Food and Drug Administration did not approve of its use for this purpose. (The FDA does not "approve" of many treatments commonly employed by medical doctors.)

Ralph C. Teall, M.D., of Sacramento, California, rose to support Dr. Bigelow's resolution. Dr. Teall is a former vice president of the American Medical Association and full-time acting medical director for the California-Western States Life Insurance Company, which is controlled by the Occidental Life Insurance Company. The Occidental Life Insurance Company is the Medicare health insurance carrier for Southern California. Dr. Teall said that he had researched chelation and there was nothing whatsoever to support its use. Even as he spoke, however, Dr. Teall had on his reference committee desk two recently published Russian articles.[1,2] Both articles reported beneficial effects on cerebral, coronary and peripheral circulation on all the patients studied with use of EDTA, as well as with another chelating agent, Unithiol, which employes a sulfhydryl group as the chelator.[3]

Dr. Teall also said a doctor in Sacramento (meaning Garry F. Gordon, M.D.) operated a chelation therapy clinic. (The Sacramento Medical Preventics Clinic was a private health care facility engaged in the active application of preventive medicine concepts within a holistic framework. Dr. Gordon gave up his affiliation with the clinic when he assumed duties as president of the American College for Advancement in Medicine in September 1976.) This doctor, said Dr. Teall, was supporting a staff with an annual payroll of more than $600,000.

Then Dr. Teall described the heated legal battle between the chelation therapy clinic and the Sacramento Medical Care Foundation, which had rejected the clinic's insurance claims. The clinic had brought suit and an injunction against the Sacramento Medical Care Foundation. For the first time in California history, depositions were taken in open court before a judge, said Dr. Teall.

This insurance company medical director also warned his colleagues that other clinics were being formed for this chelation treatment. He said that the Sacramento doctor was being bankrolled by other doctors from all over the country. Dr. Teall emphasized that various patients were being sold a bill of goods and lulled into believing the efficacy of the treatment with "literature that was old." To his knowledge, he told the committee, nothing new had been printed on the subject since 1963 (while the pro-chelation articles *on his desk* had been published in 1972 and 1973.)

What Dr. Teall did *not* tell the members of the CMA's Reference Committee D-1 was possibly the real reason for his interest in having this antichelation resolution passed. The CMA could take the blame while his insurance company refused to pay potential health insurance claims for reimbursement by patients who were being treated in Dr. Gordon's clinic or in other chelation facilities. The resolution's passage would give Dr. Teall's employer a valid excuse to deny payments.

Franklin Ashley, M.D., a member of the Scientific Board of the California Medical Association, stood up to support the Bigelow resolution. He claimed the CMA needed to run the charlatans and thieves out of the medical profession, and that none of the information on chelation therapy for arteriosclerosis had even been presented to the CMA Scientific Board.

Leonard Asher, M.D., from the Los Angeles delegation added that CMA should do something to inform the AMA and the public about this type of treatment which was not approved by the FDA.

The CMA Reference Committee D-1 then took the matter under submission when no one rose in opposition to the House of Delegates Resolution 151–75. No one was present from the American College for Advancement in Medicine (ACAM) who could have presented the facts in defense of chelation therapy, because the ACAM members were *not* informed of the pending resolution. And there was no known opposition when the CMA House of Delegates voted to approve the following amended resolution:

RESOLVED: That the CMA opposes the use of chelation therapy in the treatment of arteriosclerotic disease except in recognized research centers; and, be it further

RESOLVED: That the CMA inform physicians and the public of the documented dangers and lack of proven benefit of chelation therapy as a treatment for arteriosclerotic diseases.

Effects of the Resolution's Adoption

The resolution warns against "documented dangers." This stems from the EDTA overdosage in two patients in 1954, reported in 1955, that we told you about in Chapter Seven. Dr. Clarke's explanation and Dr. Halstead's interpretation of those overdosages with EDTA were presented then. More than two million treatments on many thousands of patients have been given since 1954 with no reports of deleterious results.

The resolution also charges "lack of proven benefit." But what is the proof required? Over and over, published clinical journal articles report chelated patients whose electrocardiograms (EKGs) get better; their plethysmographs improve. They can walk where they could not before receiving chelation therapy. Patients don't die! What more proof has been needed in medicine until now?

Resolution 151–75 was introduced into the House of Delegates of the CMA with no thought to its fairness. It went through as a matter of routine and became the rule of the California state medical society.

The effects of the resolution's adoption filtered down to the general CMA membership quickly. A sixty-eight-year-old physician in Northern California, who is a benevolent person supporting his twelve adopted children, received a telephone call declaring that he was being kicked out of his local medical society because he was a chelating doctor. He was losing all the professional and economic advantages of membership. Almost immediately his professional life began to decline. He felt a distinct loss of respect from his fellow physicians almost at once. Worse still, his medical malpractice insurance, disability insurance, health insurance, hospital insurance and life insurance were being canceled. He had purchased these various insurance coverages through the CMA's group plans, which were part of the benefits of medical society membership.

Without a hearing, with no due process, he was told, "You are out!" Consequently, under pressure the physician signed a paper which read in part: "I hereby promise not to use chelation therapy . . ."

Harvard University medical graduate Yiwen Y. Tang, M.D., F.A.B.F.P., then of San Francisco, received a similar declaration by mail from the San Francisco Medical Society. He was threatened with expulsion unless he stopped using chelation therapy. Dr. Tang's response was not one of anxiety or fear but of anger. He telephoned Garry F. Gordon, M.D., and said, "We can't let this go on. We have to stand up and be counted!"

Dr. Gordon agreed. "Let's call their bluff," he said, and gathered together the defense forces of the then 300-member American College for Advancement in Medicine. (Now ACAM has nearly 1,000 member physicians.)

The American College for Advancement in Medicine (with executive offices at 23121 Verdugo Drive, Suite 204, Laguna Hills, California 92653; (800)532-3688 or (714)583-7666; FAX (714)455-9679; Edward A. Shaw, Ph.D, executive director), is a professional organization formed for the research and development of the clinical applications of any vascular therapy. It educates physicians and the public about cardiovascular disease and the application of chelation to that disease. The college also works toward the widespread recognition of vitamin/mineral supplementation, diet modification, anti-stress factors, exercise and other changes in lifestyles that might alter the course of this disease.

ACAM is attempting to do basic research and has contacted the FDA to proceed with clinical testing of EDTA under a physician-sponsored IND (Investigational New Drug Application). Academy members hope to see EDTA moved from "possibly effective" to "proven effective" for the purposes of FDA regulations. Unfortunately, this seemingly simple task appears virtually impossible for a small group of private physicians. Estimates of potential cost vary from $500,000 to $5 million. Apparently, pressure must be applied before government funds are put to this use. This requires informed people who will write their representatives in Washington to request such research funding.

ACAM member physicians use alternative cardiovascular therapies that involve early detection, identifying the risk factors of the patient, and then intensive education in modifying the patient's lifestyle to alter those risk factors. Chelation therapy may be employed to further modify the course of the patient's disease process before it reaches crisis proportions. As a result, there may be substantial early treatment for large numbers of patients and little need for vascular or other bypass surgery later.

These ACAM physicians practice *holistic preventive medicine*. The holistic approach is a full program that dedicates itself to reversal of our major killer disease, hardening of the arteries, and other diseases. The organization maintains a referral list of physician members in various parts of the country. To learn of a physician near you who uses rehabilitative exercise, nutritional therapy and chelation therapy against arteriosclerosis, write to the American College for Advancement in Medicine at the Laguna Hills address.

The ACAM versus the CMA

The San Francisco Medical Society conducted a peer review of their "errant" member. Dr. Tang went to the committee meeting with two slide projectors full of "before and after" slides of his patients' chelation treatment results (see Dr. Tang's photographs 1, 2, 3, 4 of Roland Hohnbaum in Chapter One). He also supplied quantities of the basic medical journal documents which his San Francisco colleagues apparently had never seen. He said, "Gentlemen, you are interested in chelation; you wish to know about it; now you are going to learn."

Dr. Tang was an hour and a half into his peer review presentation when the committee chairman noted that more than half of his committee members had left. They had come to censor their colleague and not to learn from him. The chairman was embarrassed and called a halt to the documentation. Dr. Tang then handed the peer review chairman a letter prepared in advance. The letter read:

Yiwen Y. Tang, M.D., Inc.
345 Portal Avenue
San Francisco, California 94118
Telephone (415) 566-1000

San Francisco Medical Society
Professional Relations Committee
250 Masonic Ave.
San Francisco, California 84118

Sirs:

As a member of this medical society and as a physician whose practice includes the use of EDTA Chelation Therapy, I am requesting formally that my Society initiate action to rectify a serious error on the part of our parent organization, the California Medical Association. Specifically, I am referring to the CMA's resolution, passed in February of this year, which effectively proscribes the clinical use of EDTA Chelation Therapy. The language of that resolution claims that the Federal FDA has found chelation to be dangerous and unsubstantiated by scientific and clinical research. My personal documentation and the documentation of the American College for Advancement in Medicine (a professional society which specializes in Chelation Therapy and in which I am a member) overwhelmingly supports the opposite conclusions. In fact, correspondence with the FDA in no way supports the statement that chelation is dangerous.

I formally request you to determine on what basis this erroneous information was allowed to be introduced into a resolution and subsequently passed without prior notification to physicians who are engaged in the practice of chelation, of which there are approximately 120 in the State of California. The existence of the resolution threatens the availability of this modality to my patients and my particular practice of medicine. Since medical doctors in this state are being harassed by their local medical societies to discontinue this treatment for their patients or lose their society membership with the attendant loss of malpractice insurance, this resolution denies an effective alternative therapy in cardiovascular disease to the citizens of California. The "ban" on EDTA Chelation Therapy appears to have been initiated out of concern for potential costs to insurance carriers rather than concern for the health of people.

I request that some document signed by FDA showing EDTA to be dangerous be made available to myself, my college, and my patients. If such document cannot be produced, the faulty language must be brought to the attention of the CMA so that the unfortunate error can be corrected. Further, I request that proof regarding the alleged ineffectiveness of chelation be substantiated and made public to me, my college, and my patients. If such evidence cannot be provided, the CMA resolution must be rescinded as being without basis in fact.

The documentation which I presented to you tonight is overwhelmingly positive regarding EDTA's effectiveness in the removal of calcium in arteriosclerotic conditions in cadavers, experimental animals, and in living patients. I am appealing to your sense of objectivity and my rights to require proof of accusation. My actions here are in the best interest of The Society and medicine-at-large. . . .

Should you require additional information, please contact me directly.

Sincerely,
(signed)
Yiwen Y. Tang, M.D.

A letter arrived in Dr. Tang's office from Robert Mandle, M.D., chairman of the Professional Relations Committee of the San Francisco Medical Society, four weeks after that meeting. It stated unceremoniously that Dr. Tang's letter had been taken under advisement. The San Francisco Medical Society would inform him of whatever action it took, the letter promised. Until this day, however, that letter from Dr. Mandle was the last Dr. Tang has heard from the San Francisco Medical Society.

Harassment continued for other chelating physicians in the state of California. Some doctors considered giving up being crusaders for patients' rights. It was easier to abandon the fight and flow with the mainstream of "cookbook" medicine, a few decided. Therefore, on October 20, 1975, Dr. Tang and the ACAM filed a petition for a hearing before the Scientific Board of the California Medical Association. The hearing petition read:

To:
C. John Tupper, M.D.
Chairman, Scientific Board
California Medical Association
731 Market Street
San Francisco, California 94103

From:
Yiwen Y. Tang, M.D.
345 Portal Avenue
San Francisco, California 94118
and
American College for Advancement in Medicine

23121 Verdugo Drive, Suite 204
Laguna Hills, California 92653

On behalf of myself, my immediate colleagues and the American College for Advancement in Medicine, I HEREBY PETITION FOR A FORMAL HEARING BEFORE THE SCIENTIFIC BOARD BY VIRTUE OF THAT BOARD'S FUNCTION ACCORDING TO CHAPTER 4, SECTION 1, OF THE BY-LAWS OF THE CALIFORNIA MEDICAL ASSOCIATION.

Subject of the hearing is EDTA Chelation Therapy and the scientific basis thereof. Purpose of this hearing is to validate the right of the patient to receive this therapy, and the right of the physician who performs that modality to maintain his or her status as member in good standing of his local medical society and its related organizations. Specifically, we challenge the substance of CMA Resolution 151–75, which effectively proscribes Chelation Therapy to clinical practitioners who choose to use that treatment in arteriosclerotic diseases.

Passage of this resolution represents, in our opinion, a travesty of objective deliberation and due-process . . .

. . . The proscription of EDTA Chelation Therapy was approved by the CMA under dubious conditions. There was no notification to practitioners in the field nor to our professional organization, all of whom were well known to all parties involved backing Resolution 151–75 before the CMA Reference Committee in Los Angeles. Thus, we seek a redress of due-process at the level of the Scientific Board, where the initial inquiries should have occurred in the first place, not in the political arena.

Resolution 151–75 was enacted by the CMA. It claimed that EDTA Chelation Therapy is dangerous, and that its efficacy has not been demonstrated. We are prepared to provide overwhelming evidence to the contrary on both points. For that purpose, then, we petition the following specific actions from the Scientific Board:

1. THAT WRITTEN ACKNOWLEDGEMENT OF THIS PETITION BE SENT BY REGISTERED MAIL WITHIN 15-DAYS FROM DATE OF DELIVERY TO THE OFFICES OF THE AMERICAN COLLEGE FOR ADVANCEMENT IN MEDICINE (address above),

2. THAT YOUR SCIENTIFIC BOARD MAKE A DETAILED AND COMPLETE ANALYSIS OF THE SCIENTIFIC LITERATURE REGARDING CHELATION THERAPY UPON WHICH RESOLUTION 151–75 WAS ENACTED, AND IF THAT DATA IS INSUFFICIENT TO SUBSTANTIATE THE RESOLUTION ACCORDING TO ACCEPTABLE SCIENTIFIC CRITERIA, THAT YOU INITIATE APPROPRIATE REMEDIAL PROCEDURES;

3. THAT IF, IN YOUR OPINION, YOUR REVIEW OF THE DATA SUSTAINS THE RESOLUTION, YOU ISSUE A FORMAL REQUEST TO THE CMA FOR A MORATORIUM ON THE ENFORCEMENT OF RESOLUTION 151–75 UNTIL OUR FULL RECOURSE HAS BEEN EXHAUSTED (such a moratorium is not necessary if our requested hearing will be held within 60-days of this petition; otherwise we believe that the lives and health of our patients are at risk);

4. THAT, AS PART OF THIS RECOURSE, A FULL FORMAL HEARING BE SCHEDULED WITH THE FULL SCIENTIFIC BOARD TO EVALUATE OFFICIALLY THE TWO ISSUES WE ARE CONTESTING. THIS INCLUDES THE TOXICITY OF EDTA AND ITS EFFICACY IN ARTERIOSCLEROSIS WHICH, WE BELIEVE, IS SUFFICIENTLY ESTABLISHED AS AN ACCEPTABLE MEDICAL TREATMENT IN RELATION TO EXISTING ALTERNATIVES TODAY;

5. THAT WE RECEIVE, 30 DAYS PRIOR TO ANY SCHEDULED HEARING, A STATEMENT WHICH OUTLINES THE CRITERIA BY WHICH YOUR BOARD, OR THE CMA, DETERMINES ANY THERAPY TO BE ACCEPTABLE MEDICAL TREATMENT: THAT IF SUCH CRITERIA ARE NOT A MATTER OF PUBLISHED POLICY, OR IF SUCH CRITERIA DO NOT EXIST, WE REQUEST THAT WHATEVER STANDARDS ARE TO BE EMPLOYED IN THIS INSTANCE BE DETAILED FOR US IN A WRITTEN STATEMENT WHICH IS ENDORSED BY YOURSELF OR OTHER AUTHORITATIVE OFFICIAL SOURCE;

6. THAT WE BE ALLOWED AT LEAST TEN EXPERT WITNESSES AND A MINIMUM OF THREE HOURS TO MAKE OUR PRESENTATION: AND THAT A TRANSCRIPTION OF THE ENTIRE PROCEEDINGS BE PERMITTED SO THAT THE INFORMATION MAY BE MADE AVAILABLE TO INTERESTED PARTIES.

The above concludes our formal petition. In the following section, we should like to explore several relevant areas in order to amplify your general understanding of the issues as we see them.

In reference to the specific allegation that EDTA is dangerous:

The toxicity of EDTA has been studied in depth and the literature is extensive on this subject. The substance is essentially an innocuous chemical when administered in the currently accepted dosage schedules (3 grams over a 2-plus-hour period is the standard protocol today). EDTA is a standard analytical chemical extensively employed in laboratories and industry (it has been used to clean lime deposits from the inside of boilers for years, and it is a common food preservative—you eat it frequently). Its LD-50, in relation to therapeutic dose, is considerably safer than aspirin. We are enclosing several relevant citations to this issue.

1. Meltzer, L. E., et al.
   "The Long Term Side Effects and Toxicity of Disodium Ethylenediamine Tetracetic Acid (EDTA)." *American Journal of Medical Sciences,* July 1961.
2. Oser, B.
   "Safety Evaluation Studies of Calcium EDTA." *Toxicology and Applied Pharmacology* 5:142–162, 1963.
3. Doolan, P. D., et al.
   "An Evaluation of the Nephrotoxicity of Ethylene diamine tetraacetate and Diethylene triamine pentaacetate in the Rat." *Toxicology and Applied Pharmacology* 10:481–500, 1967.
4. Foreman, H.
   "Toxic Side Effects of Ethylene diamine Tetraacetic Acid." *Journal of Chronic Disease* 16:319–323, 1963.

In reference to Dr. Teall's statement that nothing has been published since 1963 regarding EDTA's efficacy:

We would make reference to the Biological Abstracts, Medline Computer Retrieval, and particularly the citations published by the National Library of Medicine on EDTA from 1967 to 1970 which reports 517 citations alone . . . See also the Federal Register which lists EDTA as possibly effective in vascular occlusive disease.

A collateral issue in the controversy is the subject of the package insert. We all realize that in medicine, there are always proponents of particular therapeutic approaches, from psychiatry to acupuncture, who believe they demonstrate efficacy, and opponents who dispute the position. The lack of a specific indication on the package insert for vascular occlusive disease does not make its use unacceptable in medicine. In the case of EDTA, the package insert was removed voluntarily by Abbott several years ago when they were unable to justify the expense of proving their claim about efficacy in arteriosclerotic disease and in light of a rapidly expiring patent on the chemical. Package inserts have recently been the subject of concern of the AMA Board of Trustees, who have requested the FDA to put a disclaimer at the bottom of these inserts so that physicians would not feel so governed and limited by the listed indications. The use of Diphenylhydantoin for many therapeutic applications not mentioned on the package insert, as well as Propanolol Hydrochloride, must serve to remind us that the FDA has no jurisdiction over the practice of medicine, and its authority is concerned primarily with marketing claims—at least as far as the package insert is concerned. The FDA states that the use of a locally obtained drug in a physician's office is the "practice of medicine" over which they have no jurisdiction. See: R. Crout, M.D. *The Lowly Package Insert,* Dir. Bureau of Drugs—FDA.

The legal ramifications of the proscription against Chelation Therapy for arteriosclerosis by the CMA, although perhaps a more subtle issue, are potentially the most explosive. Every physician has the duty to disclose all available choices of therapy to the patient, and if he fails to do so, he may be held liable (ref. *Cobbs vs Grant* 8 Cal 3d 240, 104C.R. 505). This might well be held applicable to a group or organization of physicians. We believe EDTA Chelation Therapy is a viable alternative in vascular disease for many patients and that it is significantly less dangerous than the alternatives made available at present.

There are other issues which are germane to this controversy, namely:

1. the current trend to politicize science and medicine, making certain therapies acceptable, such as acupuncture when sufficient public pressure is brought to bear, while other therapies are made illegal and their practitioners subject to arrest.
2. the subversion of organized medicine away from the role of protecting the rights of the patient to receive unfettered care of a physician who is practicing under his essentially unlimited license in California toward becoming the enforcer of "cost control medicine," etc. . . .

But these issues are not intended to be adjudicated by the Scientific Committee. Our fondest hope is that the name of science can be vindicated by objective evaluation instead of the sham of Resolution 151–75 being allowed to set the standard. We hope that we will not have to join the present exodus away from the organized medical institutions in the name of justice and fair treatment. This is a major responsibility on you as a representative of official judgment, but we are entering a period in which these issues are coming to a head across the nation and precedence must be established. The established institutions cannot continue to rule by fiat but must, instead, substantiate their positions in fact, upon reason, and in open forum. We trust that you are worthy of the task and, as a colleague in a tradition which transcends prejudice and ephemeral vested interest, we extend to you our firm regards.

Sincerely,

(signed)
Yiwen Y. Tang, M.D.

(signed)
Garry F. Gordon, M.D.
as Board Member and on behalf
of the American College for
Advancement in Medicine

Months passed during which the following actions took place:

November 17, 1975: The CMA replied to Dr. Tang with no mention of any acceptance of the conditions as requested in the petition.

November 26, 1975: CMA attorneys responded to Dr. Gordon's letter, which was mailed to them on October 31, 1975. He requested resolution 151–75 be placed in moratorium until adequate hearing of the facts had been held. The attorneys answered, "CMA policy position is not a direct mandate which all physicians must follow." (Of course, if doctors don't follow it they apparently stand to lose their CMA membership and all related insurance benefits.)

December 1, 1975: The Federal Appeals Court in Atlanta, Georgia, ruled that chelation therapy is a reasonable and necessary treatment and that Medicare, Part A, may pay Mr. D. D. Dominey for this treatment (as reported in Chapter Thirteen).

January 26, 1976: ACAM-Dr. Tang replied to the vague CMA November 17, 1975 letter and demanded again a *full and fair hearing in an open forum with recording of the entire proceedings.*

February 26, 1976: The CMA sent notice that it was granting a tape recorded hearing to Dr. Tang and the ACAM to be held at the Los Angeles Airport Marriott Hotel on March 26, 1976 at 2:00 P.M.

With notice of a hearing to be held, the ACAM gathered together its witnesses and evidence of treatment efficacy. The College's relevant request was ignored, however, and at no time were any criteria by which EDTA could be found acceptable ever established by the CMA. The officers of ACAM submitted repeated written requests right up to the meeting-time for those guidelines. Also, no right to question the opponents of chelation therapy and force them to document their negative statements was granted. These denials or lack of actions constituted a serious disallowance of due process on the part of the CMA. It foretold of the probable negative conclusion of the proceedings.

The CMA's Ad Hoc Committee Meeting

The hearing began as scheduled by an ad hoc committee of the *Advisory Panel on Internal Medicine of the Scientific Board of the California Medical Association*. It related to the resolution passed by the CMA's House of Delegates. "The Scientific Board and the House of Delegates are two clearly distinct and different organizations," said C. John Tupper, M.D., chairman of the CMA Scientific Board. "The Scientific Board is responsible for the scientific and educational activities of the California Medical Association, and so quite separate."

In its attempt to prove the issues, the American College for Advancement in Medicine provided the CMA ad hoc committee with an enormous amount of medical documentation, plus color slides showing the beneficial effects of EDTA chelation. In verification, Dr. Tupper said, "I want you to know that we have received through Dr. Garry Gordon five boxes of reprints and other printed material that for your information weighs 102 pounds. We have them behind us here."

Although the ACAM members would have welcomed more time, in the three hours allowed it did furnish evidence for the following:

- EDTA is nontoxic when administered under proper medical supervision.
- EDTA is effective in the majority of cases of arteriosclerosis and its complications.

- Since arteriosclereosis is invariably fatal, compared with other presently used and acceptable modalities, the EDTA chelation therapy for arteriosclerosis has a very promising and highly acceptable benefit/ risk ratio. In fact, the risk is exceedingly low and as such, constitutes an acceptable medical treatment for the palliation of arteriosclerosis and its complications.

Subsequent to its presentation, the ACAM urged the CMA Scientific Board's Advisory Panel to make a speedy decision to rescind Resolution 151–75 by the CMA House of Delegates, for the reasons indicated in its petition.

Following the ACAM three-hour presentation, another hour went by while the CMA ad hoc committee members randomly questioned the ACAM members. During their questioning, the CMA ad hoc committee presented no opponents of chelation therapy. Although the ACAM had petitioned for and expected to "meet with the appropriate panels in an open forum, face-to-face, for a free and open exchange of information" and to counter the arguments of medical opponents, none appeared. The notorized transcript of that hearing which we hold indicates that there was no exchange of information—only questions asked by the CMA and answers given by the ACAM.

ACAM members anticipated that the open hearing would "provide both sides with better access to each other's information regarding the use of EDTA chelation therapy as a palliative in arteriosclerosis and enable our college [ACAM] to learn first hand of any information that you have that may indicate a possible danger or harmful effect of this therapy of which we are unaware, as well as the facts upon which any opposition is based. Possibly we may learn of an alternative therapy that offers equal opportunity for symptomatic relief in arteriosclerosis and which is less controversial." The CMA Scientific Board was unresponsive to this portion of the petition.

Dr. Gordon told us of an exchange between two CMA committee members overheard in the men's washroom by an ACAM member. It went like this.

"How long do we have to listen to this s**t?"

"Just long enough to let these idiots dump out their stuff. We'll soon get rid of them and finish them off."

Following the four-hour meeting, the CMA decision was seemingly arrived at within fifteen minutes. One of the ACAM medical witnesses, Lester I. Tavel, D.O., of Houston, Texas, had to catch a plane immediately at the conclusion of the meeting. He left for the airport, which was across the street, to check in for his flight. Fifteen minutes later he saw three of the CMA ad hoc committee members arrive at the airport bar. Each committee member had left behind at the place where he had been sitting his huge pile of exhibit and reference material supplied by the ACAM. And the CMA ad hoc committee of the Scientific Board never met again. Was this a "full and fair" hearing?

The CMA Ad Hoc Committee's Recommendation

The Advisory Panel on Internal Medicine and the Executive Committee of the Scientific Board April 14, 1976 endorsed the following recommendation to serve as official CMA policy regarding chelation therapy in the treatment of arteriosclerosis in lieu of House of Delegates Resolution 151–75:

THE EFFICACY OF CHELATION THERAPY IN THE TREATMENT OF ARTERIOSCLEROSIS IS UNPROVEN AND IT IS NOT NOW AN AC-CEPTED THERAPY. WHEN USED FOR SUCH TREATMENT, DISODIUM EDETATE (ENDRATE, EDTA) IS AN EXPERIMENTAL DRUG. THUS, THE CALIFORNIA MEDICAL ASSOCIATION RECOMMENDS THAT SUCH USE, IN EACH PATIENT, BE REPORTED TO THE FDA AND FURTHER, THAT IT REQUIRE THE PATIENT'S INFORMED CONSENT.

During the summer of 1976, newspapers around the country printed nearly similar stories that were critical of chelation therapy. They appeared in towns and cities where chelation physicians practiced and were adapted to include local or regional medical personnel in authority. The following article, from the *Salt Lake City Tribune* of August 8, 1976, is typical:

The Salt Lake City-County Health Department has questioned the use of chelation therapy for arteriosclerosis and multiple sclerosis.
   Dr. Harry L. Gibbons, city-county health director, said there is inadequate evidence that chelation therapy, which uses trace metal elements in a nutrient solution may be beneficial to arteriosclerosis and multiple sclerosis patients and may, in fact, be harmful.

The health official pointed out that the manufacturer states chelation therapy does not benefit arteriosclerosis and the Federal Food and Drug Administration backs up the manufacturer's statement.

In view of this vehement opposition, it is a wonder that courageous doctors continue to administer chelation therapy.

SUGGESTED GENERAL REFERENCES FROM THE MEDICAL, NUTRITIONAL AND LABORATORY LITERATURE BY SUBJECT

CARDIOVASCULAR SYSTEM

Arrhythmias

The effect of Na_3EDTA-induced hypocalcemia on the general and coronary hemodynamics of the intact animal. (MAXWELL, G. M., Elliott, R. B. and Robertson, E.) *Am Heart J* 66:82–87, 1963.

Rate of rise of left ventricular pressure. Indirect measurement and physiologic significance. (LANDRY, JR., A. B. and Goodyer, A. V. N.) *Am J. Cardiol* 15:660–664, 1965.

Quinidine toxicity and its treatment. An experimental study. (LUCHI, R. J., Helwig, Jr., J. and Conn, Jr., H. L.) *Am Heart J* 65:340–348, 1963.

Intensification of the effects of quinidine on experimental auricular fibrillation in the dog previously treated with the disodium salt of ethylene diamine tetra-acetate. (BOYADJIAN, N.) *C R Soc Biol* 155:414–416, 1961.

Ventricular arrhythmias following the administration of Na_2EDTA. (NAYLER, W. G.) *Pharmacol Exp Ther* 137:5–13, 1962.

Treatment of cardiac arrhythmias with salts of ethylene diamine tetraacetic acid (EDTA). (SURAWICZ, B., MacDonald, M. G., Kaljot, V., Bettinger, J C., Carpenter, A. A., Korson, L. and Starcheska, Y. K.) *Am Heart J* 58:493–503, 1959.

Myocardial responses to chelation. (SOFFER, A., Toribara, T. and Sayman, A.) *Brit Heart J* 23:690–694, 1961.

Clinical applications and untoward reactions of chelation in cardiac arrhythmias. (SOFFER, A., Toribara, T., Moore-Jones, C. and Weber, D.) *AMA Arch Intern Med* 106:824–834, 1960.

The effect of calcium chelation on cardiac arrhythmias and conduction disturbances. (JICK, S. and Karsh, R.) *Am J Cardiol* 4:287–293, 1959.

Effects of pacemaker impulses on latent arrhythmias produced by intramyocardial chemical stimulation. (CASTELLANOS, JR., A., Lemberg, L., Gomez, A. and Berkovits, B. V.) *Cardiologia* 51;340–348, 1967.

Arteries (Animal)

Effect of copper in thyroxine potentiation of in vitro epinephrine action on smooth muscle. (SHIDA, H., Meyers, M. A. and Barker, S. B.) *J Pharmacol Exp Ther* 141:280–284, 1963.

Role of calcium in initiation of contraction in smooth muscle. (ISOJIMA, C., and Bozler, E.) *Am J Physiol* 205:681–685, 1963.

Influence of ethylene diamine tetraacetate and calcium ions on vascular tension. (LASZT, L.) *Nature* 212:1587, 1966.

Sucrose-gap recording of prolonged electrical activity from arteries in Ca-free solution containing EDTA at low temperature. (GRAHAM, J. M. and Keatinge, W. R.) *J Physiol* 208:2P–3P, 1970.

Responsiveness of arterial smooth muscle to noradrenaline after long periods of Ca-free solution containing EDTA at low temperature. (KEATINGE, W. R.) *J Physiol* 216:31PO, 1971.

Effect of EDTA and other chelating agents on norepinephrine uptake by rabbit aorta in vitro. (NEDERGAARD, O. A. and Vagne, A.) *Proc West Pharmacol Soc* 11:87–90, 1968.

Arteriosclerosis

Chelates in the treatment of occlusive arteriosclerosis. (BRUCKNEROVA, O. and Tulacek, J.) *Vnitr Lek* 18:729–736, 1972.

1st experience with the treatment of atherosclerosis patients with calcinosis of the arteries with trilon B (disodium salt of EDTA). (ARONOV, D. M.) *Klin Med (Moskva) 41*:19–23, May 1963.

Atherosclereosis, occlusive vascular disease and EDTA. (Ed) (CLARKE, SR., N. E.) *Am J Cardiol 6*:233–236, 1960.

The treatment of coronary artery disease with disodium EDTA. A reappraisal. (KITCHELL, J. R., Palmon, Jr., F., Aytan, N. and Meltzer, L. E.) *Am J Cardiol 11*:501–506, 1963.

Chelation endarterectomy for occlusive atherosclerosis. (LAMAR, C. P.) *J Am Geriat Soc 14*:272–294, 1966. (28)

Arteriosclerosis therapy with mucopolysaccharides and EDTA. (FRIEDEL, W., Schulz, F. H. and Schroder, I.) *Deutsch Gesundh 20*:1566–1570, 1965.

Reduction of elevated plasma lipid levels in atherosclerosis following EDTA therapy. (OLWIN, J. H. and Koppel, J. L.) *Proc Soc Exp Biol Med 128*:1137–1140, 1968.

Treatment of occlusive vascular disease with disodium ethylene diamine tetraacetic acid (EDTA). (CLARKE, SR., N. E., Clarke, Jr. N. E. and Mosher, R. E.) *Am J Med Sci 239*:732––744, 1960.

Depression of cholesterol levels in human plasma following ethylene diamine tetraacetate and hydralazine. (PERRY, JR., H. M. and Schroeder, H. A.) *J Chron Dis 2*:520–533, 1955.

The effects of chelating agents upon the atherosclerotic process. (ANONYMOUS) *Nutr Rev 21*:352, 1963.

Mobilization of atherosclerotic plaque calcium with EDTA utilizing the isolation-perfusion principle. (WILDER, L. W., De Jode, L. R., Milstein, S. W. and Howard, J. M.) *Surgery 52*:793–795, 1962.

Arteriosclerosis (Animal)

Effect of calcium disodium ethylene diamine tetraacetate on hypercholesterolemic rabbits. (SAUNDERS, J. R., Princiotto, J. V. and Rubin, M.) *Proc Soc Exp Biol Med 92*:29–31, 1956.

Effect of chelation on phosphorus metabolism in experimental atherosclerosis. (McCANN, D. S., Koen, Z., Zdybek, G. and Boyle, A. J.) *Circ Res 11*:880–884, 1962.

Some in vivo effects of chelation. II. Animal experimentation. (KOEN, A., McCann, D. S. and Boyle, A. J.) *J Chron Dis 16*:329–333, 1963.

Physical and chemical changes in isolated chylomicrons: prevention by EDTA. (ONTKA, J. A.) *J Lipid Res* 11:367–375, 1970.

Blood

Changes in hematologic values induced by storage of ethylene diamine tetraacetate human blood for varying periods of time. (LAMPASSO, J. A.) *Am J Clin Path* 49:443–447, 1968.

Failure of anticoagulants to influence the viscosity of whole blood. (GALLUZZI, N. J., DeLashmutt, R. E. and Connolly, V. J.) *J Lab Clin Med* 64:773–777, 1964.

Investigation on the influence of diamethylsulfoxide on conservation of the whole blood at low temperatures. (FIDELSKI, R., Niedworok, J. and Pniewski, T.) *Bibl Haemat* 23:667–673, 1965.

Comparative effects of anticoagulants on bacterial growth in experimental blood cultures. (EVANS, G. L., Cekoric, Jr., T. and Searcy, R. L.) *Am J Med Techn* 34:103–112, 1968.

Studies on the origin and significance of blood ammonia. I. Effect of various anticoagulants on the blood ammonia determination. (CONN, H. O.) *Yale J Biol Med* 35:171–184, 1962.

Blood (Animal)

Effect of manganese edetate on blood formation in rats. (SULLIVAN, T. J.) *Nature* 186:87, 1960.

The effect of heparin and EDTA on DNA synthesis by marrow in vitro. (LOCHTE, JR., H. L., Ferrebee, J. W. and Thomas, E. D.) *J Lab Clin Med* 55:435–438, 1960.

Blood Clotting

The effect of EDTA on human fibrinogen and its significance for the coagulation of fibrinogen with thrombin. (GODAL, H. C.) *Scand J Clin Lab Invest* 12 (Suppl 53):1–20, 1960.

Barium sulphate adsorption and elution of the 'prothrombin complex' factors. (VOSS, D.) *Scand J Clin Lab Invest* 17 (Suppl 84):119–128, 1965.

The precipitation of fibrinogen by heparin at pH 4.8. (TEMPERLEY, I. J.) *Irish J Med Sci* 448:159–166, 1963.

Role of calcium in the structure of fibrinogen. (CAPET-ANTONINI, F. C.) *Biochim Biophys Acta* 200:497–507, 1970.

Effect of various anticoagulants on carbon dioxide-combining power of blood. (ZARODA, R. A.) *AM J Clin Path* 41:377–380, 1964. (8)

Delayed fibrin polymerization due to removal of calcium ions. (GODAL, H. C.) *Scand J Clin Lab Invest* 24:29–33, 1969.

Blood Erythrocytes

Oxidation of hemoglobin by ethylene diamine tetraacetate and leukocytes. (NORDQVIST, P., Persson, E., Ryttinger, L. and Ljunggren, M.) *Scand J Clin Lab Invest* 15:62–66, 1963.

Observations on the hexokinase activity in intact human erythrocytes. (GARBY, L. and De Verdier, C. H.) *Folia Haemat* 83:313–316, 1965.

Effects of ethylene diamine tetraacetate and deoxycholate on kinetic constants of the calcium ion-dependent adenosine triphosphatase of human erythrocyte membranes. (WOLF, H. U.) *Biochem J* 130:311–314, 1972.

The effect of the anticoagulant EDTA on oxygen uptake by bone-marrow cells. (GESINSKI, R. M. and Morrison, J. H.) *Experientia* 24:296–297, 1968.

Hemorrhagic and hemolytic transfusion reaction due to anti-Le$_a$. (MACPHERSON, C. R., Teteris, N. J. and Claassen, L. G.) *Transfusion* 3:392–396, 1963.

Sedimentation rate of stored blood, using sequestrene as the anticoagulant. (MELVILLE, I. D. and Rifkind, B. M.) *Brit Med J* 1:107–109, 1960.

Error in hematocrit value produced by excessive ethylene diamine tetraacetate. (LAMPASSO, J. A.) *Techn Bull Regist Med Techn* 35:109–110, 1965.

Elimination of error in hematocrit produced by excessive EDTA. Experience with the Coulter Counter Model S. (BRITTIN, G. M., Brecher, G. and Johnson, C. A.) *Techn Bull Regist Med Techn* 39:246–249, 1969.

The effect of anticoagulant concentration on centrifuged and electronic hematocrits. (FERRO, P. V. and Sena, T.) *Am J Clin Path* 51:569–577, 1969.

Error in hematocrit determination due to too high concentration of anticoagulant. (CULLUM, C. and Lepow, M. L.) *Pediatrics* 40:1027–1028, 1967.

The Westergren sedimentation rate, using K$_3$EDTA. (GAMBINO, S. R., Di Re, J. J., Montellone, M. and Budd, D. C.) *Techn Bull Regist Med Techn* 35:1–8, 1965.

Effect of ethylene diamine tetraacetic acid (dipotassium salt) and heparin on the estimation of packed cell volume. (PENNOCK, C. A. and Jones, K. W.) *J Clin Path* 19:196–199, 1966.

The inhibitory action of EDTA on erythrocyte agglutination by lectins. (TUNIS, M.) *J Immun* 95:876–879, 1965.

Separation of haemoglobins Lepore and H from A and A_2 in starch or acrylamide gels buffered with tris-EDTA. (CURTAIN, C. C.) *J Clin Path* 15:288–289, 1962.

Error in hematocrit value produced by excessive ethylene diamine tetraacetate. (LAMPASSO, J. A.) *Am J Clin Path* 44:109–110, 1965.

5-Year controlled trial of chelating agents in treatment of thalassaemia major. (FLYNN, D. M.) *Arch Dis Child* 48:829, 1973.

A serum agglutinating human red cells exposed to EDTA. (GILLUND, T. D., Howard, P. L. and Isham, B.) *Vox Sang* 23:369–370, 1972.

Study of human red blood cell membrane using sodium deoxycholate. II. Effects of cold storage, EDTA and small deoxycholate concentrations on ATPase activities. (PHILPPOT, J. and Authier, M. H.) *Biochim Biophys Acta* 298:887–900, 1973.

Blood Erythrocytes (Animal)

The effects of metallic edetates on the growth and blood formation of rats. (SULLIVAN, T. J.) *Arch Int Pharmacodyn* 124:225–236, 1960.

The inhibition of hematopoietic action of iron by ethylene diamine tetraacetic acid (EDTA). (ITOH, H., Yamaguchi, T. and Yamasawa, S.) *Yokohama Med Bull* 13:9–16, 1962.

Blood Leukocytes

Pathogenesis of acute inflammation, VI. Influence of osmolarity and certain metabolic antagonists upon phagocytosis and adhesiveness by leucocytes recovered from man. (ALLISON, JR., F. and Lancaster, M. G.) *Proc Soc Exp Biol Med* 119:56–61, 1965.

Studies on factors which influence the adhesiveness of leukocytes in vitro. (ALLISON, JR., F. and Lancaster, M. G.) *Ann NY Acad Sci* 116:936–944, 1964.

The action in vitro and in vivo of sodium versenate on the phagocytic activity of neutrophile leukocytes. (FORSSMAN, O. and Nordqvist, P.) *Acta Haemat* 31:289–293, 1964.

The relationship between phagocytosis of polystyrene latex particles by polymorphonuclear leucocytes (PML) and aggregation of PML. (TALSTAD, I.) *Scand J Haemat* 9:516–523, 1972.

The prevention of clumping of frozen-stored leukocyte populations by EDTA. (BOCK, G. N., Chess, L. and Mardinay, Jr., M. R.) *Cryobiology* 9:216–218, 1972.

EDTA-Na$_2$ and leukocytes. (KISSMEYER-NIELSEN, F. and Andresen, E.) *Bibl Haemat* 19:434–438, 1964.

Rapid collection of human leukocytes or lymphocytes from peripheral blood. (SEVERSON, C. D., Frank, D. H., Stokes, G., Seepersad, M. F. and Thompson, J. S.) *Transplantation* 8:535–538, 1969.

Histochemical studies on leucocyte alkaline phosphatase in non-leukaemic granulocytosis: effects of anticoagulants and role of zinc and magnesium. (PERILLIE, P. E. and Finch, S. C.) *Brit J Haemat* 13:289–293, 1967.

Isolation of leococytes from human blood. Further observations. Methylcellulose, dextran, and ficoll as erythrocyte-aggrevating agents. (BOYUM, A.) *Scand J Clin Lab Invest* 21 (Supl 97):31–50, 1968.

The technique and interpretation of tests for leucocidin with special reference to the value of ethylene diamine tetraacetic acid (EDTA). McLEOD, J. A. and McLeod, J. W.) *Brit J Exp Path* 42:171–178, 1961.

Blood Plasma

Cholesterol measurement in serum and plasma. (GRANDE, F., Amatuzio, D. S. and Wada, S.) *Clin Chem* 10:619–626, 1964.

Measurement of renin activity in human plasma. (PICKENS, P. T., Bumpus, F. M., Lloyd, A. M., Smeby, R. R. and Page, I. H.) *Circ Rest* 17:438–448, 1965.

Serum-insulin or plasma-insulin? (Letters) (GRANT, D. B.) *Lancet* 1:207, 1972.

The distribution of EDTA and citrate in blood and plasma. (REUTER, H., Niemeyer, G. and Gross, R.) *Thromb Diath Haemorrh* 19:213–220, 1968.

Binding of EDTA, histidine and acetylsalicylic acid to zinc-protein complex in intestinal content, intestinal mucosa and blood plasma. (SUSO, F. A. and Edwards, Jr., H. M.) *Nature* 136:230–232, 1972.

Change in plasma phosphate concentration on infusion of calcium gluconate or Na$_2$-EDTA. (HAUSMANN, E.) *Proc Soc Exp Biol Med* 134:182–184, 1970.

Blood Platelets

Pseudothrombocytopenia: manifestation of a new type of platelet agglutinin. (SHREINER, D. P. and Bell, W. R.) *Blood* 42:531–549, 1973.

Influence of cryoprofibrin on the antiglobulin consumption test with platelets. (VAN DER WEERDT, C. M. and Vreeken, J.) *Vox Sang* 10:536–542, 1965.

Release reaction in washed platelet suspensions induced by kaolin and other particles. (CRONBERG, S. and Caen, J. P.) *Scand J Haemat* 8:151–160, 1971.

Effects of ethylene diamine tetraacetate (EDTA) and citrate upon platelet glycolysis. (ROSSI, E. C.) *J Lab Clin Med* 69:204–216, 1967.

Studies on the ultrastructure of pseudopod formation in human blood platelets. I. Effect of temperature, period of incubation, anticoagulants and mechanical forces. (SKJORTEN, F.) *Scand J Haemat* 5:401–414, 1968.

Effect of aggregating agents and their inhibitors on the mean platelet shape. (O'BRIEN, J. R. and Heywood, J. B.) *J Clin Path* 19:148–153, 1966.

Platelet sequestration in man. I. Methods. (ASTER, R. H. and Jandl, J. H.) *J Clin Invest* 43:843–855, 1964.

Effect of glass contact on the electrophoretic mobility of human blood platelets. (HAMPTON, J. R. and Mitchell, J. R. A.) *Nature* 209:470–472, 1966.

The role of chelation and of human plasma in the uptake of serotonin by human platelets. (KERBY, G. P. and Taylor, S. M.) *J Clin Invest* 40:44–51, 1961.

The evaluation of anticoagulant solutions used in the preparation of platelets for transfusion. (DAVEY, M. G., Lander, H. and Robson, H. N.) *Bibl Haemat* 23:1358–1361, 1965.

Platelet preservation. III. Comparison of radioactivity yields of platelet concentrates derived from blood anticoagulated with EDTA and ACD. (COHEN, P., Cooley, M. H. and Gardner, F. H.) *New Eng J Med* 273:845–850, 1965.

Evaluation of a technic for counting dog and human platelets. (WEED, R. I., Crump, S. L., Swisher, S. N. and Trabold, N. C.) *Blood* 25:261–266, 1965.

Platelet aggregation by ristocetin in EDTA plasma: extensive clumping with high concentrations of EDTA. (TS'AO, C. H.) *Haemostasis* 1:315–319, 1972/73.

A macromolecular serum component acting on platelets in the presence of EDTA—'platelet stain preventing factor.' (STAVEM, P. and Berg, K.) *Scand J Haemat* 10:202–208, 1973.

Effects of ethylene diamine tetraacetic acid (EDTA) on platelet structure. (WHITE, J. G.) *Scand J Haemat* 5:241–254, 1968.

Blood Pressure

Renal and cardiovascular effects induced by intravenous infusion of magnesium chelates. (KELLEY, H. G., Turton, M. R. and Hatcher, J. D.) *Canad Med Assoc J* 84:1124–1128, 1961.

Blood Pressure (Animal)

Action of a chelate of zinc on trace metals in hypertensive rats. (SCHROEDER, H. A. Nason, A. P. and Mitchener, M.) *Am J Physiol 214*:796–800, 1968.

Antihypertensive effects of metal binding agents. (SCHROEDER, H. A., Perry, Jr., H. M., Menhard, E. M. and Dennis, E. G.) *J Lab Clin Med 46*:416–422, 1955.

On the cardiovascular activities of the socium salt of ethylene diamine tetraacetic acid. (MARCELLE, R. and LeComte, J.) *C R. Soc Biol 153*:1483–1485, 1959.

Blood Serum

Changes in serum and spinal fluid calcium effected by disodium ethylene diamine tetraacetate. (SOFFER, A., and Toribara, T.) *J lab Clin Med 58*:542–547, 1961.

The binding of EDTA to human serum albumin. (ANGHILERI, L. J.) *Naturwissenschaften 55*:182, 1968.

Serum calcium and phosphorus homeostatis in man studied by means of the sodium-EDTA test. (KALLIOMAKI, J. L., Markkanen, T. K. and Mustonen, V. A.) *Acta Med Scand 170*:211–214, 1961.

Determination of calcium in solutions containing ethylene diamine tetraacetic acid. (TORIBARA, T. Y. and Koval, L.) *J Lab Clin Med 57*:630–634, 1961.

Semimicro method for determination of serum uric acid using EDTA-hydrazine. (PATEL, C. P.) *Clin Chem 14*:764–775, 1968.

Digitalis

Effects of calcium chelation on digitalis-induced cardiac arrhythmias. (SZEKELY. P. and Wynne, N. A.) *Brit Heart J 25*:589–594, 1963.

The effect of disodium EDTA on digitalis intoxication. (ROSENBAUM, J. L., Mason, D. and Seven, M.J.) *Am J Med Sci 240*:77–84, 1960.

Use of the chelating agent, EDTA, in digitalis intoxication and cardiac arrhythmias. (SURAWICZ, B.) *Progr Cardiov Dis 2*:432–443, 1960.

Antagonism of the contractile effect of digitalis by EDTA in the normal human ventricle. (COHEN, S., Weissler, A. M. and Schoenfeld, C. D.) *Am Heart J 69*:502–514, 1965.

Calcium, chelates, and digitalis. A clinical study. (ELIOT, R. S. and Blount, Jr., S. G.) *Am Heart J 62*:7–21, 1961.

Treatment of digitalis intoxication with EDTA Na₂. (NGUYEN-THE-MINH) *Presse Med* 71:2385–2386, 1963.

Lymph

Interaction of lymphocytes and phytohaemagglutinin: inhibition by chelating agents. (KAY, J. E.) *Exp Cell Res* 68:11–16, 1971.

'Radial segmentation' of the nuclei in lymphocytes and other blood cells induced by some anticoagulatns. (NORBERG, B. and Soderstrom, N.) *Scand J Haemat* 4:68–76, 1967.

Veins

Topical chelation therapy for varicose pigmentation. (MYERS, H. L.) *Angiology* 17:66–68, 1966,.

DENTISTRY

Human Studies

Scanning electron microscope stuidies of dental enamel. (HOFFMAN, S., McEwan, W. S. and Drew, C. M.) *J DentRes* 48:242–250, 1969.

Disodium ethylene diamine tetraacetate as an aid for the reconstitution of lyophilized human salivary proteins before paper electrophoresis. (DAWES, C.) *Arch Oral Biol* 8:653–656, 1963.

Differences in the shape of human enamel crystallites after partial destruction by caries, EDTA and various acids. (JOHNSON, N. W.) *Arch Oral Biol* 11:1421–1424, 1966.

The relative efficiency of EDTA, sulfuric acid, and mechanical instrumentation in the enlargement of root canals. (WEINREB, M. M. and Meier, E.) *Oral Surg* 19:247–252, 1965.

The effects of different demineralizing agents on human enamel surfaces studied by scanning electron microscopy. (POOLE, D. F. G. and Johnson, N. W.) *Arch Oral Biol* 12:1621–1634, 1967.

In vivo and in vitro studies of the effect of the disodium salt of ethylene diamine tetraacetate on human dentine and its endodontic implications. (PATTERSON, S. S.) *Oral Surg* 16:83–103, 1963.

An in vitro comparison of the amount of calcium removed by the disodium salt of EDTA and hydrochloric acid during endodontic procedures. (HELING, B., Shapiro, S. and Sciaky, I.) *Oral Surg* 19:531–533, 1965.

The pharmacokinetics of fluoride in mouth rinses as inidcated by a reference substance (^{51}Cr-EDTA). (BIRKELAND, J. M. and Lokken, P.) *Caries Res* 6:325–333, 1972.

The solubility rate of calcified dental tissues and of calculus in sodium EDTA solutions. (SHAPIRO, S., Perez, G., Gedalia, I. and Sulman, F. G.) *J Periodont* 39:9–10, 1968.

Enamel conditioning for fluoride treatments. (KATZ, S., Muhler, J. C. and Beck, C. W.) *J Dent Res* 50:816–831, 1971.

Solubility of calcified dental tissue and of calculus in EDTA and 2% NnaF. (SHILOAH, J., Gedalia, I., Shapiro, S. and Jacobowitz, B.) *J Dent Res* 52:845, 1973.

Two-site model for human dental enamel dissolution in EDTA. (FOX, J. L., Higuchi, W. I., Fawzi, M., Hwu, R. C. and Hefferren, J. J.) *J Dent Res* 53:939, 1974.

The dissociation of EDTA and EDTA-sodium salts. (SAND, H. F.) *Acta Odont Scand* 19:469–482, 1961.

DERMATOLOGY

Allergies

Nickel sensitization and detergents. (MALTEN, K. E., Schutter, K., Van Senden, K. G. and Spruit, D.) *Acta Dermatovener* 49:10–13, 1969.

The relative importance of various environmental exposures to nickel in causing contact hypersensitivity. (MALTEN, K. E. and Spruit, D.) *Acta Dermatovener* 49:14–19, 1969.

EDTA: preservative dermatitis. (RAYMOND, J. Z. and Gross, P. R.) *Arch Derm* 100:436–440, 1969.

Burns (Animal)

Combinations of edetic acid and antibiotics in the treatment of rat burns infection with *Pseudomonas aeruginosa*. (WEISER, R.) *J Infect Dis* 128:566–569, 1973.

Porphyria

Acute intermittent porphyria. (RITOTA, M. C. and Sanowski, R.) *J Med Soc New Jersey* 61:101–103, March 1964.

Hexachlorobenzene-induced porphyria: effect of chelation on the disease, porphyrin and metal metabolism. (PETERS, H. A., Johnson, S. A. M., Cam, S., Oral, S., Muftu, Y. and Ergene, T.) *Am J Med Sci* 251:314–322, 1966.

Current concepts of cutaneous porphyria and its treatment with particular reference to the use of sodium calciumedetate. (DONALD, G. F., Hunter, G. A., Roman, W. and Taylor, A. E. J.) *Brit J Derm* 82:70–75, 1970.

Chelation therapy in cutaneous porphyria. A review and report of a five-year recovery. (WOODS, S. M., Peters, H. A. and Johnson, S. A. M.) *Arch Derm* 84:920–927, 1961.

Porphyria. Its manifestations and treatment with chelating agents. (PAINTER, J. T. and Morrow, E. J.) *Texas State J Med* 55:811–818, 1959.

Sclerosis

Use of the chelating agent edathamil disodium in acrosclerosis, sarcoidosis and other skin conditions with comments on tryptophan metabolism in sarcoidosis. (JOHNSON, S. A. M.) *Wisconsin Med J* 59:651–655, 1960.

Use of ethylene diamine tetraacetic acid (EDTA) and tetrahydroxyquinone on sclerodermatous skin. Histologic and chemical studies. (KEECH, M. K., McCann, D. S., Boyle, A. J. and Pinkus, H.) *J Invest Derem* 47:235–246, 1966.

Calcinosis universalis complicating dermatomyositis—its treatment with Na₂EDTA. Report of two cases in children. (HERD, J. K. and Vaughan, J. H.) *Arthritis Rheum* 7:259–271, 1964.

Treatment of calcinosis universalis with chelating agents. (FINK, C. W. and Baum, J.) *Am J Dis Child* 105:390–392, 1963.

Edathamil (EDTA) therapy of interstitial calcinosis. (LECKERT, J. T., McHardy, G. G. and McHardcy, R. J.) *South Med J* 53:728–731, 1960.

The treatment of progressive systemic sclerosis with disodium edetate. (MONGAN, E. S.) *Arthritis Rheum* 8:1145–1151, 1965.

Edathamil in the treatment of scleroderma and calcinosis cutis. (WINDERE, P. R. and Curtis, A. C.) *AMA Arch Derm* 82:732–736, 1960.

An objective evaluation of the treatment of systemic scleroderma with disodium EDTA, pyridoxine and reserpine. (FULEIHAN, F. J. D., Kurban, A. K., Abboud, R. T., Beidas-Jbran, N. and Farah, F. S.) *Brit J Erm* 80:184–189, 1968.

Scleroderma. An evaluation of treatment with disodium edetate. (NELDNER, K. H., Winkelmann, R. K. and Perry, H. O.) *Arch Derm* 86:305–309, 1962.

Favorable response of calcinosis universalis to edathamil disodium. (DAVIS, H. and Moe, P. J.) *Pediatrics* 24:780–785, 1959.

Symposium on scleroderma. (Medical Grand Rounds from the University of Alabama Medical Center). (UNIVERSITY OF ALABAMA MEDICAL CENTER.

C., OWEN, JR., W. H. DODSON AND W. J. Hammack, Editors) *South Med J* 59:1320–1326, 1966.

The treatment of systemic sclerosis with disodium EDTA, pyridoxine and reserpine. (BIRK, R. E. and Rupe, C. E.) *Henry Ford Hosp Med Bull* 14:109–118, 1966.

Systemic sclerosis. Fourteen cases treated with chelation (disocium EDTA) and/ or pyridoxine, with comments on the possible role of altered tryptophan metabolism in pathogenesis. (BIRK, R. E. and Rupe, C. E.) *Henry Ford Hosp Med Bull* 10:523–553, 1962.

Therapy of scleroderma with the disodium salt of ethylene diamine tetraacetic acid; a contribution to the toxicology of versenate. Part I. (HOSLI, P.) *Arzneimittelforschung* 10:65–74, 1960.

DIABETES

Chelation therapy of occlusive arteriosclereosis in diabetic patients. (LAMAR, C. P.) *Angiology* 15:379–395, 1964.

Hypoglycaemia induced by disodium ethylene diamine tetraacetic acid. (MELTZER, L. E., Palmon, Jr., F. P. and Kitchell, J. R.) *Lancet* 2:637–638, 1961.

Some physical-chemical variables affecting insulin migration in vitro. I. Electrophoresis. (FREEDLENDER, A. E., Rees, S. B. and Soeldner, J. S.) *Proc Soc Exp Biol Med* 115:21–25, 1964.

EDTA

Spectrophotometric determination of microgram quantities of (ethylenedinitrilo) tetraacetic acid with bis (2, 4, 6-tripyridyl-s-triazine) iron(II). (KRATOCHVIL, B. and White, M. C.) *Anal Chem* 37:111–113, 1965.

Separation of NTA and EDTA chelates by thin-layer chromatography. (RAJABALEE, F. J. M., Potvin, M. and Laham, S.) *J Chromatogr* 79:375–379, 1973.

Infrared spectra and correlations for the ethylene diamine tetraacetic acid metal chelates. (SAWYER, D. T.) *Ann NY Acad Sci* 88:307–321, 1960.

Separation of metal-EDTA complexes by thin-layer chromatography. (VANDERDEELEN, J.) *J Chromatogr* 39:521–522, 1969.

Ion-exchange characteristics of the radium-ethylene diamine tetraacetate complex. (BAETSLE, L. and Bengsch, E.) *J Chromatogr* 8:265–273, 1962.

Effect of buffer equilibrium on paper electrophoresis. (KABARA, J. J., Zyskowski, D. and Spafford, N.) *J Chromatogr* 13:556–557, 1964.

Coordination chain reactions. II. The ligand-exchange reaction of tetraethylene-pentamine-nickel(II) and ethylene diamine tetraacetatocuprate(II). (MARGERUM, D. W. ad Carr, J. D.) *J Am Chem Soc* 88:1639–1644, 1966.

Coordination chain reactions. III. The exchange of N, N, N^1, N^1-tetrakis (2-aminoethyl) ethylene diaminezinc(II) and ethylene diamine tetraacetocupra-te(II). (CARR, J. D. and Margerum, D. W.) *J Am Chem Soc* 88:1645–1648, 1966.

Alkali metal binding by ethylene diamine tetraacetate, adenosine 5'-triphosphate, and pyrophosphate. (BOTTS, J., Chashin, A. and Young, H. L.) *Biochemistry* 4:1788–1798, 1965.

Base-catalyzed hydrogen-deuterium exchange in bivalent metal-EDTA chelates. (TERRILL, J. B. and Reilley, C. N.) *Anal Chem* 38:1876–1881, 1966.

Anomalous behaviour of EDTA during gel filtration. Studies on the possible contamination of the S100 protein. (LEVI, A., Mercanti, D., Calissano, P. and Alema, S.) *Anal Biochem* 62:301–304, 1974.

EDTA prevents the photocatalyzed destruction of the products of catecholamine oxidation. (KARASAWA, T., Funakoshi, H., Jurukawa, K. and Yoshida, K.) *Anal Biochem* 53:278–281, 1973.

Computation of metal binding in bi-metal—bi-chelate systems. (BOTTS, J., Chashin, A. and Schmidt, L.) *Biochemistry* 5:1360–1364, 1966.

Binding of EDTA to DEAE-cellulose and its interference with protein determinations. (WARD, W. W. and Fastiggi, R. J.) *Anal Biochem* 50:154–162, 1972.

Interference of sodium ethylene diamine tetraacetate in the determination of proteins and its elimination. (NEURATH, A. R.) *Experientia* 22:290, 1966.

Formation constants of certain zinc-complexes by ion-exchange method. (VOHRA, P., Krantz, E. and Kratzer, F. H.) *Proc Soc Exp Biol Med* 121:422–425, 1966.

GASTROINTESTINAL SYSTEM

Intestines (Human & Animal)

Effects of ethylene diamine tetraacetate and metal ions in intestinal absorption of vitamin B12 in man and rats. (IKUDA, K. and Sasayama, K.) *Proc Soc Exp Biol Med* 120:17–20, 1965.

Intestines (Human)

The action of EDTA on human alkaline phosphatases. (CONYERS, R. A. J.,

Birkett, D. J., Neale, F. C., Posen, S. and Brudenell-Woods, J.) *Biochim Biophys Acta* 139:363–371, 1967.

Liver (Animal)

The dissociation of rat liver ribosomes by ethylene diamine tetraacetic acid; molecular weights, chemical composition, and buoyant densities of the subunits. (HAMILTON, M. G. and Ruth, M. E.) *Biochemistry* 8:851–856, 1969.

Analytical study of rat liver microsomes treated by EDTA or pyrophosphate. (AMARCOSTESEC, A.) *Arch Int Physiolo Biochem* 81:358–359, 1973. (4)

Effect of metal ions and EDTA on the acitivity of rabbit liver fructose 1,6-diphosphatase. (TATE, S. S.) *Biochem Biophys Res Commun* 24:662–667, 1966.

Liver (Human)

Hepato-lenticular degeneration (Wilson's disease) treated by penicillamine. (RICHMOND, J., Rosenoer, V. M., Tompsett, S. L., Draper, I. and Simpsons, J. A.) *Brain* 87:619–638, 1964.

Hepatolenticular degeneration. Clinical, biochemical and pathologic study of a patient with fulminant course aggravated by treatment with BAL and versenate. (HOLLISTER, L. E., Cull, V. L., Gonda, V. A. and Kolb, F. O.) *Am J Med* 28:623–630, 1960.

Hepatic and renal studies with iron-59 EDTA in patients with and without liver or kidney disease. (McLAREN, J. R., Galambos, J. T. and Drew, W. D.) *Radiology* 81:447–454, 1963.

GENITOURINARY SYSTEM

Kidneys (Human)

The effect of glucose on the glomerular filtration rate in normal man. A preliminary report. (BROCHNER-MORTENSEN, J.) *Acta Med Scand* 180:109–111, 1971.

^{51}Cr-EDTA biological half life as an index of renal function. (Letters) (BRIEN, T. G. and Fay, J. A.) *J Nucl Med* 13:339–340, 1972.

Glomerular filtration rate measurement in man by the single injection method using ^{51}Cr-EDTA. (CHANTLER, C., Garnett, E. S., Parsons, V. and Veall, N.) *Clin Sci* 37:169–180, 1969.

^{51}Cr-edetic-acid clearance and G. F. R. (Letters) (STAMP, T. C. B.) *Lancet* 2:1348, 1968.

Comparison between inulin and ^{51}Cr-labelled edetic acid for the measurement of glomerular filtration-rate. (HEATH, D. A., Knapp, M. S. and Walker, W. H. C.) *Lancet* 2:1110–1112, 1968.

Comparison of glomerular filtration rate measurements using inulin, ^{51}Cr.EDTA, and a phosphate infusion technique. (STAMP, T. C. B., Stacey, T. C. and Rose, G. A.) *Clin Chim Acta* 30:351–358, 1970.

A comparison between the clearances of inulin, endogenous creatinine and ^{51}Cr-EDTA. (TRAUB, Y. M., Samuel, R., Lubin, E., Lewitus, Z. and Rosenfeld, J. B.) *Isr J Med Sci* 9:487–489, 1973.

Simultaneous ^{51}Cr edetic acid, inulin, and endogenous creatinine clearances in 20 patients with renal disease. (FAVRE, H. R. and Wing, A. J.) *Brit Med J* 1:84–86, 1968.

Estimation of glomerular filtration rate from plasma clearance of 51-chromium edetic acid. (CHANTLER, C. and Barratt, T. M.) *Arch Dis Child* 47:613–617, 1972.

Dialysance of molecules of different size in reused Kiil, Ab-Gambro, and Rhone-Poulence dialysers. (KRAMER, P., Matthaei, D., Go, J. G., Tonnis, H. J. and Scheler, F.) *Brit Med J* 2:320–322, 1972.

Chemotherapy in nephrolithiasis. (TIMMERMANN, A. and Kallistratos, G.) *Isr J Med Sci* 7:689–695, 1971.

Instrumental chemolysis of renal calculi: indications and dangers. (MISCHOL, H. R. and Wildbolz, R.) *J Urol* 105:607–610, 1971.

Modern aspects of chemical dissolution of human renal calculi by irrigation. (TIMMERMANN, A. and Kallistratos, G.) *J Urol* 95:469–475, 1966.

Uterus (Human)

Effect of EDTA on human cumulus granulosa cells. (DEKEL, N., Shahar, A., Soferman, N. and Kraicer, P. F.) *Isr J Med Sci* 8:2004–2007, 1972.

IMMUNOLOGY

Human Studies

Role of calcium in complement dependent hemolysis. (YACHNIN, S. and Ruthenberg, J.) *Proc Soc Exp Biol Med* 117:179–181, 1964.

Studies on human C'l-esterase. I. Purification and enzymatic properties. (HAINES, A. L. and Lepow, I. H.) *J Immun* 92:456–467, 1964.

Further studies on the effect of Ca + + on the first complement of human complement (C'l). (YOUNG, F. E. and Lepow, I. H.) *J Immun* 83:364–371, 1959.

Lupus Erythematosus

Inhibition oif L. E. phenomenon by EDTA. (SAUMUR, J.) *J-Lancet* 82:240–242, 1962.

Methods for the estimation of the second component and third component complex of complement using intermediates of the complement sequence. (TOWNES, A. S. and Stewart, Jr., C. R.) *Bull Hopkins Hosp* 117:331–347, 1965.

LABORATORY

Insulin Assay

The immunoassay of insulin in human serum treated with sodium ethylene diamine tetraacetate. (SHELDON, J. and Taylor, K. W.) *J Endocr* 33:157–158, 1965.

Observations on the precipitation reaction in a double-antibody immunoassay for insulin. (GRANT, D. B.) *Acta Endocr* 59:139–149, 1968.

Influence of heparin-plasma, EDTA-plasma, and sereum on the determination of insulin with three different radioimmunoassays. (THORELL, J. I. and Lanner, A.) *Scand J Clin Lab Invest* 31:187–190, 1973.

Urinalysis

Transport of urine specimens for bacteriological examination. Experiment with addition of calcium disodium edathamil. (ODEGAARD, K. and Odegaard, A.) *Nord Med* 81:607–609, 1969.

Chelatometric magnesium determination in urine. (WUNSCH, L.) *Clin Chim Acta* 30:157–163, 1970.

Quantitative determination of EDTA and other polyamino acetic acids in urine and serum. (STAHLAVSKA, A. and Malat, M.) *Clin Chim Acta* 41:181–186, 1972.

Spectrophotometric determination of ethylene diamine tetraacetic acid in plasma and urine. (LAVENDER, A. R., Pullman, T. N. and Goldman, D.) *J Lab Clin Med* 63:299–305, 1964.

A simple method for the determination of EDTA in serum and urine. (BLIJEN-BERG, B. G. and Leijnse, B.) *Clin Chim Acta* 26:577–579, 1969.

Simple and precise micromethod for EDTA titration of calcium. (COPP, D. H., Cheney, G. A. and Stokoe, N. M.) *J Lab Clin Med* 61:1029–1037, 1963.

Determination of calcium in urine with EDTA by means of a cation exchange resin. (VEDSO, S. and Rud, C.) *Scand J Clin Lab Invest* 15:395–398, 1963.

Potentiometric determinations of calcium, magnesium, and complexing agents in water and biological fluids. (RIET, B. VAN'T and Wynn. J. E.) *Anal Chem* 41:158–162, 1969.

LIPIDS

Human Studies

A procedure for in vitro studies on fatty acid metabolism by human subcutaneous adipose tissue. (OSTMAN, J.) *Acta Med Scand* 177:183–197, 1965.

MICROBIOLOGY

Enzymes (Lysozyme)

Effects of organic cations on the gram-negative cell wall and their bactericidal activity with ethylene diamine tetraacetate and surface active agents. (VOSS, J. G.) *J Gen Microbiol* 48:391–400, 1967.

Effect of ethylene diamine tetraacetic acid, Triton X-100, and lysozyme on the morphology and chemical composition of isolated cell walls of *Escherichia coli*. (SCHNAITMAN, C. A.) *J Bact* 108:553–563, 1971.

Lysis of *Escherichia coli* with a neutral detergent. (GODSON, G. N. and Sinsheimer, R. L.) *Biochim Biophys Acta* 149:476–488, 1967.

The role of amine buffers in EDTA toxicity and their effect on osmotic shock. (NEU, H. C.) *J Gen Microbiol* 57:215–220, 1969.

Sensitization of *E. coli* to the serum bactericidal system and to lysozyme by ethyleneglycol-tetraacetic acid. (BRYAN, C. S.) *Proc Soc Exp Biol Med* 145:1431–1433, 1974.

MUSCULOSKELETAL SYSTEM

Muscles (Human)

Reversal of the ATPase reaction in muscle fibres by EDTA. (DREWS, G. A. and Engel, W. K.) *Nature* 212:1551–1553, 1966.

Myositis ossificans traumatica with unusual course. Effect of EDTA on calcium, phosphorus and manganese excretion. (LIBERMAN, U. A., Barzel, U., De Vries, A. and Ellis, H.) *Am J Med Sci 254*:35–47, 1967.

Capillary permeability to human skeletal muscle measured by local injection of ^{51}Cr-EDTA and ^{133}Xe. (TRAP-JENSEN, J., Korsgaard, O. and Lassen, N. A.) *Scand J Clin Lab Invest 25*:93–99, 1970.

Tendons (Human)

An electron microscopic study of the effect of crude bacterial a-amylase and ethylene diamine tetraacetic acid on human tendon. (DIXON, J. S., Hunter, J. A. A. and Steven, F. S.) *J Ultrastruct Red 38*:466–472, 1972.

NEUROPSYCHIATRIC

Human Studies

ACTH and a chelating agent for schizophrenia. (KEBE, S. R.) *West Med 4*:46, 48, 1963.

Porphyric psychosis and chelation therapy. (PETERS, H. A.) *Recent Adv Biol Psychiat 4*:204–217, 1961.

Abnormal copper and tryptophan metabolism and chelation therapy in anticonvulsant drug intolerance. (PETERS, H. A., Eichman, P. L., Price, J. M., Kozelka, F. L. and Rseese, H. H.) *Dis Nerv Syst 27*:97–107, 1966.

Pyruvic and lactic acid metabolism in muscular dystrophy, neuropathies and other neuromuscular disorders. (GOTO, I., Peters, H. A. and Reese, H. H.) *Am J Med Sci 253*:431–448, 1967.

NUCLEIC ACIDS

Animal Studies

The release of radioactive nucleic acids and mucoproteins by trypsin and ethylene diamine tetraacetate treatment of baby-hamster cells in tissue culture. (SNOW, C. and Allen A.) *Biochem J 119*:707–714, 1970.

Structural studies on ribosomes, II. Denaturation and sedimentation of ribosomal subunits unfolded in EDTA. (MIALL, S. H. and Walker, I. O.) *Biochem Biophys Acta 174*:551–560, 1969.

The dissociation of rabbit reticulocyte ribosomes with EDTA and the location of messenger ribonucleic acid. (NOLAN, R. D. and Arnstein, H. R. V.) *Europ J Biochem* 9:445–450, 1969.

Evidence for the detachment of a ribonucleoprotein messenger complex from EDTA-treated rabbit reticulocyte polyribosomes. (TEMMERMAN, J. and Lebleu, B.) *Biochim Biophys Acta* 174:544–550, 1969.

The degradation of deoxyribonucleic acid by L-cysteine and the promoting effect of metal chelating agents and of catalase. (BERNEIS, K. and Kofler, M.) *Experientia* 20:16–17, 1964.

A differential sovent effect on thermal stability of genetic markers in DNA. (PETERSON, J. M. and Guild, W. R.) *J Mol Biol* 20:497–503, 1966.

The influence of chelating agents on the prooxidative effect of a hydrogen peroxide producing methylhydrazine compound. (BERNEIS, K., Kofler, M. and Bollag, W.) *Experientia* 20:73–74, 1964.

NUCLEOTIDES AND NUCLEOSIDES

Animal Studies

Studies of the 105,000 X g supernatant of different rat tissues. (MORGAN, W. S.) *Lab Invest* 12:968–977, 1963.

Coelomocyte aggregation in *Cucumaria frondosa*: effect of ethylene diamine tetraacetate, adenosine, and adenosine nucleotides. (NOBLE, P. B.) *Biol Bull* 139:549–556, 1970.

NUTRITION

Animal Studies

Calcium utilization and feed efficiency in the growing rat as affected by dietary calcium, buffering capacity, lactose and EDTA. (EVANS, J. L. and Ali, R.) *J Nutr* 92:417–424, 1967.

Effects of dietary EDTA and cadmium on absorption, excretion and retention of orally administered ^{65}Zn in various tissues of zinc-deficient and normal goats and calves. (POWELL, G. W., Miller, W. J. and Blackmon, D. M.) *J Nutr* 93:203–212, 1967.

Quantitative relation of EDTA to availability of zinc for turkey poults. (KRATZER, F. H. and Starcher, B.) *Proc Soc Exp Biol Med* 113:424–426, 1963.

Metabolism of ethylene diamine tetraacetic acid (EDTA) by chickens. (DARWISH, N. M. and Kratzer, F. H.) *J Nutr* 86:187–192, 1965.

Effects of the apical ectodermal ridge on growth of the Versene-stripped chick limb bud. (GASSELING, M. T. and Saunders, Jr., J. W.) *Develop Biol* 3:1–25, 1961.

Iron Metabolism (Animal)

A study of the prolonged intake of small amounts of ethylene diamine tetraacetate on the utilization of low dietary levels of calcium and iron by the rat. (HAWKINS, W. W., Leonard, V. G., Maxwell, J. E. and Rastogi, K. S.) *Canad J Biochem* 40:391–395, 1962.

The effect of ingestion of disodium ethylene diamine tetraacetate on the absorption and metabolism of radioactive iron by the rat. (LARSEN, B. A. Bidwell, R. G. and Hawkins, W. W.) *Canad J Biochem* 38:51–55, 1960.

The effect of prolonged intake of ethylene diamine tetraacetate on the utilization of calcium and iron by the rat. (LARSEN, B. A., Hawkins, W. W., Leonard, V. G. and Armstrong. J. E.) *Canad J Biochem* 38:813–817, 1960.

Fe^{59}-amino acid complexes: are they intermediates in Fe^{59} absorption across intestinal mucosa? (MANIS, J. and Schachter, D.) *Proc Soc Exp Biol Med* 119:1185–1187, 1965.

Iron Metabolism (Human)

Clinical usefulness of iron chelating agents. (WAXMAN, H. S. and Brown, E. B.) *Progr Hematol* 6:338–373, 1969.

A comparative study of iron absorption and utilization following ferrous suphate and sodiuym ironedetate ("Sytron®"). (HODGKINSON, R.) *Med J Aust* 1:809–811, 1961.

Factors influencing the clinical use of chelates in iron storage disease. (WEINER, M.) *Ann NY Acad Sci* 119:789–796, 1964.

Effect of orally administered chelating agents EDTA, DTPA and fructose on radioiron absorption in man. (DAVIS, P.S. and Deller, D.J.) *Aust Ann Med* 16:70–74, 1967.

Life Extension (Animal)

Life extension in the rotifer *Mytilina brevispina var redunca* by the application of chelating agents. (SINCOCK, A. M.) *J Geront* 30:289–293, 1975.

Zinc Metabolism (Human)

Fate of intravenously administered zinc chelates in man. (ROSOFF, B., Hart, H., Methfessel, A. H. and Spencer, H.) *J Appl Physiol* 30:12–16, 1971.

OPHTHALMOLOGY

Human Studies

Scleromalacia perforans associated with Crohn's disease treated with sodium versenate (EDTA). EVANS, P. J. and Eustace, P.) *Brit J Ophthal* 57:330–335, 1973.

Effect of intravenous sodium bicarbonate, disodium edetate (Na^{2}EDTA), and hyperventilation on visual and oculomotor signs in multiple sclerosis. (DAVIS, F. A., Becker, F. O., Michael, J. A. and Sorensen, E.) *J Neurol Neurosurg Psychiat* 33:723–732, 1970.

Treatment of blepharitis. (BARAS, I.) *Eye Ear Nose Throat Mon* 44:68, 70, 118, Feb. 1965.

Corneal contact lens solutions. (GOULD, H. L. and Inglima, R.) *Eye Ear Nose Throat Mon* 43:39–49, Apr. 1964.

A new technique of contact lens storage, soaking and cleaning. (DABEZIES, Jr., O. H. and Naugle, T.) *Eye Ear Nose Throat Mon* 50:378–382, Oct. 1971.

OTOLARYNGOLOGY

Animal Studies

Biological study of a chelating agent with an affinity for calcium in the field of otology. (CHEVANCE, L. G.) *Acta Otolaryng* 51:46–54, 1960.

Human Studies

Chelation therapy in Wegener's granulomatosis. Treatment with EDTA. (HANSOTIA, P., Peters, H., Bennett, M. and Brown, R.) *Ann Otol* 78:388–402, 1969.

Chelation in clinical otosclerosis. (STECKER, R. H. and Bennett, M.) *AMA Arch Otolaryng* 70:627–629, 1959.

POISONING

Chelation in medicine. (SCHUBERT, J.) *Sci Am* 214:40–50, 1966.

Chelation. (RENOUX, M. and Mikol, C.) *Presse Med* 72:3317–3319, 1964.

Clinical uses of metal-binding drugs. (CHENOWORTH, M. B.) *Clin Pharmacol Ther* 9:365–387, 1968.

Lead (Alcohol)

Clinical manifestations and therapy of acute lead intoxication due to the ingestion of illicitly distilled alcohol. (CRUTCHER, J. C.) *Ann Intern Med* 59:707–715, 1963.

Lead intoxication and alcoholism: a diagnostic dilemma. (CRUTCHER, J. C.) *J Med Assoc Georgia* 56:1–4, Jan. 1967

Chelation therapy in lead nephropathy. (MORGAN, J. M.) *South Med J* 68:1001–1006, 1975.

Treatment of lead intoxication. Combined use of peritoneal dialysis and edetate calcium disodium. (MEHBOD, H.) *JAMA* 201:972–974, 1967.

Porphyrin metabolism during Versenate® therapy in lead poisoning. Intoxication from an unusual source. (FROMKE, V. L., Lee, M. Y. and Watson, C. J.) *Ann Intern Med* 70:1007–1012, 1969.

Lead (Children)

Treatment of lead encephalopathy. The combined use of edetate and hemodialysis. (SMITH, H. D., King, L. R. and Margolin, E. G.) *Am J Dis Child* 109:322–324, 1965.

Erythrocyte hypoplasia due to lead poisoning. A devastating, yet curable disease. (MOOSA, A. and Harris, F.) *Clin Pediat* 8:404–402, 1969.

Successful calcium disodium ethylene diamine tetraacetate treatment of lead poisoning in an infant. (KNELLER, L. A., Uhl, H. S. M. and Brem, Jr.) *New Engl J Med* 252:338–340, 1955.

Lead intoxication in children: a current problem in Providence, Rhode Island. Appearance of 19 cases of lead poisoning in children in two year period constitutes epidemic. (ORSON, J. and May, J. B.) *Rhode Island Med J* 48:608–611, 1965.

Ambulatory treatment of lead poisoning: report of 1,155 cases. (SACHS, H. K., Blanksma, L. A., Murray, E. F. and O'Connell, M. J.) *Pediatrics* 46:389–396, 1970.

Lead poisoning from home remedies. (McNEIL, J. R. and Reinhard, M. C.) *Clin Pediat* 6:150–156, 1967.

Lead neuropathy in children. (SETO, D. S. Y. and Freeman, J. M.) *Am J Dis Child* 107:337–342, 1964.

The use of chelating agents in the treatment of acute and chronic lead intoxication in childhood. (CHISOLM, JR., J. J.) *J Pediat* 73:1–38, 1968.

Treatment of lead encephalopathy in children. (COFFIN, R., Phillips, J. L., Staples, W. I. and Spector, S) *J Pediat* 69:198–206, 1966.

Reversible myocarditis due to chronic lead poisoning in childhood. (FREEMAN, R.) *Arch Dis Child* 40:389–393, 1965.

Lead poisoning. (Accidental chemical poisonings.) (JACOBZINER, H. and Raybin, H. W.) *New York J Med* 63:2999–3001, 1963.

Treatment of lead poisoning with intramuscular edathamil calcium-disodium. (SHRAND, H.) *Lancet* 1:310–312, 1961.

Chelation therapy in children with subclinical plumbish. (CHISOLM, JR., J. J.) *Pediatrics* 53:441–443, 1974.

Lead poisoning in children. (Clinical Rounds from the Massachusetts General Hospital). (FEIGIN, R. D., Shannon, D. C., Reynolds, S. L., Shapiro, L. W. and Connelly, J. P.) *Clin Pediat* 4:38–45, 1965.

Calcium disodium edathamil therapy of lead intoxication. The significance of aminoaciduria. (ANDREWS, B. F.) *Arch Environ Health* 3:563–567, 1961.

Lead poisoning in children. (MONCRIEFF, A. A., Koumides, O. P., Clayton, B. E., Patrick, A. D., Renwick, A. G. C. and Roberts, G. E.) *Arch Dis Child* 39:1–13, 1964.

Lead (Pregnancy)

Lead poisoning during pregnancy. Fetal tolerance of calcium disodium edetate. (ANGLE, C. R. and McIntire, M. S.) *Am J Dis Child* 108:436–439, 1964.

Mercury

The treatment of chronic intoxications due to lead, arsenic and mercury. (LEWIS, C. E.) *GP* 27:128–132, 1963.

Acrodynia. A long-term study of 62 cases. (CHAMBERLAIN, 3rd, J. L. and Quillian, II, W. W.) *Chin Pediat* 2:439–443, 1963.

A controlled trial of edathamil calcium disodium in acrodynia. (McCOY, J. E., Carre, I. J. and Freeman, M.) *Pediatrics* 25:304–308, 1960.

Plutonium (Human)

Plutonium excretion. Study following treatment with zirconium citrate and edathamil calcium-disodium. (SANDERS, JR., S. M.) *Arch Environ Health* 2:474–483, 1961.

Selenium (Animal)

The treatment of acute selenium, cadmium, and tungsten intoxication in rats with calcium disodium ethylene diamine tetraacetate. (SIVJAKOV, K. I. and Braun, H. A.) *Toxicol Appl Pharmacol* 1:602–608, 1959.

Snakes

The chemical modification of necrogenic and proteolytic activities of venom and the use of EDTA to produce *Agkistrodon piscivorus,* a venom toxoid. (GOUCHER, C. R. and Flowers, H. H.) *Toxicon* 2:139–147, 1964.

The effect of EDTA on the extent of tissue damage caused by the venoms of *Bothrops atrox* and *Agkistrodon piscivorus.* (FLOWERS, H. H. and Goucher, C. R.) *Toxicon* 2:221–224, 1965.

Studies on the improvement of treatment of Habu snake *(Trimeresurus flavoviridis)* bite. 2. Antitoxic action of monocalcium disodium ethylene diamine tetraacetate on Habu venom. (SAWAI, Y., Makino, M., Miyasaki, S., Kawamura, Y., Mitsuhashi, S. and Okonogi, T.) *Jap J Exp Med* 31:267–275, 1961.

Radiology

Promotion of radioisotope excretion. (STRAIN, W. H., Danahy, D. T., O'Reilly, R. J., Thomas, M. R., Wilson, R. M. and Pories, W. J.) *J Nucl Med* 8:110–116, 1967.

Effect of multiple injections of calcium compounds on the survival of x-irradiated rats. (RIXON, R. H. and Whitfield, J. R.) *Nature* 199:821–822, 1963. (15)

Distribution of cobalt-60 in the rat as influenced by chelating agents. (DU KHUONG LE) *Nature* 204:696–697, 1964.

Respiratory System

Animal Studies

Intravascular concentrations of calcium and magnesium ions and edema formation in isolated lungs. (NICOLAYSEN, G.) *Acta Physiol Scand* 81:325–339, 1971.

Ultrastructural studies of the alveolar-capillary barrier in isolated plasma-perfused rabbit lungs. Effects of EDTA and of increased capillary pressure.

(HOVIG, T., Nicolaysen, A. and Nicolaysen, G.) *Acta Physiol Scand* 82:417–431, 1971.

The importance of decalcification in the treatment of tuberculosis. II. The influence of decalcification of the course of experimental tuberculosis in guinea pigs infected with tubercle bacilli of low degree resistance to izoniazid. (GARA-PICH, M., Jelonek, A. and Kulig. A.) *Acta Med Pol* 8:313–318, 1967.

The importance of decalcification in the treatment of tuberculosis. I. The influence of decalcification in the course of healing in experimental tuberculosis in guinea pigs. (GIZA, T., Hjanicka, M., Jelonek, A., Kulig, A., Rembiesowa, H. and Garapich, M.) *Acta Paediat Scand* 55:33–37, 1966.

Human Studies

Measurement of sputum viscosity in a cone-plate viscometer. II. An evaluation of mycolytic agents in vitro. (LIEBERMAN, J.) *Am Rev Resp Dis* 97:662–672, 1968.

RHEUMATOID ARTHRITIS

Some in vivo effects of chelation. I. Rheumatoid arthritis. (BOYLE, A. J., Mosher, R. E. and McCann, D. S.) *J Chron Dis* 16:325–328, 1963.

Case histories of rheumatoid arthritis treated with sodium or magnesium EDTA. (LEIPZIG, L. J., Boyle, A. J. and McCann, D. S.) *J Chron Dis* 22:553–563, 1970.

TOXICITY STUDIES

Animal Studies

Safety evaluation studies of calcium EDTA. (OSER, B. L., Oser, M. and Spencer, H. C.) *Toxicol Appl Pharmacol* 5:142–162, 1963.

The toxicity and pharmacodynamics of EGTA: oral administration to rats and comparisons with EDTA. (WYNN, J. E., Riet, B. Van't and Borzelleca, J. F.) *Toxicol Appl Pharmacol* 16:807–817, 1970.

The relative toxicity in rats of disodium ethylene diamine tetraacetate, sodium oxalate and sodium citrate. (PAYNE, J. M. and Sansom, B. F.) *J Physiol* 170:613–620, 1964.

Metabolic changes in experimental poisoning with ethylene diamine tetraacetic acid. (REMAGEN, W., Hiller, F. K. and Sanz, C. M.) *Arzneimittelforschung* 11:1097–1099, 1961.

Contribution to the metabolism of MnNa$_2$ edathamil. (SYKORA, J., Kocher, Z. and Eybl, V.) *AMA Arch Indust Health* 21:24–27, 1960.

The toxic effect of CoCl$_2$, Co(Co-EDTA) or Na$_2$(Co-EDTA) containing aerosols on the rat and the distribution of (Co-EDTA)—in guinea pig organs. (HOBEL, M., Maroske, D., Wegener, K. and Eichler, O.) *Arch Int Pharmacodyn Ther* 198:213–222, 1972.

Human Studies

Chelation therapy. (CRAVEN, P. C. and Morrelli, H. F.) *West J Med* 122:277–278, 1975.

Toxic side effects of ethylene diamine tetraacetic acid. (FOREMAN, H.) *J Chron Dis* 16:319–323, 1963.

The long term use, side effects, and toxicity of disodium ethylene diamine tetraacetic acid (EDTA). MELTZER, L. E., Kitchell, J. R. and Palmon, Jr., F.) *Am J Med Sci* 242:11–17, 1961.

Acute versenate nephrosis occurring as the result of treatment for lead intoxication. (REUBER, M. D. and Bradley, J. E.) *JAMA* 174:263–269, 1960.

Fatal nephropathy during edathamil therapy in lead poisoning. (BRUGSCH, H. G.) *AMA Arch Indust Health* 20:285–292, 1959.

Pathologic changes associated with the use of sodium ethylene diamine tetraacetate in the treatment of hypercalcemia. (DUDLEY, H. R., Ritchie, A. C., Schilling, A. and Baker, W. H.) *New Eng J Med* 252:331–337, 1955.

Hazards of edathamil (EDTA) therapy in lead intoxication. (Letters) (ANDREWS, B. F.) *Pediatrics* 28:161–162, 1961.

Lesions resembling vitamin B complex deficiency and urinary loss of zinc produced by ethylene diamine tetraacetate. (PERRY, JR., H. M. and Schroeder. H. A.) *Am J Med* 22:168–172, 1957.

Edetic acid therapy. (Letters) (NODINE, J. H.) *JAMA* 212:628, 1970.

Kidneys (Animal)

A comparative study of the toxic effects of calcium and chromium chelates of ethylene diamine tetraacetate in the dog. (AHRENS, F. A. and Aronson, A. L.) *Toxicol Appl Pharmacol* 18:10–25, 1971.

Study of the mechanism of renal vacuologenesis induced in the rat by ethylene diamine tetraacetate. Comparison of the cellular activities of calcium and chromium chelates. (SCHWARTZ, S. L., Johnson, C. B. and Doolan, P. D.) *Mol Pharmacol* 6:54–60, 1970.

Calcium disodium edetate nephrosis in female rats of varying ages. (REUBER, M. D.) *J Path* 97:335–338, 1969.

Subcellular localization of ethylene diamine tetraacetate in the proximal tubular cell of the rat kidney. (SCHWARTZ, S. L., Johnson, C. B., Hayes, J. R. and Doolan, P. D.) *Biochem Pharmacol* 16:2413–2419, 1967.

An evaluation of the nephrotoxicity of ethylene diamine tetraacetate and diethylene triamine pentaacetate in the rat. DOOLAN, P. D., Schwartz, S. L., Hayes, J. R., Mullen, J. C. and Cummings, N. B.) *Toxicol Appl Pharmacol* 10:481–500, 1967.

Calcium disodium edetate nephrosis in inbred rats. Variation in Marshall, Buffalo, Fisher, and ACI strains. (REUBER, M. D. and Lee, C. W.) *Arch Environ Health* 13:554–557, 1966.

Studies of the nephrotoxicity of ethylene diamine tetraacetic acid. (SCHWARTZ, S. L., Hayes, J. R., Ide, R. S., Johnson, C. B. and Doolan, P. D.) *Biochem Pharmacol* 15:377–389, 1966.

Effects of edathamil disodium on the kidney. (ALTMAN, J., Wakim, K. G. and Winkelmann, R. K.) *J Invest Derm* 38:215–218, 1962.

Edetate kidney lesions in rats. (REUBER, M. D. and Schmieler, G. C.) *Arch Environ Health* 5:430–436, 1962.

Kidneys (Human & Animal)

Nephrotoxic hazard from uncontrolled edathamil calcium-disodium therapy. (FOREMAN, H., Finnegan, C. and Lushbaugh, C. C.) *AMA* 160:1042–1046, 1956.

Accentuation of Ca edetate nephrosis by cortisone. (REUBER, M. D.) *Arch Path* 76:382–386, 1963.

Liver (Animal)

'Phenergan' and versene in dietary liver necrosis. (McLEAN, A. E. M.) *Nature* 185:191–192, 1960.

Hepatic lesions in young rats given calcium disodium edetate. *Pharmacol* 11:321–326, 1967.

Teratology (Animal)

Chelating agents and teratogenesis. (Letters) (MARSH, L. and Fraser, F. C.) *Lancet* 1:846, 1973.

A direct analysis of early chick embryonic neuroepithelial responses following exposure to EDTA. (DANIELS, E. and Moore, K. L.) *Teratology* 6:215–225, 1972.

Teratogenic effects of a chelating agent and their prevention by zinc. (SWENER-TON, H. and Hurley, L. A.) *Science* 173:62–64, 1971.

TUMORS AND VIRUSES

Animal Studies

Studies on cell deformability. II. Some effects of EDTA on sarcoma 37 cells. (WEISS, L.) *J Cell Biol* 33:341–347, 1967.

Chelating agents for the binding of metal ions to macromolecules. (SUNDBERG, M. W., Meares, C. F., Goodwin, D. A. and Diamanti, C. L.) *Nature* 250:587–588, 1974.

Inhibition of DNA synthesis in animal cells by ethylene diamine tetraacetate, and its reversal by zinc. (RUBIN, H.) *Proc Natl Acad Sci USA* 69:712–716, 1972.

Some effects of disodium ethylene diamine tetraacetate on the growth of transplantable mouse tumors. (ASANO, M.) *Jap J Med Sci Biol* 12:365–374, 1959.

Local inhibition and enhancement of growth of transplanted tumor cells in mice. (GITLITZ, G. F., Ship. A. G., Glick, J. L. and Glick, A. H.) *J Surg Res* 3:370–376, 1963.

Human Studies

Studies of cell deformability. IV. A possible role of calcium in cell contact phenomena. (WEISS, L.) *J Cell Biol* 35:347–356, 1967.

Metals, ligands, and cancer. (WILLIAMS, D. R.) *Chem Rev* 72:203–213, 1972.

The effect of anticoagulants on the volume of normal and leukemic leukocytes. (LADINSKY, J. L. and Westring, D. W.) *Cancer Res* 27:1689–1695, 1967.

NEW REFERENCES

ACAM compilation of EDTA abstracts and references. American College for Advancement in Medicine, 23121 Verdugo Drive, Suite 204, Laguna Hills, CA 92653, 1990.

Altura BM, Altura BT: Magnesium withdrawal and contraction of arterial smooth muscle: effects of EDTA, EGTA, and divalent cations. Proc Soc Exp Biol Med 1976; 151: 752–755.

Badimon L, Badimon JJ, Lassila R, Heras M, and other: Thrombin regulation of platelet interaction with damaged vessel wall and isolated collagen type-I at arterial flow conditions in a procine model—effects of hirudins, heparin and calcium chelation. Blood 1991; 78: 423–434.

Boyle AJ, Clarke NE, Mosher RE, McCann DS. Chelation therapy in circulatory and sclerosing diseases. Fed Proc 1961; 29:243–251.

Bjorksten J. Possibilities and limitations of chelation as a means for life extension. J Adv Med 1989; 2:77–78.

Bjorksten J: Possibilities and limitations of chelation as a means for life extension. J Adv in Med 1989; 2: 77–78.

Brucknerova O, Malinovska V. First clinical experience with combined treatment with chelation III and glucagon in ischaemic disease of the lower extremities. Cas Lek Ces 1980; 119:814–815.

Busch L, Tessler J, Bazerque PM: Effects of calcium and EDTA on rat skin capillary permeability and on its response to histamine, serotonin, and bradykinin. Acta Physiol Pharmacol Latinoam (Argentina) 1989; 39: 227–234.

Casdorph HR, Farr CH. EDTA chelation therapy III, treatment of peripheral arterial occlusion, an alternative to amputation. J Hol Med 1983; 5:3–15.

Casdorph HR. EDTA chelation therapy, efficacy in arteriosclerotic heart disease. J Hol Med 1981; 3:53–59.

Casdorph HR. EDTA chelation therapy II, efficacy in brain disorders. J Hol Med 1981; 3:101–117.

Chappell LT, Kienow NT. The cost effectiveness of alternative medicine in the workplace. Chicago, Great Lakes Association of Clinical Medicine, Jack Hank, Executive Director, 70 West Huron Street, Chicago, IL 60610, 1993.

Chappell LT, Stahl JP. The correlation between EDTA chelation therapy and improvement in cardiovascular function: a meta-analysis. J Adv Med 1993; 6: 139–160.

Chelation bibliography—a collection of 80 articles. American College for Advancement in Medicine, 23121 Verdugo Drive, Suite 204, Laguna Hills, CA 92653, 1979.

Clarke NE, Clarke C, Mosher R. Treatment of angina pectoris with disodium ethylene tetraacetic acid. Am J. Med Sci 1956 Dec:654–666.

Clarke NE, Clarke CN, Mosher RE. The "in vivo" dissolution of metastatic calcium: an approach to atherosclerosis. Am J Med Sci 1955; 229:142–149.

Clarke NE. Arteriosclerosis, occlusive vascular disease and EDTA. Am J Cardiology 1960; 2:233–236.

Clarke NE. Treatment of occlusive vascular disease with disodium ethylene diamine tetraacetic acid (EDTA). AmJ Med Sci 1960 June: 732–744.

Cook DJ, Guyatt GH, Ryan G, et al. Should unpublished data be included in meta-analyses? JAMA 1993; 269:2749–2753.

Cranton EM, Brecher A. Bypassing Bypass. New York, Stein and Day 1984.

Cranton EM; ed: A textbook on EDTA chelation therapy. J Adv Med 1989; 2:1–416.

Cranton EM, Frackelton JP: Current status of EDTA Chelation Therapy on occlusive arterial disease. J of Adv in Med 1989; 2: 107–119.

Cranton EM, Frackelton JP: Free radical pathology in age-associated diseases; treatment with EDTA chelation, nutrition and antioxidants. J Hol Med 1984; 6: 6–37

Cranton EM, Frackelton JP. Free radical pathology in age-associated diseases; treatment with EDTA chelation, nutrition and antioxidants. J Hol Med 1984; 6:6–37.

Cranton EM, Frackelton JP. Negative Danish study of EDTA chelation biased. Townsend Letter for Doctors 1992 July:604–605.

Cranton EM. Protocol of American College of Advancement in Medicine for the safe and effective administration of EDTA chelation therapy. J Adv Med 1989; 2:269–306.

Cranton EM. The current status of EDTA chelation therapy. J Hol Med 1985; 7:3–7.

DeBoer DA, Clark RE: Iron chelation in myocardial preservation after ischemia-reperfusion injury: The importance of pretreatment and toxicity. Ann Thorac Surg 1992; 53: 412–8.

Deucher DP: EDTA Chelation Therapy: an antioxidant strategy. J Advancement in Med 1988; 1: 182–190.

Deucher DP. EDTA chelation therapy: an antioxidant strategy. J Adv Med 1988; 1:182–190.

Diehm C. "Wonder remedy chelation"—Claims and actuality. Zeitschrift der Deutschen Herzstiftung 1986; 10:11–15.

Dudley HR, Ritchie AC, Schilling A, Baker WH. Pathologic changes associated with the use of sodium ethylene diamine tetra-acetate in the treatment of hypercalcemia. N Engl J Med 1955; 252:331–337.

Editorial: Diagnostic and therapeutic technology assessment: chelation therapy. JAMA 1983; 250–672.

Editorial: EDTA chelation: a rebuttal. J Adv Med 1992; 5:3–5.

Editorial: EDTA chelation therapy for arteriosclerotic heart disease. Med Lett Drugs Ther 1981; 23:51.

Evers R. Chelation of vascular atheromatous disease (experience with 3000 patients). Private communication 1975; see ref. 10.

Freeman AP, Giles RW, Berdoukas VA, Walsh WR, Choy D, Murray PC: Early left ventricular dysfunction and Chelation Therapy in thalassemia major. Ann Intern Med 1983; 99: 450–4.

Glass G, McGaw B, Smith M. Meta-Analysis in Social Research. Newberry Park, CA, Sage Publications 1981:123–125, 218.

Godfrey ME, EDTA chelation as a treatment of arteriosclerosis. NZ Med J 1990; 103:162–163.

Gordon GB, Vance RB. EDTA chelation therapy for atherosclerosis: history and mechanisms of action. Ost Ann 1976; 4:38–62.

Gordon GB, Vance RB: EDTA Chelation Therapy for atherosclerosis: history and mechanisms of action. Ost Ann 1976; 4: 38–62.

Guldager B, Jelnes R, Jorgensen SJ, et al. EDTA treatment of intermittent claudication—a double-blind, placebo-controlled study. J Int Med 1992; 231: 261–267.

Gutteridge, JMC. Ferrous-salt-promoted damage to deoxyribose and benzoate, the increased effectiveness of hydroxyl-radical scavengers in the presence of EDTA. Biochem J 1987; 243:709–714.

Gutteridge, JMC: Ferrous-salt-promoted damage to deoxyribose and benzoate, the increased effectiveness of hydroxylradical scanvengers in the presence of EDTA. Biochem J 1987; 243: 709–714.

Hagen PO, Davies MG, Schuman RW, Murray JJ: Reduction of vein graft intimal hyperplasia by ex vivo treatment with Desferrioxamine Manganese. J of Vasc Res 1992; 29: 405–409.

Halstead BM: The Scientific Basis of EDTA Chelation Therapy, Colton, California, Golden Quill Publishers 1979.

Halstead BM. The Scientific Basis of EDTA Chelation Therapy, Colton, California, Golden Quill Publishers 1979.

Hancke C, Flytlie K. Benefits of EDTA chelation therapy on arteriosclerosis.

Pre-publication draft, presented in 1992 in Frankfort, Germany and Milano, Italy. Testcenter Kredslobsklinik, Lyngby Hovegade 17, DK-2800-Lyngby 45 42 88 09 00 (Denmark).

Hancke C, Flytlie K. Manipulation with EDTA. Ugeskar Laegar 1992; 154:2213–2215.

Hinkle DE, Wiersma W, Jurs SG. Applied Statistics for the Behavioral Sciences. Boston, MA, Houghton Mifflin 1979:85–101.

Hoekstra PP III, Gedye JL, Hoekstra P, et al. Serial infusions of magnesium disodium ethylene diamine tetraacetic acid enhance perfusion in human extremities. Pre-publication draft. Therma-Scan, Inc. 26711 Woodward Ave, Huntington Woods, MI 48070, 1993.

Juneja S, Wolf M, McLennan R: Clumping of lymphoma cells in peripheral blood induced by EDTA. J Clin Pathol 1992; 45: 538–40.

Kaman RL, Rudolph CJ, McDonagh EW, Walker FM. Effect of EDTA chelation therapy on aortic calcium in rabbits on atherogenic diets: quantitative and histochemical studies. J Adv Med 1990; 3:13–22.

Kaman RL, Rudolph CJ, McDonagh EW, Walker FM: Effect of EDTA Chelation Therapy on aortic calcium in rabbits on atherogenic diets: quantitative and histochemical studies. J Adv in Med 1990; 3: 13–22.

Kindness G, Frackelton JP. Effect of ethylene diamine tetraacetic acid (EDTA) on platelet aggregation in human blood. J Adv Med 1989; 2:519–530.

Kindness, G, Frackelton JP: Effect of ethylene diamine tetraacetic acid (EDTA) on platelet aggregation in human blood. J Adv in Med 1989; 2: 519–30.

Kitchell JR, Palmon F, Aytan N, Meltzer L. The treatment of coronary artery disease with disodium EDTA: a reappraisal. Am J Cardiol 1963; 11:501–506.

Kaman RL, Rudolph CJ, Galewaler J: Mineral excretion patterns during EDTA Chelation Therapy. J Amer Osteo Assoc 1977; 76: 471.

Lamar CP. Chelation endarterectomy for occlusive atherosclerosis. J Am Ger Soc 1966; 14:272–294.

Lamar CP. Chelation therapy of occlusive artheriosclerosis in diabetic patients. Angiology 1964; 15:379–394.

Lamb DJ, Leake DS. The effect of EDTA on the oxidation of low density lipoprotein. Atherosclerosis 1992; 94:35–42.

Lamb DJ, Leake DS: The effect of EDTA on the oxidation of low density lipoprotein. Atherosclerosis 1992; 94: 35–42.

Langhof H, Zanbel H. Voelkner E. Treatment of arteriosclerosis with Na ethyl-enediaminetetraacetate (EDTA). metab Parietis Vasorum, Papers Intern Congr Angiol 5th 1961; 1021–1024.

Lanza F, Stierle A, Gachet C, Cazenave JP: Differential effects of extra- and intracellular calcium chelation on human platelet function and glycoprotein-IIB–IIIA complex stability. Nouvelle Revue Francaise D Hematologie 1992; 34: 123–131.

Lau J, Antman EM, Jimenez-Silva J, Kupelnick B. Cumulative meta-analysis of therapeutic trials for myocardial infarctioin. N Engl J Med 1992; 327:248–255.

Lermer N, Blei F, Bierman F, Johnson L. Chelation therapy and cardiac status in older patients with thalassemia major. Am J Ped Hem Onc 1990; 12:56–60.

Levy RJ, Howard SL, Oshry LJ: Carboxyglutamic acid (Gla) containing proteins of human calcified atherosclerotic plaque solubilized by EDTA. Molecular weight distribution and relationship to osteocalcin. Atherosclerosis 1986; 59: 155–60.

Link G, Pinson A, Hershko C: Heart cells in culture: a model of myocardial iron overload and chelation. J Lab Clin Med 1985; 106: 147–53.

Lugo-Miro VI, Green M, Mazur L. Coomparison of different metronidazole therapeutic regiments for bacterial vaginosis. JAMA 1992; 268:92–95.

Magee HR. Reply to Gibson TJB: Chelation therapy for atherosclerosis. Med J. Aust 1985; 143: 127.

Malinovska V, Zechmeister A, Malinovska L., et al. The therapeutic effects of glucagon and chelation III on the arterial wall after experimental lipidosis and calcification. Scripta Medica 1983; 56: 391–400.

Mallette LE, Hollis BW, Dunn K, Stinson M, Dunn JK, Wittels E, Gotto AM: Medical Service, Veterans Administration Medical Center, 2002 Holcombe Boulevard, Houston, TX 77030 USA. Ten weeks of intermittent hypocalcemic stimulation does not produce functional parathyroid hyperplasia. Am J Med Sci, 1991; 302: 138–141.

Marban E, Koretsune Y, Corretti M, Chacko VP, Kusuka H: Calcium and its role in myocardial cell injury during ischemia and reperfusion. Circulation 1989; 80: 17–22.

May J, Loesche W, Heptinstall S: Glucose increases spontaneous platelet aggregation in whole blood. Journal: Throm Res 1990; 59: 489–495.

McDonagh EW, Rudolph CJ. A collection of published papers showing the efficacy of EDTA chelation therapy. McDonagh Medical Center, Gladstone, MO. 1989.

McDonagh EW, Rudolph CJ, Cheraskin E. The effect of EDTA chelation therapy plus multivitamin/trace mineral supplementation upon vascular dynamics (ankle/branchial systolic blood pressure). J Hol Med 1985; 7:16–22.

McGillem MJ, Mancini GBJ. Inefficacy of EDTA chelation therapy for atherosclerosis. NEJM 1988; 318:1618–1619.

Menasche P, Pinwica A: Free radicals and myocardial protection: a surgical viewpoint. Ann Thorac Surg 1989; 47: 939–45.

Morgan K. Myocardial ischemia treated with nutrients and intravenous EDTA chelation. Report of two cases. J Adv Med 1991; 4:47–56.

Muldoon MF, Manuck SB, Matthews KA. Lowering cholesterol concentrations and mortality: a quantitative review of primary intervention trials. Br Med J 1990; 301:309–314.

Oliver LD, Mehta R, Sarles HE. Acute renal failure following administration of ethylenediamine-tetraacetic acid (EDTA). Tex Med 1984; 80:40–42.

Olszewer E, Carter JP. EDTA chelation therapy in chronic degenerative disease Med Hypoth 1988; 27:41–49.

Olszewer E, Carter JP. EDTA chelation therapy in chronic degenerative disease. Med Hypoth 1988; 27:41–49.

Olszewer E, Sabbag, FC, Carter JP. A pilot double-blind study of sodium-magnesium EDTA in peripheral vascular disease. J Nat Med As 1990; 82:173–177.

Olwin JH, Koppel JR. Reduction of elevated plasma lipid levels in artherosclerosis following EDTA therapy. Soc Exp Biol & Med Proc 1968; 128:1137–1140.

Patterson R. Chelation therapy and Uncle John. Can Med As J 1989; 40:829–831.

Peng CF, Kame JJ, Bissett JK, et al: Improvement of oxidative phosphorylation by EDTA in mitochondria from acutely ischemic myocardium which has been reperfused. Clin Res 1977; 25: 244.

Perizzolo KE, Sullivan S, Waugh DF: Effects of calcium binding and of EDTA and CaEDTA on the clotting of bocine fibrinogen by thrombin. Arch Biochem Biophys 1985, 237:520–534.

Rahko, PS, Calerni R. Uretsy BF. Successful reversal by chelation therapy of congestive cardiomyopathy due to iron overload. J Am Coll Card 1986; 8:436–440.

Rahko PS, Salerni R, Utetsky BF: Successful reversal by Chelation Therapy of congestive cardiomyopathy due to iron overload. J Am Coll Card 1986; 8: 436–40.

Riordan HD, Cheraskin E, Dirks M, et al. EDTA chelation/hypertension study: clinical patterns as judged by the Cornell Medical Index questionaire. J Ortho Med 1989; 4:91–95.

Riordan HD, Cheraskin E, Dirks M, et al. EDTA treatment of intermittent claudication—a double-blind, placebo controlled study. J Int Med 1992; 231:261–267.

Robinson DM, chelation therapy. NZ Med J 1982; 95: 750.

Rosenthal R. The "File Drawer Problem" and tolerance for null results. Psychological Bulletin 1979; 86: 638–641.

Rudolph CJ, McDonagh EW, Barbar RK. A non-surgical approach to obstructive carotid atheromatous stenosis: and independent study. J Adv Med 1991; 4:157–166.

Rudolph CJ, McDonagh EW. Effect of EDTA chelation and supportive multi vitamin/trace mineral supplementation on carotid circulation: case report. J Adv Med 1990; 3:5–12.

Rudolph CJ, McDonagh EW, Barber RK. Effect of EDTA chelation on serum iron. J Adv Med 1991; 4:39–45.

Rudloph CJ, McDonagh EW, Barber RK: Effect of EDTA chelation on serum iron. J Adv in Med 1991; 4: 39–45.

Scheafler RL, McClave JT. Probability and Statistics for Engineers. Boston, MA, PWS Publishers 1986:363–371.

Simon VC, Cohen RA: EDTA influences reactivity of isolated aorta from hypercholesterolemic rabbits. Am J Heart Circ Physiol 1992; 262: 31–5.

Sloth-Nielsen J, Guldager B, Mouritzen, C, et al. Artheriographic findings in EDTA chelation therapy on peripheral arteriosclerosis. Am J Surg 1991; 162:122–125.

Soffer A. Chelation therapy for arteriosclerosis. JAMA 1975; 233:1206–1207.

Solti F. Juhasz-Nagy S, Kecskemeti V, Czako B, Nemeth V, Kekesi V: Effect of the Ca2+ chelators EDTA and EGTA on sinoatrial-node activity and heart irritability. Acta Physiol Acad Sci Hung 1982; 60: 155–64.

Surawicz B, MacDonald MG, Kaljot V, Bettinger JC. Treatment of cardiac arrhythmias with salts of ethylenediamine tetraacetic acid. Am Heart J 1959; 58:493–503.

Suvorov AV, Markosyan RA: Some mechanisms of EDTA effect on platelet aggregation. Byull Eksp Biol Med 1981; 91: 587–590.

Uhl HS, Dysko RC, St. Clair, RW, EDTA reduces liver cholesterol content in cholesterol-fed rabbits. Atherosclerosis 1992; 96: 181–188.

Uhl HS, Dysko RC, St. Clair RW: EDTA reduces liver cholesterol content in cholesterol fed rabbits. Atherosclerosis 1992; 96:181–188.

Valles J, Martinez-Sales V, Aznar J, Santos MT: The effect of EDTA on the production of prostacyclin by rat aorta. Thromb Res 1986; 43: 479–483.

Van der Schaar P. Exercise tolerance in chelation therapy. J Adv Med 1989; 2:563–566.

Walker F, Wilson C III, Kaman RL: North Texas State Univ., Texas Coll Osteopath. Med., Denton, Tex. USA. The effects of EDTA Chelation Therapy on plaque composition and serum lipoproteins in atherosclerotic rabbits. J Am Ost Assoc, 1978, 78: 144.

Walker FM, Wilson CW III, Kaman RL: Dept. Biol., NTSU/TCOM, Denton, Tex. 76203 USA. The effects of EDTA Chelation Therapy on plaque calcium and plasma lipoproteins in atherosclerotic rabbits. Fed Proc 1979; 38 (No. 4335).

Wirebaugh SR, Geracts DR. Apparent failure of edetic acid chelation therapy for the treatment of coronary atherosclerosis. DICP Ann Ph 1990; 24:22–25.

Wolf FM. Meta-analysis: Quantitative Methods for Research Synthesis. Newberry Park, CA. Sage Publications 1986:55.

Wolf FM. Meta-Analysis Quantitative Methods for Research Synthesis. Newberry Park, CA, Sage Publications 1986:31–33.

Zechmeister A, Gulda O. Subcellular metabolism of CA2+ in smooth muscle and myocardium (an ultrahistochemical study). Folla Morphol 1981; 29: 333–335.

Zechmeister A, Malinovska V, Hadasova E, et al. Effect of glucagon on lipid and calcium deposition in arterial wall. Folla Morphol 1979: 27: 23–26.

Zurcker MB, Grant RA: Nonreversible loss of platelet aggregability induced by calcium deprivation. Blood 1978; 52:505–13.

Zylke J. Studying oxygen's life-and-death roles if taken from or reintroduced into tissue. JAMA 1988; 259: 964–965.

Zylke J: Studying oxygen's life-and-death roles if taken from or reintroduced into tissue. JAMA 1988; 259: 964–5.

Appendix C
SUPPLIERS OF CHELATING THERAPY PRODUCTS

Three commercial companies which specialize in furnishing chelation therapy supplies to health care professionals only are the following.

Gy & N Nutriment Pharmacology, located at P.O. Box 2252, Carlsbad, California 92018; telephone (619) 434–6360 or (800) 526–3030 in California and (800) 445–2122 throughout the United States, offers products and supplies for chelation therapy, injectable vitamins, minerals, amino acids and IV solutions. Gy & N also distributes a complete line of oral vitamins, minerals, glandulars and special-use oral products. Its laboratory services include analyses of hair, plasma, urine, red blood cells (RBC) and whole blood minerals as well as antibodies to candida, antibodies to chemicals, IgG$_4$ food allergy testing, immune system assessment programs and the services of a comprehensive immunology laboratory with state-of-the-art cell sorting capability.

The McGuff Company, a wholesale medical products firm specializing in competitively priced products relating to chelation therapy, is located at 3524 Lake Center Drive, Santa Ana, California 92704; telephone (714) 545–2491 or (800) 854–7220; teleFAX (714) 540–6514. With eighteen years of experience and over 2.5 million vials of EDTA sold to health professionals, the McGuff Company's greatest asset is its experience. EDTA dosage and osmolarity software along with the company personnel's expertise help simplify some of the complexity of chelation therapy. The McGuff Company's product categories offered include various injections, intravenous (IV) solutions, IV sets, IV needles and catheters, nutritional supplements and many kinds of physicians' office supplies.

Phyne Pharmaceuticals, Inc/American Pharmaceutical ENT., Inc.

is located at 7950 East Redfield Road, Suite 110, P.O. Box 12543, Scottsdale, Arizona 85267; telephone (602) 998–4142 or (800) 345–3391; teleFAX (602) 443–4775. Phyne Pharmaceuticals offers the full complement of solutions, equipment, disposables and other supplies for accomplishing chelation therapy and preventive medicine procedures. Other items in its inventory are collagen–placenta "Cridon" cosmetics plus DMSO creams and liquids. This medical supply corporation, under the chairmanship of James Critchlow, H.M.D., was a pioneer in the early days of chelation therapy. Dr. Critchlow helped to establish chelation therapy as the procedure of choice for preventing or reversing hardening of the arteries. In 1973, the Phyne Pharmaceutical Company chairman became one of only three founding members of the American Academy of Medical Preventics which grew into the current American College for Advancement in Medicine.

Note: The American Medical Association (AMA) has petitioned the FDA to put a disclaimer on the bottom of all package inserts in use for all drugs to ease this severely increased physician responsibility. However, physicians regularly utilize drugs in a manner not listed on the package insert. FDA documents point out that this physician practice is both legal and ethical. The FDA has not been instructed by Congress to interfere with the physician's use of a drug.

Previously, EDTA was indicated on the package insert for angina or peripheral vascular disease when symptomatic disease presented a threat. Any risks of use were outweighed by the benefits in the face of the symptomatic vascular disease process. For simply delaying arteriosclerosis of aging, however, the manufacturers had decided many years ago that the risk appeared too great until new information on toxicity is elaborated.[1-4]

You should be informed as well that this new information about lack of toxicity exists today. But the manufacturer is virtually powerless to change a single word on a package insert without expending millions of dollars to get the FDA to agree. As a reader of this book, you may be able to change these "catch-22" situations. New federal legislation may become necessary to facilitate the widespread availability of some form of chelation therapy for all U.S. citizens who desire it, following appropriate informed consent procedures with their physicians.

Appendix D
CHELATION RESOURCES

Rebounding Information (Chapter 10)

The Needak® brand of rebounders may be acquired by contacting Ken Seeley, Marketing Manager, Nedak Manufacturing Company, P.O. Box 776, O'Neill, Nebraska 68763; telephone (800) 232–5762 or (402) 336–4083; teleFAX (402) 336–4941. The company also has available a large selection of books and videos on rebounding.

You can learn of more than thirty rebound exercises with captioned drawings from the 1989 published book written by Dr. Morton Walker, *Jumping for Health,* $9.95 (Avery Publishing Group of Garden City Park, New York).

CHELATION FORMULATIONS (Chapter 11)

1. Dr. Michael Jude Loquasto's oral chelation product, Vita Chel Plus,™ is marketed from the offices of Healthplex Medical Center, P.O. Box 1187, Route 209, Marshalls Creek, Pennsylvania 18335; telephone (800) 228–4673 or (717) 223–0140; teleFAX (717) 223–7355. It is packaged in bottles of 60 tablets, 120 tablets and 225 tablets, and in individual daily packets for convenient carrying on day trips. To receive Vita Chel Plus™, contact the Healthplex Medical Center for the single-bottle cost, quantity discount prices, manner of payment and your preferred method of shipment.
2. Dr. Hitendrah H. Shah's formula is manufactured by Biodyne, Inc., 229 West 7th Street, P.O. Box 417, San Jacinto, California 92581; telephone (909) 487–2550 or toll free (888) 465–4782.

The Biodyne Corporation offers nutritional products for health professionals to dispense to consumers focused on oral chelation therapy, animal glandulars and detoxification of the human colon, liver, kidneys and lungs. Dr. Shah has authored a booklet entitled *Cleanse, Nourish, and Rejuvenate,* describing various techniques of whole body detoxification. The small book is being distributed by Biodyne, Inc. at a price of $2.95. Another of Dr. Shah's books, *A Guide to Natural Nutritional Alternatives for Heart Disease,* is an easy-to-understand and comprehensive treatise on various nutritional alternatives, including herbs, vitamins, minerals, enzymes, glandulars, antioxidants, plus Ayurvedic and homeopathic products.

For a list of physicians who practice preventive medicine, including chelation therapy, contact:

American College for Advancement in Medicine
23121 Verdugo Drive, Suite 204, Laguna Hills, CA 92653
Phone (714) 583–7666 or (800) 532–3688 FAX (714) 455–9679

1996–97 Membership Roster American College for Advancement in Medicine

23121 Verdugo Drive, Suite 204
Laguna Hills, CA 92653
(714) 583-7666 • (800) 532-3688 • FAX (714) 455-9679

This roster lists physician members of record of the American College for Advancement in Medicine as of June 1, 1996. Listing in this roster does not constitute a recommendation by ACAM of a particular physician's services.

ACAM physician members must have earned an M.D., D.O., or their equivalent, currently possess an unrestricted license to practice medicine issued by an applicable licensing authority, and have been accepted for membership by meeting formal procedural requirements established by ACAM's Board of Directors.

Roster Contents

Geographic Listing of ACAM Physicians:

United States   352

International   404

©1996
American College for Advancement in Medicine
All rights reserved
Revised June 1, 1996

ACAM FELLOW (FACAM)

The designation of FACAM after the physician's name indicates that he is a Fellow of the American College for Advancement in Medicine and signifies special contributions both to preventive medicine and to ACAM. Fellows must have attended ACAM's chelation therapy workshop and passed the ABCT written exam, met specified medical/scientific writing requirements, provided service to ACAM, attended at least four ACAM conference programs, and been an ACAM member in good standing for a minimum of two years.

SPECIALTY AND SUSPECIALTY CODES

A	ALLERGY	GYN	GYNECOLOGY
AN	ANESTHESIOLOGY	HGL	HYPOGLYCEMIA
AC	ACUPUNCTURE	HO	HYPERBARIC OXYGEN
AR	ARTHRITIS	HOM	HOMEOPATHY
AU	AURICULOTHERAPY	HYP	HYPNOSIS
BA	BARIATRICS	IM	INTERNAL MEDICINE
CD	CARDIOVASCULAR DISEASE	LM	LEGAL MEDICINE
		MM	METABOLIC MEDICINE
CT	CHELATION THERAPY	NT	NUTRITION
CS	CHEST DISEASE	OBS	OBSTETRICS
DD	DEGENERATIVE DISEASE	OME	ORTHOMOLECULAR MEDICINE
DIA	DIABETES	OPH	OPHTHALMOLOGY
END	ENDOCRINOLOGY	OSM	OSTEOPATHIC MANIPULATION
FP	FAMILY PRACTICE		
GE	GASTROENTEROLOGY	PD	PEDIATRICS

GP	GENERAL PRACTICE	PM	PREVENTIVE MEDICINE
GER	GERIATRICS		
PMR	PHYSICAL MEDICINE &	R	RADIOLOGY
	REHABILITATION	RHU	RHEUMATOLOGY
P	PSYCHIATRY	RHI	RHINOLOGY
PO	PSYCHIATRY	S	SURGERY
	(ORTHOMOLECULAR)	WR	WEIGHT REDUCTION
PH	PUBLIC HEALTH	YS	YEAST SYNDROME
PUD	PULMONARY DISEASES		

CERTIFICATION OF ACAM PHYSICIANS ADMINISTERING EDTA CHELATION THERAPY

Most ACAM physicians administer EDTA chelation therapy, a medical procedure involving intravenous infusion of a man-made amino acid (ethylene diamine tetraacetic acid), to treat atherosclerosis and other chronic degenerative diseases. The American Board of Chelation Therapy in Chicago, Illinois provides two levels of certification for physicians who have met the criteria listed below:

DIPLOMATE (DIPL)

a. is a graduate of an approved school of medicine (D.O. or M.D., or foreign equivalent);

b. is currently licensed to practice in the state or territory where he/she conducts practice;

c. has been recommended (by letter) by two Diplomates in Chelation Therapy;

d. has successfully completed the written examination of the American Board of Chelation Therapy;

e. shows evidence of being responsible for the administration of 1000 chelation treatments;

f. has satisfied the requirements for preceptor training as outlined in the protocol of preceptorship;

g. has successfully completed the oral examination of the American Board of Chelation Therapy;

h. submits 10 acceptable questions and answers with references for use in future written exams.

DIPLOMATE CANDIDATE (D/C)

a. is a graduate of an approved school of medicine (D.O. or M.D. or foreign equivalent);
b. is currently licensed to practice in the state or territory where he/she conducts practice;
c. has been recommended (by letter) by two Diplomates in Chelation Therapy;
d. has successfully completed the written examination of the American Board of Chelation Therapy; and is in the process of completing the remaining requirements for ABCT Diplomate status.

ACAM PHYSICIANS—GEOGRAPHIC
UNITED STATES

ALABAMA

Ashland

Robert B. Andrews, Jr., DO
544 East First Ave.
Ashland, AL 36251
(205) 354-2131, ext. 146
GP, OS, Emerg. Med.

Birmingham

Gus J. Prosch Jr., MD, D/C
759 Valley St.
Birmingham, AL 35226
(205) 823-6180—FAX (205) 823-6000
A, AR, CT, GP, NT, OME

GulfShores

Glen P. Wilcoxson, MD
1720 GulfShores Pkwy., #4
P.O. Box 1888
GulfShores, AL 36547
(334) 968-6515—FAX (334) 968-6756
BA, CT, NT, PM, RHU, YS

Huntsville

George Gray, MD
521 Madison St., #100
Huntsville, AL 35801
(205) 534-1676—FAX (205) 534-0926
BA, CT, GER, IM, NT, PM

Theodore

Claude L. Buerger Jr., MD
4270 Windsor Rd.
Theodore, AL 36582—NO REFERRALS

ALASKA

Anchorage

Sandra Denton, MD, DIPL
3201 C Street, Suite 306
Anchorage, AK 99503
(907) 563-6200—FAX (907) 561-4933

A, AC, AR, AU, CD, CT, DD, DIA, END, FP, NT

Robert Rowen, MD, DIPL
615 E. 82nd Ave., Ste. 300
Anchorage, AK 99518
(907) 344-7775—FAX (907) 522-3114
AC, CT, FP, NT, PM, HYP

Palmer

D. Lynn Mickelson, MD, D/C
440-A West Evergreen
Palmer, AK 99645
(907) 745-3880—FAX (907) 745-2631
A, CT, GP

Wasilla

Robert E. Martin, MD
P.O. Box 870710
Wasilla, AK 99687
(907) 376-5284
AU, CT, FP, GP, OS, PM

ARIZONA

Cave Creek

Frank W. George II, DO, MDH
38425 N. Spur Cross Rd.
P.O. Box 547
Cave Creek, AZ 85331
(602) 488-6331—FAX (602) 488-0297
CT, DD, GP, MM, NT, OS

Cottonwood

Darrel Parry, DO
1699 E. Cottonwood St.
Cottonwood, AZ 86326
(602) 639-2200
AC, BA, CT, FM, OS, PD, PMR

Glendale

Lloyd D. Armold, DO, DIPL
4901 W. Bell Rd., Ste. 2
Glendale, AZ 85308
(602) 939-8916—FAX (602) 978-2817
AR, CT, GP, MM, PM, OSM

Mesa

William W. Halcomb, DO
4323 E. Broadway, Suite 109
Mesa, AZ 85206
(602) 832-3014
A, CT, GP, HO, OSM, PM

Parker

S. W. Meyer, DO
332 River Front Dr.—P.O. Box 1870
Parker, AZ 85344—NO REFERRALS

Payson

Garry Gordon, DM
901 Anasazi Rd.
Payson, AZ 85541—NO REFERRALS

Phoenix

Lester Adler, MD, D/C
3333 Indian School Rd., #4
Phoenix, AZ 85018
(602) 956-8871
CT, GP, IM, MM, NT, PM

Laszlo I. Belenyessy, MD
P.O. Box 60036
Phoenix, AZ 85082—NO REFERRALS

Terry S. Friedmann, MD, DIPL
10565 N. Tatum Bl., Suite B115
Phoenix (Paradise), AZ 85254
(602) 381-0800—FAX (602) 381-0054
A, CT, FP, HGL, HYP, NT

Stanley R. Olsztyn, MD
4350 E. Camelback Rd., Suite B-220
Phoenix, AZ 85018
(602) 840-8424—FAX (602) 840-8545
A, CT, PM, DD

Bruce H. Shelton, MD
2525 W. Greenway Rd., #300
Phoenix, AZ 85018
(602) 993-1200/993-0160
A, AC, DD, FP, HOM, PO, YS

Scottsdale

Gordon H. Josephs, DO, D/C
7315 E. Evans
Scottsdale, AZ 85260
(602) 998-9232—FAX (602) 998-1528
CT, GP, NT, PM, S

Doris J. Rapp, MD
8157 E. Del Cuarzo
Scottsdale, AZ 85258
(602) 905-9195
A, PD, Env Med, HOM

Sedona

Lester Adler, MD, D/C
40 Soldiers Pass Rd., #12
Sedona, AZ 86339
(520) 282-2520
CT, GP, IM, MM, NT, PM

Tucson

Alexander P. Cadoux, MD, D/C
5655 East River Rd., #151
Tucson, AZ 85750
(520) 529-9668—FAX (520) 529-9669
A, CT, FP, MM, NT, PM

Gordon Josephs, DO, D/C
3956 E. Pima
Tucson, AZ 85712
(520) 326-7566
CT, GP, NT, PM, S

Jesse Stoff, MD, D/C
2122 N. Craycroft Rd., #112
Tucson, AZ 85712
(520) 290-4516—FAX (520) 290-6403
A, AC, CT

ARKANSAS

Hot Springs

William Wright, MD
1 Mercy Dr., Suite 211
Hot Springs, AR 71913
(501) 624-3312
A, CT, GP, IM

Leslie

Melissa Taliaferro, MD, DIPL
Cherry Street, P.O. Box 400
Leslie, AR 72645
(501) 447-2599—FAX (501) 447-2917
AC, CT, DD, IM, NT, PM, RHU

Little Rock

Norbert J. Becquet, MD, FACAM, DIPL
613 Main Street
Little Rock, AR 72201
(501) 375-4419
CT, OPH, PM, RHU

Mena

David P. Brown, MD
622 Mena Street, #A
Mena, AR 71953
(501) 394-7570
FP, GP, GYYN, IM, NT, PM

Mountain Home

Merl B. Cox, DO
126 South Church
Mountain Home, AR 72653
(501) 424—5025
OS, PM

Springdale

G. Howard Kimball, MD, D/C
900 Dorman, Suite E
Springdale, AR 72766
(501) 756-3251—FAX (501) 756-9186
A, CT, FP, NT, YS

CALIFORNIA

Albany

Ross B. Gordon, MD, DIPL
405 Kains Ave.
Albany, CA 94706
(510) 526-3232—FAX (510) 526-3217
BA, CT, NT, PM

Azusa

William C. Bryce, MD
400 N. San Gabriel Ave.
Azusa, CA 91702
(818) 334-1407
CT, NT, PM

Bakersfield

John B. Park, MD, D/C
6501 Schirra CT., #200
Bakersfield, CA 93313
(805) 833-6562—FAX (805) 833-3498
AN, BA, FP, GP, PM, S

Carmelo A. Plateroti, DO
606-34th Street
Bakersfield, CA 93301
(805) 327-3756
DD, END, NT, OS, PM, S

Ralph G. Seibly, MD
2123 17th Avenue
Bakersfield, CA 93301
(805) 631-2000—FAX (805) 631-0914
A, CD, CT, DD, DIA, FP, PM, WR

Belmont

JoAnne Lombardi, MD
2206 Pullman Ave.
Belmont, CA 94002—NO REFERRALS

Beverly Hills

Larrian Gillespie, MD
505 S. Beverly Dr., #1233
Beverly Hills, CA 90212—NO REFERRALS

Cathie Ann Lippman, MD
291 S. La Cienega Bl., Suite 207
Beverly Hills, CA 90211
(310) 289-8430
A, AC, PM, YS

Burbank

David J. Edwards, MD
2202 W. Magnolia
Burbank, CA 91506
(818) 842-4184 or (800) 975-2202
CD, CT, FP, GP, NT, PM, YS

Douglas Hunt, MD, D/C
2625 W. Alameda, #326
Burbank, CA 91505
(818) 566-9889—FAX (818) 566-9879
A, BA, CT, HGL, MM, NT, PM, PO, YS

Campbell

Carl L. Ebnother, MD
621 E. Campbell Ave., #11A
Campbell, CA 95008
(408) 378-7970—FAX (408) 378-4908
CD, CT, IM, MM, NT, YS

Canyon Lake

John V. Beneck, MD, D/C
22107 Old Paint Way
Canyon Lake, CA 92587
(909) 244-3686—FAX (909) 244-0109
Emergency Medicine

Carlsbad

Mark Drucker, MD
4004 Skyline Rd.
Carlsbad, CA 92008
(619) 729-4777
BA, CT, NT, PM, WR

Carmel

Gerald A. Wyker, MD
25530 Rio Vista Drive
Carmel, CA 93923
(408) 625-0911
GP, MM, PM

Carmichael

J. E. Dugas, MD
4811 Cypress Ave.
Carmichael, CA 95608—RETIRED

Concord

John P. Toth, MD, D/C
2299 Bacon St., Ste. 10
Concord, CA 94520
(510) 682-5660—FAX (510) 682-8097
A, CD, CT, GP, HGL, NT

John R. Toth, DO, D/C
2299 Bacon St., Ste. 11
Concord, CA 94520
(510) 687-9447—FAX (510) 687-9483
A, CT, FP, NT, PMR

Corte Madera

Jeffrey Anderson, MD
45 San Clemente Drive, Ste. B-100
Corte Madera, CA 94925
(415) 927-7140
DD, ENV, MED, IMMUNO, MM, NT

Michael Rosenbaum, MD
45 San Clemente Drive, Suite B-130
Corte Madera, CA 94925
(415) 927-9450—FAX (415) 927-3759
A, HGL, MM, NT, P, YS

Covina

James Privitera, MD, D/C
105 No. Grandview Ave.
Covina, CA 91723
(818) 966-1618—FAX (818) 966-7226
A, CT, MM, NT

El Cajon

William J. Saccoman, MD, DIPL
505 N. Mollison Ave., Suite 103
El Cajon, CA 92021
(619) 440-3838
CT, NT, PM

Encino

Ilona Abraham, MD
17815 Ventura Blvd., Stes. 111 & 113
Encino, CA 91316
(818) 345-8721—FAX (818) 345-7150
A, AC, CD, CT, P

A. Leonard Klepp, MD, DPL
16311 Ventura Blvd., #725
Encino, CA 91436
(818) 981-5511—FAX (818) 907-1468
CT, FP, PM, HGL, NT

Fall River Mills

Charles K. Dahlgren, MD
Hwy 299 E., Hospital Annex
Fall River Mills, CA 96028
(916) 335-5354
A, NT, RHI, S

Fresno

David J. Edwards, MD
360 S. Clovis Ave.
Fresno, CA 93727
(209) 251-5066—(209) 251-5108
A, PM, CT, MM, NT, GYN, YS

Glendale

Joseph Lee Filbeck Jr., MD
1812 Verdugo Blvd.
Glendale, CA 91208
(818) 952-2243
AN, PM

Grand Terrace

Hiten Shah, MD
22807 Barton Road
Grand Terrace, CA 92324
(714) 783-2773
CT, GP, HO, NT, PM

Hollywood

James J. Julian, MD
1654 Cahuenga Blvd.
Hollywood, CA 90028
(213) 467-5555
AR, BA, CT, NT, PM

Huntington Beach

Francis Foo, MD, D/C
10188 Adams Ave.
Huntington Beach, CA 92646
(714) 968-3266—FAX (714) 968-6408
FP, S

Irvine

Ronald Wempen, MD
14795 Jeffrey Rd., Suite 101
Irvine, CA 92720
(714) 551-8751
A, AC, MM, NT, PO, YS

Lafayette

Richard Gracer, MD
895 Moraga Rd., #15
Lafayette, CA 94549
(510) 283-6590
FP, DD, OME, PM

La Jolla

Charles Moss, MD
8950 Villa La Jolla, #2162
La Jolla, CA 92037
(619) 457-1314
AC, FP, HGL, MM, NT, YS, Env. Med.

Pierre Steiner, MD
1550 Via Corona
La Jolla, CA 92037—NO REFERRALS

Lancaster

Richard P. Huemer, MD
1739 West Avenue J
Lancaster, CA 93534
(805) 945-4502—FAX (805) 945-4841
A, CT, GP, HGL, MM, NT, OME, PM

Mary Kay Michelis, MD
1739 West Avenue J
Lancaster, CA 93534
(805) 945-4502—FAX (805) 945-4841
CT, OPH

Long Beach

H. R. Casdorph, MD, PhD, FACAM, DIPL
1703 Termino Ave., Suite 201
Long Beach, CA 90804
(310) 597-8716—FAX (310) 597-4616
CD, CS, CT, DIAM, IM, NT

John Kregzde, MD
3780 Woodruff Ave., #G
Long Beach, CA 90808
(310) 420-6044
GP, IM

Los Altos

Robert F. Cathcart III, MD
127 Second St., Suite 4

Los Altos, CA 94022
(415) 949-2822
A, AR, CT, DD, OME, PM

Claude Marquette, MD
5050 El Camino Real, #110
Los Altos, CA 94022
(415) 964-6700
A, AR, CT, DD, HGL, MM, NT, PM, YS

Los Angeles

Hans D. Gruenn, MD
12732 Washington Blvd., #D
Los Angeles, CA 90066
(310) 822-4614
AC, CT, GP, NT, PM, PMR, YS

Anna Law, MD
6228 Rockcliff Drive
Los Angeles, CA 90068
(213) 957-9063
Emergency Med.

Marc R. Rose, MD
3325 N. Broadway
Los Angeles, CA 90031
(213) 221-6121—FAX (213) 225-6120
AN, CD, IM, NT, OPH

Michael R. Rose, MD
3325 N. Broadway
Los Angeles, CA 90031
(213) 221-6121—FAX (213) 225-6120
AN, CD, IM, NT, OPH

Joseph Sciabbarrasi, MD, D/C
2211 Corinth Ave., #204
Los Angeles, CA 90064
(310) 477-8151—(310) 477-5833
CT, GP, HOM, NT, YS

Malibu

Jesse Hanley, MD
22917 Pacific Coast Hwy., #220
Malibu, CA 90265
(310) 456-7721
AC, FP, HGL, NT, PM, YS

Mission Hills

Sion Nobel, MD, D/C
10306 N. Sepulveda Blvd.
Mission Hills, CA 91345
(818) 361-0115
PMR

Mission Viejo

David A. Steenblock, DO
26381 Crown Valley Pkwy., Suite 130
Mission Viejo, CA 92691
(714) 367-8870—FAX (714) 367-9779
CT, GP, Stroke Recovery

Monterey

Michael E. Davis, DO, D/C
172 Eldorado Street
Monterey, CA 93940
(408) 373-1551—FAX (408) 373-1140
FP, OS

Howard Press, MD, D/C
172 Eldorado Street
Monterey, CA 93940
(408) 373-1551—FAX (408) 373-1140
CT, DD, FP, NT, PM, YS

Newport Beach

Allen Green, MD
4019 Westerly Place, Suite 100
Newport Beach, CA 92660
(714) 251-8700—FAX (714) 251-8900
AC, CT, FP, NT, PM

Joan Resk, DO
4063 Birch Street, Suite 230
Newport Beach, CA 92660
(714) 863-1110
CD, CT, DD, OSM, NT, PM

Alan Sosin, MD, D/C
4321 Birch St., Suite 100
Newport Beach, CA 92660
(714) 851-1550—FAX (714) 851-9970
AC, CT, IM, NT

J. William Thompson, MD
4321 Birch St., #100
Newport Beach, CA 92660
(714) 851-1550—FAX (714) 851-9970
CT, PM

Fred Weisman, MD
4321 Birch, #100
Newport Beach, CA 92660
(714) 851-1550—FAX (714) 851-9970
CD, DIA, END, GE, IM, NT

Julian Whitaker, MD, DIPL
4321 Birch St., Suite 100
Newport Beach, CA 92660
(714) 851-1550—FAX (714) 851-9970
CD, CT, DIA, DD, NT, PM

North Hollywood

David C. Freeman, MD
11311 Camarillo St., #103
North Hollywood, CA 91602
(818) 985-1103
GP, NT, PM

Orange

James Vatcher, MD, D/C
872 S. Cedarwood St.
Orange, CA 92669—NO REFERRALS

Palm Springs

Edmund Chein, MD
2825 Tahquitz Way, Bldg. A
Palm Springs, CA 92262
(619) 327—8939
GP

Sean Degnan, MD
2825 Tahquitz McCallum, Suite 200
Palm Springs, CA 92262
(619) 320-4292—FAX (619) 322-9475
AC, CT, NT, PM

David Freeman, MD
2825 Tahquitz McCallum, Suite 200
Palm Springs, CA 92262
(619) 320-4292
GP, NT, PM

Porterville

John B. Park, MD, D/C
200 North G St.
Porterville, CA 93527
(209) 781-6224—FAX (209) 781-0294
AN, BA, FP, GP, PM, S

Rancho Cucamonga

Francis V. Pau, MD, D/C
9726 Foothill Blvd.
Rancho Cucamonga, CA 91730
(909) 987-4262
AC, CT, DIA, GP, IM, NT

Rancho Mirage

Charles Farinella, MD
69-730 Hwy. 111, #106A
Rancho Mirage, CA 92270
(619) 324-0734
CT, GP, PM

Redding

Bessie J. Tillman, MD, DIPL
2054 Market St.
Redding, CA 96001
(916) 246-3022
A, CT, DD, NT, PM, YS

Redlands

Felix Prakasam, MD
415 Brookside Ave.
Redlands, CA 92706
(909) 798-1614
AN, CT, DD, HO, NT, OSM

Redwood City

Rajan Patel, MD
1779 Woodside Rd., #101
Redwood City, CA 94061
(415) 365-2969
A, CT, FP, NT, PM, YS

Sacramento

Michael Kwiker, DO, D/C
3301 Alta Arden, Suite 3
Sacramento, CA 95825
(916) 489-4400—FAX (916) 489-1710
A, CT, DIA, NT

Martin Mulders, MD, D/C
3301 Alta Arden, Suite 3
Sacramento, CA 95825
(916) 489-4400—FAX (916) 489-1710
CT, GP, IM, NT, PM

San Diego

John L. May, MD
458 26th Street
San Diego, CA 92102
(619) 685-6900—FAX (619) 685-6901
CD, CT, DD, HO, MM, Stroke

San Francisco

Scott V. Anderson, MD
345 West Portal Ave.
San Francisco, CA 94127
(415) 566-1000
CT, DD, GP, MM, NT, PM

Laurens N. Garlington, MD
56 Scenic Way
San Francisco, CA 94121
(415) 751-9600—FAX (415) 750-0466
Anesthesiology

Richard A. Kunin, MD
2698 Pacific Ave.
San Francisco, CA 94115
(415) 346-2500—FAX (415) 346-4991
CT, DD, HYP, PM, P, PO

Paul Lynn, MD, DIPL
345 W. Portal Ave., 2nd Floor
San Francisco, CA 94127
(415) 566-1000—FAX (415) 665-6732
A, AR, CT, DD, NT, PM

Wai-Man Ma, MD, D/C
728 Pacific Ave., #611
San Francisco, CA 94133
(415) 397-3888
FP

Denise R. Mark, MD, DIPL
345 W. Portal Ave., 2nd Floor
San Francisco, CA 94127
(415) 566-1000—FAX (415) 665-6732
CT, DIA, DD, IM, PM, YS

Gary S. Ross, MD
500 Sutter, #300
San Francisco, CA 94102
(415) 398-0555
A, AC, CT, DD, FP, NT, PM

Bruce Wapen, MD
P.O. Box 77007
San Francisco, CA 94107
(415) 696-4500
Emergency Med.

San Jacinto

Hiten Shah, MD
229 W. 7th
San Jacinto, CA 92583
(909) 487-2550
GP, NT, PM

San Jose

F. T. Guilford, MD
2674 N. First St., #101
San Jose, CA 95134
(408) 433-0923—FAX (408) 433-0947
A, CT, NT, PM

San Leandro

Steven H. Gee, MD, DIPL
595 Estudillo St.
San Leandro, CA 94577
(510) 483-5881
AC, BA, CT, GP

San Marcos

William C. Kubitschek, DO
1194 Calle Maria
San Marcos, CA 92069
(619) 744-6991
AC, FP, NT, OSM, PM, PMR

San Rafael

Scott v. Anderson, MD
25 Mitchell Blvd., #8
San Rafael, CA 94903
(415) 472-2343
DD, GP, MM, NT, PM

Santa Barbara

Kenneth J. Frank, MD
831 State St., #280
Santa Barbara, CA 93101
(805) 730-7420—FAX (805) 730-7434
A, BA, FP, NT, PM

H. J. Hoegerman, MD, DIPL
101 W. Arrellaga, Ste. D
Santa Barbara, CA 93101
(805) 963-1824
A, CT, CD, GP, DIA, FP, RHU

James K. Kwako, MD
1805-D East Cabrillo Blvd.
Santa Barbara, CA 93018
(805) 565-3959—FAX (805) 565-3989
AC, CT, FP, NT, PM

Santa Maria

Nolan T. Higa, MD, D/C
937 E. Main St., #106
Santa Maria, CA 93454
(805) 347-0067/68—FAX (805) 929-2032
AN, CT

Santa Monica

Hyla Cass, MD
513 Wilshire Blvd., #236
Santa Monica, CA 90401—NO REFERRALS

Michael Rosenbaum, MD
2730 Wilshire Blvd., #110
Santa Monica, CA 90403
(310) 453-4424
A, HGL, MM, NT, P, YS

Murray Susser, MD, DIPL
2730 Wilshire Blvd., #110
Santa Monica, CA 90403
(310) 453-4424—FAX (310) 828-0261
A, CT, NT, OME

Cynthia Watson, MD
530 Wilshire Blvd., #203
Santa Monica, CA 90401
(310) 393-0937
FP, GYN, NT, PM, PD, YS

Chi H. Yang, MD
1260 15th Street, #1119
Santa Monica, CA 90404
(310) 587-2441
CT, GP

Santa Rosa

Ron Kennedy, MD, D/C
2460 West Thrid St., Suite 225
Santa Rosa, CA 95401
(707) 576-0100—FAX (707) 576-1700
CT, END, NT, PM, PT, YS

Terri Su, MD, D/C
95 Montgomery Dr., #220
Santa Rosa, CA 95404
(707) 561-7560—(707) 571-8929
AC, AN, CT, FP, NT, PM

Sherman Oaks

Rosa M. Ami Belli, MD
13481 Cheltenham Dr.
Sherman Oaks, CA 91423—
NO REFERRALS

Simi Valley

Derrick D'Costa, MD
2816 Sycamore Dr., #101
Simi Valley, CA 93065
(805) 522-1344—FAX (805) 522-2074
BA, FP, HYP, MM, NT, PM

Smith River

JoAnn Vipond, MD
12559 Hwy. 101 North
Smith River, CA 95567
(707) 487-3405
CT, NT, PM

Stanton

William J. Goldwag, MD
7499 Cerritos Ave.
Stanton, CA 90680
(714) 827-5180
CT, NT, PM

Stockton

Luigi Pacini, MD
1307 N. Commerce St.
Stockton, CA 95202
(209) 464-7757
CT, CT, IM, PM

Walter S. Yourchek, MD
4553 Quail Lakes Dr.
Stockton, CA 95207
(209) 951-1133
Dermatology, S

Studio City

Charles E. Law Jr., MD
3959 Laurel Canyon Blvd., Suite I
Studio City, CA 91604
(818) 761-1661
AC, BA, CT, GP, NT, PM

Upland

Bryan P. Chan, MD
1148 San Bernardino Rd., #E-102
Upland, CA 91786
(909) 920-3578—FAX (909) 949-1238
FP

Van Nuys

Salvacion Lee, MD
14428 Gilmore St.
Van Nuys, CA 91401
(818) 785-7425
BA, CT, GP, HGL, NT, PM

Walnut Creek

Ingrid A. Bellwood, MD
1300 Boulevard Way
Walnut Creek, CA 94595—NO REFERRALS

Alan Shifman Charles, MD
1414 Maria Lane
Walnut Creek, CA 94596
(510) 937-3331
AC, CT, DD, FP, OM

COLORADO

Boulder

Michael A. Zeligs, MD
1000 Alpine, #211
Boulder, CO 80304
(303) 442-5492
AN, END, MM, NT, PM

Colorado Springs

James R. Fish, MD, DIPL
3030 N. Hancock
Colorado Springs, CO 80907
(719) 471-2273
CT, HYP, PM

M. Martin Hine, MD, D/C
303 S. Circle, #202
Colorado Springs, CO 80910
(719) 632-7003
GP

George Juetersonke, DO, DIPL
5455 N. Union, #200
Colorado Springs, CO 80918
(719) 528-1960—FAX (719) 528-5607
A, AC, CT, HGL, NT. OSM, P

Carl Osborn, DO
6050 Erin Park, #200
Colorado Springs, CO 80918
(719) 260-8122
CT, DD, OS, PMR, YS

Denver

Lauren E. Mitchell, DO
2222 E. 18th Ave.
Denver, CO 80206
(303) 333-3733—FAX (303) 333-1351
CT, DD, OSM, PM, WR, YS

Durango

Michele A. Fecteau, DO
1911 Main Ave., #101
Durango, CO 81301
(970) 247-1160
CT, DD, OS, PMR, YS

Carl E. Osborn, DO
1911 Main, #101
Durango, CO 81301
(970) 247-1160
CT, DD, OS, PMR, YS

Grand Junction

William L. Reed, MD
2700 G Road, #1-B
Grand Jct., CO 81505—NO REFERRALS

Lakewood

Terry Grossman, MD, D/C
255 Union St., #440
Lakewood, CO 80228
(303) 986-9455
CT, FP, NT, MM

Littleton

Milt Hammerly, MD, D/C
5161 E. Arapahoe Rd. #290
Littleton, CO 80122
(303) 694-2626—FAX (303) 796-8174
FP, NT, PH, PM

CONNECTICUT

Bridgeport

Tadeusz A. Skowron, MD, D/C
50 Ridgefield Ave., #317
Bridgeport, CT 06610
(203) 368-1450
GP, IM

Middlebury

Henry Sobo, MD
900 Straits Turnpike
Middlebury, CT 06762
(203) 598-0400
GP

Milford

Alan R. Cohen, MD, D/C
67 Cherry Street
Milford, CT 06460
(203) 877-1936
FP, NT, PD, PM, YS

Orange

Robban Sica, MD, D/C
325 Post Rd.
Orange, CT 06477
(203) 799-7733—FAX (203) 799-3560
A, AC, NT, PM, P, YS

Torrington

Jerrold N. Finnie, MD, D/C
333 Kennedy Dr., #204
Torrington, CT 06790
(203) 489-8977
A, CT, CS, NT, RHI, YS

Weston

Sidney M. Baker, MD
40 Hillside Rd. No.
Weston, CT 06883-1514—NO REFERRALS

Westport

Marie A. Di Pasquale, MD
29 Old Hill Farms Rd.
Westport, CT 06880—NO REFERRALS

DELAWARE

Millsboro

George Yossif, MD, PhD, DIPL
559 E. Dupont Hwy.
Millsboro, DE 19966
(302) 855-6949 or (800) 858-3370
FAX (302) 934-7949
CT, END, IM, NT, P, PM

DISTRICT OF COLUMBIA

Washington

Andrew Baer, MD
4123 Connecticut Ave. N.W.
Washington, D.C. 20008—NO REFERRALS

Paul Beals, MD, D/C
2639 Connecticut Ave N.W., Suite 100
Washington, D.C. 20037
(202) 332-0370
CT, FP, NT, PM

George H. Mitchell, MD
2639 Connecticut Ave. NW, Suite C-100
Washington, DC 20008
(202) 265-4111
A, NT

Aldo M. Rosemblat, MD, D/C
5225 Wisconsin Ave. N.W., #401
Washington, DC 20015
(202) 237-7000—FAX (202) 237-0017
AC, S

FLORIDA

Altamonte Springs

Donald Colbert, MD, D/C
100 Lakeshore Dr., #100
Altamonte Springs, FL 32714
(407) 776-6100
FP

Atlantic Beach

Richard Worsham, MD, D/C
303 1st Street
Atlantic Bch., FL 32233—NO REFERRALS

Boca Raton

Leonard Haimes, MD
7300 N. Federal Hwy., Suite 107
Boca Raton, FL 33487
(407) 994-3868—FAX (407) 997-8998
A, BA, CT, IM, NT, PM

Eric Hermansen, MD, DIPL
951 N.W. 13th St., #4B
Boca Raton, FL 33486
(407) 392-4920—(407) 392-4979
CT, HOM, IM, NT, PM

Robert Knight, MD, D/C
2900 N. Military Trail, #200
Boca Raton, FL 33431
(407) 995-7600
CT, Phlebology, Ultrasound

Robert D. Willix Jr., MD, D/C
1515 S. Federal Hwy., #306
Boca Raton, FL 33432
(407) 362-0724
CD, HGL, MM, NT, PM, PMR

Bradenton

Eteri Melinkov, MD, DIPL
116 Manatee Ave. East
Bradenton, FL 34208
(813) 748-7943
CD, CT, DIA, GP, PM, YS

Joseph Ossorio, MD
101 River Front Blvd., #150
Bradenton, FL 34205
(941) 748-8704—FAX (941) 741-8066
HYP, PM, P

Brandon

Carol Roberts, MD
1209 Lakeside Drive
Brandon, FL 33510
(813) 661-3662
A, CT, DD, GP, GYN, MM, PM

Cooper City

Murray Zedeck, DO, D/C
9100 Griffin Rd.
Cooper City, FL 33328
(407) 347-0007
FP, OS, RHU

Crystal River

Azael Borromeo, MD, DIPL
700 S.E. 5th Terrace, #7
Cryustal River, FL 34429
(904) 795-4711—FAX (904) 795-7559
BA, GP, PATHOLOGY, S

Fort Lauderdale

Stefano DiMauro, MD
1333 S. State Road 7, Tam O'Shanter Plaza
N. Lauderdale, FL 33068—NO REFERRALS

Bruce Dooley, MD, D/C
500 S.E. 17th Street
Fort Lauderdale, FL 33316
(305) 527-9355—FAX (305) 527-4167
A, CT, GP, NT, PM, YS

Bruce Dooley, MD, D/C
2583 E. Sunrise
Fort Lauderdale, FL 33304
(305) 564-8888—(305) 527-4167
A, CT, GP, NT, PM, YS

Adam Frent, DO
2583 E. Sunrise Blvd.
Fort Lauderdale, FL 33304
(313) 425-0235—FAX (313) 425-9003
CT, DIA, DD, FP, GER, HGL, PM

Anthony J. Sancetta, DO, D/C
4001 Ocean Dr., #206
Ft. Lauderdale, FL 33308
(954) 491-7796
CT, GP, NT, OS, PM, PMR

Fort Myers

Gary L. Pynckel, DO, DIPL
3840 Colonial Blvd., #1
Fort Myers, FL 33901
(941) 278-3377—FAX (941) 278-3702
CT, FP, GP, OSM, PM

Gainesville

George G. Feussner, MD
6717 N.W. 11th Place, #D
Gainellsville, FL 32605
(352) 331-7303—FAX (352) 332-8732
EEG, Chronic Pain Mgmt., Neurology

Leonard Smith, MD, D/C
720 S.W. 2nd Ave., #202
Gainesville, FL 32601
(352) 378-6262—(352) 378-0779
NT, S

Hollywood

S. Marshall Fram, MD
1425 Arthur St., #211
Hollyywood, FL 33020—NO REFERRALS

Herbert Pardell, DO, DIPL
210 S. Federal Hwy., Suite 302
Hollywood, FL 33020
(954) 922-0470—FAX (954) 921-5555
CT, DD, IM, MM, NT, PM

Homosassa

Carlos F. Gonzalez, MD, DIPL
7991 So. Suncoast Blvd.
Homossassa, FL 32646
(352) 382-8282
A, CD, CS, END, PMR, RHU

Indialantic

Glen Wagner, MD, D/C
121 6th Ave.
Indialantic, FL 32903
(407) 723-5915
A, AC, CT, GP, NT, YS

Jacksonville

Stephen Grable, MD
4205 Belfort Rd., #3075
Jacksonville, FL 32216
(904) 296-4977
DD, IM, PM, YS

John Mauriello, MD, D/C
4063 Salisbury Rd., #206
Jacksonville, FL 32216
(904) 296-0900—FAX (904) 296-8346
AN, CD, CT, NT, PM

Jupiter

Neil Ahner, MD, DIPL
1080 E. Indiantown Rd.
Jupiter, FL 33477
(407) 744-0077—FAX (407) 744-0094
CT, NT, PM

Lady Lake

Nelson Kraucak, MD, D/C
8923 N.E. 134th Ave.
Lady Lake, FL 32159
(904) 750-4333
AC, FP

Lakeland

Harold Robinson, MD, D/C
4406 S. Florida Ave., Suite 27
Lakeland, FL 33803
(813) 646-5088
CT, FP, GP, HGL, NT, PM

S. Todd Robinson, MD, D/C
4406 S. Florida Ave., Suite 30
Lakeland, FL 33803
(813) 646-5088
CT, FP, GP, HGL, NT, PM

Lake Worth

Sherri W. Pinsley, DO
2290 10th Ave. North, #605
Lake Worth, FL 33461
(407) 547-2264—FAX (407) 220-7332
CT, DD, GP, NT, OS, PMR

Largo

Carlos M. Garcia, MD, D/C
6519 126 Ave. North
Largo, FL 34643
(813) 532-9720—FAX (813) 532-9621
AN, CD, CT, IM, PM, Pain Mgmt.

Lauderhill

Herbert R. Slavin, MD, DIPL
7200 W. Commercial Blvd., Suite #210
Lauderhill, FL 33319
(305) 748-4991—FAX (305) 748-5022
CT, DIA, DD, GER, IM, NT

Maitland

Joya Lynn Schoen, MD, D/C
341 No. Maitland Ave., Suite 200
Maitland, FL 32751
(407) 644-2729—FAX (407) 644-1205
A, CT, HGL, HOM, OSM

Eileen M. Wright, MD
340 N. Maitland Ave., #100
Maitland, FL 32751
(407) 740-6100
GP, PM

Jack E. Young, MD
341 No. Maitland Ave., Suite 200
Maitland, FL 32751
(407) 644-2729—FAX (407) 644-1205
FP, GE, GP, MM, NT, PM

Marco Island

Richard Saitta, MD
1010 N. Barfield Dr.
Marco Island, FL 33937
(813) 642-8488
AC, CT, HO, IM, NT, PM

Merritt Island

James M. Parsons, MD, D/C
5 Minna Lane, #201
Merritt Island, FL 32953
(407) 452-0332
A, CT, HO, MM, NT, RHU

Miami

Joseph G. Godorov, DO
9055 S. W. 87th Ave., Suite 307
Miami, FL 33176
(305) 595-0671
CT, END, FP, HGL, NT, PM

Victor A. Marcial-Vega, MD, D/C
4037 Poinciana Ave.
Miami, FL 33133
(305) 442-1233—FAX/Phone (305) 445-4504
CT, DD, FP, GP, PM, Oncology

Herbert Pardell, DO, DIPL
7980 Coral Way
Miami, FL 33155
(305) 267-5790—FAX (305) 267-5855
CT, DD, IM, MM, NT, PM

Milton

Willliam Watson, MD, D/C
600 Stewart St. N.E.
Milton, FL 32570
(904) 623-3836—FAX (904) 623-2201
BA, GP, S

Naples

Bruce Dooley, MD, D/C
Grand Central Station 322, Goodlette Rd.
South
Naples, FL 33940
(813) 435-0543—FAX (813) 435-9011
A, CT, GP, NT, PM, YS

Myron B. Lezak, MD, D/C
800 Goodlette Rd. N., #270
Naples, FL 33940
(941) 649-7400—FAX (941) 649-6370
GE, IM

David Perlmutter, MD
800 Goodlette Rd. North, #270
Naples, FL 33940-5461
(813) 262-8971
DD, END, FP, NT, PM, Neurology

New Port Richey

Michael H. Beilan, DO
5211 U.S. Hwy 19 North, #200
New Port Richey, FL 34652
(813) 842-3111
FP, NT, OS, PM

North Miami Beach

Martin Dayton, DO, DIPL
18600 Collins Ave.
N. Miami Beach, FL 33160
(305) 931-8484
CT, FP, GER, NT, OSM, PM

Stefano DiMauro, MD
16666 N.E. 19th Ave., #101
N. Miami Beach, FL 33162
(305) 940-6474
A, CT, DIA, FP, NT, PMR

Sylvan R. Lewis, MD, D/C
18260 N.E. 19th Ave., #204
N. Miami Beach, FL 33162
(305) 940-4848—FAX (305) 936-8059
CD, IM, NT

Ocala

George Graves, DO
P.O. Box 2220
11512 County Road 316
Ft. McCoy (Ocala), FL 32134-2220
(352) 236-2525—FAX (352) 236-8610
A, AR, BA, CT, GP, OS

Orange City

Travis L. Herring, MD, D/C
106 West Fern Dr.
Orange City, FL 32763
(904) 775-0525
CT, FP, HOM, IM

Orlando

Kenneth Hoover, MD
2909 N. Orange Ave., #108
Orlando, FL 32804-4639
(407) 897-6002—FAX (407) 897-0907
A, CT, P., Env. Med.

Robert M. Knight, MD, D/C
2045 Glenwood Drive
Orlando, FL 32792
(407) 647-0808
CT, Phlebology, Ultrasound

Ormond Beach

Hana Chaim, DO
595 W. Granada Blvd., #D
Ormond Beach, FL 32174
(904) 672-9000
A, CT, Env. Med., FP, Sclerotherapy

Peter D. Hsu, DO
1650 Ocean Shore Blvd.
Ormond Beach, FL 32716
(904) 441-1477
A, FP, GP, NT, OS, PM

Palm Bay

Neil Ahner, MD, DIPL
1663 Georgia St.
Palm Bay, FL 32907
(407) 729-8581—FAX (407) 729-6079
CT, NT, PM

Palm Harbor

Glenn Chapman, MD, D/C
34621 US Hwy. 19 N.
Palm Harbor, FL 34684
(813) 786-1661
FP, GP, NT, PM

Panama City

Naima Abdel-Ghany, MD, PhD, DIPL
340 W. 23rd Street, Suite E
Panama City, FL 32405
(904) 763-7689
A, CD, CT, IM, PUD, PH, PM

James W. De Ruiter, MD, D/C
2202 State Ave., #311
Panama City, FL 32405
(904) 785-1517—FAX (904) 784-1271
OBS-GYN

Pembroke Pines

Eric Rosenkrantz, MD, D/C
1551 N. Palm Avenue
Pembroke Pines, FL 33026
(954) 432-8511
CD, CT, GER, IM

Pensacola

Ward Dean, MD
P.O. Box 11097
Pensacola, FL 32524
(904) 484-0595
CT, DD, END, NT, Anti-aging, Wght. Red.

Plantation

Robert M. Knight, MD, D/C
8200 W. Sunrise Blvd., #D4
Plantation, FL 33322
(305) 452-0529
CT, Phlebology, Ultrasound

Pompano Beach

Fariss D. Kimbell Jr., MD, D/C
3450 Park Central Blvd. N.
Pompano Beach, FL 33064
(305) 977-3700
CT, FP, GER, NT, Neurology, Neurosurgery

Dan C. Roehm, MD
3400 Park Central Blvd. N., Suite 3450
Pompano Beach, FL 33064
(305) 977-3700—FAX (305) 977-0180
CD, CT, IM, MM, NT, OME

Anthony J. Sancetta, DO, D/C
3450 Park Central Blvd. N.
Pompano Beach, FL 33064
(954) 977-3700
CT, GP, NT, OS, PM, PMR

Port St. Lucie

Ricardo V. Barbaza, MD, D/C
1874 S.E. Port St. Lucie Blvd.
Port St. Lucie, FL 34952
(561) 335-4994
GP, NT, PM

Sarasota

Thomas McNaughton, MD
1521 Dolphin St.
Sarasota, FL 34236
(941) 365-6273—FAX (941) 365-4269
CT, GP, NT, PM

Joseph Ossorio, MD
2345 Bee Ridge Rd., #5
Sarasota, FL 34239
(941) 921-1412
HYP, PM, P

Sebastian

Peter Holyk, MD, D/C
680 Jordan Ave.
Sebastian, FL 32958
(407) 388-1222
A, CT, DIA, DD, Ophthal.

St. Petersburg

Daniel S. Stein, MD, D/C
3527 1st Ave. South
St. Petersburg, FL 33711
(813) 328-8000
CT, GYN, OBS, PM, S

Ray Wunderlich Jr., MD, DIPL
1152 94th Ave. North
St. Petersburg, FL 33702
(813) 822-3612—FAX (813) 578-1370
A, BA, CT, DD, HGL, MM, PO

Stuart

Neil Ahner, MD, DIPL
705 North Federal Hwy.
Stuart, FL 34994
(407) 692-9200—FAX (407) 692-9888
CT, NT, PM

Sherri W. Pinsley, DO
7000 S.E. Federal Hwy., Suite #302
Stuart, FL 34997
(407) 220-1697—(407) 220-7332
CT, DD, GP, NT, OS, PMR

Tallahassee

Royce V. Jackson, MD, D/C
1630-A N. Plaza Drive
Tallahassee, FL 32317
(904) 656-8846
CT, NT, PM

Tampa

Donald J. Carrow, MD
3902 Henderson Blvd., Suite 206
Tampa, FL 33629
(813) 832-3220—FAX (813) 282-1132
AR, CD, CT, DIA, HGL, HO

James C. Etheridge, MD, PA, D/C
13615 Bruce B. Downs Blvd., #113
Tampa, FL 33613
(813) 971-9850—FAX (812) 971-9867
CT, DIA, IM, S

Eugene H. Lee, MD
1804 W. Kennedy Blvd. #A
Tampa, FL 33606
(813) 251-3089—FAX (813) 251-5668
AC, CT, NT, PM, GP, HGL

Tavares

James Coy, MD, D/C
204 Texas Ave.
Tavares, FL 32778
(904) 742-7344
A, CT, GP

Vero Beach

John Song, MD
1360 U.S. 1, #1
Vero Beach, FL 32960
(407) 569-3566
FP, GP, IM, NT, PM, S

West Palm Beach

Antonio L. Court, MD, D/C
2260 Palm Beach Lakes Blvd., #213
West Palm Beach, FL 33409
(407) 684-8137—FAX (407) 478-2155
CT, IM, HYP, NT, PH, PM

Winter Park

James M. Parsons, MD, D/C
Great Western Bank Bldg.
#303 2699 Lee Rd.
Winter Park, FL 32789
(407) 628-3399
A, CT, MM, NT, RHU, HO

Winter Springs

Peter D. Hsu, DO
116 W. SR 434
Winter Springs, FL 32708
(407) 327-3322—FAX (407) 327-3324
A, FP, GP, NT, OS, PM

GEORGIA

Albany

Thomas C. Paschal, MD, D/C
715 West Third Ave.
Albany, GA 31701-1875—NO REFERRALS

Atlanta

Stephen Edelson, MD, DIPL
3833 Roswell Rd, #110
Atlanta, GA 30342
(404) 841—0088
CT, NT, FP, Env Med, PM

David Epstein, DO
427 Moreland Ave., #100
Atlanta, GA 30307
(404) 525-7333—FAX (404) 521-0084
BA, CT, GP, NT, OSM, PM

Milton Fried, MD, DIPL
4426 Tilly Mill Road
Atlanta, GA 30360
(770) 451-4857—FAX (404) 451-8492
A, CT, IM, NT, PM, PO

Bernard Mlaver, MD, DIPL
4480 North Shallowford Rd.
Atlanta, GA 30338
(770) 395-1600
CT, NT, PM

Lavonne M. Painter, MD, D/C
99 Butler Street S.E.
Atlanta, GA 30303
(404) 730-1491
NT, PD, PH

William E. Richardson, MD, DIPL
1718 Peachtree St. N.W., #552
Atlanta, GA 30309
(404) 607-0570
CD, CT, FP, NT, PM, YS

Calhoon

Patricia Tygrett, DO
P.O. Box 1988
Calhoon, GA 30701
(706) 625-5204
FP

Camilla

Bertha Gunter, MD, D/C
24 N. Ellis Street
Camilla, GA 31730
(912) 336-7343—FAX (912) 336-7400
GP

Oliver L. Gunter, MD, DIPL
24 N. Ellis Street
Camilla, GA 31730
(912) 336-7343
CT, DIA, DD, GP, NT, PU

Clayton

William J. Lee, MD, D/C
P.O. Box 229
Clayton, GA 30525
(706) 782-4044
CT, S

College Park

D. Robert Howard, MD, D/C
1650 Virginia Ave.
College Park, GA 30337-2824
(404) 761-9500
DD, DIA, FP, NT, PMR

Covington

Gloria Freundlich, DO, D/C
4122 Tate Street
Covington, GA 30209
(770) 787-0880
CT, FP, NT, OSM, PM

Cumming

James L. Bean, MD
4575 Piney Grove Dr.
Cumming, GA 30130
(770) 887-9418 phone/FAX
GYN, NT, OBS

Gainesville

Kathryn Herndon, MD
530 Spring St.
Gainesville, GA 30503
(404) 503-7222
AC, AU, CT, NT, OS, PMR

Macon

James T. Alley, MD
380 Hospital Dr., #125
Macon, GA 31201
(912) 745-1575—FAX (912) 745-1974
Addiction Med., Rehab

Pooler

Carlos Tan, MD
4 Pooler Prof. Plaza
Pooler, GA 31322
(912) 748-6631
CT, GP, S

Smyrna

William Stafano, MD
645 Windy Hill Rd.
Smyrna, GA 30080—NO REFERRALS

Warner Robins

Terril J. Schneider, MD
205 Dental Drive, Ste. 19
Warner Robins, GA 31088
(912) 929-1027
A, CT, FP, NT, PM, PMR

HAWAII

Hilo

Douglas Miller, MD, D/C
400 Hualani St., #191-B
Hilo, HI 96720
(808) 961-5700—FAX (808) 961-3355
A, ENT, ENV MED

Honolulu

Wendell K. S. Foo, MD
2357 S. Beretania St., A-349
Honolulu, HI 96826
(808) 373-4007
AN, DD, Pain Mgmt.

Frederick Lam, MD, D/C
1270 Queen Emma St., #501
Honolulu, HI 96813
(808) 537-3311
A, AC, CT, FP, HGL

David Miyauchi, MD
1507 South King St., #407
A. Y. Wong Bldg.
Honolulu, HI 96826
(808) 949-8711 or (808) 988-2188
CT, GP, NT, PM

Kailua-Kona

Clifton Arrington, MD
P.O. Box 649
Kealakekua, HI 96750
(808) 322-9400
BA, CT, FP, NT, PM

IDAHO

Coeur d'Alene

Charles T. McGee, MD
226 Ironwood Dr., #4116
Coeur d'Alene, ID 83814—NO REFERRALS

Nampa

Stephen Thornburgh, DO, DIPL
824 17th Ave. So.
Nampa, ID 83651
(208) 466-3517
AC, CT, HOM, OS

ILLINOIS

Arlington Heights

Terrill K. Haws, DO, D/C
121 So. Wilke Road, Suite 111
Arlington Heights, IL 60005
(847) 577-9451—FAX (847) 577-8601
CT, DD, FP, GP, OSM

William J. Mauer, DO, FACAM, DIPL
3401 N. Kennicott Ave.
Arlington Heights, IL 60004
(800) 255-7030—FAX (847) 255-7700
CT, DIA, GP, NT, OSM, PM

Aurora

Thomas Hesselink, MD
688 So. Edgelawn Dr., Suite 1735
Aurora, IL 60506
(708) 844-0011—FAX (708) 844-0500
A, CT, GP, NT, PM, Candida

Belvidere

M. Paul Dommers, MD
554 S. Main St.
Belvidere, IL 61008
(815) 544-3112
AR, AU, CT, MM, PM

Braidwood

Bernard Milton, MD, D/C
233 E. Reed St.
Braidwood, IL 60408
(815) 458-6700
AC, AU, CT, FP, HGL, YS

Chicago

Alan F. Bain, DO, D/C
104 S. Michigan Ave., #705
Chicago, IL 60603
(312) 236-7010
AC, CT, IM, NT, OS

David Edelberg, MD, D/C
990 W. Fullerton Ave., #300
Chicago, IL 60614
(312) 296-6700
AC, DD, CT, IM, NT, YS

Razvan Rentea, MD
3525 W. Peterson, Suite 611
Chicago, IL 60659
(312) 583-7793—FAX (312) 583-7796
GP, MM, PM

Geneva

Richard E. Hrdlicka, MD, D/C
302 Randall Rd., #206
Geneva, IL 60134
(708) 232-1900
A, BA, FP, NT, PM, YS

Homewood

Frederick Weiss, MD
3207 W. 184th St.
Homewood, IL 60430—NO REFERRALS

Metamora

Betty Sy Go, MD
205 S. Engelwood Dr.
Metamora, IL 61548
(309) 367-2321—FAX (309) 367-2324
A, AC, CT, FP, NT, PM

Thomas Hesselink, MD
205 S. Engelwood
Metamora, IL 61548
(309) 367-2321—FAX (309) 367-2324
A, CT, GP, NT, PM, Candida

Moline

Terry W. Love, DO, DIPL
2610 41st Street
Moline, IL 61252
(309) 764-2900
CT, NT, PM

Naperville

Robert C. Filice, MD
1280 Iroquois Dr., #200
Naperville, IL 60563
(708) 369-1220
A, CT, END, NT, PM, YS

Oak Park

Paul J. Dunn, MD
715 Lake St.
Oak Park, IL 60301
(708) 383-3800
CT, HGL, NT, OSM, PM, YS

Ross A. Hauser, MD, D/C
715 Lake St.
Oak Park, IL 60301
(708) 848-7789—FAX (708) 848-7763
AN, CT, DD, NT, PMR, RHU

Ottawa

Terry W. Love, DO, DIPL
645 W. Main
Ottawa, IL 61350
(815) 434-1977
AR, CT, GP, OSM, RHU, PM

Schaumburg

Joseph Mercola, DO, D/C
1443 W. Schaumburg Rd., #250
Schaumburg, IL 60194
(708) 980-1777
A, AR, CT, GP, NT, RHU, YS

Skokie

John H. Olwin, MD
9631 Gross Point Road
Skokie, IL 60076
(708) 676-4030
CT, S

Sugar Grove

H. B. De Bartolo Jr., MD
11 De Bartolo Dr.
Sugar Grove, IL 60554
(708) 859-1818—FAX (708) 859-2021
A, ENT, LM, NT, PM, Chron. Fatigue,
Snoring

Woodstock

John R. Tambone, MD
102 E. South St.
Woodstock, IL 60098
(815) 338-2345
A, CT, GP, NT, PM, HYP

INDIANA

Clarksville

George Wolverton, MD, DIPL
647 Eastern Blvd.
Clarksville, IN 47130
(812) 282-4309
CD, CT, FP, GYN, PM, PD

Elkhart

Douglas W. Elliott, MD, D/C
1506 Osolo Rd., #A
Elkhart, IN 46514
(219) 264-9635
FP

Evansville

Harold T. Sparks, DO, DIPL
3001 Washington Ave.
Evansville, IN 47714
(812) 479-8228—FAX (812) 479-7327
A, AC, BA, CT, FP, PM

Franklin

Merrill Wesemann, MD
251 E. Jefferson
Franklin, IN 46131
(317) 736-6121
AC, AU, FP, HYP

Highland

Cal Streeter, DO, DIPL
9635 Saric Court
Highland, IN 46322
(219) 924-2410—FAX (219) 924-9079
A, CD, CT, FP, OSM, PM

Indianapolis

Kevin Cantwell, MD
11715 Fox Rd., #400-227
Indianapolis, IN 46236-8923
(317) 870-9360
GP

David A. Darbro, MD, DIPL
2124 E. Hanna Ave.
Indianapolis, IN 46227
(317) 787-7221
A, AR, CT, DD, FP, PM

Gary L. Moore, MD, D/C
3351 N. Meridan St. #202
Indianapolis, IN 46208
(317) 923-8978—FAX (317) 923-8982
A, CT, DD, MM, NT, PM

Laurence Webster, MD
6801 Lake Plaza Dr., #B-208
Indianapolis, IN 46220
(317) 841-9046
A, CT, DD, NT, PM, YS, WR

Lynn

David Chopra, MD
P.O. Box 636
Lynn, IN 47355
(317) 874-2411
AC, BA, CT, DD, GER, IM

Mooresville

Norman E. Whitney, DO
P.O. Box 173—492 S. Indiana St.
Mooresville, IN 46158
(317) 831-3352
AR, CD, DD, DIA, FP, NT

North Manchester

Marvin D. Dziabis, MD
300 W. Seventh Street
North Manchester, IN 46962
(219) 569-2274
Anatomic Pathology, Clin. Pathology,
Nuclear Med.

South Bend

Keim T. Houser, MD
515 N. Lafayette Blvd.
South Bend, IN 46601
(219) 232-2037
GYN, OBS

David E. Turfler, DO
336 W. Navarre St.
South Bend, IN 46616
(219) 233-3840
A, FP, GP, HGL, OBS, OSM

Valparaiso

Myrna D. Browbridge, DO, D/C
850-C Marsh St.
Valparaiso, IN 46383
(219) 462-3377
AC, AR, CT, GP, NT, OSM

Winchester

Oscar Ordonez, MD
400 South Oak
Winchester, IN 47394
(317) 584-6600
IM

IOWA

Davenport

David Nebbeling, DO
622 E. 38th Street
Davenport, IA 52807
(319) 391-0321—FAX (319) 391-5741
CT, GP, HGL, NT, OS, PM

Sioux City

Horst G. Blume, MD
700 Jennings St.
Sioux City, IA 51105
(712) 252-4386
CT, DD, Neuro, NT, OS, Pain Mgmt., S

KANSAS

Coffeyville

J. E. Block, MD, D/C
1501 W. 4th
Coffeyville, KS 67337
(316) 251-2400
CD, IM

Garden City

Terry Hunsberger, DO, D/C
602 N. 6th St.—P.O. Box 679
Garden City, KS 67846
(316) 275-7128
BA, CT, FP, NT, OSM, PM

Hays

Roy N. Neil, MD
105 West 13th
Hays, KS 67601
(913) 628-8341
BA, CD, CT, DD, NT, PM

Kansas City

John Gamble, Jr., DO
1606 Washington Blvd.
Kansas City, KS 66102
(913) 321-1140
GP, FP, DIA, DD, NT, OSM

Topeka

John Toth, MD
2115 S.W. 10th
Topeka, KS 66604
(913) 232-3330—FAX (913) 232-4066
FP, NT, PM, Sclerotherapy

KENTUCKY

Berea

Edward K. Atkinson, MD, D/C
448 Calico Rd.
Berea, KY 40403
(606) 925-2252
AN, CT

Bowling Green

John C. Tapp, MD
414 Old Morgantown Rd.
Bowling Green, KY 42101
(502) 781-1483
CT, GYN, MM, PD, P. RHU

Louisville

Kirk Morgan, MD, FACAM, DIPL
9105 U.S. Hwy. 42

Louisville, KY 40059
(502) 228-0156—FAX (502) 228-0512
CD, CT, FP, MM, NT, YS

Somerset

Stephen S. Kiteck, MD
1301 Pumphouse Rd.
Somerset, KY 42501
(606) 678-5137
FP, IM, PD, PM

LOUISIANA

Chalmette

Saroj T. Tampira, MD
800 W. Virtue St., Ste. 207
Chalmette, LA 70043
(504) 277-8991
CD, DD, DIA, IM

Gretna

Diana Betancourt, MD
522 3rd Street
Gretna, LA 70053
(504) 363-0101
GP, NT, PD, PUD

Jefferson

Charles C. Mary Jr., MD
1201 S. Clearview Pkwy., #100
Jefferson, LA 70121
(504) 737-4636
IM, GE

Kenner

Maria Hernandez-Abril, MD
3814 Williams Blvd.
Kenner, LA 70065
(504) 443-4306—FAX (504) 443-4547
GP

Lafayette

Sydney Crackower, MD, D/C
701 Robley Dr., #100
Lafayette, LA 70503
(318) 988-4116
CT, FP, GER

Mandeville

James Carter, MD
800 Hwy. 3228
Mandeville, LA 70448
(504) 626-1985
CT, FP, NT, PM

Roy M. Montalbano, MD
120 Century Oaks Lane
Mandeville, LA 70471—NO REFERRALS

Newellton

Joseph R. Whitaker, MD
P.O. Box 458
Newellton, LA 71357
(318) 467-5131
CT, GP, IM

New Iberia

Adonis J. Domingue, MD, DIPL
602 N. Lewis, #600
New Iberia, LA 70560
(318) 365-2196
GP

New Orleans

James P. Carter, MD
1430 Tulane Avenue
New Orleans, LA 70112
(504) 588-5136—FAX (504) 584-3540
GP, NT, PM

Janet Perez Chiesa, MD
360 Millaudon St.
New Orleans, LA 70118-3761
(504) 484-6655
GP, IM, PM, Neurology

Simmesport

Steve Kuplesky, MD, D/C
296 Christine Lane
Simmesport, LA 71369
(318) 941-2671
CT, GP, NT, Emerg. Med.

MAINE

Eliiot

Dayton Haigney, MD, D/C
46 Dow Highway
Eliot, ME 03903
(207) 439-1068
A, CT, DD, NT, PM, PMR, HYP

Van Buren

Joseph Cyr, MD
47 Main Street, P.O. Box 448
Van Buren, ME 04785
(207) 868-5273
CT, GP, OBS

Waterville

Arthur B. Weisser, DO
184 Silver St.
Waterville, ME 04901
(207) 873-7721—FAX (207) 873-7724
CT, FP, GP, NT, OS, PM

MARYLAND

Annapolis

Cheryl Brown-Christopher, MD
1419 Forest Dr., #202
Annapolis, MD 21403
(410) 268-5005
AR, CT, DIA, FP, HYP, PM, WR

Baltimore

Lisa P. Battle, MD, MPH
3100 Wyman Park Dr.
Baltimore, MD 21211
(410) 338-3059/522-9933
FP

Alexander P. Cadoux, MD, D/C
2324 W. Joppa Road, #100
Baltimore, MD 21093
(410) 296-3737—FAX (410) 296-0650
A, CT, FP, MM, NT, PM

Ronald Parks, MD, D/C
3655B Old Court Rd., #19
Baltimore, MD 21208-3905
(410) 486-5656
CT, GP, NT, PM, PO

Binyamin Rothstein, DO, DIPL
2835 Smith Ave., #209
Baltimore, MD 21209
(410) 484-2121
A, CT, GP, NT, OS, RHU

Laurel

Paul V. Beals, MD, D/C
9101 Cherry Lane Park, Suite 205
Laurel, MD 20708
(301) 490-9911
CT, FP, NT, PM

Rockville

Norton Fishman, MD, D/C
11140 Rockville Pike, #520
Rockville, MD 20852
(301) 816-3000
CT, GER, IM, PM

Harry Lai, MD
21 Wall Street
Rockville, MD 20850—NO REFERRALS

Bruce Rind, MD, D/C
11140 Rockville Pike, #520
Rockville, MD 20852
(301) 816-3000—-FAX (301) 816-0011
AC, CT, NT, OS, CH, PN, MUSIC
DISORDERS

MASSACHUSETTS

Barnstable

Michael Janson, MD, FACAM, DIPL
275 Mill Way—P.O. Box 732
Barnstable, MA 02630
(508) 362-4343—FAX (508) 362-1525
A, CD, CT, NT, OME, YS

Boston

Ruben Oganesov, MD, D/C
39 Brighton Ave.
Boston, MA 02134
(617) 783-5783—FAX (617) 783-1519
AC, CT, GP, NT, PMR

Brookline

Judith K. Shabert, MD
125 Rockwood Street
Brookline, MA 02146
(617) 738-0370
OBS, GYN, NT

Cambridge

Guillermo Asis, MD, DIPL
2500 Massachusetts Ave.
Cambridge, MA 02140
(617) 661-6225—FAX (617) 492-2002
A, CD, CT, NT, OME, YS

Hanover

Richard Cohen, MD, DIPL
51 Mill Street, #1
Hanover, MA 02339
(617) 829-9281—FAX (617) 829-0904
A, CD, CT, NT, PM, YS

Lowell

Svetlana Kaufman, MD, D/C
24 Merrimack St., #323
Lowell, MA 01852
(508) 453-5181
A, CT, GP, GER, PM, RHI

Newton

Carol Englender, MD, D/C
1126 Beacon St.
Newton, MA 02161
(617) 965-7770
A, FP, NT, PM, Env. Medicine

Northampton

Barry D. Elson, MD
52 Maplewood Shops—Old South St.
Northampton, MA 01060
(413) 584-7787—FAX (413) 584-7778
A, CT, NT, PM, YS

Wellesley

Richard Cohen, MD, DIPL
70 Walnut Street
Wellesley, MA 02181
(617) 239-0231
A, CD, CT, NT, PM, YS

West Boylston

Vera Jackson, MD, D/C
360 West Boylston St., #107
West Boylston, MA 01583
(508) 854-1380
A, CT, DD, GP, NT, PM

N. Thomas La Cava, MD
360 West Boylston St., Suite 107
West Boylston, MA 01583
(508) 854-1380—(508) 854-1377
NT, PD, PM

MICHIGAN

Atlanta

Leo Modzinski, DO, MD, DIPL
12394 State St.
Atlanta, MI 49709
(517) 785-4254—FAX (517) 785-2273
BA, CT, FP, GP, NT, OSM

Bay City

Parveen A. Malik, MD
808 N. Euclid Ave.
Bay City, MI 48706
(517) 686-3760
BA, CT, FP, GP, NT, PM

Canton

Jarmina Ramirez-Salcedo, MD, D/C
2038 Otter Pond Lane
Canton, MI 48188
(313) 397-5842 phone/FAX
FP

Clarkston

Nedra Downing, DO
5639 Sashabaw Road
Clarkston, MI 48346

(810) 625-6677
A, GP, NT, OS, PM, YS

Farmington Hills

Paul A. Parente, DO, DIPL
30275 Thirteen Mile Rd.
Farmington Hills, MI 48018
(810) 626-7544
BA, CT, GP, PM

Albert J. Scarchilli, DO, DIPL
30275 Thirteen Mile Rd.
Farmington Hills, MI 48018
(810) 626-7544
BA, CT, FP, GP, MM, OSM, PM

Mary E. Short, DO
30275 Thirteen Mile Rd.
Farmington Hills, MI 48334
(810) 626-7544
FP, DD, NT, PM, GYN, YS

Flint

William M. Bernard, DO, D/C
1044 Gilbert Street
Flint, MI 48532
(810) 733-3140
A, CT, FP, GER, OSM, PM

Kenneth Ganapini, DO, D/C
1044 Gilbert St.
Flint, MI 48532
(810) 733-3140
FP, GP, OSM, PM, YS

Grand Rapids

Grant Born, DO, DIPL
2687 44th St. S.E.
Grand Rapids, MI 49512
(616) 455-3550—FAX (616) 455-3462
A, CT, FP, GYN, PM, PMR

Tammy Geurkink-Born, DO, D/C
2687 44th St. S.E.
Grand Rapids, MI 49512
(616) 455-3550—FAX (616) 455-3462
CT, GP, PM, YS, Laser

Highland Park

Elizabeth M. Gidney, MD
12850 Woodward Ave.
Highland Park, MI 48203
(313) 869-5070—FAX (313) 869-5072
GP

Jackson

J. Daniel Clifford, MD
300 W. Washington, #270
Jackson, MI 49201
(517) 787-9510
A, CT, IM

Linden

Marvin D. Penwell, DO, DIPL
319 S. Bridge Street
Linden, MI 48451
(313) 735-7809
A, CT, FP, GE, GYN, OSM

Livonia

Thomas A. Padden, DO, D/C
16828 Newburgh Rd.
Livonia, Mi 48154
(313) 432-1010—FAX (313) 432-9080
FP, PM

Norway

F. Michael Saigh, MD, D/C
411 Murray Rd. West U.S. 2
Norway, MI 49870
(906) 563-9600
FP

Parchment

Eric Born, DO
100 Maple Street
Parchment, MI 49004
(616) 344-6183
DIA, FP, NT, OS, PM, YS

Pontiac

Vahagn Agabian, DO
28 N. Saginaw St. Suite 1105
Pontiac, MI 48058
(810) 334-2424
CT, DD, DIA, GER, IM, OME

Saline

John G. Ghuneim, MD
Saline Prof. Office Bldg.
420 Russell, #204
Saline, MI 48176
(313) 429-2581—FAX (313) 429-3955
AC, AU, CT, IM, NT, PM,
Prolo-sclerotherapy

St. Clair Shores

Adam Frent, DO
23550 Harper Ave.
St. Clair Shores, MI 48080
(810) 779-5700—(810) 779-9296
CT, DIA, DD, FP, GER, HGL, PM

Washington

James Ziobron, DO, D/C
58060 Van Dyke
Washington, MI 48094
(810) 781-6523
A, CT, DD, F, P, YS

MINNESOTA

Minneapolis

Michael Dole, MD, DIPL
10700 Old County Rd. 15, Suite 350
Minneapolis, MN 55441
(612) 593-9458—FAX (612) 593-0097
FP, PM, YS

Jean R. Eckerly, MD, DIPL
10700 Old County Rd. 15, Suite 350
Minneapolis, MN 55441
(612) 593-9458—FAX (612) 593-0097
CT, IM, NT, OME, PM

MISSISSIPPI

Coldwater

Pravinchandra Patel, MD
P.O. Drawer DD
Coldwater, MS 38618
(601) 622-7011
CT, FP

Ocean Springs

James H. Waddell, MD
1520 Government Street
Ocean Springs, MS 39564
(601) 875-5505
AC, AN, AU, CT

Shelby

Robert Hollingsworth, MD
Drawer 87, 901 Forrest St.
Shelby, MS 38774
(601) 398-5106
CT, FP, GYN, OBS, PD, S

MISSOURI

Des Peres

Garry A. Johnson, MD, D/C
1926 Firethorn Drive
Des Peres, MO 63131
(314) 821-7616
AN

Florissant

Tipu Sultan, MD
11585 W. Florissant
Florissant, MO 63033
(314) 921-7100
A, AR, CT, HGL, PM

Independence

Lawrence Dorman, DO
9120 E. 35th Street
Independence, MO 64052
(816) 358-2712
AC, CT, MM, OSM, PM

Joplin

Ralph D. Cooper, DO
1608 E. 20th Street
Joplin, MO 64804
(417) 624-4323
FP, GP, GYN, OS, S

Kansas City

James F. Holleman, DO, D/C
3100 Main St., #201
Kansas City, MO 64111
(816) 561-6555—FAX (816) 561-6777
GP

Edward W. McDonagh, DO, FACAM, DIPL
2800-A Kendalwood Pkwy.
Kansas City, MO 64119
(816) 453-5940—FAX (816) 453-1140
CD, CT, DD, FP, HO, PM

James Rowland, DO
8133 Wornall Rd.
Kansas City, MO 64114
(816) 361-4077
AC, CT, DD, GP, HYP, OSM

Charles J. Rudolph, DO, PhD, FACAM, DIPL
2800-A Kendallwood Pkwy.
Kansas City, MO 64119
(816) 453-5940—FAX (816) 453-1140
CD, CT, DD, FP, HO, PM

Mountain Grove

Doyle B. Hill, DO
600 No. Bush
Mountain Grove, MO 65711
(417) 926-6643
A, CT, FP, GP, NT, OSM

Springfield

William C. Sunderwirth, DO
2828 N. National
Springfield, MO 65803
(417) 869-6260
CT, DIA, GP, OSM, PM, S

St. Louis

Octavio R. Chirino, MD
9701 Landmark Pdwy. Dr., #207
St. Louis, MO 63127
(314) 842-4802
OBS, GYN

Harvey Walker Jr., MD, PhD, FACAM, DIPL
138 N. Meramec Ave.
St. Louis, MO 63105
(314) 721-7227—FAX (314) 721-7247
CT, DIA, HGL, IM, NT, PM

Simon M. Yu, MD, D/C
11709 Old Ballas Rd., #200
St. Louis, MO 63141
(314) 605-5111—FAX (314) 991-5200
CD, CT, DIA, IM, NT, PM

Sullivan

Ronald H. Scott, DO
131 Meredith Lane
Sullivan, MO 63080
(314) 468-4932
GP, GER, GYN, NT, PM, OSM

Union

Clinton C. Hayes, DO
100 W. Main
Union, MO 63084
(314) 583-8911
CT, GP

MONTANA

Billings

David C. Healow, MD
1242 North 28th, #1001
Billings, MT 59102
(406) 252-6674
AC, AN

Richard A. Nelson, MD, D/C
1001 S. 24th West
Creekside Two, #202
Billings, MT 59108
(406) 656-7416
AC, IM, Neurology, NT, P, RHU

Red Lodge

Oliver B. Cooperman, MD
P.O. Box 707
Red Lodge, MT 59068
(406) 446-3055
P. Herbal Psychiatry

Shelby

Robert Stanchfield, MD, D/C
925 Oilfield Ave.
Shelby, MT 59474
(406) 434-5595—FAX (406) 434-2701
FP

White Sulphur Springs

Daniel J. Gebhardt, MD
Box 338-12 E. Main
White Sulphur Springs, MT 59645
(406) 547-3384
CT, GP, GYN, IM, PM, RHU

NEBRASKA

Hartington

Steve Vlach, MD, D/C
405 W. Darlene St.
Hartington, NE 68739
(402) 254-3935—FAX (402) 254-2393
CD, CT, DIA, FP, NT, WR, YS, Em Med

McCook

Kenneth W. Ellis, MD, D/C
1401 East "H" St., #A
McCook, NE 69001
(308) 345-8376
Osteopathic Surgery

Omaha

Richard J. Holcomb, MD, D/C
248 N. 129th Street
Omaha, NE 68154
(402) 334-7964—FAX (402) 391-6818
AN

Eugene C. Oliveto, MD
10804 Prairie Hills Dr.
Omaha, NE 68144
(402) 392-0233
CT, HYP, NT, PM, P, PO

Jeffrey Passer, MD, D/C
9300 Underwood Ave., Suite 520
Omaha, NE 68114
(402) 398-1200—FAX (402) 398-9119
BA, CT, IM, PM

Ord

Otis W. Miller, MD, D/C
408 So. 14th Street
Ord, NE 68862
(308) 728-3251
CT, FP, NT, P, YS

NEVADA

Gardnerville

Frank Shallenberger, MD
1524 Hwy. 395
Gardnerville, NV 89410
(702) 782-4164
CT, GP, HOM, NEURL THER, OXID MED

Las Vegas

Steven Holper, MD
3233 W. Charleston, #202
Las Vegas, NV 89102
(702) 878-3510—FAX (702) 878-1405
Phys. Rehab.

Ji-Zhou (Joseph) Kang, MD
5613 S. Eastern
Las Vegas, NV 89119
(702) 798-2992
A, AC, GP, IM, NT

Robert D. Milne, MD
2110 Pinto Lane
Las Vegas, NV 89106
(702) 385-1393
A, AC, CT, FP, NT, PM

M. Michael Robertson, MD
1150 S. Eastern Ave.
Las Vegas, NV 89104
(702) 385-4429—FAX (702) 385-1383
AN, CT, FP, NT, PMR, PM

F. Fuller Royal, MD
3663 Pecos McLeod
Las Vegas, NV 89121
(702) 732-1400
A, AC, CT, GP, HYP

Overton

William O. Murray, MD
P.O. Box 305
Overton, NV 89040
(702) 397-2677—FAX (702) 397-2420
FP

Reno

W. Douglas Brodie, MD
309 Kirman Ave., #2
Reno, NV 89502
(702) 324-7071
CT, DD, FP, GP, HOM, IM, NT, PM

David A. Edwards, MD, DIPL
6490 S. McCarran Bl., Ste. C24
Reno, NV 89509
(702) 827-1444—FAX (702) 827-2424
A, AC, CT, DD, PM, YS

Michael L. Gerber, MD, DIPL
3670 Grant Drive
Reno, NV 89509
(702) 826-1900
CT, MM, OME

Corazon Ibarra-Ilarina, MD, DIPL
6490 S. McCarran Blvd., Ste. C24
Reno, NV 89509
(702) 827-1444—FAX (702) 827-2424
CT, PM, Biol Med

Donald E. Soli, MD
708 North Center St.
Reno, NV 89501
(702) 786-7101
A, AR, CT, HGL, HO, PUD

Yiwen Y. Tang, MD
429 Plumb Lane
Reno, NV 89509—NO REFERRALS

NEW HAMPSHIRE

Derry

Keith D. Jorgensen, MD, D/C
44 Birch St., #304
Derry, NH 03038
(603) 432-8104
Otolaryngology

New London

Savely Yurkovsky, MD
12 Newport Road
New London, NH 03257-1999
(603) 526-2001
A, CD, CS, CT, NT, PM

NEW JERSEY

Bloomfield

Majid Ali, MD
320 Belleville Ave.
Bloomfield, NJ 07003
(201) 586-4111
A, PM, Pathology

Cherry Hill

Brian Karlin, DO
1916 Old Cuthbert Rd., #A-1
Cherry Hill, NJ 08034
(609) 429-3335
GP

Allan Magaziner, DO, DIPL
1907 Greentree Rd.
Cherry Hill, NJ 08003
(609) 424-8222—FAX (609) 424-2599
CT, NT, OSM, PM

Denville

Majid Ali, MD
95 E. Main Street
Denville, NJ 07834
(201) 586-4111—FAX (201) 586-8466
A, PM, Pathology

Edison

C. Y. Lee, MD, DIPL
952 Amboy Avenue
Edison, NJ 08837
(908) 738-9220—FAX (908) 738-1187
A, AR, AU, CT, DD, OME

Ralph Lev, MD, MS, FACAM, DIPL
952 Amboy Avenue
Edison, NJ 08837
(908) 738-9220—FAX (908) 738-1187
CD, CT, S

Richard B. Menashe, DO, DIPL
15 South Main St.
Edison, NJ 08837
(908) 906-8866—FAX (908) 906-0124
A, CD, CT, HGL, NT, YS

Egg Harbor Township

Edward M. Andujar, MD, D/C
3003 English Creek Center, #210
Egg Harbor Township, NJ 08234
(800) 606-8483—FAX (609) 646-3436
GP

Englewood Cliffs

Uttam L. Munver, MD, D/C
P.O. Box 1746
Englewood Cliffs, NJ 07632
(718) 991-8310
FP, P

Fort Lee

Gary Klingsberg, DO, DIPL
1355 15th St., #200
Fort Lee, NJ 07024
(201) 585-9368
A, CT, Env. Med., NT, PM, YS

Hackensack

Robin Leder, MD, D/C
235 Prospect Ave.
Hackensack, NJ 07601
(201) 525-1155
A, CT, NT, PM

Hackettstown

Robert A. Siegel, MD
2-B Doctors Park
Hackettstown, NJ 07840
(908) 850-1810
OB/GYN

Lakewood

Ivan Krohn, MD, D/C
117 E. County Line Rd.
Lakewood, NJ 08701
(908) 367-2345—FAX (908) 367-2727
CD, DD, GP

Middletown

David Dornfield, DO, D/C
18 Leonardville Rd.
Middletown, NJ 07748
(908) 671-3730—FAX (908) 706-1078
CT, DD, FP, NT, PM, PMR

Neil Rosen, DO, D/C
18 Leonardville Rd.
Middletown, NJ 07748
(908) 671-3730—FAX (908) 706-1078
FP, NT, OS, PM, PMR

Milburn

James Neubrander, MD, D/C
96 Milburn Ave., #200
Milburn, NJ 07041
(201) 275-0234—FAX (201) 275-1646
A, CT, MM, NT, PM, YS

Millville

Charles H. Mintz, MD
10 East Broad Street
Millville, NJ 08332
(609) 825-7372—FAX (609) 327-6588
GP, NT, PM

Passaic

Jose R. Sanchez-Pena, MD, D/C
124 Gregory Ave., #201
Passaic, NJ 07055
(201) 471-9800—FAX (201) 471-9240
CT, GER, IM, PUD

Paterson

Marvin Gastman, DO
100 Hamilton Plaza/Clark St., #317
Paterson, NJ 07501—NO REFERRALS

Piscataway

Laurence Rubenstein, DO
10 Plainfield Ave.
Piscataway, NJ 08854
(908) 469-1155—FAX (908) 457-9420
FP, OS

Princeton

Eric Braverman, MD, DIPL
212 Commons Way, Bldg. #2
Princeton, NJ 08540
(609) 921-1842—FAX (609) 921-6092
A, CT, DD, FP, IM, PM

Leonid Magidenko, MD, D/C
212 Commons Way Blvd., #2
Princeton, NJ 08540
(609) 921-1842—FAX (609) 921-6092
IM, PM

Ridgewood

Constance Alfano, MD, D/C
104 Chestnut
Ridgewood, NJ 07450
(201) 444-4622
A(food), Candida, BA, CT, GP, NT

Shrewsbury

David Dornfield, DO, D/C
167 Avenue at the Common, #1
Shrewsbury, NJ 07702
(908) 389-6455—FAX (908) 389-6365
CT, DD, FP, NT, PM, PMR

Neil Rosen, DO, D/C
167 Avenue at the Common, #1
Shrewsbury, NJ 07702
(908) 389-6455—FAX (908) 389-9365
FP, NT, OS, PM, PMR

Somerset

Marc Condren, MD
15 Cedar Grove Lane, #20
Somerset, NJ 08873
(908) 469-2133
A, FP, MM, NT

Toms River

Ivan Krohn, MD, D/C
2008 Rt. 37 E., #1
Toms River, NJ 08753
(908) 506-9200
CT, CD, DDP, GP

West Creek

Robert D. Miller, DO, D/C
196 Main St., P.O. Box 232
West Creek, NJ 08092
(609) 296-4643—FAX (609) 296-3393
FP, OS

West Orange

Faina Munits, MD, DIPL
51 Pleasant Valley Way
West Orange, NJ 07052
(201) 736-3743
A, CD, DIA, DD, HGL, PM

Woodcliff Lake

Joseph Spektor, MD
54 Indian Drive
Woodcliff Lake, NJ 07675—
NO REFERRALS

NEW MEXICO

Albuquerque

Ralph J. Luciani, DO, DIPL
2301 San Pedro N.E., Suite G
Albuquerque, MN 87110
(505) 888-5995
AC, AU, CT, FP, OSM, PM

Gerald Parker, DO
9577 Osuna N.E.
Albuquerque, NM 87111
(505) 271-4800
A, CT, AC, AR, GP, HO

John T. Taylor, DO
9577 Osuna N.E.
Albuerque, NM 87111
(505) 271-4800
A, AC, AR, CT, GP, HO

Las Cruces

Adex Cantu, MD
301 Perkins Dr.
Las Cruces, NM 88005
(505) 523-4858
A, AR, CT, GER, P, REHAB

Roswell

Annette Stoesser, MD
112 S. Kentucky
Roswell, NM 88201
(505) 623-2444—(505) 623-9693
A, CT, DIA, DD, FP, NT

Santa Fe

John L. Laird, MD, DIPL
1810 Calle de Sebastian, #H-4
Santa Fe, NM 87505
(505) 989-4690
CD, CT, DIA, END, GER

Bert A. Lies, Jr., MD
539 Harkle Rd., #D
Santa Fe, NM 87501
(505) 982-4821
AC, NT, PMR, R, RHU, Orth

Shirley B. Scott, MD
P.O. Box 2670
Santa Fe, NM 87504
(505) 986-9960
GE, MM, PM, YS

NEW YORK

Albany

Kenneth A. Bock, MD, FACAM, DIPL
Pinnacle Place, Suite 210
10 McKown Road
Albany, NY 12203
(518) 435-0082—FAX (518) 435-0086
A, CD, CT, FP, NT, PM

Brentwood

Juan J. Nolasco, MD, D/C
78 Wicks Rd., #1
Brentwood, NY 11717
(516) 434-4840
AC, GP, GYN, IM, PMR

Brewster

Jeffrey C. Kopelson, MD, D/C
221 Clock Tower Commons
Brewster, NY 10509
(914) 278-6800—FAX (914) 278-6897
CT, FP, NT, PM

Bronx

Richard Izquierdo, MD
1070 Southern Blvd., Lower Level
Bronx, NY 10459
(212) 589-4541
A, FP, GP, NT, PD, PM

Uttam L. Munver, MD, D/C
1963-A Daly Ave.
Bronx, NY 10460
(718) 991-8300
FP, P

Shashikant Patel, MD, D/C
405 East 187th Street
Bronx, NY 10458
(718) 365-7777—FAX (718) 365-1179
FP, IM

Brooklyn

Asya Benin, MD
2116 Ave. P
Brooklyn, NY 11229
(718) 338-1616
CD, DD, DIA, END, FP, GE, GER

Aldrick F. Chu-Fong, MD, D/C
185 Prospect Park S.W., #102
Brooklyn, NY 11218
(718)438-6565—FAX (718) 438-1361
CT, IM, Hematology, Oncology

Tova Rosen, MD
5001 14th Ave., #A-7
Brooklyn, NY 11219
(718) 435-9695
GP, PD, Minor Surg

Yelena Shvarts, MD, D/C
1309 West 7 Street
Brooklyn, NY 11204
(718) 259-2122—FAX (718) 259-3933
GP, PD

Tsilia Sorina, MD
2026 Ocean Ave.
Brooklyn, NY 11230
(718) 375-2600
CT, GP, NT, PM

Joseph Spektor, MD
2116 Avenue P
Brooklyn, NY 11229
(718) 377-3232
AN

Michael Teplitsky, MD
415 Oceanview Ave.
Brooklyn, NY 11235
(718) 769-0997—FAX (718) 646-2352
A, CD, CT, DIA, IM, PM

Pavel Yutsis, MD, DIPL
1309 W. 7th St.
Brooklyn, NY 11204
(718) 259-2122—FAX (718) 259-3933
A, CT, FP, NT, PD, PM, YS

Buffalo

Kalpana Patel, MD
65 Wehrle Drive
Buffalo, NY 14225
(716) 833-2213—FAX (716) 833-2244
A, CT, NT, PD, PM, HGL, YS

East Meadow

Christopher L. Calapai, DO, DIPL
1900 Hempstead Tnpke
East Meadow, NY 11554
(516) 794-0404—FAX (516) 794-0332
A, CT, FP, NT, OSM, YS

Falconer

Reino Hill, MD
230 West Main St.
Falconer, NY 14733
(716) 665-3505
CT, FP, PM

Forest Hills

Tsilia Sorina, MD
109-40 71st Road
Forest Hills, NY 11375
(718) 261-9400
GP, NT, PM

Fredonia

Robert F. Barnes, DO, D/C
3489 E. Main Rd.
Fredonia, NY 14063
(716) 679-3510—FAX (716) 679-3512
CT, NT, PM

Great Neck

Mary F. DiRico, MD, D/C
1 Kingspoint Rd.
Great Neck, NY 11024—NO REFERRALS

Hauppauge

Vincent C. Parry, DO
236 Northfield Road
Hauppauge, NY 11788
(516) 724-2233
FP, OS, S

Huntington

Serafina Corsello, MD, FACAM, DIPL
175 E. Main Street
Huntington, NY 11743
(516) 271-0222—FAX (516) 271-5992
CT, DD, MM, NT, OME, PM

Huntington Station

Michael Fass, MD, D/C
A-Plaza 680 E. Jericho Tnpke
Huntington Station, NY 11746
(516) 549-4607
CD, FP, GYN, NT

Lawrence

Mitchell Kurk, MD, D/C
310 Broadway
Lawrence, NY 11559
(516) 239-5540—(516) 371-2919
CT, FP, GER, NT, OME, PM

Lewiston

Donald M. Fraser, MD
5147 Lewiston Rd.
Lewiston, NY 14092
(716) 284-5777
Orth Surg

Mamaroneck

Monica Furlong, MD, D/C
921 W. Boston Post Rd.
Mamaroneck, NY 10543
(914) 381-7687—FAX (914) 381-0942
GP

Massena

Robert W. Snider, MD, D/C
284 Andrew Street
Massena, NY 13662
(315) 764-7328
A, CT, FP

Middletown

Henry C. Sobo, MD, D/C
825 Route 211E
Middletown, NY 10940
(914) 344-3278
A, BA, CD, CT, IM, NT, PM, HGL, WR, YS

Newburgh

Henry C. Sobo, MD, D/C
133 South Plank Rd.
Newburgh, NY 12550
(914) 561-6477
BA, IM

New York

Richard N. Ash, MD, D/C
860 Fifth Ave.
New York, NY 10021
(212) 628-3113—FAX (212) 249-3805
A, CD, CT, HYP, NT, MM, IM

Robert C. Atkins, MD
152 E. 55th St.
New York, NY 10022
(212) 758-2110—FAX (212) 751-1863
CT, HGL, OME

Tom Bolte, MD
133 E. 73rd Street
New York, NY 10021
(212) 861-9000 or (516) 897-8386
CD, CT, DIA, IM, NT, YS

Christopher L. Calapai, DO, DIPL
18 East 53 Street
New York, NY 10022
(212) 838-9100—FAX (212) 838-8803
A, CT, FP, NT, OSM, YS

Edward S. Cheslow, MD, D/C
107 W. 82nd St., #103
New York, NY 10024
(212) 362-0449
IM

Serafina Corsello, MD, FACAM, DIPL
200 W. 57th St., #1202
New York, NY 10019
(212) 399-0222
CT, DD, MM, NT, OME, PM

Robert Faylor, MD
377 Park Ave. South, #3
New York, NY 10016
(212) 679-6717—FAX (212) 679-6714
CT, IM

Leo Galland, MD
133 E. 73 St.
New York, NY 10021
(212) 861-9000
A, GE, IM, MM, NT, PO

Sheila George, MD
226 West 26th St., 5th Floor
New York, NY 10001
(212) 924-5900—FAX (212) 924-7600
AC, FP

Ronald Hoffman, MD, FACAM, DIPL
40 E. 30th Street
New York, NY 10016
(212) 779-1744—FAX (212) 779-0891
A, FP, HGL, NT, PM

Robin Leder, MD, D/C
159 W. 53rd St., #18D
New York, NY 10019
(212) 333-2626
A, CT, NT, PM

Warren M. Levin, MD, DIPL
24 W. 57th Street, #701
New York, NY 10019
(212) 397-5900—FAX (212) 397-6054
A, AC, CT, NT, OME, PM

Fred Pescatore, MD
152 East 55 Street
New York, NY 10022
(212) 758-2110
CT, DIA, END, GP, PM, PH

Jose R. Sanchez-Pena, MD, D/C
451 Park Ave. South, 2nd Floor
New York, NY 10016
(212) 779-0202—FAX (212) 779-1521
CT, GER, IM, PUD

Michael J. Teplitsky, MD
31 East 28th Street
New York, NY 10016
(212) 679-3700—FAX (212) 679-9730
A, CD, CT, DIA, IM, PM

Nancy Weiss, MD
109 East 36 Street
New York, NY 10016
(212) 683-8105
IM, RHU

Niagara Falls

Paul Cutler, MD, FACAM, DIPL
652 Elmwood Ave.
Niagara Falls, NY 14301
(716) 284-5140
A, CT, NT

Oneonta

Richard J. Ucci, MD, DIPL
521 Main Street
Oneonta, NY 13820
(607) 432-8752
CT, FP

Orangeburg

Neil L. Block, MD
14 Prel Plaza
Orangeburg, NY 10962
(914) 359-3300
A, CD, FP, IM, NT, PO

Plainview

Thomas K. Szulc, MD, D/C
720 Old Country Rd.
Plainview, NY 11803
(516) 931-1133—FAX (516) 931-1167
AC, AN, AU, Pain Mgmt.

Plattsburgh

Driss Hassam, MD, D/C
50 Court Street
Plattsburgh, NY 12901
(518) 561-2023
GE, S

Quogue

Lewis S. Andreder, MD
33 Montauk Hwy. P.O. Box 1555
Quogue, NY 11959
(516) 653-6000—FAX (516) 288-8208
FP, IM, NT, PM

Rhinebeck

Kenneth A. Bock, MD, FACAM, DIPL
108 Montgomery St.
Rhinebeck, NY 12572
(914) 876-7082—FAX (914) 876-4615
A, CD, CT, FP, NT, PM

Smithtown

Michael Jardula, MD
60 Terry Rd.
Smithtown, NY 11787
(516) 361-3363
A, DIA, FP, IM, PM

Suffern

Bruce Oran, DO, D/C
Two Executive Blvd., #202
Suffern, NY 10901
(914) 368-4700—FAX (914) 368-4727
BA, CT, FP, OS, NT, PM

Michael B. Schachter, MD, FACAM, DIPL
Two Executive Blvd., #202
Suffern, NY 10901
(914) 368-4700—FAX (914) 368-4727
A, CT, NT, PO

Syosset

Steven Rachlin, MD
8 Greenfield Road
Syosset, NY 11791
(516) 625-6884—FAX (516) 921-8278
A, CT, IM, NT, PM

Westbury

Savely Yurkovsky, MD
309 Madison St.
Westbury, NY 11590
(516) 333-2929
A, CD, CS, CT, NT, PM

Woodside

Fira Nihamin, MD
39-65 52nd Street
Woodside, NY 11377
(718) 429-0039—FAX (718) 429-6965
CD, DIA, DD, GP, GER, IM

NORTH CAROLINA

Aberdeen

Keith E. Johnson, MD
1111 Quewhiffle
Aberdeen, NC 28315
(919) 281-5122
DD, GP, GER, NT, PM, PMR

Asheville

Ron Rosedale, MD, D/C
Park Terrace Center, 1312 Patton Ave.
Asheville, NC 28806
(704) 252-9833—(800) 445-4762
FAX (704) 876-0640
GP

John Wilson, MD, DIPL
Park Terrace Center, 1312 Patton Ave.
Asheville, NC 28806
(704) 252-9833—(800) 445-4762
FAX (704) 876-0640
A, CT, Env Med, NT, PM

Banner Elk

Charles Wiley, MD, D/C
P.O. Box 307-Hwy. 184, High Country
Square
Banner Elk, NC 28604
(704) 898-6949—FAX (704) 898-6950
GP

Black Mountain

James Biddle, MD, D/C
465 Crooked Creek Rd.
Black Mountain, NC 28711
(704) 669-7762—FAX (704) 669-4255
IM

Cary

Loghman Zaiim, MD
1817 N. Harrison Ave.
Cary, NC 27513
(919) 677-8383—FAX (919) 677-8380
PD

Locust

Clarence E. Norris, MD, D/C
P.O. Box 699
Locust, NC 28097—NO REFERRALS

Raleigh

John Pittman, MD, D/C
4505 Fair Meadow Lane, #111
Raleigh, NC 27607
(919) 571-4391—FAX (919) 571-8968
GP

Roanoke Rapids

Bhaskar D. Power, MD, D/C
1201 E. Littleton Rd.
Roanoke Rapids, NC 27820
(919) 535-1411
A, FP, PD, PUD, RHI, S

Statesville

Ron Rosedale, MD, D/C
Plaza 21 North
Statesville, NC 28677
(704) 876-1617
GP

John L. Wilson, MD, DIPL
Plaza 21 North
Statesville, NC 28677
(704) 876-1617
A, CT, Env. Med., NT, PM

Winston-Salem

Walter Ward, MD, D/C
1411B Plaza West Road
Winston-Salem, NC 27103
(910) 760-0240
A, CT, ENT, NT, RHI, YS

NORTH DAKOTA

Grand Forks

Richard H. Leigh, MD, DIPL
2314 Library Circle
Grand Forks, ND 58201
(701) 775-5527
CT, GYN, MM, NT

Minot

Brian E. Briggs, MD, D/C
718 6th Street S.W.
Minot, ND 58701
(701) 838-6011—(701) 838-5055
CT, FP, NT

OHIO

Akron

Josephine Aronica, MD
1867 W. Market St.
Akron, OH 44313
(330) 867-7361
AC, CT, NT

Francis J. Waickman, MD
544 "B" White Pond Drive
Akron, OH 44320
(216) 867-3767—FAX (216) 867-4857
A, Env Med, CI Imm, YS

Bluffton

L. Terry Chappell, MD, FACAM, DIPL
122 Thurman St. Box 248
Bluffton, OH 45817
(419) 358-4627—FAX (419) 358-1855
AU, CT, FP, HYP, NT, PMR

Jay Nielsen, MD
122 Thurman St.—Box 248
Bluffton, OH 45817
(419) 358-4627—FAX (419) 358-1855
A, CT, FP, GP, NT, YS

Canton

Jack E. Slingluff, DO, DIPL
5850 Fulton Rd. N.W.
Canton, OH 44718
(330) 494-8641
CD, CT, FP, HGL, MM, NT

Centerville

John H. Boyles Jr., MD
7076 Corporate Way
Centerville, OH 45459—NO REFERRALS

Cincinnati

Ted Cole, DO
9678 Cincinnati-Columbus Road
Cincinnati, OH 45241
(513) 779-0300
A, CT, FP, NT, OSM, PD

Leonid Macheret, MD, D/C
375 Glensprings Dr., #400
Cincinnati, OH 45246
(513) 851-8790
CT, GP, NT, PM

Cleveland

Radha Baishnab, MD, D/C
7225 Old Oak Park Blvd., #2B
Cleveland, OH 44130
(216) 234-8080
CD, CT, IM, NT, PM

John M. Baron, DO, DIPL
4807 Rockside, Ste. 100
Cleveland, OH 44131
(216) 642-0082
CT, NT, PO

Robert B. Casselberry, MD, D/C
2132 W. 25th Street
Cleveland, OH 44113
(216) 771-5855—FAX (216) 771-4534
AC, CT, DD, NT, OS, PM

James P. Frackelton, MD, FACAM, DIPL
24700 Center Ridge Rd.
Cleveland, OH 44145
(216) 835-0104—FAX (216) 871-1404
CT, HO, NT, PM

Derrick Lonsdale, MD, FACAM, DIPL
24700 Center Ridge Rd.
Cleveland, OH 44145
(216) 835-0104—FAX (216) 871-1404
NT, PM, PD

Lawrence Porter, MD, D/C
36001 Euclid Ave., #A-10
Cleveland, OH 44094
(216) 942-5838
GP, IM

Douglas Weeks, MD, D/C
24700 Center Ridge Rd.
Cleveland, OH 44145
(216) 835-0104—FAX (216) 871-1404
CT, HO, NT, PM, AC, PMR

Columbus

David C. Korn, DO
3278 Maize Rd.
Columbus, OH 43224
(614) 268-6170
CT, DD, MM, NT, PM, RHU

William D. Mitchell, DO, DIPL
3520 Snouffer Rd.
Columbus, OH 43235
(614) 761-0555—FAX (614) 761-8937
CD, CT, GP, IM, PM, OSM

Hubbard

James P. Dambrogio, DO
212 N. Main St.
Hubbard, OH 44425
(216) 534-9737—FAX (216) 534-9739
CT, NT, OS

Lorain

Robert Stevens, DO, D/C
2160 Reid Ave.
Lorain, OH 44052
(216) 246-3993
GP

Lyndhurst

Robert B. Casselberry, MD, D/C
5576 Mayfield Rd.
Lyndhurst, OH 44124
(216) 460-1880
AC, CT, DD, NT, OS, PM

Maumee

Elizabeth C. Christenson, MD
219 West Wayne Street
Maumee, OH 43537
(419) 893-8438—FAX (419) 893-1465
GP

Paulding

Don K. Snyder, MD
11573 State Rt. 111
Paulding, OH 45879
(419) 399-2045
CT, FP

Russels Point

Paul Bonetzky, DO
Aries Medical
One Aries Center
Russels Point, OH 43348
(513) 843-5000
A, FP, GER, GYN, NT, Laser Surg.

Salem

William Z. Kolozsi, MD
2380 Southeast Blvd.
Salem, OH 44460
(216) 337-1152
GE, HYP, NT

Springfield

Narinder K. Saini, MD
1911 E. High St.
Springfield, OH 45505
(513) 325-1155
IM, PM

Toledo

James C. Roberts, Jr., MD, D/C
4607 Sylvania Ave.
Toledo, OH 43623
(419) 882-9620—FAX (419) 882-9628
BA, CD, IM, PM

Versailles

Charles W. Platt, MD, D/C
552 South West Street
Versailles, OH 45380
(513) 526-3271
A, CT, FP, GP

Youngstown

James Ventresco Jr., DO
3848 Tippecanoe Rd.
Youngstown, OH 44511
(330) 792-2349
CT, FP, NT, OSM, RHU

OKLAHOMA

Jenks

Leon Anderson, DO, DIPL
121 Second Street
Jenks, OK 74037
(918) 299-5039
CT, NT, OSM

Oklahoma City

Charles H. Farr, MD, PhD, FACAM, DIPL
5419 S. Western Ave.
Oklahoma City, OK 73109
(405) 634-7855—FAX (405) 634-7320
A, CT, NT, PM

Charles D. Taylor, MD, DIPL
4409 Classen Blvd.
Oklahoma City, OK 73118
(405) 525-7751—FAX (405) 525-0303
GP, GYN, OBS, PM, PMR

Paul Wright, MD
608 N.W. 9th St., #1000
Oklahoma City, OK 73102
(405) 272-7494
CD, DIA, FP, GYN, OBS, PD

Pawnee

Gordon P. Laird, DO, D/C
304 Boulder
Pawnee, OK 74058
(918) 762-3601
CT, FP, GE, PM, S

Valliant

Ray E. Zimmer, DO, D/C
602 No. Dalton
Valliant, OK 74764
(405) 933-4235
S

OREGON

Albany

Monty Ross Ellison, MD
909 Elm Street
Albany, OR 97321
(541) 928-6444
PMR, S

Ashland

Ronald L. Peters, MD
1607 Siskiyou Blvd.
Ashland, OR 97520
(541) 482-7007
A, CT, DD, FP, NT, PM, YS

Coos Bay

David H. Tang, MD
1775 Thompson Road
Coos Bay, OR 97420—NO REFERRALS

Grants Pass

James Fitzsimmons Jr., MD
591 Hidden Valley Rd.
Grants Pass, OR 97527
(541) 474-2166
A, CT

Portland

Richard C. Heitsch, MD
Professional Plaza 102, Bldg. V
177 N.E. 102nd Avenue
Portland, OR 97220
(503) 261-0966—FAX (503) 252-2691
A, CT, FP, GP, HGL, NT

J. Stephen Schaub, MD
9310 S.E. Stark Street
Portland, OR 97216
(503) 256-9666—FAX (503) 253-6139
AC, CT, IM, NT, OS

Jeffrey Tyler, MD
163 N.E. 102nd Ave.
Portland, OR 97220
(503) 255-4256
CT, IM, GER, PD, PM

Salem

Terence Howe Young, MD, D/C
1205 Wallace Rd. NW
Salem, OR 97304
(541) 371-1558
A, CT, GP, OSM, PM

PENNSYLVANIA

Allentown

Frederick Burton, MD
321 E. Emmaus Ave.
Allentown, PA 18103
(610) 791-2453—FAX (610) 791-9974
IM, CT, NT, PM

D. Erik von Kiel, DO, DIPL
Liberty Square Med. Cntr., Suite 200
Allentown, PA 18104
(610) 776-7639
CT, FP, MM, NT, OSM

Bangor

Francis J. Cinelli, DO
153 N. 11th Street
Bangor, PA 18013
(610) 588-4502—FAX (610) 588-6928
CT, GP, HYP

Bedford

Bill Illingworth, DO, DIPL
120 West John St.
Bedford, PA 15522
(814) 623-8414
AN, CT, GP, NT, OSM, PM, Pain Mgmt

Bensalem

Robert J. Peterson, DO
2169 Galloway Rd.
Bensalem, PA 19020
(215) 579-0330
AR, CD, CT, DD, DIA, NT, PM, YS

Bethlehem

Sally Ann Rex, DO
1343 Easton Ave.
Bethlehem, PA 18018
(215) 866-0900
CT, GP, OS, PM, Occ. Med.

Darby

Lance Wright, MD, D/C
112 S. 4th Street
Darby, PA 19023
(610) 461-6225—FAX (610) 583-3356
DD, END, HYP, NT, PM, PO

Elizabethtown

Dennis L. Gilbert, DO, DIPL
50 North Market Street
Elizabethtown, PA 17022
(717) 367-1345
A, AR, CT, NT, YS, Pain Mgmt

Fountainville

Harold H. Byer, MD, PhD, DIPL
5045 Swamp Rd., #A-101
Fountainville, PA 18923
(215) 348-0443
AR, CT, DIA, S

Greensburg

Alfonso S. Arevalo, MD, D/C
100 West Point Dr.
Greensburg, PA 15601
(412) 836-6041
BA, FP, GP, GYN, NT, PD

Ralph A. Miranda, MD, FACAM, DIPL
RD. #12-Box 108
Greensburg, PA 15601
(412) 838-7632—FAX (412) 836-3655
CT, FP, NT, OME, PM

Greenville

Roy E.. Kerry, MD
17 Sixth Avenue
Greenville, PA 16125
(412) 588-2600
A, DD, EM, NT, OTO, YS

Haverford

Conrad G. Maulfair, Jr., DO, FACAM,
DIPL
600 Haverford Rd., #200
Haverford, PA 19041
(610) 658-0220 or (800) 733-4065
A, CT, HGL

Hazleton

Arthur L. Koch, DO, DIPL
57 West Juniper St.
Hazleton, PA 18201
(717) 455-4747
CT, GP, PM

Jeannette

R. Christopher Monsour, MD, D/C
70 Lincoln Way East
Jeannette, PA 15644
(412) 527-1511
Addiction, P

Lehighton

P. Jayalakshmi, MD, DIPL
330 Breezewood Rd.
Lehighton, PA 18235
(215) 473-7453
A, AC, AR, BA, CT, DIA, DD

K. R. Sampathachar, MD, DIPL
330 Breezewood Rd.
Lehighton, PA 18235
(215) 473-7453
AC, AN, CT, DD, HYP, NT

Levittown

Joseph A. Maxian, DO, D/C
56 Highland Park Way
Levittown, PA 19056
(215) 945-0707—FAX (215) 945-9120
FP

Lewisburg

George C. Miller II, MD, D/C
3 Hospital Drive
Lewisburg, PA 17837
(717) 524-4405—FAX (717) 523-8844
GYN, OBS, YS

Meadville

Paul Peirsel, MD, D/C
751 Liberty Street
Meadville, PA 16335
(814) 333-5501
CT, NT, Emerg. Med., Crit. Care

McMurray

Dennis J. Courtney, MD, D/C
4198 Waashington Rd., #1
McMurray, PA 15317
(412) 941-1193
AN, AU, CT, NT, OS, PM, PMR

Mechanicsburg

John M. Sullivan, MD, D/C
1001 S. Market St., #B
Mechanicsburg, PA 17055
(717) 697-5050—FAX (717) 697-3156
A, CT, DIA, FP, PD, YS

Mt. Pleasant

Mamduh El-Attrache, MD
20 E. Main St.
Mt. Pleasant, PA 15666
(412) 547-3576
BA, CT, DIA, GER, OBS, PO

Narberth

Andrew Lipton, DO, D/C
822 Montgomery Ave., #315
Narberth, PA 19072
(610) 667-4601
GP

Newtown

Robert J. Peterson, DO
1614 Wrightstown Rd.
Newtown, PA 18940
(215) 579-0330
AR, CD, CT, DD, DIA, NT, PM, YS

Penndel

George Danielewski, MD, D/C
142 Bellevue Ave.
Penndel, PA 19047
(215) 757-4455
GP

Philadelphia

Frederick Burton, MD
69 W. Schoolhouse Lane
Philadelphia, PA 19144
(215) 844-4660
IM, CT, NT, PM

George Danielewski, MD, D/C
7927 Fairfield St.
Philadelphia, PA 19152
(215) 338-8866
CD, CT, FP, GER, NT, PM

Sarah M. Fisher, MD
530 South 2nd Street, #106-B
Philadelphia, PA 19147
(215) 627-6000—FAX (215) 291-3986
CT, DD, GP, NT, PM, YS

Mura Galperin, MD
824 Hendrix St.
Philadelphia, PA 19116
(215) 677-2337
CT, FP

Larry S. Hahn, DO
9892 Bustleton Ave., #301
Moss Plaza
Phildelphia, PA 19115
(215) 464-4111
FP, GP, GER

P. Jayalakshmi, MD, DIPL
6366 Sherwood Road
Philadelphia, PA 19151
(215) 473-4226
A, AC, AR, BA, CT, DIA, DD

Brian Karlin, DO, D/C
2500 S. Sheridan St.
Philadelphia, PA 19148
(215) 465-5583
GP

Robert J. Peterson, DO
2528 S. Broad Street
Philadelphia, PA 19145
(800) 870-0222
AR, CD, CT, DD, FP, NT, YS

K. R. Sampathachar, MD, DIPL
6366 Sherwood Road
Philadelphia, PA 19151
(215) 473-4226
AC, AN, CT, DD, HYP, NT

Robert A. Smith, MD, D/C
1420 Locust St., #200
Philadelphia, PA 19102
(215) 545-2828
AC, BA, CT, DD, FP, HYP

Brij Srivastava, MD, D/C
3309 N. Friend St.
Philadelphia, PA 19118
(215) 634-1920/1921
CT, GP, IM

Joseph Steingard, MD, D/C
2601 S. 12th Street
Philadelphia, PA 19148
(215) 389-6461
FP

Mark Testa, DO, D/C
2601 S. 12th Street
Philadelphia, PA 19148
(215) 389-6461
FP

Pittsburgh

Paul Del Bianco, MD, DIPL
8075 Saltsburg Rd.
Pittsburgh, PA 15239
(412) 795-8022—FAX (412) 795-8222
CT, IM

David Goldstein, MD
9401 McKnight Rd., #301-B
Pittsburgh, PA 15237
(412) 366-6780
A, DD, MM, NT, PM, PMR

Quakertown

Harold Buttram, MD, DIPL
5724 Clymer Road
Quakertown, PA 18951
(215) 536-1890
A, CT, FP, NT

William G. Kracht, DO, D/C
5724 Clymer Rd.
Quakertown, PA 18951
(215) 536-1890
A, CT, FP, NT, OS, YS

Sharon

Andrew Baer, MD
92 West Connelly Blvd.
Sharon, PA 16146
(412) 346-6500
AC, CT, IM, PM, Sclerotherapy, Addict.
Med.

Silverdale

Brian V. Melito, MD, D/C
P.O. Box 539
Silverdale, PA 18962—NO REFERRALS

Springfield

Joseph Bellesorte, DO, D/C
930 West Sproul Rd.
Springfield, PA 19064
(610) 328-3000
CT, FP, YS, Chronic Fatigue

Robert J. Peterson, DO
920 W. Sproul Rd.
Springfield/Lima, PA 19064
(800) 870-0222
AR, CD, CT, DD, FP, NT, YS

Topton

Conrad G. Maulfair, Jr., DO, FACAM, DIPL
403 North Main St.
P.O. Box 98
Topton, PA 19562
(610) 682-2104 or (800) 733-4065
FAX (610) 682-9781
A, CT, HGL

Upper Darby

Brij Srivastava, MD, D/C
434 Long Lane
Upper Darby, PA 19082
(610) 626-5122
CT, GP, IM

Wilkes Barre

William N. Clearfield, DO, D/C
318 S. Franklin St.
Wilkes Barre, PA 18702
(717) 824-0953
AC, FP, OS

Williamsport

Francis M. Powers, Jr., MD, D/C
1100 Grampian Blvd.
Williamsport, PA 17701
(717) 326-8203
CT, NT, OME, YS, Therapeutic Radiology

Wyncote

Steven C. Halbert, MD, D/C
1442 Ashbourne Rd.
Wyncote, PA 19095
(215) 886-7842
A, AC, CT, IM, NT, YS

Yardley

Paul Michael Kosmorsky, DO
303 Floral Vale Blvd.
Yardley (Buck Co.), PA 19067
(215) 860-1500
CD, CT, DD, FP, NT, OS

York

Kenneth E. Yinger, DO
1561 E. Market St.
York, PA 17403
(717) 848-2544
CT, FP

SOUTH CAROLINA

Charleston

Arthur M. LaBruce, MD, D/C
9275 G Medical Plaza Dr.
N. Charleston, SC 29406
(803) 572-1771
A, CT, NT, PM, RHI, S

Judy Kameoka, MD
3815 W. Montague Ave., #200
Charleston, SC 29418
(803) 760-0770
AN, BA, MM, NT

Columbia

Theodore C. Rozema, MD, DIPL
2228 Airport Road
Columbia, SC 29169
(803) 796-1702—(800) 992-8350 (NAT)
CT, FP, NT, PM

James M. Shortt, MD, D/C
2228 Airport Road
Columbia, SC 29169
(803) 796-1702—(800) 992-8350 (NAT)
AC, CT, FP, NT

Landrum

Theodore C. Rozema, MD, DIPL
1000 E. Rutherford Rd.
Landrum, SC 29356
(864) 457-4141—(800) 992-8350 (NAT)
FAX (864) 457-4144
CT, FP, NT, PM

James M. Shortt, MD, D/C
1000 E. Rutherford Rd.
Landrum, SC 29356
(864) 457-4141—(800) 992-8350 (NAT)
AC, CT, FP, NT

Little River

David Croland, DO
4326 Baldwin Ave., P.O. Box 1009
Little River, SC 29566
(803) 249-6755—FAX (803) 249-3323
FP

Myrtle Beach

Donald W. Tice, DO
4301 Dick Pond Rd.
Myrtle Beach, SC 29575
(803) 215-5000—FAX (803) 215-5005
FP, OS, PMR

Rock Hill

Theodore C. Rozema, MD, DIPL
2915 No. Cherry Rd.
Rock Hill, SC 29730
(800) 992-8350
CT, FP, NT, PM

James M. Shortt, MD, D/C
2915 No. Cherry Rd.
Rock Hill, SC 29730
(800) 992-8350
AC, CT, FP, NT

SOUTH DAKOTA

Chamberlain

Theodore R. Matheny, MD, D/C
1005 S. Sanborn St.
Chamberlain, SD 57325
(605) 734-6958
CT, FP

Custer

Dennis R. Wicks, MD, D/C
1 Holiday Trail, HCR 83, Box 21
Custer, SD 57730-9703
(605) 673-2689
GP, S

Vermillion

Harold J. Fletcher, MD, D/C
38 E. Cherry
Vermillion, SD 57069
(605) 624-2222
CT, FP, GE

Watertown

Mary Goepfert, MD
P.O. Box 513
Watertown, SD 57201—NO REFERRALS

TENNESSEE

Athens

H. Joseph Holliiday, MD, DIPL
1005 W. Madison Ave.
Athens, TN 37303
(423) 744-7540
CT, CD, CS, S

Chattanooga

Williami B. Findley, MD, D/C
1404 Dodds Ave.
Chattanooga, TN 37404
(423) 622-5113
CT, FP, GP

Dyersburg

Lynn A. Warner, Jr., MD
503 E. Tickle, #3
Dyersburg, TN 38024
(901) 285-4910
S

Knoxville

James Carlson, DO
509 N. Cedar Bluff Rd.
Knoxville, TN 37923
(423) 691-2961
CT, GP, OS, Sclerotherapy

Memphis

Jerre Minor Freeman, MD
6485 Poplar Ave.
Memphis, TN 38119—NO REFERRALS

Nashville

Stephen L. Reisman, MD
28 White Bridge Pike, Suite 400
Nashville, TN 37205
(615) 356-4244
CT, GP, HGL, NT, PM, YS

TEXAS

Abilene

William Irby Fox, MD
1227 N. Mockingbird Ln.
Abilene, TX 79603
(915) 672-7863 or 672-1124
CT, DIA, GP, GER, PMS, S

Amarillo

Gerald Parker, DO
4714 S. Western
Amarillo, TX 79109
(806) 355-8263
A, AC, AR, CT, GP, HO

John T. Taylor, DO
4714 S. Western
Amarillo, TX 79109
(806) 355-8263
A, AC, AR, CT, GP, HO

Arlington

R. E. Liverman, DO, D/C
1111 San Juan Ct.
Arlington, TX 76012—NO REFERRALS

Austin

Vladimir Rizov, MD
911 W. Anderson Lane, #205
Austin, TX 78757
(512) 451-8149—FAX (512) 451-0895
AR, CT, DD, DIA, GP, IM

Brownwood

Larry Doss, MD
1501 Burnett Dr.
Brownwood, TX 76801
(915) 646-8541
GP

Dallas

James M. Murphy, MD, D/C
400 S. Zang, #1218
Dallas, TX 75208
(214) 941-3100—FAX (214) 941-1979
AN, AU, BA, CD, CT, PMR

Peter Rivera, MD
7150 Greenville Ave., #200
Dallas, TX 75231
(214) 891-0466
AN

Michael G. Samuels, DO
7616 LBJ Freeway, #230
Dallas, TX 75251
(214) 991-3977—FAX (214) 788-2051
CT, NT, PM, OSM

Theodore J. Tuinstra, DO, D/C
7505 Scyene Rd., #302
Dallas, TX 75227
(214) 275-1141—FAX (214) 275-1370
GYN, OS, S

Donald R. Whitaker, DO, D/C
8345 Walnut Hill Lane, #230
Dallas, TX 75231
(214) 373-3016
DD, GP, NT, PM, YS

J. Robert Winslow, DO
5025 Arapaho, #550
Dallas, TX 75248
(214) 702-9977
A, CD, CT, END, PM, R

Fort Worth

Charles M. Hawes, DO, D/C
6451 Brentwood Stair Rd., #115
Fort Worth, TX 76112
(817) 446-8416—(817) 446-8413
CT, GP

Gerald Harris, DO, D/C
1002 Montgomery, #103
Ft. Worth, TX 76107
(817) 732-2878—FAX (817) 732-9315
CT, Pain Mgmt, Sclerotherapy

James J. Mahoney, DO
6451 Brentwood Stair Rd., #115
Fort Worth, TX 76112
(817) 446-8416—FAX (817) 446-8413
FP, OS

Ricardo Tan, MD
3220 North Freeway, #106
Ft. Worth, TX 76111
(817) 626-1993
AC, AU, CT, FP, NT, PM

Grand Prairie

Chris J. Renna, DO, D/C
2705 Hospital Blvd., #206
Grand Prairie, TX 75051
(214) 641-6660
END, FP, MM, NT, OS, PM

Harlingen

Robert R. Somerville, MD, D/C
712 N. 77 Sunshine Strip, #21
Harlingen, TX 78550
(210) 428-0757
A, S

Houston

Robert Battle, MD, DIPL
9910 Long Point
Houston, TX 77055
(713) 932-0552—FAX (713) 932-0551
A, BA, CD, CT, FP, HGL

Jerome L. Borochoff, MD
8830 Long Point, Suite 504
Houston, TX 77055
(713) 461-7517
CD, CT, FP, HO, PM

Moe Kakvan, MD, DIPL
3838 Hillcroft, #415
Houston, TX 77057
(713) 780-7019—FAX (713) 780-9783
CT, PM

Kenneth W. O'Neal, MD
1800 W. Loop S., #1650
Houston, TX 77027
(713) 871-8818
DD, EMERG MED, FP, IM, NT, PM

Stephen O. Rushing, MD
16856 Royal Crest Dr.
Houston, TX 77058
(713) 286-2195—FAX (713) 286-2197
DD, NT, P, PO

Stephen Weiss, MD
7333 North Freeway, #100
Houston, TX 77076
(713) 691-0737
Ortho Surg

Humble

John P. Trowbridge, MD, FACAM, DIPL
9816 Memorial Blvd., Suite 205
Humble, TX 77338
(713) 540-2329—FAX (713) 540-4329
CT, NT, PM, YS, A, MM

Hurst

Antonio Acevedo, MD, D/C
729 W. Bedford-Euless Rd., #203
Hurst, TX 76054
(817) 595-2580
AC, AN, AU, Pain Mgmt.

Irving

Frances J. Rose, MD, D/C
1701 W. Walnut Hill, #200
Irving, TX 75038
(214) 594-1111—FAX (214) 518-1867
A, AC, CT, FP, HGL, NT, PD, PM

Jefferson

Donald R. Whitaker, DO, D/C
210 E. Elizabeth Street
Jefferson, TX 75657
(903) 665-7781—FAX (903) 665-7887
DD, GP, NT, PM, YS

Kirbyville

John L. Sessions, DO, DIPL
1609 South Margaret
Kirbyville, TX 75956
(409) 423-2166
CT, IM, OSM

Laredo

Ruben Berlanga, MD
649-B Dogwood
Laredo, TX 78041—NO REFERRALS

Lubbock

Mark R. Wilson, MD
4002 21st St., #A
Lubbock, TX 79410
(806) 795-9494
GP

Pasadena

Carlos Nossa, MD
4010 Fairmont Pkwy., #274
Pasadena, TX 77504
(713) 768-3151
GP

Plano

Linda Martin, DO
1524 Independence, #C
Plano, TX 75075
(214) 985-1377—FAX (214) 612-0747
CT, GP, HOM, NT, OSM, PM, YS

Cornelius Matwijecky, MD
3900 W. 15th St., #305
Plano, TX 75075
(214) 964-8889—FAX (214) 964-0026
GP

Pleasanton

Gerald Phillips, MD, D/C
111 Smith Street
Pleasanton, TX 78064
(210) 569-2118—FAX (210) 569-5958
CD, CT, FP, HGL, NT, PM

San Angelo

Benjamin Thurman, MD, D/C
102 N. Magdalen, #290
San Angelo, TX 76903
(915) 653-3562—FAX (915) 944-1162
AC, HOM, NT, NEURO SCLEROTHERAPY

San Antonio

Jim P. Archer, DO
8673 Fredericksburg Rd., #150
San Antonio, TX 78240
(210) 697-8445—FAX (210) 697-0631
A, CT, HO, NT, PM

Ron L. Nelms, DO
8637 Fredericksburg Rd., #150
San Antonio, TX 78240
(210) 697-8445—FAX (210) 697-0631
A, CT, END, MM, NT, YS

Seabrook

Ronald M. Davis, MD, D/C
5002 Todville
Seabrook, TX 77586—NO REFERRALS

Sweeny

Elisabeth-Anne Cole, MD, DIPL
1002 Brockman St.
Sweeny, TX 77480
(409) 548-8610—FAX (409) 548-8614
BA, FP, NT, PM, OBS

Wichita Falls

Thomas R. Humphrey, MD
2400 Rushing
Wichita Falls, TX 76308
(817) 766-4329
BA, FP, GP, HYP

UTAH

Murray

Dennis Harper, DO, D/C
5263 S. 300 W., #203
Murray, UT 84107
(801) 288-8881—FAX (801) 262-4860
A, CT, OSM, YS

Park City

Kenneth Wolkoff, MD
3065 W. Fawn Drive
Park City, UT 84098—NO REFERRALS

Provo

D. Remington, MD, D/C
1675 N. Freedom Blvd., Suite 11E
Provo, UT 84604
(801) 373-8500—FAX (801) 373-5370
A, CT, FP, Env. Med.

VERMONT

Essex Junction

Charles Anderson, MD
175 Pearl Street
Essex Junction, VT 05452
(802) 879-6544
A, FP, NT, YS

VIRGINIA

Aldie

Elhadi Omer Abdelhalim, MD, D/C
Route 50 West
39070 John Mosby Highway
Aldie, VA 22001
(703) 327-2434—FAX (703) 327-2729
FP, GYN, OBS, PD

Norman W. Levin, MD, D/C
Route 50 West
39070 John Mosby Highway
Aldie, VA 22001
(703) 327-2434—FAX (703) 327-2729
CT, IM, PM, RHU

Annandale

Andrew Baer, MD
7023 Little River Turnpike
Annandale, VA 22003
(703) 941-3606
AC, CT, IM, PM, Sclerotherapy, Addict.
Med.

Falls Church

Sohini P. Patel, MD, D/C
5201 Leesburg Pike, #301
Falls Church, VA 22041
(703) 845-8686—(703) 845-2662
A, CT, NT, PM

Aldo M. Rosemblat, MD, D/C
6316 Castle Place, #200
Falls Church, VA 22044
(703) 241-8989—FAX (703) 532-6347
AC, S

Hinton

Harold Huffman, MD, DIPL
P.O. Box 197
Hinton, VA 22831
(703) 867-5242
CT, FP, PM

Louisa

David G. Schwartz, MD
P.O. Box 532
Louisa, VA 23093
(540) 967-2050
CT, FP, NT

Midlothian

Peter C. Gent, DO, DIPL
11900 Hull Street
Midlothian, VA 23112
(804) 744-3551
CT, GP, OSM

Norfolk

Vincent Speckhart, MD, DIPL
902 Graydon Ave.
Norfolk, VA 23507
(804) 622-0014
IM, Medical Oncology

South Hill

Frederick C. Sturmer Jr., MD, D/C
416 Durant Street
South Hill, VA 23970
(804) 447-3162
CT, GE, GYN, S

Trout Dale

Elmer M. Cranton, MD, FACAM, DIPL
Ripshin Road Box 44
Trout Dale, VA 24378
(540) 677-3631—FAX (540) 677-3843
A, CD, CT, FP, HO, NT

William C. Douglass, Jr., MD, D/C
Ripshin Road Box 44
Trout Dale, VA 24378
(540) 677-3631—FAX (540) 677-3843
CT, FP, NT, PM

Virginia Beach

Nelson M. Karp, MD
460 S. Independence Blvd.
Virginia Beach, VA 23452
(804) 497-3439
DIA, FP, GP, NT, PM, PMR

Robert A. Nash, MD, D/C
921 First Colonial Rd., #1705
Virginia Beach, VA 23454
(804) 422-1295
AC, CT, NT, PM, NEURO, PAIN MED

WASHINGTON

Bellevue

Leo Bolles, MD
15611 Bel Red Rd.
Bellevue, WA 98008
(206) 881-2224
AC, CT, HGL, PM

David Buscher, MD
1370 116th N.E., Ste. 102
Bellevue, WA 98004-3825
(206) 453-0288
Env Med/Cln Ecol, GP, NT

Clinton

Brad Weeks, MD, D/C
P.O. Box 740-6456 S. Central Ave.
Clinton, WA 98236
(360) 341-2303—FAX (360) 341-2313
GP, HOM, NT, PM, PO

Elk

Stanley B. Covert, MD, D/C
42207 N. Sylvan Road
Elk, WA 99009
(509) 292-2748
CT, FP, GP, Emerg.

Kent

Thomas A. Dorman, MD, DIPL
515 West Harrison St., #200
Kent, WA 98032-4403
(206) 854-4900—FAX (206) 850-5639
CD, CT, IM

Jonathan Wright, MD
515 West Harrison, #200
Kent, WA 98032
(206) 854-4900—FAX (206) 850-5639
A, CT, FP, MM, NT, END

Kirkland

Jonathan Collin, MD, FACAM, DIPL
12911 120th Ave. NE, #A-50. POB 8099
Kirkland, WA 98034
(206) 820-0547—FAX (206) 385-0699
CT, NT, PM

Longview

Jake Bergstrom, MD
#7 Jeffrey Place
Longview, WA 98632—NO REFERRALS

Port Townsend

Jonathan Collin, MD, FACAM, DIPL
911 Tyler Street
Port Townsend, WA 98368
(360) 385-4555—FAX (360) 385-0699
CT, NT, PM

J. Douwe Rienstra, MD
242 Monroe Street
Port Townsend, WA 98368
(360) 385-5658—FAX (360) 385-5142
GP, MM, NT, PM

Richland

Stephen Smith, MD
1516 Jadwin
Richland, WA 99352
(509) 946-1695
A, Env Med, MM, NT, YS

Spokane

William Correll, MD
South 3424 Grand
Spokane, WA 99203
(509) 838-5800—FAX (509) 838-4042
FP, NT, PM, HGL, YS, MM

Burton B. Hart, DO
E. 12104 Main
Spokane, WA 99206
(509) 927-9922—FAX (509) 927-9922
CT, PM, OSM

Vancouver

Richard P. Huemer, MD
3303 N.E. 44th Street
Vancouver, WA 98663
(360) 696-4405
A, CT, GP, HGL, MM, NT, OME, PM

Steve Kennedy, MD, D/C
406 S.E. 131st Ave., #202 B
Vancouver, WA 98683
(360) 256-4566—FAX (360) 253-3060
Reconstructive Surgery (hand), CT, PM

Harry C. S. Park, MD
1412 N.E. 88th Street
Vancouver, WA 98665
(360) 574-4074
A, AC, DD, FP, GP, GE

Yakima

Murray L. Black, DO
609 S. 48th Ave.
Yakima, WA 98908
(509) 966-1780
A, CT, FP, GP, OSM

Yelm

Elmer M. Cranton, MD, FACAM, DIPL
503 First Street South, Suite 1
P.O. Box 7510
Yelm, WA 98597
(360) 458-1061—FAX (360) 458-1661
A, CD, CT, FP, HO, NT

Carol Knowlton, MD
503 First Street South, Suite 1
P.O. Box 7510
Yelm, WA 98597
(360) 458-1061—FAX (360) 458-1661
AN, CT, NT, PM

WEST VIRGINIA

Beckley

Prudencio Corro, MD
251 Stanaford Rd.
Beckley, WV 25801
(304) 252-0775
A, CT, RHI

Michael Kostenko, DO
114 E. Main St.
Beckley, WV 25801
(304) 253-0591
A, AC, CT, FP, OSM, PM

Charleston

Steve M. Zekan, MD
1208 Kanawha Blvd. E.
Charleston, WV 25301
(304) 343-7559
CT, NT, PM, S

Logan

Thomas A. Horsman, MD
Doctors Park, 20 Hospital Dr.
Logan, WV 25601
(304) 792-1624
IM, PM

R. L. Toparis, DO
Doctors Park, 20 Hospital Dr.
Logan, WV 25601
(304) 792-1662
FP, GP, OS

Summersville

John R. Ray, DO
3029 Webster Rd.
Summersville, WV 26651
(304) 872-6583
FP

WISCONSIN

Delafield

Carol Uebelacker, MD
1760 Milwaukee St.
Delafield, WI 53018
(414) 646-4600—FAX (414) 646-4215
A, AC, BA, CT, FP, HYP

Green Bay

Eleazar M. Kadile, MD, DIPL
1538 Bellevue St.
Green Bay, WI 54311
(414) 468-9442
A, CT, P

Milwaukee

William J. Faber, DO
6529 W. Fond du Lac Ave.
Milwaukee, WI 53218
(414) 464-7680
Neuro-Musculo Skeletal

J. Allan Robertson, Jr., DO, D/C
1011 N. Mayfair Rd., #301
Milwaukee, WI 53226
(414) 302-1011—FAX (414) 302-1010
CT, FP, GP, NT, OS, YS

Robert R. Stocker, DO, DIPL
2505 N. Mayfair Rd.
Milwaukee, WI 53226—RETIRED

Jerry N. Yee, DO, D/C
2505 N. Mayfair Rd.
Milwaukee, WI 53226
(414) 258-6282
BA, CT, GP, OSM

Neillsville

Bahri O. Gungor, MD
216 Sunset Place
Neillsville, WI 54456
(715) 743-3101
FP, GP, GER, OBS-GYN

Wisconsin Dells

Robert S. Waters, MD, DIPL
Race & Vine Streets, Box 357
Wisconsin Dells, WI 53965
(608) 254-7178—FAX (608) 253-7139
CT, PM, OME

WYOMING

Gilette

Rebecca Painter, MD, DIPL
201 West Lakeway
Gilette, WY 82717
(307) 682-0330—FAX (307) 686-8118
CD, CT, DIA, IM, PUD, RHU

ACAM PHYSICIANS—GEOGRAPHIC INTERNATIONAL

ARGENTINA

Buenos Aires

Eduardo Katsiyannis, MD
Arenales 1917 PB
Buenos Aires, Argentina
NO REFERRALS

Eduardo Mydlarski, MD
Arce 957-6A
1426 Buenos Aires, Argentina
011-54-1-776-0606
CD, CT, IM, P

ARUBA

Oranjestad

A. E. Hart, MD, D/C
L. G. Smith Blvd. 14
Oranjestad, Aruba
011-297-8-20840—FAX 011 297-8-35664

AUSTRALIA

NEW SOUTH WALES

Bondi

Jonathan Bentley, MB, BS
P.O. Box 9
Bondi, NSW 2026
Australia
011-61-2-3651333—
FAX 011-61-2-3009167
GP

Gosford

Heather M. Bassett, MB, BS, D/C
91 Donnison Street
Gosford, NSW 2250, Australia
011-61-43-247388—
FAX 011-61-43-236785
A, AR, CT, GE, MM, WR, YS

Sydney

Heather M. Bassett, MB, BS, D/C
125 Beecroft Road
Beecroft NSW, 2119, Australia
011-61-2-8768969—
FAX 011-61-2-8763429
A, AR, CT, GE, MM, WR, YS

Tony Goh, MB, BS, D/C
196 Victoria Ave.
Chatswood NSW 2067, Australia
011-61-2-4115011—
FAX 011-61-2-4117836
A, AC, FP, GP, HGL, YS

E. Varipatis, MB, BS, D/C
2 Brady Street
Mosman NSW 2088, Australia
011-61-2-9604133—
FAX 011-61-2-8746118
A, CT, GP, NT, PM

QUEENSLAND

Gold Coast

Glen McCabe, MB, BS
80 Nerang Street
Southport QLD 4215, Australia
011-61-7-5911866—
FAX 011-61-7-5912857
CT, NT, PM, Imm. Therapies

Kevin Treacy, MB, BS
#11-A Evandale Medical Chambers
45 Bundall Rd.
Bundall QLD 4217, Australia
011-61-75-382288—
FAX 011-61-75-382013
GP

SOUTH AUSTRALIA

Elizabeth

James Siow, MD, D/C
#10 Sydney Chambers
Elizabeth City Centre-Elizabeth
South Australia, Australia
011-61-8-2562943
GP

VICTORIA

Melbourne

R. B. Allen, MB, BS, D/C
5/90 Mitcham Rd.
Donvale VIC 3111, Australia
011-61-3-8428611—
FAX 011-61-3-8426472
A, AC, CT, HGL, NT, PM

Robert Hanner, MB, BS, D/C
593 Whitehorse Road
Mitcham VIC 3132, Australia
011-61-3-9-8748777—
FAX 011-61-3-9-8746118
A, CT, GP, NT, PM

Peter Holsman, MB, BS, D/C
10 Glen Iris Road
Camberwell VIC 3124, Australia
011-61-3-9889-4534
CT, GP, NT, PM

Iggy Soosay, MB, BS, D/C
984 Toorak Road
Camberwell VIC 3124, Australia
011-61-3-8896616—
FAX 011-61-3-8896721
NT, PM, Herbal Medicine

BELGIUM

Antwerpen

Rudy Proesmans, MD, DIPL
Prins Boudewijnlaan 137
2610 Wilrijk-Antwerpen, Belgium
011-32-3-449-7024
FAX 011-32-3-449-8445
A, AR, CD, CT, DD, DIA

Gent

Michel De Meyer, MD, DIPL
Nekkersberglaan 11
9000 Gent, Belgium
011-32-9-222-33-42
CT, DD, FP, GP, GER, OS, PM

St. Niklaas

Antony de Bruyne, MD
Ankerstraat 134
B-9100 St. Niklaas, Belgium
011-32-3-777-4150
DD, FP, GP, GER, OBS, PM

Tienen

Marc Verheyen, MD, DIPL
3 Dr. Geensstraat
Tienen, Belgium 3300
011-32-1-681-8393
AC, CT, NT

BRAZIL

Brasilia

Edurado Freire, MD
SQS 211, Bloco F, Apt. 502
70.274-060 Brasilia DF, Brazil
FAX 011-55-61-321-6141
GP

Iler J. Oliveira, MD
SHIS-QL-24 conj.06-casa 09
Brasilia DF, Brazil 71665.065
011-55-61-2482630
CD, CS, GER, GP, IM, PM, PUD

Cuiaba-MT

Marco Aurelio S. Ribeiro, MD
Rua Joao Bento, 143, Quilombo
78045-450-Cuiaba-MT, Brazil
011-55-65-6240044
CT, DD, GP, IM, NT, P, PM

Curitiba

Oslim Malina, MD
Rua Itupava, 157
80060-Curitiba-PR, Brazil
011-41-55-2524395
CT, Vascular Surgery

Florianopolis

Jose P. Figueredo, MD
PCA Getulio Vargas, 1280
Florianopolis, SC, Brazil
011-55-48-2224960
CD, CT, GER, IM, NT, PM

Londrina-Parana

Tsutomu Higashi, MD
Rua Pernambuco, 390 2° Andar
Sala 201
Londrina-Parana CEP:86020-070, Brazil
011-55-43-323-8744
CT, GP, IM

Minas Gerais

Adjar Mendes da Silva, MD
St. Av Celso Porfirio, Machado 1739
Belo Horizonte 30320-400
Minas Gerais, Brazil
011-55-31-2862287
A, CD, CT, DD, END, GER, IM, RHU

Osorio-RS

Jose Valdai de Souza, MD
Rua Lobo da Costa, 1427
Cx. Postal 134

Osorio-RS-CEP 95.520, Brazil
011-55-51-6631269
CD, CT, DD, GP, GER, PM

Pelotas-RS

Antonio C. Fernandes, MD
Rua Santa Tecla 470A
Pelotas, RS 96010, Brazil
011-55-53-2224699
CD, CT, GER, GP, IM, PM

Porto Alegre

Moyses Hodara, MD
Rua Jose De Alencar
207 Suite 203
Porto Alegre-RS, 90880-481, Brazil
011-55-51-2243557
CS, CT, DD, FP, GP, RHU

Carlos J. P. de Sa, MD
Marcilio Dias-1056
Porto Alegre-RS 90060, Brazil
011-55-51-2334832—
FAX 011-55-51-2294852
CD, CT, DIA, HGL, S

Sao Jose-RP

A. O. Passos Correa, MD
Ave. Alberto Andalo
3314 Sao Jose do Rio Preto
CEP: 15015, Brazil
011-55-17-2334455
CT, CD, GER, IM, NT, PM

Sao Paulo

G. J. Da Encarnacao, MD
Rua Domingos Leme, 785
CEP: 04510-040
Sao Paulo, Brazil
011-55-11-8220264
CD, CT, DD, GER, GP, IM

Shirley De Campos, MD, D/C
Rua Bento de Andrade, 496
Jardim Paulista
Sao Paulo-SP 04503-001, Brazil
011-55-11-4463900—
FAX 011-55-11-884-4478
GP, PD

George S. De Moraes, MD
Praca Bart Bueno 55
San Jose Campos, Sao Paulo
Brazil-C.P. 302.12.201-970
011-55-123-21-2583-41-1011
FAX 011-55-123-22-7831-41-1048
GP

Klaus Dieter Dillner, MD
Taques Alvim 462
Cd. Jardim
Sao Paulo, Brazil
011-55-11-2112255
GP

Wagner, Fiori, MD, DIPL
Rua Prof. Artur Ramos, 183-Ap. 33
Jd. Europa-Sao Paulo
CEP 01454-011, Brazil
011-55-11-2112019
FAX 011-55-11-8134945
CT, CT, DD, GER, IM, PM

Fernando L. Flaquer, MD, D/C
Rua Prof. Artur Ramos, 183-Ap. 33
Jd. Europa-Sao Paulo
CEP 01454-011, Brazil
011-55-2112019
CT, CS, DD, GER, IM, PM

Luiz A. Raio Granja, MD
Rua do Simbolo 380, Casa 31
Sao Paulo-S.P.-CEP: 05715-570, Brazil
Phone/FAX 011-55-11-8223335
GP

Efrain Olszewer, MD
Rua Campevas 211
05016 Perdizes-Sao Paulo, Brazil
011-55-11-62-3000—
FAX 011-55-11-8852654
A, CD, CT, GER, IM, RHU

Wilson Rondo, MD, D/C
Rua Pernambuco, 167, 3° andar-Higienopolis
CEP. 01240.020, Sao Paulo, Brazil
011-55-11-825-2190
FAX 011-55-11-8200930
CT, S

Sergio Vaisman, MD
Rua Hilo Torres 123
Sao Paulo, SP 04650, Brazil
011-55-11-2108210
CD, CT, DD, GER, IM, PM

Vila Velha

Marcos Andre M. Dantas, MD
Antonio Ataide, #468
Vila Velha-Espirito Santo-Brazil
011-55-27-3290194
A, CD, CT, DD, END, GER, IM, RHU

CANADA

ALBERTA

Calgary

Bruce Hoffman, MD, D/C
#202-4411 16th Ave. NW
Calgary, Alberta, Canada T3B 0M3
(403) 286-7311 or (403) 286-7437
FAX (403) 286-4767
AC, FP, Env Med

W. James Mayhew, MD, D/C
#102-3604 52 Ave. NW
Calgary, Alberta, Canada T2L 1V9
(403) 284-2261—FAX (403) 284-9434
DD, FP, GER, HYP, IM, OBS

F. Logan Stanfield, MD, D/C
#206-215 12th Ave. SE
Calgary, Alberta, Canada T2G 1A2
(403) 265-6171
CT, HYP, MM, NT, P, PO

Edmonton

Godwin O. Okolo, MD, DIPL
9535 135 Avenue
Edmonton, Alberta, Canada T5E 1N8
(403) 476-3344—FAX (403) 478-5248
CD, CS, DIA, DD, GP, GER

Andrew W. Sereda, MD, D/C
#100-4936 87th
Edmonton, Alberta, Canada T0E 5W3
(403) 450-1991—FAX (403) 450-1990
NT, Neuro., PM

Tris Trethart, MD, DIPL
8621 104 Street
Edmonton, Alberta, Canada T6E 4G6
(403) 433-7401
NT, PM

K. B. Wiancko, MD, DIPL
#205-9509 156 Street
Edmonton, Alberta, Canada T5P 4J5
(403) 483-2703—FAX (403) 486-5674
FP, GE, GP, S

Fairview

A. Cooper, MD, DIPL
Box 283
Fairview, Alberta, Canada T0H 1L0
(403) 835-2525
CT, GP, S

Grand Centre

Richard Johnson, MD, D/C
Box 96-4818 51st Street
Grand Centre, Alberta, Canada T0A 1T0
(403) 594-7574
GP, NT, OME, PM

High Prairie

P. V. Edwards, MD, D/C
Box 449
High Prairie, Alberta, Canada T0G 1E0
(403) 523-4501—FAX (403) 523-4800
CD, DIA, DD, GP, GYN, OBS

R. Laughlin, MB, CHB, D/C
Box 449
High Prairie, Alberta, Canada T0G 1E0
(403) 523-4501—FAX (403) 523-4800
FP, GE, GP, HYP, OBS, S

BRITISH COLUMBIA

Penticton

Dietrich Wittel, MD
P.O. Box 70
Penticton, B.C., Canada V2A 6J9
(604) 492-9849
A, CT, FP, NT, PM

Port Alberni

John Cline, MD
3855 9 Avenue
Port Alberni, B.C., Canada V9Y 4T9
(604) 723-1434
CT, FP, PM

Surrey

Zigurts Strauts, MD
#304-16088 84th Avenue
Surrey, B.C., Canada V3S 2P1
(604) 543-5000—FAX (604) 543-5002
AC, CT, FP, Thermpography, Manipulative Therapy

Vancouver

Donald W. Stewart, MD, DIPL
2184 W. Broadway, #435
Vancouver, B.C., Canada V6K 2E1
(604) 732-1348—FAX (604) 732-1372
CT, GP

Williams Lake

Dale R. Loewen, MD
177 Yorston St., #202
Williams Lake, B.C., Canada V2G 1G6
(604) 398-7777—FAX (604) 398-7734
FP, GP, PM, PH

Winfield

Alex A. Neil, MD, DIPL
#216-3121 Hill Road
Winfield, B.C., Canada V0H 2C0
(604) 766-0732
CT, GP, HYP, NT

NOVA SCOTIA

Chester

J. W. LaValley, MD
227 Central Street
Chester, N.S., Canada B0J 1J0
(902) 275-4555
A, AC, GP, PM, YS

ONTARIO

Blythe

Richard W. Street, MD, D/C
Box 100 Gypsy Lane
Blythe, Ontario, Canada N0M 1H0
(519) 523-4433
GP, NT, PM

Hamilton

Angelica Fargas-Babjak, MD
1200 Main St. West
Hamilton, Ontario, Canada L8N 3Z5
(905) 521-2100—FAX (905) 523-1224
AC, AN, AU, NT, PM, PMR

Smiths Falls

Clare Minielly, MD, D/C
33 Williams Street E.
Smiths Falls, Ontario, Canada K7A 1C3
(613) 283-7703
AN, CT, GP, NT

Toronto

Paul Jaconello, MB, BS
751 Page Ave., #201
Toronto, Ontario, Canada M4K 3T1
(416) 463-2911—FAX (416) 469-0538
A, DD, GP, MM, NT, YS

COLOMBIA

Bogota

Carlos A. Acuna Ospino, MD
Ave. 19 No. 4-20 (901)
Santafe de Bogota, D.C., Colombia
011-57-1-2862695
CD, CT, CS, DIA, DD, S

Medellin

Jaime Velez, MD
Calle 57, #50-24
Medellin, 5020, Colombia
011-574-5115857—
FAX 011-574-8472126
A, CT, GE, HO, NT, RHU

COSTA RICA

San Jose

Fabio Solano, MD
P.O. Box 6629-1.000
San Jose, Costa Rica
(506) 221-81-20—FAX (506) 221-81-20
GP

DENMARK

Aabyhoej

Kurt Christensen, MD, DIPL
Sophus Bauditzvej 16
DK-8230 Arabyhoej, Denmark
011-45-6-126141—
FAX 011-45-86752185
AC, CT, GP, NT

Copenhagen

Sven Feddersen, MD
Amagerbrogade 73, 2300 S
Copenhagen, Denmark
011-45-31-584114—
FAX 011-45-31-584113
AC, AU, CT, PM, PMR, S

Lyngby

Claus Hancke, MD, DPL
Lyngby Hovedgade 17[1]
DK-2800-Lyngby, Denmark
011-45 45 88 09 00—FAX 011-45-45-
880947
CT, FP, GP, NT, OSM, PM

Vejle

Knut T. Flytlie, MD, DIPL
Gludsmindevej 39
DK-7100 Vejle, Denmark
011-45-75726090—
FAX 011-45-75726089
A, AC, AU, GP, OSM, PM

Viby

Bruce P. Kyle, MD, DIPL
Stravtrupvej 7A
8260 Viby J, Denmark
011-45-86-289688—
FAX 011-45-86-289644
CT, GP, NT, OME, PM

DOMINICAN REPUBLIC

Santo Domingo

Antonio Pannocchia, MD
Ave. 27 de Febrero, Suite 201
Santo Domingo 6, Dominican Republic
565-3259
CT, NT, PM

EGYPT

Cairo

Alaa E. I. Hosny, MB, BCH
25 Gamet El Dowal El Arabia St.
Mohandseen-Cairo, Egypt
011-202-3481316/707205
CT, GYN, OBS

Madiha M. Khattab, MD, D/C
12 Hassan Assem St.
Zamalek-Cairo, Egypt
011-202-3407585
CT, IM

ENGLAND

Buckinghamshire

Hugh J. E. Cox, MB, ChB, D/C
14 Ayleswater, Watermead
Buckingham Rd., Aylesbury
Buckinghamshire, HP 19 3FB, England
011-44-296-398801—FAX 011-44-296
A, CT, IM, NT, PM, YS

Kent

F. Schellander, MD, D/C
8 Chilston Rd.
Tunbridge Wells
Kent TN4 9LT, England
011-44-892-543535—
FAX 011-44-892-545160
CT, GP, HO, MM, NT, PM

Lancashire

Tarsem Lal Garg, MD
70 The Avenue Leigh
Lancashire WN7 1ET, England
011-44-1942 676617—
FAX 011-44-1942 260285
CD, CT, DIA, DD, FP, HO

London

Rodney O. C. Adeniyi-Jones, MB, BS, D/C
21 Devonshire Place
London W1N 1PD, England
011-44-171-486-6354—
FAX 011-44-171-486-6359
A, AC, DIA, HGL, PM, YS

Lydia S. Boeken, MD, DIPL
7 Park Crescent
London W1N 3HE, England
011-44-171-631-0156—
FAX 011-44-171-323-1693
CD, CT, DD, GP, NT, OME, PM

John Diamond, MD
50 Chandos Ave.
London N20 9DX, England
011-44-181-446-2401—
FAX 011-44-181-446-0570
AC, NT, PM, PO, PMR, Applied
Kinesiology

Wayne Perry, MD, ChB
57a Wimpole Street
London W1M 7DF, England .
011-44-171-486-1095
CD, CT, DIA, END, IM, MM

Richmond

Simi Khanna, MB, BS
129 Sheen Rd.
Richmond TW9 1YJ, England
011-44-181-332 6685—
FAX 011-44-181-332 6571
CT, HOM, NT

FRANCE

Paris

Paul Musarella, MD
96 Rue de Miromesnil
75008 Paris, France
011-33-1-45621938
GER, NT, PM, S

GERMANY

Bad Fussing

Karl Heinz Caspers, MD
Beethovenstrasse 1
D 8397 Bad Fussing, Germany—
NO REFERRALS

Bad Steben

Helmut Keller, MD
Am Reuthlein 2
D-8675 Bad Steben, Germany
011-49-9288-5166—
FAX 011-49-9288-7815
IM, PD, S. Oncology

Rottach-Egern

Claus Martin, MD
P.O. Box 244
8183 Rottach-Egern, Germany
011-49-8022-6415
CT, DD, GER

Werne

Jens-Ruediger Collatz, MD
Fuerstenhofklinik
Fuerstenhof 2
D-59368 Werne, Germany
011-49-2389-3883—
FAX 011-49-2389-536155
AC, CT, DD, GER, HO, PM

GREECE

Spyridon V. Joannides, MD
342 Kifissias Ave.
152 33 Chalandri
Athens, Greece
011-301-6890100
AN, GP, IM, NT, OS, S

HONG KONG

Hong Kong

K. Francis Siu, MD, DIPL
Rm 702, Capitol Centre
5—19 Jardine's Bazaar
Hong Kong, Hong Kong
011-852-808-0370
AC, CT, GP, IM

Kowloon

Annie S. M. Choi, MD, D/C
1413B Champion Bldg.
301-309 Nathan Rd.
Kowloon, Hong Kong
011-852-782-2988—
FAX 011-852-770-4999
CT, FP, GP, IM, PD, S

Kenneth Y. K. Ng, MB, BS
Rm. 1004-5, Champion Bldg.
301-309 Nathan Road
Kowloon, Hong Kong
011-852-2384-6118—
FAX 011-852-2780-5156
CT, GP, NT, PM

HUNGARY

Budapest

Judit Szalontai, MD, D/C
Budapest 1221
Korompai u.3.—Hungary
011-36-1-227-3651
AN, CD, CT, GP, IM, Emerg. Med.

INDIA

Bangalore

P. Jayalakshmi, MD, DIPL
166 43rd Cross
8th Block Jayanagar
Bangalore, India 5600082
011-91-80-644066
A, AC, AR, BA, CT, DIA, DD

K. R. Sampathachar, MD, DIPL
166 43rd Cross
8th Block Jayanagar
Bangalore, India 5600082
011-91-80-644066
AC, AN, CT, DD, HYP, NT

Bombay

Bhaskar Dayaram Pawar, MD, D/C
13 Lotus Court, Sir J. Tate Road
Bombay, India 400 021

011-91-22-202-3995—
FAX 011-91-22-202-9034
A, FP, PD, PUD, RHI, S

INDONESIA

Cirebon

Iwan Gunawan, MD, D/C
Jl. Lemahwungkuk 131
Cirebon 45111, Indonesia
011-62-231-202659—
FAX 011-62-231-209310
AC, GP

Jakarta

Maimunah Affandi, MD, DIPL
Jl. Gandaria VIII, #13
Kebayoran Baru, Jakarta 12130
Indonesia
Phone/FAX 011-62-21-7246927
CD, CT, DD, OME, PD

Adjit Singh Gill, MD
Jln. Tanah Abang V, #27A
Jakarta, Indonesia, 10160
011-62-21-357359
CD, CT, PM

Yahya Kisjanto, MD, DIPL
71 Diponegoro
Jakarta, Indonesia
011-62-21-334636
CD, CT, DIA, GER, IM, PMR

Otto Maulana, MD, D/C
Jl. Raden Saleh 13
Jakarta 10430, Indonesia—RETIRED

Rijanto T. Santjaka, MD, D/C
Jln. Merpati G 46
Kompleks Hankam Slipi
Jakarta-Barat, Indonesia—RETIRED

Hendra Setiady, MD, DIPL
Pulo MAS Timur IIA #2.
Jakarta Timur 13210, Indonesia
011-62-21-4713880—
FAX 011-62-21-4717147
A, CD, CT, DIA, FP, GE

Hendra Setiady, MD, DIPL
Gading Putih Raya Utara
CB 2 #12A
Kelapa Gading Permai
Jakarta Utara, Indonesia
011-62-21-4713880—
FAX 011-62-21-4717147
A, CD, CT, DIA, FP, GE

Dien G. H. Tan, MD, D/C
Gandaria 1, #45
Jakarta 13130, Indonesia
011-62-21-7203476
CT, DD, GP, NT

Semarang

Benny Purwanto, MD, DIPL
Jl. Kalimas Raya 29
Semarang 50177, Indonesia
011-62-24-549000—
FAX 011-62-24-543691
CT, GP, DD

Tangerang

Aloysius Dharmawan, MD, D/C
Jl. H. Abdullah #1—P.O. Box 169
Tangerang, Jawa Barat, Indonesia
011-62-21-5522604
FP, GR, R

IRELAND

Killaloe, Co. Clare

Paschal Carmody, MB, BCH
The East Clinic
Killaloe, Co. Clare, Ireland
011-61-376349—FAX 011-61-376773
A, AC, CT, FP, GP, NT, OS

Carrigaline, Co. Cork

Mary Dunphy, MB, BCH
Cork Rd. Clinic
Carrigaline, Co. Cork, Ireland
011-61-21371-77—
FAX 011-61-21371417
CT, DD, GP, NT, PMR, RHU

ISRAEL

Jerusalem

Fischel Goldman, MD
13 Bergman St., Bayt V'Gan
Jerusalem 96467, Israel
011-2-423207
GP

Stanley Shapiro, MD, D/C
Canfei Nesharim 24
Jerusalem, Israel
011-972-2-6526295—
FAX 011-972-2-6526298
AC, FP, GP, P

ITALY

Palermo

Michele Ballo, MD
Via Ruggero Settimo, 55
90139 Palermo, Italy
91-580301
CD, CT, GER, IM, PM, PMR

JORDAN

Amman

Mohammad M. Abu-Lughod, MB, BCh, D/C
Ibn. Khaldoon St. near
Khalidi Hospital
Amman-Jordan
011-9626-652148
GYN/OBS

LEBANON

Jounieh

Tony G. Licha'a, MD, D/C
P.O. Box 245
Jounieh, Lebanon
011-961-9-911875—
FAX 011-961-9-914195
CD, CT, IM, PM

MALAYSIA

Kuala Lumpur

Noor L. Abu Bakar, MD, DIPL
#2 Jln. Keramat
Hujung Atas
5400 Kuala Lumpur, Malaysia
011-60-3-457-8943—
FAX 011-60-3-451-1030
GP

Melaka

Mohamed S. A. Ishak, MD
40 Jalan Kee Ann,
75100 Melaka, Malaysia
011-60-6-235878/06-239396
FP, GP, RHI

Perak

Philip Chan Kwong Chow, MB, BS
61 Jalan Raja Ekram, 30450 Ipoh
Perak, Malaysia
011-605-2419625
FP, GP, IM, PD, P

Pram Singh, MB, BS
446 Back Street
32300 Pangkor, Perak, Malaysia
011-60-5-951796
AC, CT, GP, HYP, PM, NT

Selangor

M. S. Balajeyagaran, MD, D/C
#7, 2C/28 Jl. P.J.S. 46000
Petaling Jaya, Selangor, Malaysia
011-60-3-7194679
FAX 011-60-3-2740170
CT, FP, NT, YS

Soon Tong Kho, MD, D/C
183, Batu 17 Jalan Ipoh
48000 Rawang, Selangor, Malaysia
011-60-36918705—
FAX 011-60-3-617-5617
AC, FP, GP, GYN, OBS, PM

MEXICO

Chihuahua

H. Berlanga Reyes, MD, DIPL
Antonio de Montes 2118
Col. Szan Felipe
Chihuahua, Chih. 31240, Mexico
(95) 141-3-92-71 or (95) 141-3-92-75
CT, GER, GP, PM

Guadalajara, Jalisco

Eleazar A. Carrasco, MD
Chapultepec Norte 140-203
Guadalajara, Jalisco 44600, Mexico
25-16-55
CT, GP, GYN, OBS, S

F. Navares Merino, MD, DIPL
Lopez Mateos Nte. 646, S.H
Guadalajara, Jal. 44680, Mexico
(36) 16-88-70
CT, NT, PM

Juarez, Chih.

H. Berlanga Reyes, MD, DIPL
Insurgentes 2516
Cd. Juarez, Chih. 32330, Mexico
Phone/FAX 011-52-16-138023
CT, GP, GER, PM

Francisco Soto, MD
Ave. Lopez Mateos, #1281
Cd. Juarez, Chih., Mexico
011-52-16-138458—
FAX 011-52-16-137055
CT, HO, NT, PM, S

Matamoros, Tamp.

Frank Morales Jr., MD, D/C
1a y Nardos, Cal. Jardin
H. Matamoros, Tamp., Mexico
3-31-07
GP

Mexicali, B.C.

Fernando Agundez, MD, D/C
Ave Lerdo 1515, #11&14
Mexicali, B.C., Mexico
011-5265-528925
CT, DIA, DD, FP, GYN, PD

Ricardo Rocha, MD
Ave Lerdo 1515, #11&14
Mexicali, B.C., Mexico
011-5265-528925
A, CD, CT, DD, GP, NT, PM

Mexico City

Barbara Sanders Esparaza, MD, D/C
Ave. Lomas Sotelo, #201
Colonia Loma Hermosa
Mexico City, 11200, Mexico
011-525-527-95-96
DD, DIA, GP, IM, PM

Dmitriy Osmanchuk, MD, DIPL
Ave Angel 73
Mexico City, San Joe-Insurgentes, Mexico
011-52-5-393-3029
Phone/FAX 011-52-5-393-2814
AC, AN, CT, HYP, MM, PM

Ignacio Vazquez, MD
Matias Romero No. 1353-4
Colonia Narvarte
Mexico City, D.F., Mexico CP. 03650
(5) 6012135/6055240
AR, CT, HOM

N. Laredo, Tamps.

Ruben Berlanga-Garza, MD
3435 Guerrero
N. Lardeo, Tamps., Mexico
GER, P, PM

Tijuana

Francisco Contreras, P., MD
Paseo de Tijuana #19
Playas de Tijuana, B.C. 22700, Mexico
011-52-66-801850—
FAX 011-52-66-801855
CT, GP

Francisco Rique, MD
Azucenas 15
Frac. del Prado
Tijuana, B.C., Mexico
706) 681-3171
AC, AR, CT, DD, NT, PM

Rodrigo Rodriguez, MD
Azucenas 15
Frac. del Prado
Tijuana, B.C., Mexico
(706) 681-3171
CD, CT, DD, GER, MM, PM

Torreon, Coahuila

Carlos Lopez Moreno, MD
Tulipanes 475
Col. Torreon, Jardin
Torreon, Coahuila 27200, Mexico
011-52-17-138140
CT, NT, PM

NETHERLANDS

Amsterdam

Lydia Boeken, MD, DIPL
Reigersbos 100
1107 ES Amsterdam, Netherlands
011-20-697-5361—
FAX 011-20-697-5367
CD, CT, DD, GP, NT, OME, PM

Paul van Meerendonk, MD, DIPL
Paasheuvelweg 26
1105 BJ Amsterdam Z.O., Netherlands
011-31-20-69-15-140—
FAX 011-31-20-69-73-268
CD, CT, DD, GP, NT, PM

Bilhoven

Eduard Schweden, MD, DIPL
Prof. Bronkhorstlaan 10
3723 MB Bilthoven, Netherlands
011-31-10-251114/284444—
FAX 011-31-30-288810
CT, DD, NT, OS, PM

Leende

P. van der Schaar, MD, PhD, DIPL
Renheide 2
Leende 5595XJ, Netherlands
011-31-495-592232—
FAX 011-31-495-592418
CD, CT, DD, OME, S

Raymond Pahlplatz, MD, D/C
Renheide 2
Leende 559 XJ, Netherlands
011-31-495-592232—
FAX 011-31-495-592418
GP

Marc Verheyen, MD, DIPL
Renheide 2
Leende 5595XJ, Netherlands
011-31-495-592232—
FAX 011-31-495-592418
CD, CT, DD, OME, S

Maastricht

Rob van Zandvoort, MD, DIPL
Burg. Cortenstraat 26
6226 GV Maastricht, Netherlands
011-31-4362-3474
CT

Rotterdam

J. Dalmulder, MD, D/C
Joostbanckertsplaats 24-29
Rotterdam Centrum 3012 HB, Netherlands
01131 10 4126362/4147633—
FAX 011-31-10-414-7990
CT, DD, HO, HGL, NT, PM

Robert T. H. K. Trossel, MD, DIPL
Joostbanckertsplaats 24-29
Rotterdam Centrum 3012 HB, Netherlands
01131 10 4126362/4147633—
FAX 011-31-10-414-7990
A, DD, S, CT, GP, NT, PM, HO

NETHERLANDS ANTILLES

St. Maarten

Dirk van Lith, MD, DIPL
Almond Grove #9

Cole Bay-Sint Maarten
Netherlands Antilles
011-5995-42249
A, DD, CT, GP, NT, HO, PM, S

NEW ZEALAND

Auckland

Maurice B. Archer, DO
3 Warborough Ave.
P.O. Box 26227 Epsom
Auckland, New Zealand
011-64-9-524-7743,45 or 48—
FAX 011-64-9-524-7745
CT, NT, PM

R. H. Bundellu, MB, BS, DIPL
157 A. Worsdworth Rd.
Manurewa, Auckland, New Zealand
011-64-9-266-7007—-
FAX 011-64-9-266-7238
CT, FP, OBS

Christchurch

R. Blackmore, MB, CHB, DIPL
196 Hills Road
Christchurch 1, New Zealand
(03) 853-015—FAX 011-64-3-385-3014
AC, CT, FP, GP, NT, OBS

Masterton

T. J. Baily Gibson, MB, BS, DIPL
P.O. Box 274
Masterton, New Zealand
011-64-6-377-1250—
FAX 011-64-6-377-5689
A, CT, FP, OBS, OME

Napier

Tony Edwards, MB, BS
30 Munroe St.
Napier, New Zealand
(070) 354-696
CT, FP, NT, OBS, PM

Tauranga

Michael Godfrey, MB, BS, FACAM, DIPL
157 Fraser St.
Tauranga, New Zealand
011-64-75-785-899—
FAX/phone 011-64-75-782-362
CT, PM, OME

Wanaka

Andrew I. McLeod, MB, ChB, D/C
39 Russel Street
Wanaka, New Zealand
011-64-3-443-7811
AC, FP, GP, OBS

Wellington

Mark G. Hackner, MD, D/C
P.O. Box 33-244
Detone, Wellington, New Zealand
011-64-4-5684904 or 011-64-4-2368200
CT, GP, NT, PM

Tessa Jones, MB, CHB, D/C
102 Adelaide Rd.
Newtown, Wellington, New Zealand
011-64-4-389-1200—
FAX 011-64-43862646
CT, DD, FP, GP, OBS, PM

NORWAY

Svinndal

Arild Abrahamsen, MD, D/C
Svinndal 11
1523 Svinndal, Norway
011-47-9-286065—
FAX 011-47-9-286015
AC, GP, NT

PAKISTAN

Islamabad

Shahid Abbas, MB, BS, D/C
Block 7 Civic Center, Melody Market
Islamabad, Pakistan
011-92-51-210977
A, CT, Env. Med.

Lahore

M. R. Randhawa, MB, BS
446 Shadman Colony 1
Lahore, Pakistan
011-92-42-7587528/7586703
CD, DIA

PANAMA

Panama City

D. Dutari-Estevez, MD, D/C
Tercer Piso Oficina 324
Apartado 8895
Panama 5, Panama
011-507-691977—
FAX 011-507-2694368
GER, IM

Frank Ferro, MD, D/C
622-47 Eldorado
Panama City, Panama
011-507-27-4733, ext. 190—
FAX 011-507-2-27-3019
CT, GER, IM, NT, PM

PARAGUAY

Asuncion

Edelmira Grimaldo, MD
Calle Rio de Janeiro y Rosa Pena, noveno
piso
Asuncion, Paraguay
011-595-21-214-075—
FAX 011-595-21-212-602
CT, GER, NT, PM, PO, RHU

PHILIPPINES

Manila

Edgardo Aguinaldo, MD, D/C
4th Floor, Cacho-Gonzales Building
101 Aguirre cor. Trasierra Sts.
Legaspi Village, Makati City, Philippines
011-632-812-7754—FAX   011-632-893-
4256
A, CT, DD, GER, NT, OPH, PM, YS

Nelia T. Aguinaldo, MD, D/C
4th Floor, Cacho-Gonzales Building
101 Aguirre cor. Trasierra Sts.
Legaspi Village, Makati City, Philippines
011-632-812-7754—
FAX 011-632-893-4256
A, CT, DD, NT, PD, PM, RHU, YS

Rosa M. Ami Belli, MD
PDC Bldg. Ste 303-501
1440 Taft Avenue
Manila, Philippines
50-03-23
CT, HGL, NT, P

Marietto D. Ibarra, MD, D/C
Balilihan-Bohol-Philippines
011-632-834-2766
AN, CT, GP, Bio/Med

Corazon Ibarra Ilarina, MD, DIPL
Marbella Bldg. I, #904
2223 Roxas Blvd.
Pasy City, Metro Manila, Philippines
011-632-834-2766 (Tele/FAX)
CT, PM, Biol Med

Edna S. Lao, MD, D/C
#2 Mupra Condominium
Galilee St., Multinational Village
Paranaque, Metro Manila, Philippines
011-918-80354-26
CT, DD, DIA, FP, GP, PM

Leonides R. Lerma, MD, PhD
Ste 302, Pearl Garden Hotel
1700-M Adriatico, Malate
Manila, Philippines
011-632-524-3594/525-9461
A, AC, AU, CT, DD, GER, PM

Remedios L. Reynoso, MD
PDC Bldg. Ste 303-501
1440 Taft Avenue
Manila, Philippines
50-03-23
CT, NT, PM

Mario I. Saldana, MD
#405 Midland Mansions, 839
Paray Rd.
Makati, Manila, Philippines
011-632-843-3398
CT, DD, NT, PM

Quezon City

Rosario R. Austria, MD, D/C
18 Mariposa St., Cubao
Quezon City, Philippines
Phone/FAX 011-632-724-3242
CT, DIA, IM, NT, PM, Biol. Med.

Corazon Macawili-Yu, MD
19 Queens Road
Mendoza Village
Project 8, Quezon City, Philippines
96-69-04
CT, NT, PM

PUERTO RICO

Aguadilla

Edgardo Carazo, MD, D/C
Carretera #110, Km. 8.8
Aguadilla, PR 00604
(787) 890-1087
CT, DD, NT, OME, PM

Bayamon

Carlos M. Acevedo, MD, D/C
K-6 Plaza 20 Quintas del Rio
Bayamon, PR 00961
(787) 740-3049
GP

Edgardo Carazo, MD, D/C
Ave Main Bloque 54, #11, Local #2
Santa Rosa, Bayamon, PR 00960
(787) 780-3885
CT, DD, NT, OME, PM

Cabo Rojo

Werner M. Fernandez, MD
Carr 313, K07 B750
Cabo Rojo, PR 00623
(809) 255-4148
AC, AU, DIA, FP, PD, DD

Corozal

Luis Joy, MD, DIPL
Rd. 159 Km 15.5
Corozal, PR 00783
(787) 859-8318
AC, DD, GER, OME, OM, Pain Mgmt.

Guayanilla

Miguel A. Santos, MD, DIPL
HC-01, Box 6507
Bo Magas Abajo
Guayanilla, PR 00656-9715
(809) 835-0649—FAX (809) 836-3701
CT, NT, PM

Guillermo Cruz Palomo, MD, D/C
Calle Pinero 101
Rio Piedras, PR 00925
(809) 765-5715
CD, CT, DD, DIA, IM, NT, PM, PUD, YS

San Juan

Hector R. Stella Arrillaga, MD
421 Munoz Rivera Ave.
Midtown Building #103
San Juan, PR 00918
(787) 754-0145/754-0135—
FAX (787) 764-3342
AC, Neurology, Neurophisiology,
Neurovascular

Santurce

Pedro Zayas, MD
P.O. Box 14275
B.O. Obrero Station
Santurce, PR 00916
(809) 727-1105
AC, BA, CT, FP, HGL, NT

SAUDIA ARABIA

Jeddah

Alaa E. Hosny, MB, BCH
3rd Floor, Al Hifini Center
Madina Rd.
Jeddah 21463, Saudi Arabia
011-966-2-665-6241—
FAX 011-966-2-660-9779
CT, GYN, OBS

Salah A-Gader Hussein, MD, DIPL
P.O. Box 430
Jeddah, Saudia Arabia
011-966-2-6726658—
FAX 011-966-2 6711727
CD, CT, CS, IM, NT

Khalili Zarrouk, MD, D/C
Box 9862
Jeddah 21159, Saudi Arabia
011-966-2-696-3036
CD, CS, DIA, GE, GP, IM, RHU

SOUTH AFRICA

Edenvale

Lawrence P. Retief, MB, BCH, D/C
9 Wald Ave.
Dunvegan, Edenvale 1610, South Africa
011-2711-453-7551/7555
AC, GP, DOH

Pretoria

Edwin C. Boegman, MB, ChB, D/C
209 Hay Street, Brooklyn
0181 Pretoria, South Africa
011-2712-435951
CD, CT, DD

SPAIN

Madrid

Dirk van Lith, MD, DIPL
c/o Prof. Joaquin Prieto Cortez
Av. General Moscardo 39 (5B)
28020 Madrid, Spain
A, DD, CT, GP, NT, HO, PM, S

SWITZERLAND

Netstal (Glarus)

Walter Blumer, MD
8754 Netstal
(Glarus bei Zurich), Switzerland
058-61-28-46
HONORARY LIFE MEMBER
CT

VENEZUELA

Puerto La Cruz

Rosella Mazzuka, MD
Ave. Muncipal, #50
Puerto La Cruz
Venezuela 6023
011-58-81-691272—
FAX 011-58-81-773509
AC, AU, GP, FP

WEST INDIES

Jamaica

H. Marco Brown, MD
6 Corner Lane
Montego Bay, Jamaica
1-809-952-3454—FAX 1-809-952-1222
CT, NT, PM

Index